Subterranean Struggles

Number Eight
Peter T. Flawn Series in Natural Resources

Subterranean Struggles

New Dynamics of Mining, Oil, and Gas in Latin America

EDITED BY ANTHONY BEBBINGTON AND JEFFREY BURY

University of Texas Press ⌁ *Austin*

The Peter T. Flawn Series in Natural Resource Management and Conservation is supported by a grant from the National Endowment for the Humanities and by gifts from various individual donors.

Requests for permission to reproduce material from this work should be sent to:
 Permissions
 University of Texas Press
 P.O. Box 7819
 Austin, TX 78713-7819
 http://utpress.utexas.edu/index.php/rp-form

♾ The paper used in this book meets the minimum requirements of ANSI/NISO Z39.48-1992 (R1997) (Permanence of Paper).

Library of Congress Cataloging-in-Publication Data
Subterranean struggles : new dynamics of mining, oil, and gas in Latin America / edited by Anthony Bebbington and Jeffrey Bury. — First edition.
  pages   cm. — (Peter T. Flawn series in natural resources ; number eight)
  Includes bibliographical references and index.
  ISBN 978-0-292-74862-0 (cloth : alk. paper)
  ISBN 978-1-4773-0206-4 (paperback)
1. Mines and mineral resources—Latin America.   2. Social ecology—Latin America.   I. Bebbington, Anthony, 1962–   II. Bury, Jeffrey.
  TN27.5.S834   2013
  333.8098—dc23

                                                         2013008507

doi:10.7560/748620

Contents

Abbreviations

AAA   American Anthropological Association

AAG   Association of American Geographers

AIDESEP   Asociación Interétnica de Desarrollo de la Selva Peruana (Inter-ethnic Association for the Development of the Peruvian Jungle)

APDNR   Asamblea para la Defensa de Nuestros Ríos (Assembly for the Defense of Our Rivers)

ASM   artisanal and small-scale miners

BNDES   Banco Nacional de Desenvolvimento Económico e Social (Brazilian Development Bank)

BRICS   Brazil, Russia, India, China, and South Africa

CAF   Corporación Andina de Fomento (Andean Development Corporation)

CAFTA   Central American Free Trade Agreement

CAINCO   Cámara de Industria y Comercio (Chamber of Industry and Commerce)

CAO   Cámara Agropecuaria del Oriente (Agriculture Chamber for the Eastern Lowlands)

CAO   World Bank Compliance Advisor/Ombudsman

CBC   community-based conservation

CBNRM   community-based natural resource management

CCGTT   Consejo de Capitanes Guaraní-Tapiete de Tarija (Council of Guaraní and Tapiete Captains of Tarija)

CDES   Centro de Derechos Económicos y Sociales (Center for Economic and Social Rights)

CEADES   Colectivo de Estudios Aplicados al Desarrollo Social (Collective for Applied Social Development Studies)

CEDHU   Comisión Ecuménica de Derechos Humanos (Ecumenical
    Commission for Human Rights)

CENSOPAS-INS   Centro Nacional de Salud Ocupacional y Protección
    del Ambiente para la Salud, Instituto Nacional de Salud (National
    Health Institute's Centre for Occupational and Environmental
    Health Protection)

CEP   complementary environmental plan

CERD   Committee for the Elimination of Racial Discrimination (United
    Nations)

CHRZ   Cordillera Huayhuash Reserved Zone

CI   Conservation International

CNDVS   Coordinadora Nacional por la Defensa de la Vida y la Soberanía
    (National Coordinating Committee for the Defense of Life and
    Sovereignty)

COMIBOL   Corporación Minera de Bolivia (a state mining company in
    Bolivia)

COMSUR   Compañía Minera del Sur

CONAIE   Confederación de Nacionalidades Indígenas del Ecuador
    (Confederation of Indigenous Nationalities of Ecuador)

CONAMAQ   Consejo Nacional de Ayllus y Markas del Qullasuyu
    (National Council of Ayllus and Markas of Qullasuyu)

CONAP   Confederación de Nacionalidades de la Amazonía Peruana
    (Confederation of Amazonian Nationalities of Peru)

CONFENIAE   Confederación de las Nacionalidades Indígenas de la
    Amazonia Ecuatoriana (Confederation of Indigenous Nationalities
    of the Ecuadorian Amazon)

CPESC   Coordinadora de Pueblos Étnicos de Santa Cruz (Coordinating
    Body for Ethnic Peoples of Santa Cruz)

CPILAP   Central de Pueblos Indígenas de La Paz (Confederation of
    Indigenous Peoples of La Paz)

CPR   common property resources

DECOIN   Defensa y Conservación Ecólogica de Intag (Intag Ecological
    Defense and Conservation)

DIRESA   Dirección Regional de Salud (the Ministry of Health's
    subnational office)

EIA   environmental impact assessment

EIS   environmental impact study

EMIPA   Empresa Minera Paititi S.A. (Paititi Mining Company Ltd.)

EPE   Empresa Productora de Energía Ltda. (Energy Producing
    Company)

ETAPA   Empresa Municipal de Telecomunicaciones, Agua Potable,
    Alcantarillado y Saneamiento (Cuenca's municipal telecommu-
    nications, water, and wastewater company)
FDI   foreign direct investment
FECONACO   Federación de Comunidades Nativas del Río Corrientes
    (Federation of Native Communities of Río Corrientes)
FEPIBAC   Federación de Pueblos Indígenas del Bajo y Alto Corrientes
    (Federation of Indigenous People of the Lower and Upper Río
    Corrientes)
FOBOMADE   Foro Boliviano sobre Medio Ambiente y Desarrollo
    (Bolivian Forum on Environment and Development)
GASYRG   Yacuiba To Rio Grande Gas Pipeline
GOM   GasOccidente do Mato Grosso Ltda.
HDPE   high density polyethylene
ICCM   International Council for Mining and Metals
IDB   Inter-American Development Bank
IDH   impuesto directo de hidrocarburos (direct hydrocarbons tax)
IFC   International Finance Corporation (of the World Bank)
IIRSA   Integración de la Infraestructura Regional Suramericana (Initiative
    for the Integration of Regional Infrastructure in South America)
ILO 169   International Labor Organization Convention 169
IMC   International Minerals Corporation
IMF   International Monetary Fund
INDEPA   Instituto Nacional de Desarrollo de Pueblos Andinos, Ama-
    zónicos y Afroperuano (National Institute for the Development
    of Andean, Amazonian, and AfroPeruvian Peoples)
INRENA   Instituto Nacional de Recursos Naturales (National Institute
    for Natural Resources)
ITT (Yasuní-ITT)   Yasuní Ishpingo Tambococha Tiputini (a conservation
    initiative)
JEXIM   Export-Import Bank of Japan
LASA   Latin American Studies Association
LMZ   lower mineralized zone
LNG   liquid natural gas
MAS   Movimiento al Socialismo (Movement for Socialism)
MEF   Ministerio de Economía y Finanzas (Ministry of Economy and
    Finance)
MEM   Ministerio de Energía y Minas (Ministry of Energy and Mines)
MINAM   Ministerio del Ambiente (Ministry of the Environment)
MINEM   Ministerio de Energía y Minas (Ministry of Energy and Mines)

MMBO   million barrels of oil
MMP   Ministerio de Minas y Petróleo (Ministry of Mines and Petroleum)
MNR   Movimiento Nacionalista Revolucionario (Nationalist Revolutionary Movement)
NGO   nongovernmental organization
NNPC   Nigerian National Petroleum Company
NOC   national oil company
OECD   Organization for Economic Co-operation and Development
OICH   Organización Indígena Chiquitana (Chiquitano Indigenous Organization)
OLADE   Organización Latinoamericana de Energía (Latin American Energy Organization)
OPIC   Overseas Private Investment Corporation
ORAI   Organización Regional de Aidesep Iquitos (AIDESEP's Regional Organization in Iquitos)
OSINERG   Organismo Supervisor de Energía (Energy Oversight Organization)
OSINERGMIN   Organismo Supervisor de Energía y Minería (Oversight Organization for Energy and Mining)
OT   ordenamiento territorial (land use planning)
OXY   Occidental Petroleum Corporation
PCA   private conservation area
PDI   Plan de Desarrollo Indígena (Indigenous Peoples Development Plan)
PDVSA   Petróleos de Venezuela S.A. (Venezuelan Petroleum Ltd.)
PEIA   preliminary environmental impact assessment
PEPISCO   Proyecto Especial Plan Integral de Salud del Corrientes (Río Corrientes Comprehensive Health Plan Special Project)
PID   programa integral de desarrollo (comprehensive development plan)
PRAS   Plan de Reparación Ambiental y Social (Environmental and Social Reparation Planning group, of the Ministry of Environment, Ecuador)
PRONAA   Programa Nacional de Asistencia Alimentaria (a national food program)
RED   Red Ética y Democracia (Ethics and Democracy Network, a political party in Ecuador)
ROW   right-of-way
SERNAP   Servicio Nacional de Areas Protegidas (National Service of Protected Areas, of the state)
SIS   Seguro Integral de Salud (National Basic Health Service)

SNIP   Sistema Nacional de Inversión Pública (National Public Investment System)

TARP   Troubled Asset Relief Program

TCF   trillion cubic feet

TNC   The Nature Conservancy

UMZ   upper mineralized zone

UNAGUA   Unión de Sistemas Comunitarios de Agua Azuay (Coordinating Committee for Community Water Systems of Azuay)

UNDP   United Nations Development Programme

WWF   World Wildlife Fund

YABOG   Yacimientos-Bolivian Gulf (a pipeline)

YPFB   Yacimientos Petrolíferas Fiscales de Bolivia (the state-owned hydrocarbons company in Bolivia)

Preface and Acknowledgments

This book is the product of interlinked networks and many years of research. One of these networks grows out of discussions about natural resources and development that occurred at the University of Colorado-Boulder in the late 1990s and early 2000s. Tony Bebbington, Jeff Bury, Tom Perreault, and Denise Humphreys Bebbington were each part of these discussions, as were other wonderful colleagues and graduate students at Boulder. A second network is the product of research that, between 2004 and 2010, focused specifically on extractive industry and social conflict in the Andes and Amazon. That research was based at the University of Manchester, UK, and through a close collaboration between Manchester and the Centro Peruano de Estudios Sociales (CEPES) in Lima, it brought together Tony Bebbington, Leonith Hinojosa, Denise Bebbington, Mari Burneo, Martin Scurrah, Ximena Warnaars, Jen Moore, Teresa Velásquez, and Jeff Bury. The third set of research initiatives concerned with climate change, water, environment, and society in the Peruvian Andes has brought Jeff Bury, Tim Norris, Ken Young, and other scholars together in a series of collaborations. Finally each of these networks is part of a loose but very productive web of relationships that link cultural and political ecologists working in Latin America.

In this sense, *Subterranean Struggles* reflects the convergence of several different political ecological research initiatives in the Andes that are led by, but not limited to, geographers. One important moment in this convergence was when Tony Bebbington, Jeff Bury, and Ken Young organized a series of sessions on the topic of "Subterranean Political Ecologies in Latin America" at the 2008 Annual Meetings of the Association of American Geographers in Boston. A number of the chapters in this book were first presented in their germinal form in those sessions. Since then the idea of the collection slowly matured, some chapters were lost along the way, and others were added. The conversion of the idea into a book proposal was made possible by an Economic and Social Research Council/Social Science Research Council Visiting Scholar Fellowship that allowed Jeff Bury to collaborate with an ESRC Professorial Research Program (Grant No. RES-051-27-0191), which Tony Bebbington was coordinating. The same ESRC Professorial Research Program supported the preparation of several chapters in this book—Chapters 1, 2, 5, 8, 10, and 11—while a National Science Foundation support (Grant No. BCS-0002347) to Bury supported the preparation of Chapters 1, 2, 6, and 11. A further ESRC-DfID grant (RES-167-25-0171) to Bebbington supported the preparation of Chapter 7, and the final preparation of the manuscript was supported by a Ford Foundation grant to Bebbington for work on social conflict and institutional change in extractive industries. We are immensely grateful to the ESRC, SSRC, DfID, NSF, and Ford Foundation for this support. We also acknowledge the support of Clark University, the University of Manchester, and the University of California at Santa Cruz.

In addition to these funding agencies and others that are noted in the individual chapters, we thank the following. First, we are grateful to Ken Young who was actively involved in the early stages of this project. For work at the other end of the project, our thanks go to Emily Gallagher of Clark University for her meticulous copyediting and preparation of the text for publication. We also wish to thank, in no particular order: all the authors of the book for their patience and willingness to deal with many proposed revisions; Marta Fole, Jean Heffernan, and Pamela Dunkle for administering the grants that have supported the production of the book; Leonith Hinojosa-Valencia for her intellectual and administrative support of these different research projects; Allison Faust, Casey Kittrell, and Victoria Davis at the University of Texas Press for all their help and patience; Fernando Eguren and Juan Rheineck of CEPES as well as Fernando Romero, Javier Torres, Martin Scurrah, and so many other friends and colleagues in Peru for our discussions on these issues; Guido Cortes, Miguel Urioste, Juan Pablo Chumacero, and colleagues in CER-DET and Fundación Tierra in Bolivia; Pablo Ospina, Manuel Chiriboga, and various colleagues at FLACSO-Ecuador; Julio Berdegué and friends at Rimisp, a remarkably stimulating group of colleagues; and our graduate students at Manchester, Clark, and Santa Cruz for all the insights and stimulation that come from our debates with them.

Finally, Tony thanks Denise, Anna, and Carmen for tolerating his increasing desperation when the project was not getting any closer to the finish line. Their love and support—and occasionally perceptive comment telling him to get things in perspective—are what keep him going. Jeff would like to thank his family for offering their unwavering support for his efforts, particularly because he has been gone for such long periods into the back of beyond.

ANTHONY BEBBINGTON
Director, Graduate School of Geography and
Higgins Professor of Environment and Society
Clark University
Professorial Research Fellow, University of Manchester
Research Associate, Centro Peruano de Estudios Sociales, Lima

JEFFREY BURY
Department of Environmental Studies,
University of California at Santa Cruz

Subterranean Struggles

CHAPTER 1

Political Ecologies of the Subsoil

ANTHONY BEBBINGTON AND JEFFREY BURY[1]

If the 2009 box-office hit *Avatar* showed anything, it was that the political ecology of the subsoil can make for great commercial success. Indeed, the film has it all. At a macropolitical economy level, it deals with resource wars (cf. Le Billon 2008); the interactions between (galactic) commodity chains and territorial dynamics (cf. Bridge 2008); extraction, dispossession, and the viability of capitalism (cf. Harvey 2003); and the endogenization of the subsoil to global political economy (cf. Huber and Emel 2008). It offered a critique of corporate social and environmental responsibility (cf. Emel 2002; Watts 2004b), a take on subaltern resistance, and an exploration of the challenges of alliance-building within a socioenvironmental movement (Horowitz 2010; Bebbington 2007b).

And yet, while the extractive economy may make for great films, the topic has, until very recent times, remained relatively marginal to the wider political ecological enterprise. Indeed, it would seem fair to say that in the quarter century since Piers Blaikie's and Harold Brookfield's classic treatises on soil erosion and land degradation (Blaikie 1985; Blaikie and Brookfield 1987)—two books widely seen as launching the field of political ecology, at least within Geography (Walker 2005)—the subsoil has remained fairly hidden from view while the core enterprise of political ecology has moved forward with something of a surface bias. The *ecology* in *political ecology* has typically referred to land, forests, crops, water, and livestock (Zimmerer and Bassett 2003), expanding its reach in more recent years to include nondomesticates, mosquitoes, lawns, and bugs more generally (Raffles 2002; Robbins 2007). What lies beneath, however, has received far less attention (though see Emel, Bridge, and Krueger 1994; Bridge 2000; Watts 2004b). A run through the primers in political ecology is one indicator of this lacuna. The matter of the subsoil—minerals, oil, and gas—appears neither in the essays collected in

Bassett and Zimmerer's statement on the field of political ecology (Bassett and Zimmerer 2003), nor in the pages of Paul Robbins' critical introduction to political ecology (Robbins 2004, though see 2012), nor of Tim Forsyth's introduction to critical political ecology (Forsyth 2003). The theme is also absent from the iconic first edition of Peet and Watts' *Liberation Ecologies* (Peet and Watts 1996), though the second edition (Peet and Watts 2004) does include a chapter by Watts himself building upon his own history of work on oil (Watts 2004c). This editorial change in the second edition perhaps reflected that the contents of the subsoil were at last slowly rising to the surface of political ecological debate, and indeed, Rod Neumann's (2005) *Making Political Ecology* identified "environmental security and violence" as one of six future directions for political ecology—a theme in which, for him, subsoil resources loom large. Meanwhile, recent excellent reviews of the field of political ecology (Walker 2005; Walker 2006; Walker 2007) and of the emerging interfaces between cultural and political ecology (Zimmerer 2004; Zimmerer 2006; Zimmerer 2007) do not refer to the subsurface.[2]

Of course, this claim that political ecology has said little about the subsoil depends considerably on where one draws the lines around the field—never an easy task (Blaikie 1999). Our comments so far have assumed that political ecology's boundaries are reflected in the reach of this last decade's clutch of texts that have aimed to define and comment on the field (Bassett and Zimmerer 2003; Forsyth 2003; Zimmerer and Bassett 2003; Robbins 2004; Neumann 2005). However, pushing the boundaries a bit further out to include research in the political economy of the environment, environmental economic geography, or resource geography more generally, then we can say that somewhat more attention has been paid to subsoil. Several authors stand out here. Philippe Le Billon (2001; 2004) has addressed the relationships between oil, minerals, and conflict and opened up important conversations with debates on the "resource curse" and greed/grievance theses on conflict (Auty 2001; Collier and Hoeffler 2004). Building on earlier collaborations with Jody Emel (Emel, Bridge, and Krueger 1994), Gavin Bridge has argued that a reflection on mining and hydrocarbons can help rethink resource governance (Bridge 2000; Bridge 2001; Bakker and Bridge 2006) and the theoretical and ontological status of relations between nature and society (Bakker and Bridge 2006). More recently, and also building on collaborations with Emel (Emel and Huber 2008; Huber and Emel 2008), Matthew Huber has tried to bring the subsoil into the very core of the political economy of space and nature (Huber 2008; Huber 2009).

As important as this work in political economy of the environment is, it has largely been oriented towards advanced industrial economies (Le Billon's work excepted). "Third world political ecology," to use Bryant and Bailey's (1997) characterization, has remained practically silent on the subsoil—with new research interested in this theme emerging only quite recently (Hilson and Yakovleva 2007; Fry 2008; Himley 2008; Tschakert 2009; Horowitz 2010, 2008; Schroeder 2010).[3] In light of these claims, our aims in this chapter are threefold. First, we argue for the analytical and political significance of the subsoil. Second, we outline theoretical and methodological foundations for a political ecology of the subsoil. Third, we discuss why recent trends and transformations in Latin America suggest the importance and urgency of elaborating and pursuing this agenda (this theme is further elaborated in Chapter 2). We argue that a political ecology of the subsoil must be central to understanding the regional transformations and shifting geopolitical insertions that are currently occurring in the continent and will continue to unfold over decades to come. Fourth, and finally, we explain our particular focus on "subterranean struggles" and offer a summary roadmap through the book.

Why the Subsoil Matters

Our remarks in the preceding section are offered neither as criticism of our colleagues' work nor of the field of political ecology, but rather as an observation that the subsoil has been a significant gap in academic political ecology.[4] Here we identify several reasons why the subsurface may merit greater attention than it has thus far received.

The most significant argument for deeper engagement with the subsoil relates to its immense power in and significance for the transformation of social life. The "perhaps obvious, but nevertheless crucial point" here is that "capitalist social life is profoundly dependent on the abundant provision of fossil fuel energy" (Huber 2008, 105). It is also deeply dependent on minerals and building materials—indeed, none of the spatial fixes and urbanization of capital (Harvey 1982; Harvey 1985), nor the increased density and reduced distance that the World Bank (2009) identifies as sine qua nons of development, would be possible without these materials, for they all involve cement, rock, iron, steel, copper, and a range of metals used in small quantities to give steel particular characteristics needed in construction. In this vein, Huber's (2008, 106) claim that "the late-eighteenth/early-nineteenth century 'energy shift' from biological to fossil modes of energy—at the time, meaning coal— coincided with the dramatic *social* shift towards the generalization of capitalist social relations" is far from being an idle one. The implication is that the extraction of the subsoil, and the transformations that accompany it, are co-constitutive of the transitions to the forms of capitalism (and socialism) known in the modern historical period. As Huber goes on to argue, this take on the subsoil makes apparent the ways in which nature and resources are not external to but are instead "an internal and necessary basis for the capitalist mode of production" (Huber 2008, 108).

Following a logic similar to Huber's, the continuing expansion of capitalist investment has become constitutive not only of "the generalization of capitalist social relations" but also of possible limits to this same process of expansion. Indeed, as capital delves ever more deeply and broadly into the earth to extract and produce new commodities, so new challenges arise. These challenges might be understood as symptomatic of the second (environmental) contradiction of capital (O'Connor 1988), a contradiction in which the very expansion of capitalism undermines the environmental conditions of its own sustainability—indicators of which might be climate change or severe environmental degradation. Of course, whether these are contradictions or merely problems that can be converted into new market opportunities, is less clear. Another way of understanding some of these challenges lies in the language of Polanyi's double movement (Polanyi 1944), "a situation where attempts to expand the reach and depth of capitalist commodification are met by more-or-less vocal (even violent) forms of resistance" (Castree 2007, 27). Indeed, the studies collected in this book document a series of struggles that may all be viewed as constitutive of such a double movement, as populations contest what they view as unacceptable consequences of extraction. For Polanyi, such double movements were not necessarily indicative of contradiction and could be offset by the evolution of forms of "market society" "where individuals and communities are somehow encouraged to 'live with' the fairly stark forms of creative destruction that are the hallmark of 'capitalism unleashed'" (Castree 2007, 27). Whatever the case, there is a clear sense—and our book is testimony to this—that resource extraction is constitutive of internal and serious tensions that threaten the expansion of this same extraction.

While the subsoil is endogenous to capitalist transformations in general, the types of transformation in which it is complicit evidently vary at a national and subnational level. In part, this variation is related to where these geographical spaces fall along the commodity chain in question and, in part, to the relative power of different actors within this chain. Thus the societal and territorial transformations linked to the extraction of silver and gold from colonial Latin America differed dramatically between, say, Bolivia and Spain:[5] while parts of Spain enjoyed wealth, accumulation, the rise of silver-based currency, and ultimately rampant inflation (Wallerstein 1974; Stein and Stein 2000), Bolivia saw much more localized accumulation coupled with exploitation, the hollowing out of mountains, the spread of tailings, wide-spread human suffering, and the slow, steady building of a miners' political consciousness that contributed in no small measure to the national revolution of 1952. Likewise, along the hydrocarbon commodity chain, the hydro-carbonized transformations of Iraq, Nigeria, or Venezuela are profoundly different from those of oil and gas consuming countries. Though all are trans-formations, let us dwell a moment on some of the ways in which the subsoil has been deeply implicated in the reworking of producer states.

At one extreme are Michael Watts' (Watts and Kashi 2008; Watts 2009) apocalyptic accounts of the environmental dislocation of the Niger Delta:

> Burning twenty-four hours a day at temperatures of 13–14,000 °C, Nige-rian natural gas produces 31.75 million tonnes of carbon dioxide and 10.89 million tonnes of methane, more than the rest of the world (and render-ing Nigeria probably the biggest single cause of global warming) (Ham-mer 1996). The oil spillage record is even worse. There are roughly 300 spills per year in the Delta, and in the 1970s alone the spillage was four times the much publicised Exxon Valdez spill in Alaska. In one year alone, almost 700,000 barrels were soiled according to a government commission. Ogoni-land itself suffered 111 spills between 1985 and 1994 (Hammer 1996, 61). Figures provided by the NNPC [Nigerian National Petroleum Company] document 2,676 spills between 1976 and 1990 . . . The consequences of flar-ing, spillage and waste for Ogoni fisheries and farming have been devas-tating. Two independent studies completed in 1997 reveal total petroleum hydrocarbons in Ogoni streams at 360 and 680 times the European Commu-nity permissible levels. (Watts 1999, 22)

The social dislocations visited through oil are no less awful:

> What I have described is the radical displacement of a specific form of customary authority (chieftainship) through the creation of a governable space of civic vigilantism . . . Community rule in Nembe is a realm of pri-vatized violence. In the context of a weak and corrupt state, the genesis of this power-nexus bears striking resemblances to the genesis of the Mafia of nineteenth-century Sicily. (Watts 2004a, 207)

If this image of the Niger Delta is the *Apocalypse Now* of the extractive option, at a quite different extreme are national political economic transfor-mations such as those of Botswana and Chile, where diamonds and copper, respectively, have been central to a steady institutional modernization and a more or less sustained process of economic growth and poverty reduction.[6] Indeed, Chile and Botswana are consistently identified (e.g., ICMM 2006) as experiences that show it is not necessarily the case that economies with a heavy dependence on extractive industries perform less well (in terms of growth and poverty reduction) than more diversified economies—the so-called resource curse relationship (e.g., Auty 2001; Weber-Fahr 2002). While such arguments about the existence (or nonexistence) of a resource curse are likely to continue for some while (Bebbington et al. 2008a), most commentators *do* seem to accept that economies that depend on their subsoil are faced by particularly knotty problems of macroeconomic management and governance that are as likely to lead to a Nigeria as to a Chile. For our purposes here, the general point is that the subsoil—its own nature, its interactions with pre-extraction political economies, the ways in which it has been governed, and its particular insertion into global circuits—appears to be implicated in the differing forms taken by national and subnational capitalisms across many parts of the globe.

The subsoil also has special resonance for political ecology's interest in social movements (Peet and Watts 1996; Peet and Watts 2004; Robbins 2004). The extraction of minerals and hydrocarbons seems to be particularly significant in the formation, deepening, and radicalization of identities (Watts 2004a). Many factors are at play here. The experience of working in hazardous extractive environments has historically been associated with strong labor identities and organizations, and we have already noted the case of Bolivian miners (Nash 1979), though the same has applied historically to British, West Virginian, or Peruvian miners (Long and Roberts 1984). While the move in the extractive economy towards a tertiarization of all manner of functions (including labor recruitment) has subsequently weakened such forms of labor movement, extraction still invokes militant identities of various forms and scales. These can derive from a sense of compromised citizenship and ownership in the face of nonlocal actors taking away "the soil beneath our feet," dumping "*our* mountains into *our* streams." But such identities can also be related to forms of resource nationalism in which the extracted product is associated with national identity, sovereignty and security, a sense that the subsoil is somehow more closely tied to nation than is any manufactured product, or even perhaps labor value itself. Moreover, such resource nationalism can exist and be exercised not only at a broadly popular level—as in Bolivia's gas wars (Perreault 2006)—but also among skilled and professional labor working for state hydrocarbons and mining companies (Valdivia 2008; Santiago 2006).

At the same time, the manifest geographical and territorial presence of extraction can interact with indigenous, regional, and sometimes separatist identities associated with territories within national boundaries (Ross 2004; Ross 2008). Indeed, the expansion of the extractive frontier has often come accompanied by territorialized conflict and social mobilization. However, because extraction so often occurs in historically marginalized locations, and because the profits at stake are often so large, the mobilizations that occur around extraction are many, varied, and ambiguous (see Bebbington et al., Chapter 10 in this book). Some mobilize against while other interests mobilize in favor of the hoped-for jobs and subcontracts that a new mine or hydrocarbon operation might generate. Still others may appear to be mobilizing against an extractive project when in fact they simply want access to its benefits (Arellano-Yanguas 2012). For their part, interests associated with the industry are happy to cultivate such splintering of identity and organization, while currying other identities and organizations in order that they can become functional to the ongoing enterprise of extraction. Watts (2004a) shows this clearly for the case of the Niger delta, explaining how oil companies supported and financed the emergence of youth vigilante groups under the aegis of "cultural organization" in return for the support proffered by these groups. He also documents (as do others) how easily this can collapse into violence.

On a more theoretical plane, the subsoil constitutes a potentially useful basis on which to think about nature–society dualisms and about how, in Bakker and Bridge's (2006, 14) words, "to express the causal role of the material without straying into object fetishism or without attributing intrinsic qualities to entities/categories whose boundaries are 'extrinsic'—defined, at least in part, socio-culturally." Put in slightly different terms, exploring how the subsoil enters the political economy might prove conceptually fruitful given the theoretical challenges to political ecology to recognize that (and analyze how) the environment can have effects on society without slipping into a form of environmental determinism, or to recognize that the environment is brought into social life through social processes without falling into positions that see nature as nothing other than "produced." This is not to imply that a concern for the subsoil will be *more* fruitful than to ask the same questions for water, forests, or other resources—but it is to suggest that it will be fruitful in different ways. Writing in the aftermath of the 2010 British Petroleum oil rig explosion in the Gulf of Mexico, or writing (as we are) from personal and professional commitments to a Peru whose La Oroya metal smelter town has twice been listed among the ten most-polluted places on Earth,[7] it seems clear that political ecologies of the subsoil can throw important light on notions of risk and hazard. For instance, following Bakker and Bridge's (2006) call for a reformulation of how nature is handled in resource geographies, one can imagine interpretations of hazards that understand them not as products of the inherent uncooperativeness of particular resources (oil, smoke, waste water), nor merely as the results of mistakes in governance or of technological limitations, but instead as artifacts of how socio-natures are produced jointly by humans and nonhumans. Linking such a reading to Huber's (2008) call to understand fossil fuels—and, we would add, minerals—as a necessary and internal basis of capitalism, it becomes only a short step to interpretations of calamity that demonstrate the endogeneity of environmental hazard to the political economy in ways perhaps reminiscent of calls made long ago by Watts (1983).

Finally, also on a theoretical plane, extraction throws an interesting twist into the geographical and political ecological preoccupation with scale (Swyngedouw and Heynen 2003; Marston, Jones III, and Woodward 2005; Zimmerer 2006; Manson 2008; Neumann 2009). Without commenting directly on these other debates regarding the existence or nonexistence of "geographical scale," the subsoil offers an interesting perspective on the notions of levels, boundaries, and the consequences for nature–society when materials cross these boundaries. To speak of the "subsoil" or "subsurface," by definition, invokes the existence of a boundary defined by the surface of the Earth. All of the transformations we have emphasized in this chapter derive from the passage of materials across this boundary and into the realms of human use. In the case of hydrocarbons and certain hard rock minerals, however, further boundaries are also crossed. The burning of hydrocarbons and the production of cement, in particular, release greenhouse gases that themselves cross the boundary between atmospheric layers (the troposphere and stratosphere), at which point they have consequences for the temperature of the Earth's surface. How and how far these boundary crossings occur and lead to various results depends on the internal qualities of the materials, as well as the ways in which they are bundled up with forms of human use. The flaring of natural gas, for example, that Watts suggests renders Nigeria possibly the "biggest single cause of global warming" (Watts 1999, 22, citing Hammer 1996), is itself a joint product of the material nature of hydrocarbons in the Niger Delta and of company technology policy. It may well be that the mineral fruits of the subsoil, along with the water with which they interact, form that part of the material world that is most effective in binding together atmospheric, surface, and subsurface dynamics into kinds of socio-nature that, in their current form, will change the world dramatically. Understanding how these minerals and hydrocarbons couple with human practices in ways that bring them across the surface boundary and into human use is, therefore, critical for any understanding of the drivers of different dimensions of global change.

Subsoil Political Ecologies: Foundations and Practices

Foundations

Political ecology being the broad umbrella that it is—or in Blaikie's (2010) terms, a "settler discipline" that finds itself treading where other disciplines have gone before—there is no particular reason to expect a political ecology of the subsoil to have distinct foundations or underlying major themes; indeed, there is already a great deal from which to choose. However, the specific concern for the subsoil may increase the relevance of particular conceptual and methodological entry points. We highlight several here, moving from concerns whose roots lie more in cultural ecology to others inspired by political economy. While these themes are not presented as a framework (and we did not ask other authors in this volume to speak to them directly) they are each present in the chapters that follow.

The first relates to an old chestnut in political ecology: the differing opinions of whether political ecology *as practiced* has been weak on politics or weak on ecology (Bebbington and Batterbury 2001). Whatever the case, there is strong reason to argue that a subsoil political ecology will gain greatly by engaging seriously with ecology, biogeography, geology, hydrology, soil sciences, and allied fields such as hydrogeochemistry. First, many of the conflicts around extraction hinge on its effects in the environment. These effects are highly contested. Hence, even if researchers themselves prefer to steer clear of measuring these impacts, it is immensely useful to be able to understand how others measure them and then make claims on the basis of such measurement. Given that much dispute hinges on the legitimacy of different forms of knowledge about impact (Cash et al. 2003; Bebbington and Bury 2009), being able to assess these knowledges and measurements on their own terms is vital. We suggest, however, that it is also important for the political ecologist to be able to measure well, while recognizing the ways in which data is socially constructed, in order to be able to understand the effects of extraction on other domains such as human health (King 2010) or agriculture. Second, given the politically charged environment in which knowledge about extraction is produced, and given that it is not easy for researchers to stay outside of this political debate (even should they wish to), we also suggest (and it has been our experience) that the legitimacy of the political ecologist is all the greater when their work involves theoretical and/or quantitative ecological analysis. Third, and more conceptually, given that so much of the political ecology of extraction involves water, this would mean that a political ecology of the subsoil would be able to engage the hydro-social complexes at stake not only through the language of the political economy of the environment, but also in terms of the relationships between changes in water chemistry and discourses and practices defining the social control of water.

The second foundation relates to another long-standing theme: the debates around adaptation. The suggestion here is not to reinvoke cybernetic approaches or the equilibrium-infused debates on whether something is adapted. Instead, our concern is more worldly. The magnitude and character of changes induced by extraction are profound, whether we are dealing with the territories where extraction occurs or with the coupled mineral, hydrological, and climatic systems whose dynamics change as a result of the extraction-induced release of carbon and other chemicals. Some of these changes operate on timescales that run across generations and are very often irreversible. The depth of such changes invokes the importance of understanding how populations of different types and scales respond (or "adapt") to environmental transformations that are more or less permanent but human caused. Understanding such adaptive dynamics and relating them to the political economies that drive transformation and regulate responses is important. Understanding the viability of these adaptations is equally critical, not only as questions of human ecological importance, but also for wresting debate back from both environmental-determinist and technocratic discourses.

This previous point regarding responses to environmental transformation relates to a third foundation, one which draws inspiration from work in the political economy of the environment and environmental economic geography. In an important paper, Bridge (2008) laid out an agenda for research on the "governance of resource based development" that would merge the concerns of global production networks/value chains approaches with those that focus on regional and territorial dynamics and on the materiality of resources. Bridge was concerned with demonstrating that the forms taken by global oil production networks are influenced by oil's material and territorial characteristics (which establish particular challenges for how to capture and valorize oil), and also that the ways in which territorialized components of the subsoil are brought into social life and affect regional development dynamics hinge on the nature of the global networks in which they are embedded. While cautioning that the precise forms of this dynamic would vary depending on the product in question, Bridge made the more general point that resource, territory, and global production network must be seen as coproduced (cf. Bakker and Bridge 2006).

Our fourth foundation relates to the centrality of the state, a long-standing focus of political ecology research (Cockburn and Ridgeway 1979; Bryant 1992; Robbins 2000; McCarthy and Prudham 2004; McCarthy 2007). As Bridge (2008, 414) notes: "The extensive territorial embeddedness of the extractive sector suggests that emphasis in the resource curse literature on the role of the state is certainly warranted." While the same may be said in a general sense for all economic sectors, there are reasons why the state is even more central to political ecologies of extraction. First, the geographical fixity of minerals and hydrocarbons, coupled with the massive up-front investments involved in extraction, mean that extractive industry is far from footloose. This, in turn, gives the host state relatively more bargaining power vis-à-vis the industry (once it is established), making the sector more subject to, but also more likely to seek to influence, domestic politics. Second, the coupling of subsoil resources and notions of sovereignty and nation also means that the state and extraction are intimately bundled together. Third, and relatedly, in many countries ownership of the subsoil is vested in the state (the United States is something of an exception in this regard). The state thus plays a far more important role in determining patterns of access and control than it does, say, for land, water, or many forest resources. For all these reasons, the state enters into political ecologies of extraction in profound and particular ways, requiring reflection on the relationships between extraction, access, nation, sovereignty, and borders (see, for instance, the chapters in this volume by Perreault and Bebbington et al.).

Our fifth foundation is the process of enclosure and struggles over access to resources, both of which have long been discussed in political ecology research (e.g., Wolf 1972; Blaikie 1985; Bebbington 1999; McSweeney 2004; Adams and Hutton 2007; Bury 2008b; Carr and McCusker 2009). Bridge (2008, 415) comments: "The extractive sector clearly illustrates how value can be created by enclosure and exclusion (via the extension of property rights). This process is not limited to extractive industries and occurs—via technological innovation and patenting—in many other sectors." However, he continues (and this is what makes enclosure so significant to a subsoil political ecology): "The non-renewable character of extraction . . . means that enclosure is a primary competitive logic in extractive industries." But of course the process of enclosing the subsurface also cordons off many surface resources that are of an equally elemental nature for preexisting livelihoods and sources of well-being among those people who lived in or from the same territories. As suggested in later sections of this chapter and more so in Chapter 2, in some countries the rate of expansion of extractive industry, primarily in the form of state-granted concessions to private companies, effectively means that these countries are undergoing a process of accelerated and extensive enclosure.

Such enclosure is significant for many reasons. On the one hand, it is central to the commodification of various parts of the landscape, laying the bases for new rounds of landscape transformation as businesses seek to gain access to these commodities. On the other hand, it transforms relations of access to a wide range of resources, politicizing these landscapes in new ways. This politicization has frequently come accompanied by conflict and struggle, as these changing relations of access are contested. Understanding these relationships between enclosure, commodification, and struggle therefore becomes central to understanding processes of landscape transformation in areas affected by extraction. This is, indeed, *the* fundamental interest that runs through all the chapters in this collection.

Practicing a political ecology of the subsoil

While we would argue that the very way in which subsoil political ecologies are practiced constitutes a further foundation to the enterprise, we discuss these questions of practice separately because the links between political ecology, political practice, and policy engagement are not easy ones. Indeed, these links were the subject of two in a series of "progress reports" on political ecology that geographer Peter Walker produced for the journal *Progress in Human Geography* (Walker 2005; Walker 2006; Walker 2007). While not all political ecologists would agree with Walker's views, the latter merit attention, not least because they were based on significant consultation with other scholars. They also merit attention for the specific case of the subsoil because the politics surrounding extraction are so contentious, violent, and not infrequently lethal, while the governance arrangements remain informal and beholden to special interests (Liebenthal, Michelitsch, and Tarazona 2005; Humphreys, Sachs, and Stiglitz 2007; Bebbington 2007b; Horowitz 2010).

Reflecting on the relationships between political ecology and politics, Walker (2007, 364–365) comments:

> With roots in peasant and development studies, social movements theory, and studies of indigenous knowledge and symbolic and discursive struggles over resources . . . one might expect political ecology to be more at home and engaged in these realms of relatively informal, non-institutional politics and power . . . Yet, in the formal institutions and products of political ecology as a profession (conferences, specialty groups, publications, and so on), this act of giving back—the act of a self-conscious, ethical *politics* of research— is often not particularly visible.

This might be, he later suggests, because authors believe their writings will one day find their way into political debate and the public sphere anyway, or "more cynically, it might be inferred that as an institutional formation political ecology does not place an especially high priority on 'giving back' to its research subjects—perhaps, even, that much of political ecology has no articulated guidelines to effect positive change" (Walker 2007, 366).

There is a similar distance, Walker (2006, 383) argues, between political ecology and policy engagement:

> The actual engagement of political ecology with fields of research and public debate outside the academy has been limited. For example, political ecology has had virtually no engagement with some of the world's most important international research programs dealing with environmental change and human–environmental relations, such as the Intergovernmental Panel on Climate Change, the International Geosphere-Biosphere Programme, the International Human Dimensions Programme on Global Environmental Change, and the Millennial Ecosystems Assessment.

Much the same could be said for initiatives such as the Extractive Industries Review (a multiyear process convened by the World Bank in response to criticisms of its financing of mineral and hydrocarbon projects), the ongoing Extractive Industries Transparency Initiative, or the Soros funded Revenue Watch International.

As Walker notes, there are many legitimate reasons for such nonengagement. Indeed, the admonition that only those without sin should cast the first stone certainly applies here, and so, once again, our point is not to criticize. Rather, we want to suggest that a "political ecology of the subsoil" may have contours that *by definition* would lead it to include such engagement. Here we build on Joan Martínez-Alier's (2002) notion of an "environmentalism of the poor" that seeks to redress the unequal distribution of environmental gains and losses incurred during economic growth. In these "ecological distribution conflicts," both poor people and activists seek to prevent the transfer of the socioenvironmental costs of growth to those areas where poor people live. They do this through various forms of political action that, in the final instance, are always oriented towards securing changes in public and corporate policy that will protect their livelihoods. We would suggest that it is no accident that so many of the cases related by Martínez-Alier, as he defines the extent of this environmentalism of the poor, involve ecological distributional conflicts surrounding mining and hydrocarbons (e.g., Martínez-Alier 2002, 54–67, 100–111).

We take Martínez-Alier as suggesting that these activists are themselves political ecologists, and we would certainly understand them as such—activists involved in the politicization of environmental and distributional questions related to extraction. If so, then activism and activists already fall *within* the bounds of a political ecology of the subsoil, and the question is not so much one of political ecology engaging with *ostensibly external* worlds of politics and policy, but rather one of component parts of the subfield engaging with one another. This is not, however, a trivial task. Levels of distrust are often extreme in areas affected by the expansion of extractive industry—a reflection of the very large amounts of money, as well as the potentially very significant impacts on livelihood and environment that are at stake. Often this distrust has also been nourished by actual experiences of violence and murder, and by the fact that extraction often becomes bundled with other illicit political processes around the laundering of drug money or acquisition of arms, be this for insurgent groups or groups organized and armed in order to protect mines and oil fields (e.g., Watts 2004a).

Methodologically, in a very practical sense, this puts a premium on building trust among researchers, activists, and communities, while making it a particularly difficult challenge. Looking across research experiences to date, there appears to be no magic solution. Certain practices do emerge as important that, while undoubtedly relevant for other subfields of political ecological inquiry, take on particular resonance in the context of extraction. They include:

- Sustained and long-term engagement with a locale and a people. Examples here would include earlier works in cultural ecology that involve entire generations of researchers in working in particular places (Geertz 1963; Sauer 1969; Nietschmann 1973; Denevan 1992a), and more recently, for the specific case of extractive industry, Stuart Kirsch's (2006) work in Papua New Guinea, and Suzana Sawyer's (2004) and Laura Rival's (2002) sustained relationships with different indigenous groups and regions in Ecuador.
- Plenty of good-quality fieldwork. This is already implicit in the previous point but we make it explicit here for two reasons. First, it can be a terribly important source of legitimacy both for the products of research and for the researcher should they engage in public debates on extraction (see next point). Second, conflicts around extraction (perhaps like all conflicts) can be terribly messy, with alliances and commitments shifting quickly and counterintuitively in the face of such massive financial incentives. Capturing these counterintuitive shifts, and simply being able to operate in the midst of such conflict, depends on the insights and legitimacy bestowed by long periods of fieldwork.
- Ongoing willingness to become a participant in public debates and, at

times, litigation. Again there are plenty of examples of this, if not always from political ecologists. They include Michael Watts' involvement in Nigerian oil struggles and the Alien Tort Claims Act in the United States (Watts 2010), Suzana Sawyer's support to legal processes in Ecuador, Stuart Kirsch's participation in similar processes related to the infamous Ok Tedi mine in Papua New Guinea, Terry Karl's participation as expert witness in a variety of legal cases, support given by Shin Imai and colleagues at the Osgoode School of Law at York University to groups affected by mining in Peru, and the more modest involvement of one of us in public debates with mining company officials and lawyers in Peru (Bebbington et al. 2007a, b).

- Publishing of material in a variety of formats and languages that are locally accessible. Again, while this is a general rule, the more charged the issues on which one works, the greater the ethical imperative to publish locally, and not only in English. There is probably also a more self-oriented interest for such a publication strategy, for in the course of such research, the likelihood that the researcher will be accused of "serving interests" is great. The more transparent the researcher about their findings and materials, the better.

Reworking Latin America: The Subsoil and New Geopolitical Ecologies?

If there is a general case to be made for a political ecology of the subsoil, this book argues that this is especially so in Latin America, which has seen a dramatic increase in investment in exploring and exploiting the subsoil. Moreover, as argued earlier, the scale of this investment, the debates that surround it, and its relationshps to broader initiatives of regional energetic and infastructural integration mean that a political ecology of extraction is not only critical to understanding more general trends and transformations in Latin America but might also be read as part of a more general reorganization of the geopolitical economy of the region. From 1990 to 1997, while global investment in mining *exploration* increased by 90 percent, in Latin America it increased by 400 percent and in Peru it increased by a remarkable 2000 percent (Banco Mundial 2005). Between 1990 and 2000, the region's share of overall global mining investment increased from 12 to 33 percent (de Echave, 2007). Bridge (2004c) recorded similar trends, noting that between 1990 and 2001, 12 of the world's 25 largest mining *investment* projects were in Latin America and the Caribbean (9 in Chile, 2 in Peru, 1 in Argentina) and that worldwide, of the 10 countries that saw most investment in mining, 4 were in Latin America (Chile ranked first, Peru sixth, Argentina ninth, and Mexico tenth). These trends continue, with foreign direct investment to both South and Central America doubling between 2004 and 2007,[8] and foreign direct investment (FDI) at a country level also increasing significantly in some countries. For instance, FDI growth in hydrocarbons from 2004 to 2007 was 223 percent in Brazil and 623 percent in Colombia; and in mining was 458 percent in Brazil, 502 percent in Bolivia, and 550 percent in Mexico.

These surges in investment have gone both to traditional areas of extraction as well as to new frontiers that have no history of extraction (see Chapter 10 in this volume, by Bebbington et al.). Thus traditional recipients of mining investment (Peru, Chile, and Bolivia) continue to receive investment, while other countries with no significant history of mining are also seeing increased interest (e.g., Ecuador, El Salvador, and others in Central America). Indeed, some of the Central American investments may become particularly important internationally because of the issues they raise. A Canadian company, Pacific Rim, is currently suing the government of El Salvador for lost revenue as a result of a de facto moratorium on mining while the government decides whether to allow mining or not. The infamous Marlin mine in Guatemala has become an iconic case for global debates on mining and human rights; indeed, the company itself felt forced to allow an independent human rights assessment of the mine that was, ultimately, quite critical.[9] Meanwhile, even in countries with a long history of mining, investment has flowed not only to traditional areas, but also to new frontiers. In Peru, these include, for instance, the highly contentious expansion into the northern department of Piura (see Chapter 10, this volume) and remote mountain corridors in the Department of Ancash (see Chapter 4, by Bury and Norris), while planned investment in Bolivia includes development of what would be the world's largest iron mine, El Mutún in the eastern department of Santa Cruz (see Chapter 8, by Hindery).

Patterns for hydrocarbons are equally striking. Of the 78.3 million hectares of Peru's Amazonia, 56.1 million are lots for oil and gas exploration—compared with just 15.5 million hectares of protected areas and 13.4 million hectares of legalized indigenous territory (Viale and Monge 2010, quoting data from the Instituto del Bien Común). Over half of both Ecuador's and Bolivia's Amazon is also available for oil and gas exploration (Finer et al. 2008), while Brazil is aggressively opening the offshore hydrocarbon frontier to its east. More than is the case for mining, these trends in hydrocarbons investment are part of regional initiatives to link energy and infrastructural investments. While the explicit plan for a so-called "energy ring" (*anillo ener-*

gético) linking suppliers and users of energy in the region (and then north to Mexico and California) no longer exists formally, elements of its logic have continued to drive investment. Thus growth of investment in gas extraction in Bolivia reflects strategic responses to supply Argentina and, above all, Brazil (see Chapter 3 in this volume, by Perreault; also Kaup 2010), while the development of the Camisea natural gas field and the dramatic increase in hydrocarbons concessions in Peru's Amazon (Viale and Monge 2010) are part of a more strategic vision to supply energy to an expanded mining sector in the south of Peru (and north of Chile), as well as to the United States (even though the result of this orientation has been to reduce availability for Lima and domestic industrialization).

These regional visions for an integrated system of extraction are part of a far larger reordering of Latin America's geopolitical economy and economic geography. Of central importance here is the so-called Initiative for Regional Infrastructural Integration in South America (Integración de la Infraestructura Regional Suramericana, IIRSA)—US$69 billion worth of 514 infrastructural investments in transport, energy, and communications.[10] The logic binding these projects together draws on the shared historical imaginary of a geographically integrated South America, in which: interoceanic roads connect the Atlantic and Pacific coasts of the continent; widened rivers (*hidrovías*) connect inland production zones (of soybean, grains, biofuels, etc.) with modernized ports; and pipelines and high-tension transmission lines link sources of hydrocarbons and hydroelectricity to consumers, exporters, and energy-hungry sites of mineral extraction and processing. While senior managers at the Inter-American Development Bank have said in interviews that there is no strategic relationship between extractive industry investments and IIRSA, the potential synergies are not lost on some of the industry representatives we have also interviewed. These synergies include the building of ports that will facilitate mineral exports, pipelines that facilitate the transport of hydrocarbons, and power lines that will, inter alia, bring electricity to extractive industry installations.

In Chapter 2, we elaborate on these trends. For our purposes here, the point is that at a regional level one can reasonably speak of the fashioning of a new geopolitical ecology in Latin America. This process reworks the territories in which extraction touches ground or through which transmission wires and pipelines pass (see Chapter 8) and involves a refashioning of the entire region through a process that is profoundly conflictive. This collection seeks to understand elements of this conflict through an approach that tacks back and forth between these broader political ecological transformations and the internal dynamics of protest and mobilization around resource extraction.

Tracing Subterranean Struggles

The agenda we have outlined for a political ecology of the subsoil is an expansive one. While the different contributors to this collection address elements of this broader agenda, they converge around the particular issue of *struggle*. The focus on struggle is not, however, a normative one and in this sense the book differs from a collection such as *Liberation Ecologies*. While normatively the temptation exists to frame political ecologies of extraction in oppositional terms—of communities against companies, of counterhegemonic discourses against hegemonies, of indigenous against modern, of peasant against large-scale capital—the authors of these chapters approach struggle in its various dimensions. They document struggles to cope with extractive industry, to respond to and resist extraction, to maneuver among and make sense of shifting contours of identity politics, and to demand new ways of governing extraction. The authors also describe struggles within movements among groups with differing interests and agendas, and, more generally, the everyday struggles and tensions that frequently accompany the rise of extraction and become embedded in everyday life within these "territories of extraction" (Humphreys Bebbington 2010).

We frame these struggles as *subterranean* partly as a play on the fact that these are struggles around and mediated through the subsoil. However, we also want to capture the sense that various elements of these struggles are hidden from easy view. Many dimensions of struggle become routinized in everyday life; these are not just the dramatic armed and organized struggles that Watts (2004a) draws attention to, but also the mundane but painful everyday calculations that Warnaars (Chapter 6 of this volume) speaks of as she describes the way in which conflicts over mining in El Pangui, Ecuador, seep into all aspects of life: "Daily activities such as buying groceries at the neighbour's food store, using the internet services from the man across the road, choosing which taxi to take or which hotel to stay in all depend on whether 'they are with us or not.'" These hidden costs of extraction never find their ways into environment and social impact assessments, yet are arguably one of the most permanent and irreversible consequences of the irruption of extraction into local societies.

A second subterranean component of these struggles is the issue of memories and histories that course through people's responses to extraction. Warnaars again offers one example of this: memories of earlier mining accidents that have transformed former artisanal and small-scale miners into some of the most assertive critics of mining in El Pangui. Other memories run yet deeper. Extraction is a territorializing project (Wilson 2004; Humphreys

Bebbington and Bebbington 2010) that may intersect with quite distinct territorializing projects that have long histories. Thus, as Bebbington et al. note in Chapter 10, conflicts around natural gas in Tarija Bolivia are also bound up with a long history of territorial loss for Guarani and Weenhayek people. This does not necessarily translate into outright rejection of gas extraction — rather, for these indigenous peoples the struggle is *how* (at once a political and an intellectual challenge) to make gas extraction functional in their efforts to regain territory, to make territorial reconsolidation a politically *and* economically viable project, and to ground this in a coherent politics of identity. Derrick Hindery also presents these issues in Chapter 8.

In Chapter 10, Bebbington et al. highlight another frequently hidden element of conflicts over extraction: the imbrications of such conflicts with other partisan political and ideological projects. The presence of political parties and movements within these conflicts is often used by companies and government in their efforts to delegitimize protests, on the grounds that the protests are politically motivated rather than based on any justifiable cause for concern. Putting on one side the untenable distinction between conflicts that are political and others that are not, the analytically significant point here is that struggles over extraction frequently become overdetermined: they serve as lightning rods for other struggles that have gone latent for a while but are then reactivated through the tensions and passions aroused by extraction. The struggles over extraction also serve as vehicles for such other struggles. This should be no great surprise — it does, though, present an analytical challenge at the point of trying to understand the struggles over extraction and simultaneously understanding the ways in which extraction is bundled up with other dimensions of the political economy. Unpicking this dimension of conflict has been systematically weak in political ecology, which in general says very little about political parties but a bit more about political movements. In this collection, the theme is especially present in Tom Perreault's discussion of gas and regional politics in Bolivia (Chapter 3).

While some of the struggles treated in this book are indeed hidden, others are prominent and often overtly violent. However, they are subterranean in yet another sense because they involve resources that have yet to be unearthed and can only be exploited using sophisticated technologies and with the deployment of massive capital-intensive machinery. Furthermore, the full environmental costs of such activities are often obscured by time horizons that can run across several generations and involve complex environmental problems such as acid mine drainage or deep water table contamination. Many of the environmental impacts of the mineral and hydrocarbon operations discussed in this book are likely to persist long into the future. Consequently, the hidden nature and moral and economic value of the resources hidden below surface ecological and social systems are generating new types of struggles over access to resources that are very sensitive to temporal and spatial considerations and are complex to evaluate. These struggles are also profound because of what is at stake. The environmental and social consequences of the most recent round of large-scale extractive operations are of such magnitude that they involve struggles over the very existence of landscapes imbued with cultural meaning, quality of life for large populations, and entire livelihood systems. Bury and Norris in Chapter 4 and Postigo, Montoya, and Young in Chapter 9 examine these struggles over landscapes and large-scale social and environmental impacts in the Andes and the Amazon.

The Chapters Introduced

This collection is concerned with exploring the political ecological transformations that have been part of the last two decades of expansion in the extractive economy. The authors address the relationships between the broader and more local manifestations of these transformations, and they trace the relations between these transformations and a range of struggles and conflicts in the region. The chapters are organized such that we begin at a regional level (Chapter 2), move to subnational scales (Chapters 3 through 8), and then draw out broader patterns by comparing across the different ways in which regional and subnational dynamics interact (Chapters 9 through 11).

In Chapter 2, Bury and Bebbington lay out the contours of the new political economy of extraction in the Andean-Amazonian region. The authors briefly analyze the historical and macroeconomic dimensions of the current growth of extractive industries and the scale and nature of investment in the natural resource sector across Latin America. They then address the recent resurgence of mineral investment and extractive activities in the wake of the global economic crisis, challenges to the neoliberal model of economic development, and the influence of new transnational actors and shifting political affairs in the region. They conclude the chapter with a brief discussion of the near-term social and environmental challenges posed by Latin America's deepening and rapidly expanding extractive-led development.

Addressing the relationships between the subsoil and national and subnational politics, Perreault (Chapter 3) examines struggles over the reterritorializations of Bolivian space and the way they are shaped by natural gas extraction, the control of gas rents, competing visions of national economic development, and the emergence and consolidation of social identities. With

South America's second largest reserves, gas extraction has fuelled competing spatial imaginaries of economic development and national identity, and this uneasy cartography of social struggle may be seen as a contest between a nationalist vision of development and an export-led model of regional autonomy. Perreault concludes that these struggles over natural gas extraction have animated latent and antagonistic social identities centered on regional divides, ethnic difference, and class struggle; they are, therefore, central to understanding contemporary struggles over national territory, development, and identity in Bolivia.

As Perreault also notes, gas has also been central to the politics of neoliberalism and post-neoliberalism in Bolivia (see also Bebbington and Humphreys Bebbington 2011). In a related vein, in Chapter 4 Bury and Norris examine competing frontiers of neoliberal change in Peru, specifically the frontiers of global mineral investment and of private conservation initatives in the Cordillera Huayhuash, Peru. Since the 1990s, each form of land use has expanded in the Huayhuash, unevenly superimposed not only upon the region's human and natural geographies but also upon each other. The authors explore the paradox of, and conflicts over, these competing forces of change, their impacts on local communities and households, and the ways in which resistance and social mobilization are shaping the future of resource governance in the region. Resonating with themes in Perreault's chapter, Bury and Norris show how conflicts related to the extractive economy are also very often conflicts over the governance of space.

Moore and Velásquez in Chapter 5 examine the nature of struggles around mineral extraction activities in Ecuador's new "Twenty-first Century Socialism" agenda. This is a revealing context in different ways. First, as Ecuador has little history of medium- or large-scale metal mining, these are struggles over the very initial moments of the establishment of a significant mining economy. Second, somewhat as in the case of Bolivia, these struggles are occurring under a progressive government brought to power with the support of many of the same social organizations and movements with which it is now in conflict over mining. Third, in the cases that Moore and Velásquez discuss, the people contesting mining are far from classic subaltern actors. These are market-oriented dairy producers and export-oriented banana farmers. Their concerns are to protect the conditions of existence of their livelihoods, and their strategies combine protest with the production of scientific and technical knowledge to contest the claims of miners. The authors explore the reach and limits of these strategies and the nature of the claims made in these protests, suggesting how important it is to understand the *actual* nature of struggles rather than read them through preexisting lenses of resistance and alterity. Moore and Velásquez also suggest the need to be cautious regarding the prospects of such struggles, and they suggest not only that the rush of an ostensibly progressive government towards extraction has reduced the political space for struggle, but also that expanded dependence on extraction constrains possibilities for progressive national political, economic, or ecological agendas.

Ximena Warnaars continues these themes in Chapter 6. She too analyzes conflicts around mining in Ecuador, but this time in the humid tropical lowlands. Like Moore and Velásquez, Warnaars emphasizes the complexity of these struggles, insisting that there is no room for Mannichean readings of conflicts among two groups: miners and the population. Understanding territory as itself a product of sedimented and overlapping conflicts, many of them living on through current memories, she describes how the arrival of mining is, in a sense, just one more layer in this process of sedimentation. It is, though, a particularly powerful layer, inducing significant polarization within the territory and bringing previously buried conflicts back to the surface. Warnaars discusses this polarization partly through a focus on moments of organized conflict. She is, however, more interested in discussing how these conflicts come to permeate everyday life—put another way, while Moore and Velásquez (Chapter 5) consider how struggle is *strategized*, Warnaars (Chapter 6) emphasizes how it is *lived*. This suggests yet another sense in which struggle is subterranean—in Warnaars reading, it is always just beneath the surface of everyday encounters in stores, hair salons, and taxis and on the street.

In Chapter 7, Bebbington and Scurrah bring the focus back to hydrocarbons with their discussion of the case of Río Corrientes, one of the most emblematic conflicts over oil extraction in the Northeast Peruvian Amazon. This conflict has waxed and waned for over three decades as a result, above all, of the environmental and health damage inflicted by different operators of the oil field. However, since the mid-2000s the conflict began to take a new course as a combined effect of (1) new strategies of struggle on the part of lowland indigenous organizations (strategies that combined forceful direct action with very explicit and specific negotiation with the company and government), and (2) a new interest on the part of the then Human Rights Ombudswoman's office to become involved in the case. The case is interesting not only because of its long (and unresolved) history but also because part of the State became an active player in seeking to move the conflict in the direction favored by indigenous organizations. That it took this role reflected specific changes in the Ombudswoman's office, as well as work conducted by the Ministry of Health demonstrating serious health impacts due to the release of waste waters into the human environment. The authors discuss in some detail the nature of the conflict, negotiation, and agreement that un-folded in the 2000s. In the process, they reveal some of the hidden aspects of the negotiations that often accompany struggle and demonstrate that details of those negotiations can have significant causal effects in the regional politi-cal ecology. The chapter is also striking in that it is something of an alphabet soup of organizations, but this only shows just how many actors can become caught up in the struggles discussed in this book—again warning against any simple Mannichean explanations.

In Chapter 8, Derrick Hindery continues with the focus on hydrocar-bons in ways that contrast with Bebbington and Scurrah (Chapter 7) while also connecting with issues raised in Chapters 1 and 2. The core of Hindery's argument is that individual extractive industry projects should not be seen in isolation—indeed to view them separately is to see them in ways that suit the interests of industry because this obscures the full social and environmental impacts of any single project. Hindery explores the synergies between gas pipeline, mining, and large-scale infrastructural investments in the Eastern Lowlands of Bolivia, tracing a series of impacts that flow from these syner-gies. Tackling these synergistic impacts presents particular challenges to in-digenous and nongovernmental organizations, both because they are rarely included in the project-specific environmental impact statements on which these groups are consulted and because to trace them requires a capacity to grasp regional-level processes that is often beyond the resources of many such organizations. Indeed, Hindery's case is testament to the limited ability of indigenous organizations to monitor and reverse the negative impacts of ex-tractive projects in their territories. Herein lies the significant contrast with the case of Río Corrientes: while Hindery does not analyze the reasons for this limited influence, his analysis would suggest that an important factor has been the involvement of international organizations and a national state fully invested in extraction. He closes the chapter wondering whether the Morales government might constitute a positive step forward for indigenous rights and environmental protection, while also noting that the violent conflicts in 2011 over road building in the Indigenous Territory and National Park of Isiboro-Securé "suggest limited progress on the ground." Indeed, other ana-lyses of Bolivia, including Humphreys Bebbington (2012b), as well as those described in Chapters 5 and 6 on Ecuador, would also argue against being sanguine in this regard.

The authors of Chapters 9 and 10 offer a comparative approach to ana-lyzing the place of struggle within subsoil political ecologies of the region. In Chapter 9, Postigo, Montoya, and Young read across four different cases of extraction in Peru, while in Chapter 10 Bebbington and colleagues draw out patterns from case studies in Bolivia, Ecuador, and Peru. Taken together, the two chapters cover experiences in the coast, highlands, humid lowlands, and drier Chaco lowlands. Notwithstanding this geographical diversity, certain patterns seem recurrent both across cases and between the two chapters. Most significant among these patterns is the absolute centrality of struggle and mobilization. For Postigo, Montoya, and Young, in the face of state-business coalitions that provide such stong support for forms of extraction that create risks to livelihood, "social mobilization is often the only tool available for local people." Meanwhile Bebbington et al. conclude that "even if some mobilizations do not achieve their goals (be these to block extractive industry, to secure its unencumbered expansion, or to negotiate the terms on which companies as well as state and local populations interact), the dynamics surrounding extraction have changed profoundly throughout the region as a result of social protest." However, the two chapters also show the different ways in which struggle affects such dynamics. As part of their larger argument that subsoil political ecologies should include significant biophysical analysis (as we also argue above), Postigo, Montoya, and Young insist that some of the variation to be found across cases has to be understood in terms of differences in ecology, hydrology, and mineralogy. For their part, Bebbington et al. draw particular attention to interactions between contemporary struggles and diverse regional political-ecological histories.

These two comparative chapters also emphasize the extent to which subterranean struggles should be understood not only in terms of existing state forms, but also as constitutive of those forms. Indeed, Bebbington et al. conclude that at their core, most struggles over extraction reflect demands for a stronger state—for stronger regulatory presence, for planning, for protection of human rights and environmental assets, and for predictability in the lived environment of rural populations. If this is so, then the final measure of the success of these struggles is the extent to which they are vehicles for institutional change.

In the concluding chapter we assess how far and in what ways the claims that we have laid out in this introduction are supported by the empirical chapters. To recap, our arguments are both regional and general. At a regional level we have argued that the contemporary dynamics of extraction in Latin America are fundamentally new. We have also argued that the newness and scale of this phenomenon mean that the political economy of extraction has become central to more general transformations in the region—or, put more bluntly, that one cannot explain the political economy of much of contemporary Latin America without considering the extractive economy. Then, beyond the specificities of Latin America, we are making the more general argument that the subsoil has an analytical significance of its own and that this merits specific attention in political ecology. In particular, we claim that to engage with the subsoil highlights the centrality of the state to political ecology, suggests a particular sense of both the ecological and the political in political ecology, makes struggle yet more central than has already been suggested by iconic texts in the subfield, suggests new avenues for linking global flows and territorial dynamics, and brings particular challenges to the practice of political ecology.

Notes

1. We are grateful to comments on this essay from Tom Perreault and Emily Gallagher. Early parts of the chapter draw on Bebbington (2012b).

2. Zimmerer (2007) does mention articles by Derrick Hindery (2004) on gas pipelines in Bolivia and Jeffrey Bury (2004) on neoliberalism and mining expansion in Peru, though he does not dwell on them.

3. This growing interest also became apparent in the Annual Meetings of the Association of American Geographers from 2007 with a growing number of papers and sessions on the subsoil in non-OECD (Organization for Economic Co-operation and Development) contexts. The Latin American Studies Association conference in 2009 also suggested increasing concern for the topic.

4. The "academic" qualification is an important one—see below.

5. More exactly, what is today called Bolivia.

6. Though it must be noted that the notion of Chile and Botswana as "success stories" is not shared by all, with the long-term viability of the Botswanan option seeming uncertain according to some (Battisteli and Guichaoua 2012).

7. See Blacksmith Institute's 2007 Press Release "The 2007 Top Ten of Worst Polluted Places," 12 September 2007, http://www.blacksmithinstitute.org/the-2007-top-ten-of-worst-polluted-places.html.

8. These figures refer to all federal direct investments (FDI), not just in extraction. The figures are US$46,907,000 in 2004 and US$92,945,000 in 2007.

9. See www.hria-guatemala.com (HRIA Guatemala) for the status of human rights impact assessments in Guatemala.

10. For more information on IIRSA, see www.iirsa.org. According to IIRSA, by the beginning of 2009, 51 of its projects had been concluded and 196 were being implemented, with a combined cost of US$38 billion; another 103 projects were being prepared, with a cost of US$17 billion; and 31 projects had been defined as strategically important and so were being given priority (IIRSA 2008). Given the scale of investment in IIRSA, and the transformations in South American environments that it will catalyze, there is remarkably little work on it in the academic literature.

CHAPTER 2

New Geographies of Extractive Industries in Latin America

JEFFREY BURY AND ANTHONY BEBBINGTON

Shortly after midnight on Friday, October 12, 1492, Christopher Columbus and his expeditionary force of three ships first hove into view of the landscapes of the Americas. The next morning the expedition made landfall on a small island in the Bahamas where Columbus claimed the lands for the Spanish Crown.[1] When the many inhabitants of the island approached them, Columbus and his men offered them a few red caps, glass beads, and "many other things of little value," which apparently "gave them great pleasure and made them so much our friends it was a marvel to see" (Columbus, as cited in Markham 1893, 33). The local people, in exchange, gave them parrots, skeins of cotton thread, darts, and some of the gold jewelry that they wore, as Columbus notes, "on their arms, legs, in their ears, around their necks, and through their noses" (Markham 1893, 39). On the first day of contact Columbus noted that he was satisfied with the results of these exchanges because the local inhabitants "would be more easily freed and converted to our holy faith by love than by force" and that "they should be good servants" (Markham 1893, 37–38). This momentous meeting on the beaches of the Bahamas, when Columbus offered the native populations of the Western Hemisphere trinkets of little value in exchange for their freedom and lands, is a well-worn moment of profound historical significance that inaugurated a centuries-long period of interhemispheric unequal exchange that transformed the planet (Crosby 1972). While history has long examined the conquest of the Americas through the triple imperatives of god, gold, and glory, from the distance of four centuries, the text of Columbus' journals is inordinately and rather obsessively focused on gold, its abundance, and how it might be extracted. From the very first moments following first contact, when Columbus notes that he "took trouble to ascertain if there was gold" and that "the men made signs that there is much gold" (Columbus, as cited in Markham

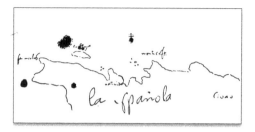

"It is certain that where there are such lands there must be an infinite number of things that would be profitable." (Christopher Columbus, November 26, 1492)

The map is purported to have been hand sketched by Columbus upon his arrival to the island of Hispaniola (currently the Dominican Republic and Haiti) two days after his "discovery" of the Americas (Bagrow and Skelton 2009). The statement is drawn from abstracts of Columbus' journal transcribed by Bartolomé de las Casas and translated by Markham (1893). The original journals have thus far been lost to history.

1893, 39, 44), the promising glimmers of its presence transforms the focus of the voyage. His subsequent five-month tour of the region becomes a frenzied quest for golden treasure, pausing, as he states in one translated version of his journals, "no longer than the winds forced me" and that this new region "may contain many things of which I have no knowledge, for I do not wish to stop, in discovering and visiting many islands, to find gold" (Columbus 1892, 11; Columbus as cited in Markham 1893, 45). The rest of the expedition's daily log entries then describe his search for gold and other items of value across the islands of what are currently Cuba, Haiti, and the Dominican Republic. The topic of gold also dominated the expedition's interactions with and treatment of local inhabitants. Anyone indicating that they knew where any measurable quantity of gold could be found was violently taken hostage until the gold was found and eventually acquired through whatever means necessary. Eventually, and perhaps not altogether coincidentally considering the fact that the presence of gold would likely lead to wholesale pillaging of their communities and peoples, local leaders began to suggest either that they had no gold or that somewhere, much farther off in the distance, there was a fabulous island literally made of gold. As Columbus notes, he "heard from an old man that there were many neighboring islands, at a distance of a hundred leagues or more, in which much gold is found." Even more enticingly, and similar to Marco Polo's description of the fabled treasure of *Cipango*, he notes that he was told that "there is even one island that was all gold [and] in the others there was so much that it was said they gather it in sieves, and they fuse it to make bars, and work it in a thousand ways" (Columbus as cited in Markham 1893, 117). Columbus thus "made sail to shape a course in search of the islands which the Indians had told him contained much gold, some of them having more gold than earth" (Markham 1893, 126). While these islands were never located by Columbus during his four voyages, edited versions of his account of the islands became some of the most widely read texts across Europe during the sixteenth century. Subsequent waves of *conquistadores* sought the fabulous treasures of the El Dorados of the Western Hemisphere, and though most were mythical constructs, Hernando Cortes and Francisco Pizarro did indeed encounter such places in the cases of the Aztec and Inca capital cities of Tenochtitlan and Cusco (Prescott 1843; Hemming 1970).

Columbus' first accounts of the region also had a much more immediate and profound impact on world affairs, largely because the expedition was, first and foremost, funded as a business venture to establish new commercial trade routes. Columbus' description of the lands of the Western Hemisphere bears a striking resemblance to what today would be referred to as a venture capital business proposal in that it was a quite accurate and thoroughly persuasive discussion of the potential profit that might be generated through the extraction of the region's many resources. Throughout the text of his journals he refers directly to his investors—in this case the King and Queen of Spain—in the hope of persuading them to invest more extensively in future operations that would, he insisted, be more profitable. In this reading of the text, Columbus, or perhaps his editor, Bartolomé de las Casas, carefully describes the key factor endowments of land, labor, and capital investment that will lead to future profits. For example, the frequency of his discussion of various elements illustrates that while the various formulations of the terms *god* and *Christian* are mentioned 36 and 51 times, respectively, and are certainly justified as noble reasons to "invest," so to speak, in the business, much more of the text is devoted to the abundance of resources that can be extracted and appraisals of the health and suitability of the local people for labor devoted to the extraction of these resources. Outside of referring to himself (the term *admiral* appears 560 times in the text), the next most common terms are formulations of land, including the terms *island* (258 times) and *land* (211). Next in frequency are various formulations and discussion of the local people (190). The terms *great* (144), *king* (111), *highnesses* (56) and *sovereigns* (53) are indeed utilized, which does provide some support for the "glory" imperative of the conquest. However, a large part of the text is devoted to a very extensive and thorough inventory of the potential resources of these new lands, including, first and foremost, gold (146), but also precious items and metals such as pearls (11), copper (7), iron (6), silver (5), and mines (15). Other resources that are detailed in the text include spices (15) and cinnamon (5)—the original purpose of the expedition was, of course, to establish new trade routes for spices to the "Indies"—trees (68), fish (29), "mastick," or resin, for ships (17), and fruits (15). Overall, the final extractive business proposition that the text outlines through its discussion of these endowments is that the Admiral's desire to "ascertain whether there were any profitable commodities" (Markham 1893, 107) resulted in the identification of "an infinite number of things" that had the potential to be profitable, and that "there is only wanting a settlement and the order to the people to do what is required" (Markham 1893, 114).

As history illustrates, Columbus' business proposal was accepted by his royal investors, which led to the extraction of remarkable quantities of natural resources from Latin America over the next 400 years. Recent estimates of just the quantity of gold and silver extracted during this period suggest that between 1492 and 1810 approximately 1,685 metric tons of gold and 85,991 metric tons of silver were shipped from the region (TePaske, Klein, and Brown 1982; Garner 1988). At current market rates (as of November 2011), the combined value of the gold and silver would be worth roughly 210 *billion* U.S. dollars. Given the enormity of the business proposal underlying the conquest, as well as the violent conquest and eventual decimation of the populous and well-organized civilizations of the Western Hemisphere, the extractive legacy in Latin America is a defining event from which much of the region's complex geographies have evolved and which inalterably transformed human affairs.

The purpose of this chapter is to provide a broad contextual background to extractive industries in Latin America. Columbus' careful description of the natural and human resources of the region provide a useful starting point for this discussion as such endowments have long been discussed by scholars across a variety of disciplines (Smith 1776; Marx and Engels 1867; Ricardo 1891; Heckscher and Ohlin 1991; Sokoloff and Engerman 2000; Engerman and Sokoloff 2005). While recent discussions have focused on the ways in which the factor endowments of land, labor, and capital resources underlying extractive industries affect international trade and economic growth (Hirsch 1974; Davis and Vásquez Cordano 2011), the focus of this chapter is much more constrained, as it seeks to illustrate the constituent factor endowments of the mining and hydrocarbons extractive sectors in Latin America and how various constellations of land, labor, and capital have affected their geographic distribution and evolution over time. This chapter is organized as follows. The first section examines recent research that is deepening our historical understanding of pre-conquest extractive industries. As part of a broader set of new research that is rewriting the historical evolution of the region, this section seeks to provide some sense of the nature of extractive industries during this emerging system of pre-Columbian exchange. The subsequent two sections then provide a very brief summary of the evolution of extractive industries across the region from just after the conquest up to the mid-twentieth century and then focus on the extractive "super cycle" of the past two decades. The final parts of the chapter examine the current state of the hydrocarbons and mineral sector across the region, explore recent technological and economic trends, and suggest that the sector has become a vast "complex" of activities that are constitutive of political, economic, and social relations throughout the countries of the region and link Latin America to the rest of the world.

Mining Histories from the Pre-Columbian Exchange

For more than 400 years our knowledge of pre-conquest mineral extraction activities was limited to the first-hand accounts of Spanish chroniclers who witnessed the conquest (de Cieza de León 1864; Estete 1535; Pizarro 1921; Xerez 1872). These observations were derived from casual surveys and first-hand impressions and were largely confined to the routes that the conquistadores followed. For example, Hernando Pizarro describes mining activities throughout Central Peru in 1532 (see Chapter 4 of this volume, by Bury and Norris). After the conquest, both the Incan and Aztec civilizations rapidly collapsed or were dismantled by the conquerors. Any comprehensive mining records that might have existed were lost in these catastrophic events and, as the native human populations of the Western Hemisphere disappeared, so too did the mines.[2] Other historical accounts were developed through interviews or reconstructed histories, often long after the conquest or outside of Latin America (de la Vega, Urquizo, and Araníbar 1967; de Las Casas 1971; Guaman Poma de Ayala 1980; de Las Casas 1992).

Recent historical research, assisted by a number of technological innovations, has enhanced the abilities of researchers to peer further into the past and into periods for which there are no human records. New technologies have been deployed to interrogate the fused ecological and social histories present in the charcoal of ancient fires, artifacts from the middens of human settlements, and the strata of lake beds and wetlands. Utilizing techniques such as radiocarbon dating, lake sediment stratigraphy, scanning electron microscopy, inductively coupled plasma-atomic emission spectroscopy, and portable X-ray fluorescence, a new period of pre-conquest histories has begun to emerge across much of the region.

The ecological record that these histories have begun to uncover with increasing resolution suggests that rather than a smooth transition between the late Pleistocene (30,000 years before present and when anatomically modern humans first appeared), the Holocene (10,000 years before present and when human civilizations first began appear), and the present, climate shifts across the region have been frequent, diverse, and often abrupt (Abbott et al. 2003; Dillehay 2008; Kuentz, Ledru, and Throuet 2011). This climatological complexity in temperature, precipitation, sea level, and glacial coverage thus led to the creation of a shifting and dynamic mosaic of landscapes and biological zones across the Americas. For example, several millennia of dry conditions during the mid-Holocene (8,000–5,000 years before present) led to the lowest water level in the Lake Titicaca basin in the past 30,000 years and a significant retreat of glaciers in Southern Peru (Baker et al. 2001; Buffen et al. 2009).

Recent research has also provided an array of new information about the presence and extent of human activities during the pre-conquest period. Contentious new evidence in what is now called the field of "first American studies" suggests that humans travelled to and occupied the Americas millennia earlier than was previously thought (Santos et al. 2003; Mann 2006; Dillehay 2009; Waters 2011). In addition, new archaeological discoveries across the region suggest that the rise of human civilizations began much earlier than was previously thought. For example, in Peru, new carbon dating techniques recently revealed that the central coastal complex of Caral was inhabited between 5,000 and 3,000 years before present (Solis, Haas, and Creamer 2001; Haas, Creamer, and Ruiz 2004). The inhabitants of Caral constructed pyramids that contain as much material as the great pyramids of Giza, though they were built nearly two millennia earlier, and materials discovered in the trash middens of the complex indicate that diverse long-distance trade routes existed that linked the coast with the highlands and Amazon Basin. While future discoveries may continue to deepen the historical record of human civilization in the region, Caral is now considered to be the oldest civilization in the Americas.

Taken together, new developments related to pre-Columbian natural and human histories suggest that the relationships between Latin American societies and their environments have been very extensive and that periods of abrupt change have occurred repeatedly (Denevan 1992a; Hodell, Curtis, and Brenner 1995; Binford et al. 1997; Erickson 1999; Sandweiss et al. 2009). The implications of these shifts in the historical record also suggest that extensive, highly organized and technologically sophisticated societies existed 4,000–5,000 years before present and that they were also engaged in numerous natural resource extraction activities. New research supports this claim, as several thousand years of successive mining and smelting centers have been identified along the Nasca-Ica coastal shelf of Peru (Eerkens et al. 2008; Eerkens, Vaughn, and Grados 2009; Van Gijseghem et al. 2011), in the Central Peruvian mountains near Morococha and Huancavelica (Burger and Mendieta 2002; Cooke et al. 2007; Vaughn et al. 2007; Cooke, Wolfe, and Hobbs 2009), across the high altiplano from Lake Titicaca to Bolivia (Abbott et al. 2003; Schultze et al. 2009; Cooke et al. 2010), and along the Chilean coast (Graffam, Rivera, and Carevič 1996; Fuller 2004; Cooke, Wolfe, and Hobbs 2009).

A synthetic analysis of this recent research indicates that pre-Columbian mineral extraction activities were widespread and included most of Peru, Bolivia and Chile. Many extractive sites were also located where later and more intensive extraction either took place or is currently taking place and include similar metals and minerals. This includes between Moquegua and the Lake Titicaca Basin (gold and silver—4,000 years before present), Ica (gold—3,800 years before present), Chuquicamata and Nasca (copper and gold, silver—1,500 years before present), Huancavelica and Cerro de Pasco (hematite and cinnabar, silver—1,400 years before present), Potosi (silver—1,000 years before present), and Morococha (copper and silver—1,000 years before present). While mineral extraction activities were widespread, they were fairly small, or as Stanish et al. (2010) suggest in the case of Lake Titicaca, "light but continuous."

Pre-Columbian extractive operations were largely developed through widespread human labor and technological advancements that included both new human knowledge and the physical resources necessary for the extraction and concentration of minerals. Extractive technologies deployed during this period were primarily limited to alluvial deposits for gold and rudimentary smelting operations for gold and silver. Alluvial mining activities, or *placer* in Spanish, have been dated to as long as 3,800 years before present in Ica, and silver refining and metallurgy have been dated to as far as 4,000 years before present at Lake Titicaca and 1,400 years before present in Cerro de Pasco (Schultz et al. 2010, 2011).

The social, economic and political systems surrounding the earliest extractive operations in the Americas are, and will perhaps always be, uncertain. While it is unclear how and under what conditions mineral extraction took place in the earliest sites, the rise of large empires such as the Tiwanaku, Inca, and Aztec was most likely responsible for a great deal of these activities. In the case of the Tiwanaku Empire, as both Schulte (2009) and Stanish (2010) argue, minerals were likely one key component of and incentive for long-distance trade due to their religious and cultural values. Finally, mining at most pre-Columbian sites was also based on relatively small encampments of human laborers, but was more intensively concentrated at major smelting sites where large deposits were located. However, the actual population of miners and how they were organized will likely remain a mystery, particularly because many of the biggest operations were located in areas that have been the site of ever-increasing production for the past 1500 years and have very likely been destroyed.

The Conquest and Its Enduring Legacy

Any adequate treatment of the 500 years in Latin America between the conquest and the extractive boom of the late twentieth century would require space far beyond that which is available here. Much of this history has been effectively addressed in other works that together have analyzed: the initial conquest and pillage of the native empires of the Americas for their treasures; the demographic collapse and disappearance of most of the people who had been living in the Western Hemisphere prior to the conquest; three centuries of colonial exploitation under the Spanish and Portuguese colonial systems; struggles for independence in the early 1800s and the long decline of capital that ensued; the devastating effects of the Great Depression and two World Wars on natural resource exports; and the emergence of state-led industrialization during the revolutionary period between the late 1940s and end of the 1970s (Rowe 1957; Samame 1984; Greaves 1985; Waszkis 1993; Walton 1994; Bethell 1995; Machado and Figueiroa 2001; Raimondi 2006; Burkholder and Johnson 2008; Humboldt and Bonpland 2008; Markham 1910; Thorp and Bertram 1978). Here we offer a brief discussion of the influence of the region's extractive heritage on subsequent historical periods and then briefly outline several key extractive periods leading up to the end of the 1980s.

During the first few decades after the conquest (de Cieza de León 1864; Prescott 1883; Hemming 1985; Estete and Ravines 1986), extractive activities across the Americas were largely engaged in plundering the precious metals of the Aztec and Inca empires and transferring massive amounts of minerals from the Americas to the rest of the world. The initial post-conquest period also involved the spatial reconfiguration of the region as native empires were dismantled and integrated into a global system of colonial control. During this period, the Spanish continued mining operations for gold and silver at a limited number of very productive native mines in Mexico and Bolivia, and labor for the mines was acquired through forced conscription, tribute,

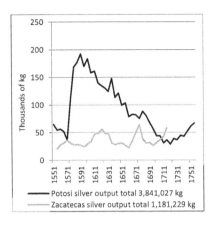

Figure 2.2. Zacatecas and Potosi annual silver output 1551–1760. Source: TePaske 1998

and taxes. As Figure 2.2 illustrates, mining at Potosi (Bolivia) and Zacatecas (Mexico) produced enormous amounts of bullion for several centuries.

Mineral processing at Potosi, one of the most productive silver mines in history, was initially dependent on native extraction and refining technologies such as *huayrachina* and *tocochimbo* furnaces and smelters and intensive human and animal labor (Galeano 1973; Bakewell 1984b; Cole 1985; Garner 1988; Van Buren and Mills 2005). In 1554, mercury amalgamation technologies were developed and spread across the region. Concentrating silver through the use of mercury (which is also referred to as the "patio process") initiated a several-centuries-long period of expansion of mining because it enabled lower-concentration ores to be profitably exploited (Brading and Cross 1972; Bakewell 1997). While the patio process was an extremely efficient technology that is still being utilized by artisanal small miners around the planet for gold extraction, Spanish control of mercury supplies and their distribution was also a key factor that influenced its adoption. Mercury is a very rare element, and during most of the colonial period the Spanish controlled the largest mercury mines in Almaden (Spain), Irija (Slovenia), and Huancavelica (Peru). Control of the mining process therefore allowed the Spanish to monopolize silver production and exploit human labor for centuries. Figure 2.3 illustrates the distribution and use of mercury across Mexico and Peru between 1558 and 1816 and the amount mined from each major source. According to TePaske, Klein, and Brown (1982), the Spanish produced 153,000 tons of mercury at these three mines that was then distributed across the Americas by colonial authorities.

Three centuries of colonial control of capital, mineral extraction technolo-

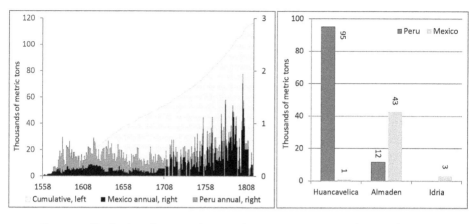

Figure 2.3. Distribution of mercury from royal treasuries in Mexico and Peru (left) and Spanish mercury mine production (right). Sources: Brown 1994; Garner 1988; TePaske, Klein, and Brown 1982

gies, and mining labor across the Western Hemisphere profoundly influenced the historical evolution of extractive industries, both during the colonial period and for many years after Latin American independence in the early 1800s. It also deeply affected the spatial configuration of most modern Latin American states and the distribution and locations of major cities. Overall, the system of mineral production that was established during the three centuries of colonial control was responsible for the creation of a global system of extraction, exchange, and production that was organized around twenty-two royal treasuries across the Americas. As Figure 2.4 illustrates, the sum total of silver and gold produced during these three centuries, according to recent estimates, was approximately 86,000 tons of silver and 1,600 tons of gold. Comparatively, the amount of gold extracted from the Americas is about 5 percent of all government gold reserves today, or roughly 50 percent of all of the gold jewelry currently on the planet (WGC 2011). The amount of silver produced in the Americas during this period is approximately 7 percent of all of the silver ever mined in human history (USGS 2012).

During the period from Latin American independence to the early twentieth century, little capital was available for new large-scale mining operations throughout the region. New mining technologies were introduced that had been developed during the gold rush in the United States and Canada in the late 1800s, but investment was fairly limited because of the lack of infrastructure and mineral processing plants (Bernstein 1964; Thorp and Bertram 1978; Purser 1971; Deustua 2000). The hydrocarbons sector also emerged in Latin

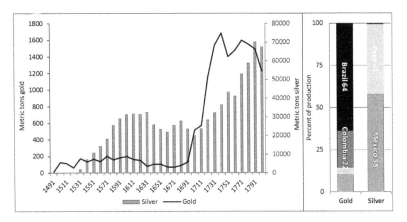

Figure 2.4. Right: Annual production of gold and silver by royal treasuries in the Western Hemisphere, 1491–1821; Left: Distribution of production by percentage and modern country boundaries. Sources: Garner 2006; TePaske, Klein, and Brown 1982

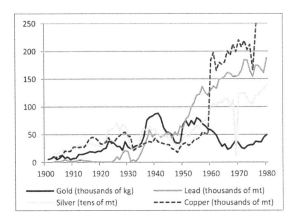

Figure 2.5. Mineral production in Peru, 1900–1980. Source: MEM 2000

America at the beginning of the twentieth century. While the first oil well was drilled in Titusville, Pennsylvania, in 1859 and the first large oil company (Standard Oil) was formed in 1870 by John D. Rockefeller, oil was not discovered in Mexico until 1901. Oil discoveries then occurred throughout the region during the next few decades.

The first half of the 1900s was characterized by a series of boom and bust cycles for extractive industries. These are reflected, for instance, in mineral production trends in Peru during the twentieth century (Figure 2.5). The Great Depression and two World Wars led to declines and surges in extractive operations. The postwar period spurred rapid growth in demand for industrial metals such as copper and lead, although gold prices declined for several decades until the global gold standard was abandoned in the 1970s. In 1969, General Juan Velasco assumed control of Peru and instituted import substitution industrialization policy reforms that provided new capital for mineral operations that enhanced mining production throughout the country. Similar patterns of growth in hydrocarbon and mineral production occurred across the region between the 1950s and 1970s (Cardoso and Faletto 1979; Becker 1983; Dore 1988). Employment and labor in the mineral sector expanded throughout the first half of the century. The mid-twentieth century also saw the widespread creation of mining syndicates and labor unions that figured prominently in the revolutionary politics of the 1960s and 1970s throughout Latin America (Long and Roberts 1984).

The Late Twentieth Century Extractives Super Cycle

During the 1990s, a number of global and regional political and economic transformations contributed to significant shifts in land, labor, and capital determinants and ushered in a new period of widespread growth of extractive industries across Latin America. At the global scale, the end of the Cold War led to a reconfiguration of geopolitical relationships (Hobsbawm 1995; Russett 1995; Gaddis 2006) that affected trade, investment, political, and development relations between Latin America and the rest of the world (Pastor 1992; Smith 1996; Sikkink 1997). Regionally, state-led industrialization and public ownership of extractive industries decreased considerably as the economic crises of the 1980s were followed by structural adjustment and neoliberal reforms. The confluence of these broad currents of change in the extractive sector initiated what has often been referred to as a "super cycle" of growth in mineral and gas production across the region (Humphreys Bebbington 2012a; Radetski et al. 2008; Silver 2008). Between the early 1990s and late 2008, the rapid growth of this cycle, though uneven in geographic extent, was historically unprecedented in terms of its magnitude and velocity.

Within Latin America, the extractive sector was seen as a critically important driver of economic growth by policymakers seeking to overcome the economic and political crises spurred by successive oil price shocks and massive national debt burdens. Import substitution industrialization policies and the nationalization of extractive industries during the decades prior to 1990 had culminated in several periods of hyperinflation and little economic growth. While there was considerable variation across the region (see Figure 2.6),

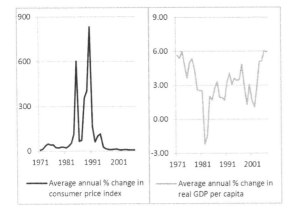

Figure 2.6. Consumer price index and real GDP change in Latin America, 1971–2007. Source: UNCTADSTAT 2011

hyperinflation of consumer prices was accompanied by declining economic growth between 1971 and 2001. Overall, the economic crises of the 1980s resulted in what is now commonly referred to as the "lost decade" of economic growth in Latin America (UNECLAC 1984; Green 2003).

Among the various effects of the spatial reordering of geopolitics that began at the end of the Cold War was the creation of new international trade and investment opportunities for many countries. In the decades since 1990, a new contingent of rapidly developing and highly populous countries has emerged, among them the so-called BRICS countries (Brazil, Russia, India, China, and South Africa), each seeking the necessary mineral and hydrocarbon supplies to support extensive urbanization and industrialization. At the same time, the developed economies have seen a decline in large-scale public construction projects and an economic slowdown partly due to a series of successive economic crises as well as in response to the continuing demographic transition. These shifts have begun to transform the global system of trade and commerce, as the BRICS countries come to account for increasingly significant shares of global economic growth. They have also become the largest sources of demand for raw materials. As Figure 2.7 illustrates, the percentage of global imports to developing and BRICS economies has nearly doubled since 1971, while the percentage of global imports to developed countries has declined by more than 25 percent.

As global demand for raw materials such as minerals and hydrocarbons has increased rapidly since 1990, commodities prices have also increased. Figure 2.8 illustrates how monthly prices for oil, gas, iron ore, copper, silver, gold, aluminum, and zinc have all increased consistently and significantly since the early 1990s. Composite indexes for these products demonstrate more clearly the sharp increase in prices that has occurred since the 1970s.

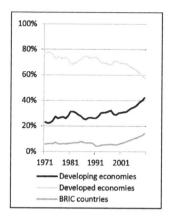

Figure 2.7. Annual shifts in global imports of goods and services. Source: UNCTADSTAT 2011

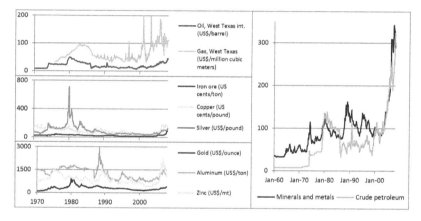

Figure 2.8. Left: Monthly hydrocarbons and select mining commodities price fluctuations, 1970–2007, adjusted for inflation; Right: Commodity price index for minerals, metals, and crude petroleum, 1960–2007, where 2000=100. Sources: GFD 2011; UNCTADSTAT 2011

In response to the political and economic shifts of the early 1990s, foreign investment surged across the globe. Between 1990 and 2007, more than US$12.7 trillion of foreign direct investment (FDI) crossed national boundaries. More than US$3.6 trillion of total FDI during this period was destined for developing countries. Figure 2.9 illustrates the rapid growth of global FDI flows beginning in 1990 as well as the volatility of investment that occurred over the period.

Between 1990 and 2007, the volatility of foreign investment to Latin America was similar to global flows. However, because the region received relatively small amounts of foreign investment prior to the year 1990, the cumulative magnitude of shifts in capital flows was much more pronounced. Overall, between 1990 and 2007, Latin America received US$969 billion in FDI. As Figure 2.10 illustrates, FDI was distributed unevenly across the region as South America accounted, on average, for roughly two thirds of all foreign investment into the region. In addition, FDI was concentrated in the largest economies. Average annual flows of FDI to the region increased by 20 percent over the period, though year-on-year changes ranged from 107

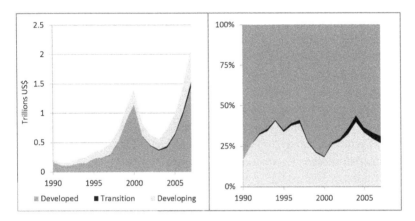

Figure 2.9. Global FDI flows 1990–2007. Source: UNCTADSTAT 2011

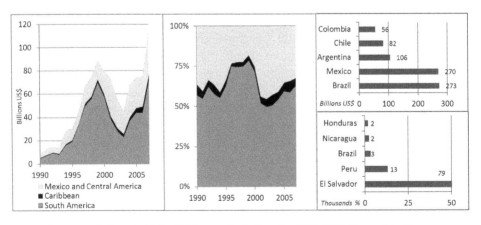

Figure 2.10. Left and middle: FDI flows to Latin America, 1990–2007; Upper right: Top five largest recipients of FDI by total amount; Lower right: Top five largest recipients of FDI by percentage change. Sources: UNECLAC 2011; UNCTADSTAT 2011

percent (1994) to minus 22 percent (2002). In the smaller economies of the region, the relative rate of increase in FDI flows was very significant. For example, between 1990 and 2007, FDI flows to El Salvador increased from US$1.9 million to US$1.5 billion, or more than 79,000 percent. Similar increases in FDI occurred throughout the Caribbean, Central America, and new investment destinations in South America.

The sources of these burgeoning FDI flows to Latin America were primarily Europe, North America, and Asia (i.e., Japan and China). While reliable comparative data are not available for much of the period, between 1999 and 2007, North American and European countries accounted for the vast majority of FDI flows across the region (UNECLAC 2011a). Figure 2.11 illustrates the variation in FDI flows by host region for Mexico and Central America, the Caribbean, and South America. Comparatively, the United States accounted for a little more than one half (53 percent) of FDI across all three regions, followed by Spain (17 percent), the Netherlands (11 percent), Japan (8 percent), the United Kingdom (4 percent), and Canada (3 percent). New flows of investment within Latin America also increased significantly during this period, though at just 3 percent of total FDI they were still relatively small in comparison to developed countries.

New flows of FDI to Latin America have financed extensive mining and hydrocarbons exploration during the past two decades. While reliable exploration investment data are mostly nonexistent and do not include the state-held operations that dominate petroleum production as well as many of the largest mining operations, between 1996 and 2007, global investments in exploration by transnational private-sector corporations accounted for approximately US$2 trillion in the hydrocarbons sector and US$91 billion in the mining sector (see Figure 2.12). Comparatively, hydrocarbons exploration in Latin America accounted for roughly 10 percent of global investment between 2005 and 2007, while mineral exploration accounted for 26 percent between 1996 and 2007.

Between 1998 and 2007, US$93.5 billion of FDI flowed into the natural resources sector in Latin America. The average annual increase of FDI in the natural resources sector was 26 percent, but, as Figure 2.13 (middle) demonstrates, in countries where potential new hydrocarbons and mineral deposits were discovered, FDI frequently increased by thousands of percent. Between 2004 and 2007, more than US$35 billion of FDI flowed into new mining operations, most of which was concentrated in just a few countries. During this same period, nearly US$12 billion of FDI flowed into the region to develop new hydrocarbons operations, primarily to develop recent oil discoveries

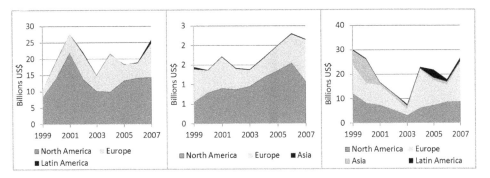

Figure 2.11. FDI flows by region of origin and destination, 1999–2007. Left: Mexico and Central America; Middle: Caribbean; Right: South America. Source: UNECLAC 2011

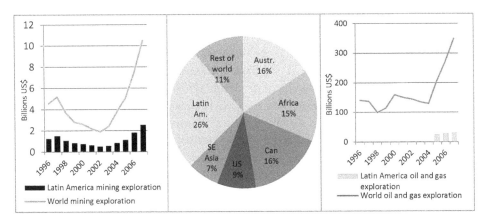

Figure 2.12. Mining and hydrocarbons exploration trends, 1996–2007. Left: Mining; Middle: World mining exploration average by percent; Right: Oil and gas exploration. Sources: Barclays 2009, 2011; Ernst & Young 2010; IFP Energies 2011; MEG 2011

in Brazil and gas deposits in the countries throughout the Amazon Basin as well as in Argentina and Bolivia (UNECLAC 2010).

The remarkable increase of extractive industry FDI across Latin America occurred in conjunction with changes in the political and economic relations governing natural resources. Largely due to the debt crises of the 1980s, many countries engaged in structural adjustment programs that were intended to attract new flows of foreign capital, generate foreign exchange for debt service, and foster economic growth. Many structural adjustment programs were

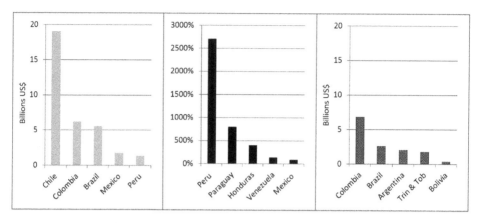

Figure 2.13. Top five recipients of extractive industry FDI in Latin America. Left: Mining, 2004–2007; Middle: FDI average annual percentage change in natural resources sector, 1998–2007; Right: Hydrocarbons, 2004–2007. Source: UNECLAC 2011

initiated during hyperinflation crises, under pressure from international lending institutions such as the World Bank and International Monetary Fund, and in accordance with the emerging "Washington Consensus" that sought to reintegrate Latin America into the global system of neoliberal trade and exchange. Aspects of the neoliberal shift that began during this period of change have been discussed and critiqued extensively in Chapter 1, by the authors of the different chapters in this text, and in an array of recent publications (e.g., Bridge 2004a; McCarthy 2004; Bury 2005; Harvey 2005; Perreault and Martin 2005; Liverman and Vilas 2006; Perreault 2006; Heynen 2007 et al.; Emel and Huber 2008; Castree 2008a, 2008b).

The features of the early neoliberal period of political and economic restructuring across the region's extractive sectors included the following key elements. First, many operations and proven mineral and hydrocarbons deposits were privatized and sold to foreign and domestic investors. Between 1990 and 1998, sales of state-run mining companies and investments in new private operations across the region generated US$140 billion for governments of the region and included a number of huge new mineral operations such as Antamina (US$5 billion), Pierina (US$800 million), and Shougang Iron (US$270 million), all in Peru (UNECLAC 2001). Second, new regulations to facilitate FDI were enacted across the region that mandated the nondiscrimination of foreign capital, freedom to remit profits abroad, reorganization and clarification of mining and hydrocarbons concessions, removal of local hiring and sourcing requirements, limitations on expropriation rights, ratification of international arbitration accords, and the creation of investment protections. Third, previous natural resource extraction legislation was either abolished or amended to limit public interest and eminent domain, reform environmental protection, establish minimal taxation regimes, formalize mineral and hydrocarbons concession taxation and leasing, and create investment incentives. Finally, many countries developed infrastructure to provide access to remote areas where new hydrocarbons and mineral deposits were being discovered. They also provided the necessary military and police support to ensure the safety of new extractive operations and their foreign personnel.

Though some countries implemented nearly all of the changes mentioned above (e.g., Peru), they were not implemented uniformly across the region, many have since been reversed or amended (e.g., Ecuador and Bolivia), and in some cases they have only recently been considered (e.g., Central America). Overall, the spatial reordering of natural resource governance has rapidly embedded the extractive sector into the global economy and fundamentally altered the social and political operating context for mining and hydrocarbons corporations across the region.

The flow of new FDI to Latin America has also been accompanied by the widespread introduction of new extractive techniques related to open pit mining, operations engineering, mineral processing, drilling, geotechnical modeling, and petroleum-intensive transportation. The introduction of these new technologies can be usefully illustrated by examining new cyanide heap leach gold mining operations that have spread rapidly throughout the region. In 1994, Newmont Mining Corporation began operating its Yanacocha cyanide heap leach gold mine in Northern Peru, which has now become the largest in the world. As the first new foreign investment in the Peruvian mining sector in more than thirty years, and the first cyanide-based gold mining operation in Latin America, Newmont deployed a host of new mining technologies to extract the diffuse gold contained in the large porphyritic domes discovered beneath the hillsides of the Cajamarca region (see also Chapter 10 in this volume, by Bebbington et al.). Porphyritic domes are igneous crustal intrusions that are often very large but only contain microscopic particles of gold that are embedded in the ore body, often at concentrations of less than one gram of gold per metric ton. In the late 1970s, drawing on more than a century of insights into the chemical properties of cyanide, new methods for dissolving and recovering gold from large tailings piles were developed in the United States (Dorr and Bosqui 1950; Habashi 1987; Krueger 2002). In order to deploy the gold cyanidation process profitably, ore must be extracted using large open pit mines, heaped onto plastic liners, and then sprayed with cyanide solution for long periods of time. Gold and other metals are dissolved as the cyanide flows through the ore. When it flows out of the heap it is then pumped to a processing facility that utilizes carbon, electrowinnowing, resin, or the patented Merrill-Crowe processes to concentrate the gold.

Constructing a large-scale cyanide heap leach gold mine thus requires access to highly guarded technical knowledge about gold cyanidation and separation. However, cyanide heap leach gold mining also requires access to a number of other skills and technologies such as sophisticated geotechnical analyses and modeling of ore deposits, mine engineering, widespread utilization of explosives, earth moving equipment to extract the ore, machinery to haul the ore, crushing or stamping mills to pulverize the ore, further engineering to design leach pads, and rigorous geochemical analyses to monitor water and soil quality in the areas surrounding the mine. Acquiring and utilizing these technologies require huge amounts of capital to gain access to the necessary infrastructure, energy, machinery, and expertise.

The other necessary requirement, if large amounts of capital are going to be "fixed" into the mine site, is that the entire process take place at a scale that is large enough to be profitable. By way of example, during Yanacocha's first year of operation, 11.1 million metric tons (mmt) of rock were excavated from two different open pits (Carachugo and Maqui Maqui), of which 7.5 mmt were piled onto heap leach pads (the other 3.6 mmt was "waste" rock). In order to dislodge, lift, and move the rock to the leach pads, tons of explosives were needed as well as giant excavators and a number of large mine haul trucks. One mine haul truck in use during the early 1990s around the world was the Caterpillar 785D, which is 16 feet tall and 22 feet wide, weighs 250,000 kilograms, and has a maximum hauling capacity of 133 metric tons (CAT 2010). Moving 11.1 metric tons of rocks would have required approximately 83,458 785D truckloads. Just one truck, operating continuously under an intermediate load for an entire year (8,760 hours), would have required approximately 25 gallons of diesel fuel per hour, or 219,843 gallons for the entire year. It can be assumed that an entire fleet of trucks was deployed during the year at the Yanacocha mine and that the mine also required significant quantities of smaller trucks for personnel transport as well as electricity for lighting and operations. Finally, the concentration of gold in each metric ton of rock excavated at Yanacocha in 1994, after it was crushed and stamped in a processing mill, was 1.85 grams per metric ton and the final recovery rate of the gold was 64.8 percent (WMCDE 2011). At the end of its first year of operations, Yanacocha produced 304,000 ounces of gold. Between 1994 and 2011, the rapidly expanding mine excavated a total of 2.3 billion metric tons (bmt) of earth and produced 33 million ounces of gold and 1,132 metric tons of silver (MCD 2012).

While Yanacocha's gold mining operations are the largest in Latin America, in 2008 more than 15 million ounces were produced across the region using similar techniques (USGS 2012). Mining operations for other minerals such as zinc, copper, iron ore, and lead, while they deploy different mineral processing and concentration technologies, utilize similar excavation, transportation, and open-pit methods. Comparatively, the largest of these operations, the Escondida copper mine operated by BHP-Billiton and Rio Tinto in Chile, excavated 6.1 billion metric tons of earth between 1994 and 2011 — even more than Yanacocha. In short, the scales of earth movements involved are spectacular.

New FDI flows, neoliberal restructuring, and the introduction of new technologies in the extractive sector over the first decade of the 2000s have had a profound impact on the growth of mineral and hydrocarbons production. The combined success of Yanacocha's operations and the discovery of a host of new mineral and gas deposits that are currently economically feasible to extract has spurred a rapid increase in the acquisition of mining and hydrocarbons concessions by global extractive operations, particularly in the northern parts of South America. As Figure 2.14 illustrates, oil, gas, and mineral concessions cover millions of hectares in Peru, Ecuador, and Colombia. In Peru, more concessions were granted between 1990 and 2010 than in the preceding two centuries (Bebbington and Bury 2009). Similar rates of increase have occurred in Ecuador and Colombia between 2000 and 2010.

Concessions to extract minerals and hydrocarbons have also increased rapidly across the rest of Latin America between 1990 and 2010. This has, in turn, led to new discoveries and operations. By 2012, the region contained 47 percent of global copper reserves, and between 1997 and 2008 accounted for 25 percent of all new global discoveries of gold (141 million ounces). In the 2000s, Latin America also accounted for significant percentages of global mineral reserves growth in iron ore (93 percent), silver (81 percent), lead (73 percent), copper (54 percent), gold (40 percent), and zinc (36 percent) (MEG 2010; USGS 2012). Exports of mineral products have also increased significantly during this period, as have the rates of extraction for nearly every mineral resource since 1995 (Figure 2.15). Mineral exports have also grown across the entire region, particularly in South America, increasing by US$123 billion between 1990 and 2006 (Figure 2.15).

Hydrocarbons exploration, production, and exports have similarly expanded, albeit at a slower rate than for minerals. Figure 2.16 details the re-

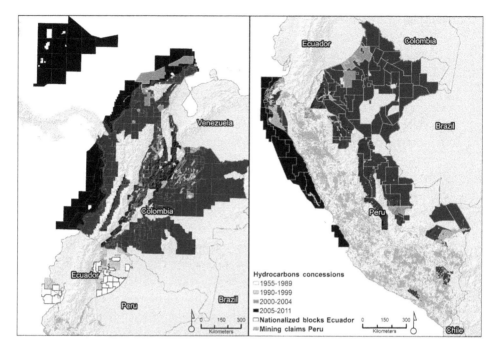

Figure 2.14. The evolution of oil, gas, and mineral concessions in the Northern Andes, 1950–2011. Sources: ANH 2011; INGEMMET 2010; MRNR 2011; PeruPetro 2011

gional growth of oil and gas reserves and exports. Petroleum reserves expanded rapidly beginning in 1980, largely as a consequence of oil discoveries in Mexico, but then slowed during the 1990s. While the largest proportional increases in oil reserves occurred in Brazil, Ecuador, and Bolivia, none of them became large exporters. Shifts in hydrocarbons exports have been divergent since the early 1990s. As there were few new discoveries of petroleum after the 1980s, rapid growth of oil production and exports in Venezuela, Mexico, and Trinidad and Tobago accounted for most of the increases in regional exports.

For most of the twentieth century, natural gas was not commercially viable, as it was difficult to store and transport. It was therefore either burned off when it was a byproduct of petroleum extraction, not developed when it was discovered, or not actively sought out by petroleum engineers and companies. Technological change has since made gas more attractive, and new natural gas discoveries have led to dramatic increases in reserves in Bolivia, Guatemala, and Peru. Natural gas exports more than tripled between 1990

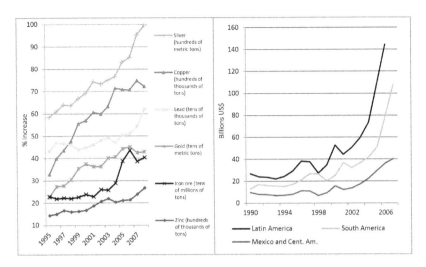

Figure 2.15. Left: Mineral production in Latin America, 1995–2008; Right: Mineral export growth for same. Source: USGS 2010

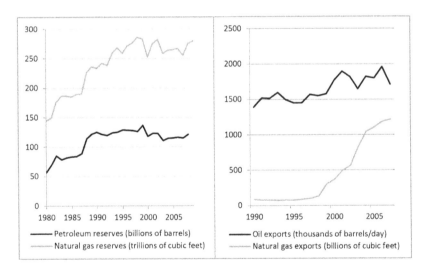

Figure 2.16. Left: Hydrocarbon reserve in Latin America 1980–2007; Right: Export growth for same. Source: USEIA 2011a

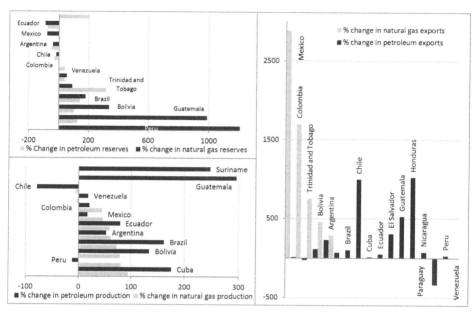

Figure 2.17. Percentage shifts by country, 1990–2007. Top left: Hydrocarbons reserves; Bottom left: Production; Right: Export. Source: USEIA 2011a

and 2007, although much of this is an arithmetic effect because natural gas production and export levels were so low in 1990. Rates of natural gas exports increased the most from Mexico, Colombia, and Trinidad and Tobago. These increases are partly due to the creation of new linkages and trading relationships with natural gas markets in the United States and partly due to producers increasing natural gas production as rapidly as possible during the temporary price spikes that occurred during the mid-2000s. Figure 2.17 illustrates the uneven nature of change that occurred in countries with either new or few hydrocarbons reserves, as well as production and export activities, between 1990 and 2007.

For most of the past century, employment in the extractive sector was closely linked to the cyclical nature of mineral and (to a lesser degree) hydrocarbons markets. Total regional employment expanded slowly until the 1960s. During the 1970s, as Figure 2.18 (left side) demonstrates, the average five-year growth rate of mining employment increased rapidly in response to the nationalization of many extractive operations and an influx of international petrodollars that provided new capital for the expansion of hydrocarbons and mineral processing facilities.[3] The discovery and development of new petroleum deposits in Mexico, Trinidad and Tobago, and Venezuela also fueled new government employment in the state-controlled hydrocarbons sector. During the 1970s, employment in the mining sector accounted for 1.8 percent of the total workforce in Latin America and was largely concentrated in a small number of countries in the region (Figure 2.18, right).

At the end of the "lost" decade of the 1980s and in the wake of successive economic crises, extractive sector employment declined precipitously. Initially, employment decreased sharply in response to the sudden scarcity of credit, hyperinflation, and a sharp contraction in global demand for raw materials. Job losses then accelerated rapidly as state-controlled operations were privatized and new capital-intensive, labor-displacing technologies were introduced. Overall, average regional employment for the 1990s was either lower than or similar to that in the 1960s. During the past decade, the relationship between mineral expansion and employment was fundamentally different in comparison to prior decades. While mineral production increased significantly across the region, overall employment growth in the mineral sector only expanded between 2000 and 2002. Since then, shifts in employment have been very uneven across the region. Employment in the mineral sector grew rapidly in Central America, Peru, and Colombia, but decreased in Brazil and Chile, and, overall, employment in the mineral sector has declined significantly during the latest period of rapid growth of mineral production. Furthermore, in comparison to the overall growth of the workforce in Latin America, mineral sector employment has declined even more significantly.

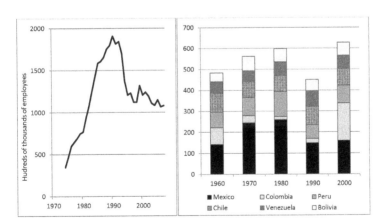

Figure 2.18. Left: Average five-year mining employment in Latin America, 1970–2010; Right: Decadal averages of mining sector employment for select countries, 1960–2008. Source: ILO 2011

Mining only accounted for an average of 0.6 percent of the workforce for the entire decade of the 2000s.[4]

The New Latin American Extractives Complex

While Latin America is home to only 9 percent of humanity (578 million people), contains 13 percent of the planet's landmass (21 million square kilometers), and accounts for 8 percent of global GDP (US$6 trillion in 2009), it contains a disproportionate amount of planetary mineral and hydrocarbon reserves and production (World Bank 2010; IMF 2010). Beginning in the 1990s, growth in extractive industries profoundly reconfigured the extraction of these minerals and hydrocarbons. By the late 2000s, the region was rearticulated into global production networks (Bridge 2008) and a new "complex" of extractive activities was rapidly expanding (cf. Watts 2009). Although hydrocarbons extraction activities increased significantly across the region, they are highly uneven because of the irregular spatial distribution of deposits. As Figure 2.19 illustrates, coal deposits are concentrated in Colombia, Brazil, and Mexico, while an irregular network of natural gas super-fields has been discovered across Mexico, Venezuela, Bolivia, and Argentina. Petroleum deposits have historically been even more asymmetrically distributed across the region as Venezuela is in control of a majority of the region's proven petroleum reserves.

The location of hydrocarbons deposits in relationship to political and ecological barriers, human population centers, transportation networks, and use patterns has also affected the ways in which these resources are used for regional energy needs. For example, as Figure 2.20 illustrates, the relative supply of hydrocarbons to meet national energy needs is proportional to such factors as overall population and the intensity of energy use by various sectors within each country.

Mineral deposits are also distributed unevenly across the region. Figure 2.21 (left side) illustrates the distribution of mineral extraction operations across the region as well as their comparative size. A number of dense mineral extraction clusters are developing in the Northern and Central Andes (copper, lead, gold, silver), Mexico (silver, gold, iron), the Amazon Basin (tin, aluminum), and Southern Brazil (iron). Figure 2.21 (right) also illustrates the total regional production of minerals and shows that Latin America accounts for nearly half of global copper and silver production as well as significant percentages of gold, zinc, and tin.

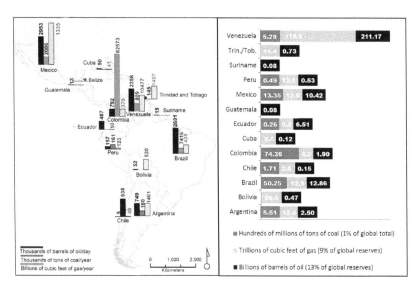

Figure 2.19. Left: Hydrocarbons production in Latin America, 2011; Right: Estimated hydrocarbons reserves of oil, coal, and natural gas in Latin America 2011. Sources: USGS 2011; USEIA 2011b

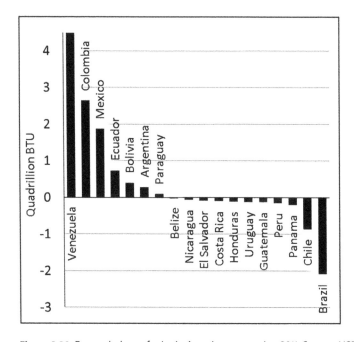

Figure 2.20. Energy balance for Latin American countries, 2011. Source: USEIA 2011a

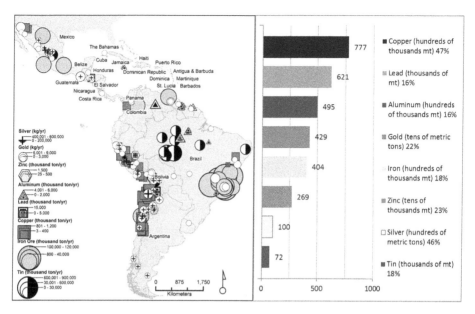

Figure 2.21. Left: Distribution of mineral production in Latin America, 2008; Right: Total mineral production in Latin America, 2008, and percentage of world production. Sources: USGS 2009; UNECLAC 2010

The subterranean intersection of hydrocarbons and minerals and the machinery and equipment being utilized to cleave, push, tear, or pump them from the earth and into the global system of production and consumption is but one component of the extractives complex in Latin America. A vast assemblage of humans, animals, plants, highways, railroads, power lines, energy infrastructure, communications networks, exploration equipment, mineral processing facilities, refineries, pipelines, storage facilities, and ports is necessary to support activities that locate, extract, process, and transport extracted materials across the region and into the global system of production and consumption. Table 2.1 and Figure 2.22 further detail the dimensions and geographic distribution of this Latin American extractives complex.

The management of hydrocarbons and minerals production through the extractives complex requires sophisticated logistics, engineering, and financial expertise as well as significant capital. Modern extractive operations are therefore generally large-scale corporations that engage in extensive extractive activities. Table 2.2 provides details for some of the largest mineral and hydrocarbons corporations. The majority of large mining operations in Latin America is controlled by transnational corporations. Four of the largest mining corporations in the world have operations across the region and control significant percentages of global reserves of minerals. Several very large Latin American corporations have significant assets and control large mineral reserves as well. In 2011, Vale was the largest mining company in the world by assets. Finally, the majority of hydrocarbons production is controlled by state-run companies in Latin America. Petróleos de Venezuela and Petróleos Mexicanos are entirely state controlled, while Petrobras of Brazil is semipublic (since it sold more than US$70 billion in shares in 2010). It is now one of the largest companies in the world.

Although large companies extract most of the industrial minerals and hydrocarbons across Latin America, artisanal small gold mining (ASM) accounts for a significant percentage of precious metal production. As Table 2.3 demonstrates, in 2005 ASM production accounted for approximately 17 percent (86 metric tons) of all gold mining in Latin America and 20 percent of global production (Valdivia and Ugaya 2011; Telmer and Veiga 2009; UNEP 2011). ASM production is concentrated throughout the Amazon basin, along the Pacific coast of Colombia, and between Panama and the Yucatan Peninsula. Most ASM mining is taking place illegally and utilizes mercury amalgamation and a variety of small-scale mobile placer technologies. In 2010, the

Table 2.1. Dimensions of the extractives complex in Latin America

Extractives Component	Quantity (2009–11)	Extractives Component	Quantity (2009–11)
Refineries	35*	Drilling rigs	436*
		land	350
Mining facilities	466	offshore	86
Pipelines	493,785 km	Port movement	8376 mmt**
operating	153,785	iron	987
proposed	340,000	coal	912
		ore	343
LNG terminals	28*	bauxite	79
existing/	8	phosphates	21
under		petroleum	2659
construction		other	1930
proposed	20	containers	1347

Notes: *count data; **millions of metric tons

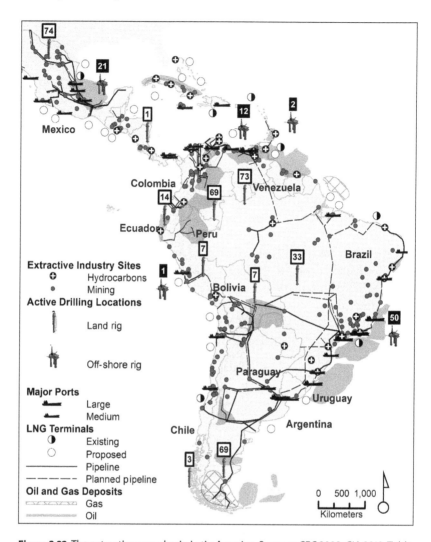

Figure 2.22. The extractive complex in Latin America. Sources: CEC 2008; CIA 2010; Tubb 2011; UNECLAC 2010; USGS 2006; National Geospatial-Intelligence Agency 2010

United Nations estimated that at least 458,000 people were engaged in ASM in South America and that they utilized 420 metric tons of mercury, most of which was released into the environment (UNEP 2011). The environmental and health consequences of ASM mercury contamination have been the focus of much recent research in Latin America (Dorea et al. 2003; Veiga, Maxson, and Hylander 2006) and Africa (Hilson, Hilson, and Pardie 2007; Tschakert and Singha 2007).

Will The Super Cycle Be Unbroken?

While extractive industries were significantly transformed during the 1990s and 2000s in Latin America, the trajectories of these changes for the near future are uncertain. In this concluding section we focus on the ways in which extractive industries are currently being reworked by continuing shifts in foreign capital investment and the development of extractive technologies that have led to significant increases in mineral and hydrocarbons reserves. These drivers of change are also likely to be areas of interest for future research, as they are rapidly evolving and have thus far received relatively little attention from scholars.

One of the most important questions regarding the most recent extractive boom in Latin America is whether or not the cycle of expansion will continue as it has for the past two decades. History has long demonstrated that patterns of growth in the extractive sector are cyclical in nature and that periods of rapid growth lead to overexpansion, overcapacity, and a collapse of commodities prices. Price collapses have historically led to periods of economic restructuring in the sector and have had significant economic and social consequences for countries heavily dependent on natural resource exports for economic growth. Latin America has been particularly vulnerable to the boom and bust of natural-resource, export-led growth throughout history, and the rate and magnitude of growth in the sector over the recent past have accelerated the region's economic vulnerability.

One test of the region's vulnerability to economic shock was the 2008 global economic crisis. As the crisis spread from housing markets to the rest of the global economy, commodities prices and flows of global foreign investment contracted very sharply. By the end of 2009, global prices for energy and base metals plummeted and FDI declined by 50 percent from its 2007 levels (see Figure 2.23, top left). FDI flows to Latin America also contracted sharply during this period (Figure 2.23, lower left). In early 2009, however, global FDI shifted in an unprecedented and unexpected fashion. For the first time since global records of foreign investment began, the total sum of FDI flows to the developing world (in this case, countries classified as developing and transitioning) exceeded flows of FDI to developed countries (FDI between developed countries has historically far exceeded flows to developing countries). Reflecting this realignment, FDI flows to Latin America began to increase. Shifts in global FDI flows to Latin America have been focused on extractive industries. So, although between 2008 and 2010 total FDI dropped in some countries—the Caribbean, Central America, Mexico (minus 18 percent) and Venezuela (minus 580 percent)—significant increases occurred in

Table 2.2. Concentration of production in the Latin American extractives complex for select corporations 2009–2011

Large Mining TNCs	Country	Operations	Product	Reserves*	Sales	Profits	Assets	Market Value***
Rio Tinto	United Kingdom	Chile	Copper	26,791,740	$56.6	$14.3	$112.4	$131.6
BHP-Billiton	Australia	Chile, Peru	Copper Silver Zinc	66,626,739 5,059 974,565	$52.8	$12.7	$84.8	$231.5
Xstrata	Switzerland	Argentina, Chile, Peru	Copper Gold Silver Zinc	40,760,859 65 5,059 974,565	$30.5	$4.7	$69.7	$64.1
Anglo American	United Kingdom	Chile	Copper Gold	35,590,594 251	$28.4	$6.6	$66.4	$66.2
Large Latin Mining TNCs								
Vale	Brazil		Copper	2,083,560	$50.1	$18.1	$127.8	$162.5
Grupo Mexico	Mexico	Mexico	Copper Silver	8,219,812 10,557	$8.3	$1.8	$14.9	$27.6

				Reserves**				
Penoles	Mexico		Copper Gold Lead Silver Zinc	13,390 6 54,536 366 149,724	$5.1	$513.7	$4.5	$13.9
Large Latin Hydrocarbon								
Petrobras	Brazil	Semi-Public	Oil	12.9	$125.9	$20.7	$328.3	$238.8
Ecopetrol	Colombia	National	Oil	1.7	$22.6	$4.3	$37.6	$84.4
Petroleos de Venezuela	Venezuela	National	Oil	211	$88.4		$141	
Petroleos Mexicanos	Mexico	National	Oil	10	$80.64	$102.6	$415.7	
Petroecuador	Ecuador	National	Oil	7			$1.7	

Sources: MCD 2012; Forbes 2012; Platts 2012; USEIA 2012
Notes: *metric tons; **billions of barrels; ***billions of US$

Table 2.3. Artisanal and small-scale gold mining (ASM) in South America

	ASM Gold Production 2005 (metric tons)	ASM Laborers 2011 (thousands)	Mercury Use 2010 (metric tons)
Bolivia	3.5	50.0	7.5
Brazil	11.2	300.0	45.0
Chile	2.1		40.0
Colombia	23.3		150.0
Ecuador	5.3		50.0
F. Guyana	10.0		7.5
Guyana	2.5	13.0	15.0
Mexico			7.5
Peru	16.5	85.0	70.0
Suriname	6.4		7.5
Venezuela	5.0		15.0
Central Am.			4.8
Total	**86**	**458**	**420**

Sources: Telmer and Veiga 2009; Valdivia and Ugoaya 2011; UNEP 2011

those countries with rapidly growing extractive industries, particularly Bolivia (52 percent), Brazil (28 percent), Peru (28 percent), and Chile (19 percent). In the context of global economic instability after 2008, much new investment has flowed into precious metals because they have historically provided "shelter" against price inflation and currency devaluations during economic crises. As Figure 2.23 (top left) illustrates, the price of gold has increased rapidly since late 2009, spurring a host of new investments in gold exploration and production, many of them in Latin America. According to one estimate, global gold exploration accounted for more than 50 percent of all mineral exploration activities in 2010 (MEG 2011).

Another explanation for the rapid shift in global FDI across Latin America is the rapid growth of demand for energy and base metals taking place in BRICS countries. As we have previously discussed, global demographic and economic shifts are moving growth in demand for natural resources and commodities to rapidly industrializing countries such as China and India. In the wake of the 2008 financial crisis in developed countries, demand for raw materials plummeted in such countries. However, during mid-2009, worldwide Chinese commodities purchases and FDI in extractive operations expanded rapidly. In Latin America, total Chinese FDI (US$15 billion) was twice as large as FDI in the region for the previous twenty years, and in 2010 China was the third largest source of FDI for the region. More than 90 percent of these investments have been in the extractives sector, particularly in hydrocarbons and industrial metals such as copper. Though perhaps of questionable quality, official Chinese FDI data (Figure 2.24) also suggest that total FDI in Latin America has increased significantly since 2005, while investments in extractive industries, as a percentage of overall investments, increased even more.

The implications of global shifts in FDI and the impacts of BRICS investment in the extractive sector in Latin America have recently emerged as topics of significant interest for policymakers and scholars. While Indian FDI investment in Latin America in 2010 (US$718 million) increased significantly (i.e. UNECLAC 2011b; IDB 2010), China has been the focal point of most recent research. A host of U.S. studies have also begun to focus on the increasing presence of China in Latin America, on shifts in Chinese investment in energy and hydrocarbons operations, and on China's unique and often misleading strategic investment behavior (U.S. Congress 2005; Santiso 2007; Roett and Paz 2008; Ellis 2009; Lederman, Olarreaga, and Perry 2009; Hearn and León 2011; Jiang and Sinton 2011; Mlachila and Takebe 2011; Salidjanova; 2011).

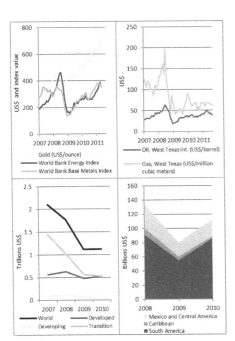

Figure 2.23. Commodities and hydrocarbons price volatility, and FDI shifts in the wake of the 2008 financial crisis (top left: gold price and Energy and Minerals Index; top right: oil and gas prices; bottom left: global FDI flows; bottom right: FDI flows, Latin America). Sources: UNCTADSTAT 2011; UNECLAC 2011; World Bank 2012

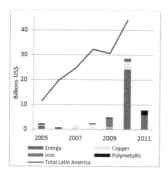

Figure 2.24. Chinese foreign direct investment in extractive industries in Latin America, 2005–2011. Source: MOFCOM 2011

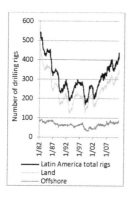

Figure 2.25. Oil and gas drilling operations in Latin America. Source: Baker-Hughes 2011

Another component of recent change in Latin American extractive industries has been the introduction of a variety of new extractive technologies that have increased hydrocarbons reserves in the region. Because global demand for hydrocarbons supplies remained strong following the 2008 economic crisis, oil and gas exploration across Latin America has continued to expand. One good indicator of exploration trends in the hydrocarbons sector is the number of current oil and gas well drilling operations. As Figure 2.25 illustrates, exploratory well drilling has returned to the levels of the early 1980s, when many of the large oil and gas fields were discovered in Mexico and Venezuela. Drilling operations on land have accounted for much of the growth in operations, which is in large part due to the introduction of new technologies such as directional drilling, super-deep ocean drilling platforms, and new "fracking" technologies that allow surface operations to hydraulically fracture subterranean rock layers to release natural gas. In 2011, the potential for these new drilling technologies to exploit new sources of hydrocarbons in Latin America became apparent when the USGS and U.S. Energy Information Administration (USEIA) completed a global assessment of tight gas

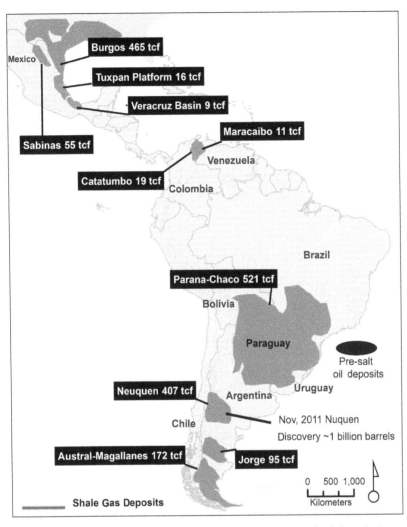

Figure 2.26. Shale gas deposits in Latin America and the Tupi pre-salt oil deposits in Brazil. Source: USEIA 2011

reserves (USEIA 2011b). While the study excluded Peru and Ecuador, the final results for the rest of Latin America were remarkable. As Table 2.4 and Figure 2.26 illustrate, a fundamental reconfiguration of hydrocarbons supplies has taken place. New super-deep oil discoveries off the coast of Brazil are currently estimated to contain more than 50 billion barrels of oil, but it is likely that more deposits will be found in the coming years as well (USEIA 2011b). In addition, new discoveries of shale gas deposits increased natural

Table 2.4. Natural gas reserves growth in the wake of new shale gas discoveries

Natural Gas and Shale Gas
Reserve Changes (tcf) 2009

	Production	Consumption	Imports	Proved Reserves	Recoverable Shale Gas	Years of Supply*
Venezuela	0.65	0.71	9%	178.9	11	**15**
Colombia	0.37	0.31	−21%	4	19	**61**
Argentina	1.46	1.52	4%	13.4	774	**509**
Brazil	0.36	0.66	45%	12.9	226	**342**
Chile	0.05	0.1	52%	3.5	64	**640**
Uruguay		n/a	100%		21	
Mexico	1.77	2.15	18%	12	681	**317**
Paraguay		1.41			62	**44**
Bolivia	0.45	0.1	−346%	26.5	48	**480**
Total, LA	**5.11**	**6.96**		**251.2**	**1906**	
World Total				**6609**	**6622**	

Sources: USEIA 2011b

Note: All measures are in trillions of cubic feet (tcf), unless otherwise noted

*Values include new shale reserve estimates.

gas estimates in mid-2011 from 251 trillion to 1,906 trillion cubic feet. Recent shale gas drilling results in Argentina suggest that the new shale gas basins of the region might contain even larger quantities of recoverable gas. There is little doubt that these new discoveries have the potential to reconfigure hydrocarbons relations in coming years and will be of significant interest to scholars.

The development of new biomining extraction technologies is also reworking mining in Latin America, modifying again the assemblage of activities that constitute the extractive complex of the region. The term *biomining* refers to new techniques that allow for the processing of metal-containing ores with biological technologies. In the early 1940s, mining engineers at Utah's Bingham Canyon Mine, the largest open pit mine in the world, discovered a new bacterium (*Acidithiobacillus ferroxidans*) that was partially responsible for chemical reactions involved in acid mine drainage. The bacterium was soon patented and utilized in new biohydrometallurgical processes to leach copper from depleted ores (Brierley 2008). Over time, a variety of new extremophiles (as these types of microorganisms are known) were discovered in extremely acidic and highly toxic heavy metal environments. Such environments typically occur near geothermal activity, on the bottom of the ocean near black smokers (hydrothermal vents), as well as at the bottom of open pit mines: in other words, in places inhospitable to any other kinds of life-forms. Because many of these new organisms actually engage in novel forms of chemosynthesis, as opposed to carbon-based life-forms that use photosynthesis, they facilitate the dissolution and release of concentrated minerals in ores, and as such can increase operational efficiencies for heap leach mining operations significantly (Rohwerder, Kinzler, and Sand 2003; Valenzuela et al. 2006; Rawlings and Johnson 2007; Jerez 2009).

Though the novel application of these new species has received little attention from regulatory authorities and researchers outside of specialized mining engineering publications, they have been widely introduced across the globe over the last several decades (Bhakta and Arthur 2002). They are currently involved in the production of roughly 25 percent of all copper on the planet and are being utilized in a number of copper mines in Chile and Peru (Olson, Brierly, and Brierly 2003; Watling 2006). Recent innovations in biomineral research suggest that there is widespread potential for the use of bioleaching techniques in other heavy metal mining operations, new bioremediation efforts, and in most of the major mining operations in Latin America (Curreli et al. 1997; Deng and Liao 2002; Brierly 2008; Siddiqui et al. 2009). These new biofrontiers of mining are well situated to inform current research discussions related to biopower and biosecurity as well as our understanding of new geographies of extraction (Rabinow and Rose 2006; Bennett 2009; Lemke 2011; Mansfield 2012).

Summary

Our purpose in this chapter has been more descriptive than analytical. We have explored dimensions of historical and contemporary change in the extractives sector in order to provide a wider geographical and temporal context to the chapters that follow. The theme of this chapter has been one of transformations on a continental scale—transformations with financial, technological, geographical, and institutional dimensions. The case study chapters that follow trace the implications of these transformations at national and, above all, subnational scales. The message of the current chapter, however, is that those territorialized processes to which the book now turns must also be understood as parts of a far larger complex reaching across space and time.

Notes

1. The precise location of Columbus' first landing is, after four centuries, still being debated. Markham (1893) argues it is Lat. 23" 55' S., Lon. 74" 28' W, which is near three different islands. In 1925, one of the islands was named San Salvador Island based on the belief that it was where the expedition landed.

2. In the case of Incan civilization, not only were the entire civilization and its records destroyed, but the means to access the records themselves disappeared as well. Incan records were kept using system of knotted cotton cords called *quipus*. After 400 years of intense scrutiny, how quipus were utilized to produce narratives remains a mystery to scholars (Urton 2008; Urton and Brezine 2005).

3. International Labour Organization, 2011, Labor Statistics Database, http://www.ilo.org/stat/lang—en/index.htm.

4. International Labour Organization, 2011, Labor Statistics Database, http://www.ilo.org/stat/lang—en/index.htm.

CHAPTER 3

Nature and Nation: Hydrocarbons, Governance, and the Territorial Logics of "Resource Nationalism" in Bolivia

TOM PERREAULT

Oil seems always to invoke a spatial lexicon in which the nation figures prominently. To the extent that oil production is located on lands populated by minorities, territorial disputes are inevitably about identity, rights, and citizenship.
WATTS 2001, 206

It is the magic of nationalism to turn chance into destiny.
ANDERSON 1991, 12

Introduction

It has been more than a decade since Bridge (2001) critiqued the *fin-de-siècle* resource triumphalism that celebrated the apparently endless abundance of natural resources and the simultaneous dematerialization of the economy. Closely linked to the neoliberal market triumphalism that heralded the end of history (Fukuyama 1992), this "post-scarcity narrative" captured the exuberant sensation of "low commodity prices, brimming resource inventories, and outward indications of resource abundance that would appear to signal this final victory over the forces of nature" (Bridge 2001, 2151). Indeed, in the frothy rhetoric of late twentieth-century capitalist globalization, the material moorings of the emergent information economy were all but erased. By all appearances, however, we are now living through a rather different historical moment. Concern over peak oil and global climate change, volatile oil prices, the collapse of global financial markets, and some of the largest bailouts of financial institutions in history have trained attention once again on the limits to growth, material and otherwise. If it is, as yet, too early to signal the end of neoliberal capitalism, it is readily apparent that the heady days of the 1990s are well behind us.

The thesis of postindustrial resource triumphalism centered, in part, on the discursive erasure of resource supply zones—those spaces at once marginal to the centers of global capital and central to capitalist processes—where natural resources are extracted. Bridge's insightful analysis focused attention on representations of resource-producing regions from the perspective of postindustrial societies, which, more often than not, portray such zones as devoid of people and free from conflict, awaiting the modernizing magic of transnational capital. Discursive representations such as these have a long history, as evidenced by the empty spaces on Spanish colonial maps, the language of *tierras baldías* (fallow or barren lands, ripe for settlement), and representations of entire regions—such as Amazonia or the American West—as pristine wilderness that is peopled, if at all, by unworthy and incapable savages. But whereas such discourses may portray these zones as empty, asocial spaces, they are in fact populated not just with people, but also with the imaginative geographies of their inhabitants, and are frequently disputed by residents and nonresidents alike. In recent years, with concern again trained on the specter of economic and environmental calamity, the narrative of "post-scarcity" has given way to one of "resource nationalism"—the supposed threat of nationalist political and economic policies limiting foreign investment in, and control over, strategically important natural resources such as oil and natural gas, thus constraining their free flow onto world markets. Such narratives have been *de rigueur* of late on the pages of trade journals for the mining, oil, and gas industries, in the business and economics blogosphere, and in business-oriented publications such as *The Economist* and the *Financial Times*. Not surprisingly, petroleum and natural gas are of particular concern to this literature, with the policies and politics of Venezuela and Russia playing leading roles. Bolivia, with its leftist president, Evo Morales, is often included in this group, usually as a junior partner to Venezuela's Hugo Chávez. Whatever this literature's faulty assumptions, it highlights a crucial relationship, which is the focus of this chapter: that of natural resources to constructions of nationalism, or, to put it more broadly, the relationship between nature and nation.

This relationship is captured nicely in the quotes by Michael Watts and Benedict Anderson that serve as epigraphs for this chapter. On the one hand, the relationship between hydrocarbons and the nation always entails claims to, and contestation over, identity, rights, and citizenship. In short, like Watts I am concerned with the way that hydrocarbons figure into expressions of nationalism and the nation. On the other hand, in this chapter I examine the nature of nationalism itself and its magic-like ability, as Anderson deftly notes, to forge destiny from mere chance—the chance of resource deposits and of elevated prices for those resources on world commodity markets. Thus, in this chapter I pose two interrelated questions. First, what is the relationship between nature and nation? And, second, how does this relationship both hinge on and inform understandings of identity, citizenship rights, and national space in Bolivia? In order to answer these questions, I argue, we must pay attention to the articulation of natural resource governance (the ways in which the relationship between nature and society is institutionalized and governed) and territorializing projects (the spatial expression of political ideologies). In what follows, I examine this articulation in the context of the politics of natural gas in Bolivia. I begin with a discussion of the emergent literature on "resource nationalism," the relationship between nature and nation, and the ideological and territorial expressions that these take. I then present a historical discussion of hydrocarbons development in Bolivia, with particular attention to nationalist ideologies and the oscillation between state and private/foreign control of hydrocarbons resources. I then move on to an examination of hydrocarbons governance and its relationship to territorializing projects in Bolivia, beginning with a consideration of President Evo Morales' "Heroes del Chaco" ("Heroes of the Chaco") decree, which sought to nationalize hydrocarbons. I then discuss alternative imaginings of natural gas and national space, with a focus on the Nación Camba (Camba Nation) and its proposals for regional autonomy in the eastern lowlands.

Nature, Nation, and Spatial Imaginary

Of Resource Nationalism, Resources, and Nationalism

In sharp contrast to the triumphal discourse of "post-scarcity" dematerialization critiqued by Bridge (2001), prevailing resource narratives now strike a more cautionary tone. The trope of "resource nationalism" has emerged with force in recent years in analyses for the energy and mining industries and the business-oriented popular press (see, for example, *Financial Times* 2009; Guriev, Kolotilin, and Sonin 2008; Stanislaw 2009; Valera 2007). This literature is concerned with the supposed threat to the free flow of natural resources onto global markets posed by economic nationalism—that is, the dismantling of neoliberal policies, which had facilitated private investment in resource sectors and the export of resources to foreign markets. For instance, in an analysis of global oil supply, Hirsch (2008, 881) argues ominously that "resource nationalism posits an Oil Exporter Withholding Scenario, which could potentially overwhelm all other considerations" (capitals in original). Adopting a similar tone, Cisneros-Lavaller (2007, 1) warns that "both Bolivia and Venezuela have adopted strong nationalist ideologies—as have most countries with strong NOCs (national oil companies)—aimed at garnering what is seen as the host governments' fair share of energy revenue . . . Though couched in ideological terms, in both cases this amounts to nothing less than . . . sharing and/or confiscating what are described, politically, as excessive windfall profits." Though most common in the oil and gas sectors, concerns over resource nationalism extend to minerals such as lithium, a vital ingredient in hybrid car batteries, the world's largest reserves of which are found on the Bolivian Altiplano. A front-page article in the New York *Times* detailed Evo Morales' dismantling of his predecessors' neoliberal resource policies and the threat this move poses to the greening of American consumerism (Romero 2009; see also *Guardian* 2009). The resource nationalism literature cautions against the nationalist politics and redistributive economic policies of "post-neoliberal" states and the threat they pose to the assumed entitlement of wealthy nations to their resources. This literature privileges the viewpoint of resource consumers potentially harmed by nationalist policies, with little concern given to the internal political and social considerations of resource-exporting states.

Whatever the failings of the resource nationalism literature (and they are as many as they are obvious), this work throws into sharp relief the uneasy relationship between nature and nation, and the ways that nature—commoditized and rendered strategic by political economy—is so often found at the heart of political and cultural struggles. This work is noteworthy as well for shedding light on the frequency and depth with which natural resources are bound up with nationalist ideologies. My objective in this chapter, then, is to examine the ways that strategically important natural resources and processes of resource extraction are integral to the production of nationalist ideologies. This is particularly the case in the global South, where processes of colonialism, both external and internal, have produced historical geographies oriented toward the production and export of raw materials and fostered social relations of production and exchange dependent on global markets for natural resources and low-value manufactures (Galeano 1973; Wolf 1982). As I will argue, examination of the relationship between nature and nation requires attention to the spatial expressions of resource extraction and nationalist sentiments, and the imbrication of nature, resource governance, and territorializing projects.

Nature and Nation

The literature on nationalism and the nation is vast and far beyond the scope of the present chapter. Indeed, the problematic of the nation has been a central focus of historical, geographical, and political scientific research over the past century, not to mention a source of innumerable conflicts both within and between nation-states. Among critical scholars, Anderson's (1991) aphorism that the nation is, above all, an "imagined community" has achieved the status of received wisdom. But if the authenticity, legitimacy, or even the very existence of a given nation—or indeed, of the very the concept of "nation"— is a point of endless contention, the political power of nationalism is not. As Gellner (1983, 48–49, cited in Hobsbawm 1990, 10) notes, "Nations as a natural, God-given way of classifying men [*sic*], as an inherent . . . political destiny, are a myth; nationalism, which sometimes takes pre-existing cultures and turns them into nations, sometimes invents them, and often obliterates pre-existing cultures: *that* is a reality." My aim in this chapter, then, is not to "prove" or "disprove" the existence or legitimacy of particular constructions of the Bolivian nation or of certain nationalist sentiments in Bolivia. Rather, I hope to interrogate the ways that nature, and more particularly natural gas, is bound up with the various forms of nationalism at play in Bolivia and with the representations of the Bolivian nation to which they give rise. Nationalism, as Smith (1991) notes, involves the (selective) articulation of history, territory, and political and/or ethnic community. As with any hegemonic ideology, however, nationalism is never stable and requires constant reproduction. In this view, then, nationalism is above all a productive force. As Breuilly (2008, xxv) asserts: "Nationalism is not a sentiment expressed by pre-existing nations; rather it creates nations where they did not previously exist." It is this productive capacity of nationalism, this ability of the ideological articulation of history, territory, and community to produce the nation and national identities that concerns me here. And in Bolivia, as in so many other nations, this productive capacity is ideologically and materially rooted, at least in part, in nature.

   In his study of oil and the Venezuelan state, Fernando Coronil (1997) represents Venezuela as having two bodies: a political body composed of citizens and a natural body composed of its subsurface resources—most importantly, petroleum. In Venezuela, Coronil argues, state authority has been produced and exercised in relation to oil, and in this regard, oil acts as both a material and ideological force. The importance of oil, not only to the authority of the Venezuelan state but also to political and economic power the world over, cannot be overestimated: "Oil, more than any other commodity, illustrates both the importance and the mystification of natural resources in the modern world" (Coronil 1997, 49). If Bolivia is not the oil nation that Venezuela is, its political fortunes have nevertheless been linked historically to its natural resource and associated productive regimes. Constructions of Bolivian national identity and regional identities within Bolivia are intimately bound up with processes of resource extraction; nationalist literature and art are animated by the historical memory of the silver mines of Potosí, the guano deposits of the Pacific coast (lost to Chile in the War of the Pacific [1879–83]), the tin mines of Oruro, and the rubber of the Amazon. In states such as Venezuela and Nigeria, which are overwhelmingly dependent on the wealth and power that flow from their massive oil reserves, oil has been integral to the process of state formation and to the construction of these states as oil nations (Watts 2004a). Similar processes are at work in Bolivia, where the country's historical identity as a *país minero* (mining nation) has largely given way to an emergent identity as a hydrocarbon state. But because of Bolivia's dependence on foreign hydrocarbons firms—some of them, such as Petrobras and Repsol YPF, among the largest and most far-reaching energy firms in the world—this national identity and state authority are attained through a sort of Faustian pact "in which a national project (modernity, development, citizenship) is purchased at the expense of sovereignty, autonomy, independence, tradition, and so on" (Watts 2001, 205). In Bolivia, it is precisely against the terms of this Faustian pact that social movements across the political spectrum are reacting. Since the discovery of massive gas reserves in the late 1990s—which overnight transformed Bolivia into a regional hydrocarbon power—natural gas has increasingly become a site of political and cultural struggle. From populist sectors based mainly in the Andean west, calls have increased for greater state control and redistribution of gas rents. By contrast, economic elites and social movements in the hydrocarbons-producing departments of Santa Cruz and Tarija have demanded greater control over the oil and gas found under their lands and a greater proportion of the rents they produce (Eaton 2007; Gustafson 2011; Humphreys Bebbington and Bebbington 2010). This scalar contest entails contrasting claims to collective rights to natural resources and their economic benefits, as well as divergent constructions of citizenship and national space.

One can argue that, in any context, the state mediates the relations between resources and society through laws governing resource and property rights, by establishing frameworks for the distribution of the benefits of resource extraction, and by regulating resource sectors. But as Valdivia (2008) has shown in the case of oil politics in Ecuador, natural resources mediate the relationship between citizens and the nation. In Bolivia, understandings of citizen identity and national belonging are constructed, in part, through the medium of natural gas (just as they have been through the media of silver, tin, nitrates, oil, and water at various other historical moments). Valdivia emphasizes the spatial nature of petro-citizenship as an imbrication and territorialization of the nation's political and natural bodies. Such territorialization — even seemingly immutable geographical "facts" as borders — is never fixed, however. As Gustafson (2011) has argued, struggles over citizenship, hydrocarbons governance, and the nation involve the reconfiguration and rescaling of national space into highly contested and unstable territories. Struggles over resources are thus simultaneously struggles over national space, the terms of citizenship, and the meaning of the nation itself.

In Bolivia and other resource-dependent countries, natural resources and their governance figure centrally into what I refer to as "territorializing projects" — the production of social and political spaces characterized by particular configurations of governance. In Bolivia in recent years, there have been many such projects, both state-sponsored and popular.[1] While the state's territorializing projects are of immense importance — Gonzalo Sánchez de Lozada's sweeping administrative decentralization known as *municipalización* and his government's legalization of communal lands as *Tierras Comunitarias de Orígen* (Original Community Lands) are examples of neoliberal governable spaces par excellence (see Rose 1999; Watts 2004a) — in this chapter I am primarily concerned with the popular production of territory. In order to understand this process, we must take into account the role of spatial imaginaries and how they are informed by historical memory and contemporary political struggle. In particular, this chapter is concerned with the ways that popular imaginaries of natural resources — especially natural gas — become territorialized, that is, endowed with spatial character, which in turn imbricates with collective identity. As I hope I will make apparent, natural gas figures prominently in the various territorializing projects at work in contemporary Bolivia.

One such territorializing project is resource governance. The concept of resource *governance* trains analytical focus on the institutional configurations through which nature and natural resources are managed, which involves state and non-state actors operating at multiple spatial scales (Bridge and Perreault 2009; Himley 2008). Of central importance here is the recognition that resource management is not only an activity of the state, but rather also occurs through ongoing negotiation and struggle over the institutions of the state, market, and civil society, which in turn involves a continual reworking of space and spatial scale (McCarthy 2005). One central problematic in the governance of natural resources is the question of property rights, and whether the control of resources is exercised by the state, by private actors, or some combination of these (Mansfield 2004). As I will detail, hydrocarbons governance in Bolivia has oscillated historically between private (mostly foreign) and state control. The tension between public/state and private/foreign control reflects, on the one hand, Bolivia's structural dependence on foreign capital and technical expertise to develop its hydrocarbons reserves and, on the other hand, popularly held aspirations to retain control of what is widely seen as national patrimony. In what follows, I examine the history of hydrocarbons development in Bolivia. The chapter then moves on to a discussion of the various territorializing projects at play in Bolivia and the role that natural gas plays in their construction and mobilization.

Gas and Its Governance: Spatial Imaginaries of "Resource Nationalism" in Bolivia

The Nature of Natural Gas

What we call natural gas is typically 70 to 80 percent methane (CH_4) in formation with other gases separated off in processing. As a gas, it is by nature expansive and volatile, and it must be contained in pipelines and holding tanks as it is extracted, transmitted, stored, and combusted. Thus, while natural gas may mediate the relationship between citizens and the nation, its entry into circuits of production and consumption is only possible thanks to complex systems of engineering, finance, and law (Bridge 2004b). This sets gas apart from resources such as water, wood, gold, or oil, whose presence is more tangible and immediate in everyday life (Perreault 2006). By contrast, our relationship with natural gas is once removed: we cannot hold, see, or smell it, and small-scale, artisanal gas producers are rare indeed.[2] Furthermore, as Bridge (2004b) has pointed out, the recent development of liquid natural gas (LNG) technology, which involves the cryogenic freezing of natural gas to its liquid phase (approximately –162 °C), has radically reshaped the geographies of global gas markets, freeing gas from the constraints of fixed, terrestrial pipelines, and allowing it to be transported off-continent, thus connecting consumers with reserves once isolated by distance and geographical barriers. Indeed, it was precisely the specter of exporting liquefied natural gas via a Chilean port to markets in California that touched off the "Gas War" in 2003, leaving more than 70 people dead and forcing the resignation of President Gonzalo Sánchez de Lozada. Thus, while nature and natural resources are not determinant in political conflict (contrary to the reactionary fantasies of Kaplan [2009]), nature's materiality is consequential in the context of political economic relations of production and exchange.

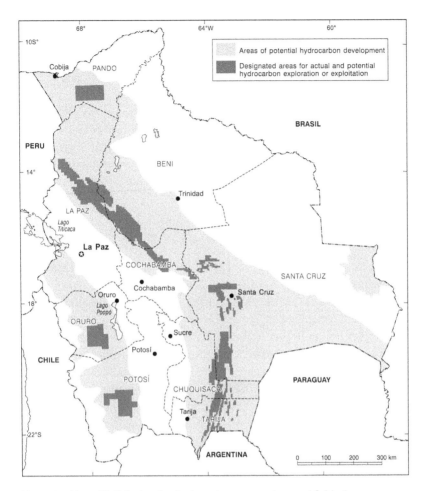

Figure 3.1. Map of Bolivia showing hydrocarbon concessions and fields. Source: Humphreys Bebbington 2012b

Another crucial aspect of the linkage between natural gas and the Bolivian nation is the basic geography of hydrocarbons deposits, which are mostly located in a broad arc at the eastern base of the Andes, in the country's Amazonian and Chaco lowlands (see Figure 3.1). This places most of the country's oil and gas riches in the eastern departments, collectively referred to as the *media luna* ("half moon," a collective term for the departments of Santa Cruz, Beni, Pando, and sometimes Tarija), which, as a group, tend to be whiter and wealthier than the departments of the Andean west. What's more, Bolivia's gas exists mostly in "nonassociated" reserves, in formations free of petroleum. Because it can be extracted alone, without the complicating presence of oil (and the requirement of separation during the extraction process), it can be extracted and harnessed more easily and cheaply than, say, Venezuelan natural gas, which is found mostly in association with oil (Miranda Pacheco 2009). These qualities increase the potential profitability of Bolivian gas, in turn placing it at the center of conflicts over regional autonomy and the control of hydrocarbon rents. Thus, the type of "chance" to which Benedict Anderson refers, as noted in the chapter's epigraph, has been turned into nationalist destiny by the elites in the eastern provinces of Santa Cruz and Tarija, where gas is found. Understanding regional contests over hydrocarbons resources requires attention to the history of oil and gas governance in Bolivia, to which this chapter now turns.

Historical Shifts in Hydrocarbons Governance in Bolivia

Hydrocarbons exploration began in Bolivia in 1916, with abortive exploratory attempts by British and Chilean firms. More sustained and successful efforts were made by the Standard Oil Company of New Jersey (now ExxonMobil), which in 1921 acquired from the government all concessions for oil exploration in Bolivia, including 2.5 million hectares of concessions in the country's eastern Amazonian and Chaco lowlands. Standard also secured agreements permitting it a range of refining, transportation, and marketing functions (Orgáz García 2002). In addition to Standard's dominance, this period was marked by the disastrous Chaco War, which Bolivia fought against (and lost to) Paraguay between 1932 and 1935. Though the causes for this war have more to do with the political and military incompetence of Bolivia's ruling elite, in nationalist representations it has been retrospectively framed as a gallant defense of the country's oil fields against the invading Paraguayans.

The catastrophe of the Chaco War led to the overthrow of the military government and the nationalization of Standard's holdings. The new government broke its contract with Standard Oil in 1936, allowing the company exploration rights only. In 1937, after Standard Oil was accused of illegally transporting petroleum to Argentina, the company's assets were expropriated and it was expelled from the country. In its place, the government established the state-run hydrocarbons company Yacimientos Petroliferos Fiscales Bolivianos (YPFB), which assumed responsibility for production, transport, refining, and commercialization of oil and natural gas (Fernández Terán 2009; Wu 1994). This has since come to represent (and be represented as) the embodiment of the state and national patrimony (Haarstad 2009). Perhaps most graphically, its weakening (and partial breakup) under the neo-liberalization of Bolivia's hydrocarbons industry in the 1990s has been referred to by Bolivian journalist Mirko Orgáz García (2002) as the "Tupacamaruzación" of YPFB, in reference to the Inca leader who led a rebellion against the Spanish and was hung, drawn, and quartered in 1572. By likening the administrative dismemberment of YPFB to the execution of this iconic Andean figure, Orgáz García is asserting YPFB's importance not just to the Bolivian state, but also (and more fundamentally) to Bolivian national identity, rooted firmly in Andean indigenous culture—an identity which transcends space and time (given that Tupac Amaru's death in Cusco preceded the establishment of the Bolivian Republic by 253 years). Ensuing shifts in governance may be seen as an oscillation between YPFB (state) and private foreign capital, a result of the tension produced by Bolivia's structural dependence on foreign capital and expertise, and demands by nationalist sectors within Bolivian society (both popular and elite) for control over the nation's natural resources (Gandarillas, Tahbub, and Rodríguez Cáceres 2008).

Following the 1952 Social Revolution, with the government facing intense international political pressure, food shortages, and the threat of U.S. sanctions, Bolivia's hydrocarbons sector was again opened to foreign involvement. The U.S. government of Dwight Eisenhower sought to prevent the leftward drift of Bolivia's Movimiento Nacionalista Revolucionario (MNR, Nationalist Revolutionary Movement) government, and in the nine-year period from 1953 to 1961 Bolivia received more U.S. aid per capita than any other country in the world (Rabe 1988). This largesse came with a cost, however. Eisenhower made it clear to Bolivian president Víctor Paz Estenssoro that continued U.S. assistance would be contingent upon Bolivia's granting concessions to U.S. oil firms. A 1956 hydrocarbons law, written by the U.S. law firm Davenport and Schuster, provided only for foreign investment in Bolivian hydrocarbons development while limiting the possibilities for national involvement, despite widespread opposition within Bolivia (Hindery 2003). The Davenport Code created a system of royalties that strongly favored American firms. This arrangement permitted Gulf Oil to emerge as the dominant player in the Bolivian hydrocarbons sector, gaining control of more than 90 percent of Bolivia's oil and gas reserves (Orgáz García 2002). Conditions changed yet again in 1969, when the military government of Alfredo Ovando Candia repealed the Davenport Code and once again nationalized the country's hydrocarbons. Nationalization of oil and gas was effected on 17 October of that year (coincidentally, the same date that President Gonzalo Sánchez de Lozada would flee the country in the wake of the Gas War, some 34 years later), with the expropriation of the assets of Gulf Oil (Fernández Terán 2009; Gandarillas, Tahbub, and Rodríguez Cáceres 2008).

Once again, however, this policy was short lived. In 1970, a coup d'etat brought to power Colonel Hugo Banzer Suárez, who quickly set out to reverse Ovando's hydrocarbons law. In March 1972, Banzer promulgated a new General Hydrocarbons Law, which permitted foreign investment and allowed for joint operations between foreign firms and YPFB. Eighteen foreign firms were promptly granted thirty-year concessions (Orgáz García 2002). Following its expulsion in 1969, Gulf Oil was promised indemnification, payment of which strained YPFB's ability to produce profitably, slowing oil exports and throwing the company into debt. This situation was exacerbated by Banzer's decision to reduce the indemnification period from 20 to 6 years, thereby increasing payments and further crippling YPFB's ability to turn a profit (Hindery 2003). Banzer pursued a policy of debt-led economic growth, which for a time produced the illusion of development. This would last until the early 1980s, when a growing debt burden and Latin America's highest hyperinflation would bring economic reality home with a vengeance. The crisis of the early 1980s, which coincided with the return of civilian government, set the stage for two decades of neoliberal reform (Kohl and Farthing 2006). Although the "New Economic Policy" brought profound structural transformation to the Bolivian economy, reform of the hydrocarbons sector would wait until the second wave of neoliberal reforms, in the 1990s (Haarstad 2009).

In 1996, the government of Gonzalo Sánchez de Lozada set forth its "energy triangle" policy, consisting of (a) a new hydrocarbons law, (b) capitalization of the state hydrocarbons firm YPFB, and (c) construction of a natural gas pipeline to Brazil. Together, these measures were intended to increase state revenues by facilitating private (mostly foreign) investment in Bolivian hydrocarbons and opening up new markets in Brazil. The new hydrocarbons law sought to promote foreign investment by restructuring the tax code and implementing a new concession system with no spatial boundaries; facilitating the import, export, and internal marketing of hydrocarbons; and allowing foreign parties to distribute, transport, refine, and industrialize oil and gas (Hindery 2003). Liberalization of the hydrocarbons sector was encouraged by the U.S. government and the Inter-American Development Bank and was explicitly promoted by the World Bank through specific sectoral loans, "institution building" programs (and associated loans), and direct lobbying of members of Bolivia's Congress to pass enabling legislation (Hindery 2004). According to the Bolivian government and World Bank representatives, the 1996 Hydrocarbons Law was expected to increase foreign investment, liberalize trade in hydrocarbons and related goods and services, create an independent regulatory agency to establish tariffs and negotiate contracts with private firms, and deregulate prices (World Bank 1994b).

International hydrocarbons firms responded enthusiastically to Sánchez de Lozada's reforms.[3] In the period from 1997 to 2001, foreign investment in hydrocarbons rose from US$296 million to US$401.3 million, an increase of 35.6 percent (Hindery 2004). Before leaving office, Sánchez de Lozada signed a presidential decree reducing the royalties paid by private firms on newly discovered oil and gas reserves from 50 percent to 18 percent (royalties on existing reserves were to remain at 50 percent [Hindery 2003]). This had the effect of reducing the percentage of state earnings provided by hydrocarbons, from some 50 percent in the early 1990s to roughly 25 percent by 1999 (Kohl 2002). If Goni sought to improve the "business climate" for foreign firms, he succeeded. In 2003, the government revealed that the Bolivian operations of Spain's Repsol YPF and British-owned BP Amoco enjoyed the lowest operating costs for hydrocarbons exploration and production anywhere in the world (Hylton and Thomson 2005). Prospects for accumulation were greatly enhanced when, shortly after capitalization, the firms announced that Bolivian oil and gas reserves were substantially greater than anticipated. Indeed, whereas existing gas reserves at the time of capitalization were 1.5 trillion cubic feet (TCF), new reserves discovered or declared following capitalization totaled 50.7 TCF. Similarly, whereas oil reserves stood at 27.8 million barrels before capitalization, new reserves announced after capitalization totaled 901.3 million barrels (Hindery 2003, 117). As a result, some 97 percent of Bolivia's oil and gas was contained in "new" reserves, subject to the lower (18 percent) tariff rate.

As is apparent in this brief recounting, the history of hydrocarbons governance in Bolivia is one of oscillation between public/state control embodied by YPFB and private/foreign control embodied first by Standard, then Gulf, and now Repsol and Petrobras. In contrast to Petrobras, Petroleos de Venezuela (PDVSA), or Mexico's Pemex, YPFB lacks the technical capacity and capital to carry out all facets of hydrocarbons exploration, development, and marketing. As a consequence, it is primarily limited to "downstream" functions—refining and marketing—and must contract foreign firms for "upstream" activities of exploration and extraction.[4] This structural dependency creates a tension between the necessary presence of foreign firms and the popular desire for national control of gas and other natural resources (Kohl and Farthing 2012). In 2006, this tension manifested itself in the latest move to "nationalize" hydrocarbons, President Evo Morales' Heroes del Chaco decree.

Heroes del Chaco

Spatial imaginaries were central to Evo Morales' 2006 nationalization of hydrocarbons, known as the Heroes del Chaco decree. The decree's name references the disastrous War of the Chaco (1932–1935), which Bolivia lost to Paraguay, and in which the majority of Bolivia's 57,000 casualties were Aymara and Quechua (i.e., Andean indigenous) conscripts. Though the causes for the war had more to do with internal Bolivian politics and gross miscalculations by Bolivia's corrupt and inept political elite, it has retrospectively been framed as a gallant defense of the country's oil (and more recently, gas) fields against the invading Paraguayan forces (Klein 1992). Who, then, were the "Heroes of the Chaco" in this telling? They were the tens of thousands of Aymara and Quechua soldiers who fought and died in the dry thornscrub of southeastern Bolivia. In the context of the war's reframing as a heroic defense of the country's hydrocarbons, the name *Heroes del Chaco* may be read as a historical claim by the indigenous population of the Altiplano and Andean Valleys to the hydrocarbon resources of the distant lowland east. Thus, the label *Heroes del Chaco* resonates both with Andean indigenous historical memory, which views the war in terms of Aymara and Quechua sacrifices for the nation, and with nationalist conceptions of sovereignty, rooted in national and cultural patrimony (Orgáz García 2002). Such indigenous and popular nationalisms emerge periodically in relation to natural gas and other resources. During the 2003 Gas War, for instance, protestors chanted "Gas para los bolivianos" ("Gas for Bolivians") and *not* for foreign aggressors such as Chile and the United States (Perreault 2006).

Drawing on similar sentiments, on Labor Day (May 1) 2006, Evo Morales "nationalized" the country's natural gas and petroleum, in response to the "October Agenda" of the 2003 Gas War. Surrounded by soldiers and representatives from the national and international press, Morales announced Presidential Decree 28701 from the San Alberto natural gas field in Tarija, a banner behind him declaring *"Nacionalizado: Propiedad de Bolivianos"* ("Nationalized: Property of Bolivians"). As he read the decree, the military simultaneously occupied 56 natural gas installations throughout the country. As Webber (2006) notes, such military theatrics served both practical and symbolic purposes. On the one hand, the armed forces were needed to prevent records and documents from being removed from the offices of hydrocarbons firms, as thorough audits would be necessary to assess company activities and profits in order to renegotiate contracts. On the other hand, the presence of the military signaled armed forces support for Morales and the nationalization plan, sending a message to opposition activists in Santa Cruz and elsewhere that a coup was out of the question. Moreover, this show of military force in the oil and gas fields was a reminder of past nationalizations under military regimes; that is, the 1936 nationalization of Standard Oil's operations in the wake of the Chaco War and associated creation of YPFB, and the 1969 nationalization of Gulf Oil. As with these previous nationalizations of oil and gas, Morales' declaration may be read as a repudiation of foreign domination and a signal that the government intends to use the nation's natural resources for the benefit of Bolivian people.

Article 1 of the Heroes del Chaco decree asserts that "the state reclaims the property, the possession and the total and absolute control of these resources." Article 2 directs oil and gas firms operating in national territory to turn their hydrocarbons production over to the national firm YPFB. Article 4 indicates that operations in the largest gas deposits—with average production in 2005 of over 100 million cubic feet per day—will be subject to an 82 percent taxation rate, with the remaining 18 percent staying with the firms. (This inverts the taxation rate introduced by Sánchez de Lozada's 1996 Hydrocarbons Law, which established an 18 percent taxation rate on profits earned by hydrocarbons firms.) Production on smaller gas and oil fields will be subject to 50 percent taxation, the rate in place prior to the implementation of the 1996 law. Notwithstanding the assertions of the international press and Morales himself, the Heroes del Chaco decree constitutes less a full nationalization (as called for by many on the Bolivian left) than a forced renegotiation of the terms of hydrocarbons development (Spronk 2007). Morales had swept into office in the wake of the Gas War and its October Agenda for nationalizing hydrocarbons, reconstituting YPFB, and industrializing the country's natural gas. In this context, Morales framed his move as "nationalization" in fulfillment of campaign pledges and in rejection of his predecessors' neoliberal policies. It should be noted that the language of "nationalization" is politically expedient both to Morales and to his detractors on the right. By calling the reconfiguration of gas contracts a "nationalization," Morales appears to be fulfilling one of the key demands of the October 2003 Gas War and one of the central tenets of the October Agenda to which it led. He is also simultaneously appealing to popular nationalism and the recurring calls, from both left and right, to protect the national patrimony from those who would exploit it and leave little behind for the benefit of Bolivia and Bolivians. Morales' critics on the right, both in Bolivia and beyond, similarly find the language of nationalism politically useful, given its resonance with leftist governments in Cuba and Venezuela, both key allies of Morales's government.

Morales may, in this way, be more easily accused of "resource nationalism," though in fact his is a significantly weaker nationalism than, say, Venezuela or Russia are capable of enacting (Kohl and Farthing 2012).

Its dubious rhetorical claims notwithstanding, the Heroes del Chaco decree represented a very real shift in the distribution of rents stemming from oil and gas development. In his analysis of current gas-related conflicts in Bolivia, Gustafson (2011) compares the royalty structures of the "neoliberal era" established by Gonzalo Sánchez de Lozada (under the hydrocarbons law of 1996), the "transition period" under Carlos Mesa, and the "nationalist era" of Evo Morales (under the Heroes del Chaco decree). Under all three royalty regimes, 11 percent of tax revenues are to be divided among producing departments (according to their share of production), 1 percent goes to Beni and Pando departments, and 6 percent goes to the national treasury. During the transition period, a 32 percent direct hydrocarbon tax (*impuesto directo de hidrocarburos*, IDH) was levied, bringing the royalty rate to 50 percent of production. While the state continues to receive 50 percent of revenues from production on smaller gas fields, Morales' decree adds a variable payment of 18 to 40 percent directly to a reconstituted YPFB for production from the so-called gas "megafields": Margarita (operated by Repsol YPF), and San Alberto and San Antonio (both operated by Petrobras). Thus, under the new regime, the state receives up to 90 percent of the revenues from gas produced by Repsol YPF and Petrobras. These royalties are assessed on the value of companies' net production (total production minus the gas and/or oil used in extractive processes). The remaining 50 percent is divided between "recoverable costs" (equivalent to firms' total operating costs, expenses, and investments) and "benefits and utilities," which are subject to the additional variable fees (Rodríguez Cáceres 2007). Thus, while the Heroes del Chaco decree did not nationalize Bolivia's gas operations, it did establish a royalty structure that benefits the Bolivian state to a much greater degree than was the case under the two previous regimes. In broader historical perspective, however, this royalty structure merely replicates the distribution of rents in place prior to neoliberalization. As Rodríguez Cáceres (2007) notes, in practice the country has returned to the pre-Goni period, insofar as foreign firms are obligated to deliver the oil and gas they extract to a reconstituted YPFB, Bolivia's state hydrocarbons company.

Morales' Heroes del Chaco decree sought to "nationalize" Bolivia's hydrocarbons resources and implement a regime of production through which a greater proportion of oil and gas rents would be captured by the state than had previously been the case. Far from being a simple matter of administrative governance, Morales' decree was discursively rooted in Bolivian national-

Figure 3.2. Wall mural, Cochabamba

ist ideology and the potent historical memory of Andean indigenous peoples, his central political constituency. As Gustafson (2011) notes, the War of the Chaco is "politically, culturally, and ideologically productive" and serves to bind Bolivian hydrocarbons, as *patrimonio nacional* (national heritage), to images of the Bolivian nation. Crucially, as Morales' appeal to the war's heroes indicates, this is, at its heart, an Andean nationalism, which draws on a sense of Aymara and Quechua marginalization, sacrifice, and enduring patriotism. This is a popular nationalism, which manifests itself discursively in various forms, as is discussed below.

Qollasuyu and Spaces of Andean Nationalism

This sense of popular Andean nationalism is at work in a mural painted on a wall in the city of Cochabamba by the guerrilla art group Grupo Willka (see Figure 3.2). It represents a powerful spatial imaginary of Bolivian gas being extracted from a cracked and bleeding earth and piped to the United States, represented as a dark and foreboding Gotham. In the foreground are silhouettes of Andean *campesinos* and miners, holding aloft a banner that reads, "Nationalization of gas now, damnit!" This is a clear reference to the 2003 Gas War, in which hundreds of thousands of citizens took to the streets of La Paz, El Alto, Cochabamba, and other cities in order to protest the government's plans to export liquefied natural gas to the United States via a Chilean port. Several days of protests paralyzed El Alto and La Paz, and more than 70 people were killed in the conflict, nearly all of them protesters shot dead by the military and police, sent into the streets by President Gonzalo Sánchez de Lozada to quell the demonstrations (Perreault 2006). As with the imagery evoked by the Heroes del Chaco decree, the mural may be read as a claim by Andean indigenous peoples to the benefits of resources developed in distant parts of the country. In this sense, then, natural gas is clearly *patrimonio nacional*, that is, a national resource that should benefit all Bolivians, regardless of where in the country they live.

This imaginary intersects with another, that of a historically continuous and spatially contiguous Qullasuyu, or southern province of the Inca Empire, Tahuantansuyu, which was divided into four provinces, or *suyus*, and centered on the Inca capital Cusco. In Bolivia, *Qullasuyu* describes the space of Aymara nationalism and is promoted as a cultural and political ideal by organizations such as the Andean indigenous organization Consejo Nacional de Ayllus y Markas del Qullasuyu, (CONAMAQ, National Council of Ayllus and Markas of Qullasuyu) (Lucero 2008). It is worth noting that Grupo Willka, which painted the mural, draws its name from the nineteenth-century Aymara cultural and military hero Pablo Zárate "el Willka." In addition to being a surname, *Willka* is an honorific term in Aymara, meaning "powerful" or "guardian of tradition." Zárate Willka was a powerful Aymara *caudillo* and military leader who fought alongside the Liberal forces of Colonel José Manuel Pando in the Federalist Revolution of 1899, on expectations of racial equality. Shortly after the Liberal victory over the Conservatives, in which his troops played an important role, he was betrayed by Pando, imprisoned, and eventually executed (Larson 2004). Though little is known about Zárate Willka personally, in Aymara and Quechua political writings and activism his image has been tightly linked to Andean nationalism and the space of Qullasuyu.[5]

Spatial Imaginaries of the Media Luna

Not to be outdone, the so-called "Cambas" of the eastern lowlands have their own elaborate spatial imaginaries, perhaps most vividly and elaborately developed by the Nación Camba, based in the city of Santa Cruz. According to the Nación Camba and its followers, the Bolivian lowlands are a land apart, rich in natural resources—forests, pasture lands, and, of course, hydrocarbons. Together with chambers of commerce in Santa Cruz and other eastern cities, as well as various civil society groups, they have helped launch an autonomy movement that seeks greater political powers and—crucially—greater control over hydrocarbons development and a larger share of oil and gas rents. The Nación Camba website contains a map that illustrates their autonomist vision.[6] In this view, Bolivia has been disarticulated, with the Andean portions of the country pertaining to the Nación Aymara Queswa, which also includes the altiplano (high plains) region of Peru and portions of northern Chile. Meanwhile, the Nación Camba is composed of Santa Cruz, Beni, Pando, and the lowland portions of La Paz and Chuquisaca departments. Perhaps most intriguingly, it is surrounded by *regiones afines*, that is, regions perceived to have cultural and/or political affinity with the Nación Camba—including the department of Tarija, the Brazilian states of Acre, Rondonia, Mato Grosso, and Mato Grosso do Sul, the Argentine provinces of Salta and Formosa, and the entire country of Paraguay (!). The nationalist vision promoted by the Nación Camba differs radically from that of Grupo Willka. As opposed to the latter's integrationist perspective, this is a separatist vision, rooted in claims to control over the region's natural resources and the rents they produce. On its website, the Nación Camba juxtaposes a modern, globalized, and economically and politically progressive "Camba nation" with an Andean Bolivia it represents as backward, conservative, illiberal, and insular. It also represents Cambas as an ethnically distinct, oppressed mestizo minority, fighting for self-determination.[7] The Nación Camba has thus skillfully co-opted the language of Latin American indigenous movements, calling for a country that is multinational, pluricultural, and multiethnic, and which officially recognizes the rights of the minority groups such as mestizos.

The Autonomy Movement

The Nación Camba's autonomist vision must be seen as part of a broader array of autonomy movements at play in Bolivia, a comprehensive analysis of which is beyond the scope of the current chapter.[8] The most thoroughly developed vision for regional autonomy for the *media luna* was articulated by the Asamblea Provisional Autonómica de Santa Cruz (Provisional Autonomic Assembly of Santa Cruz) in 2006 (Zegada 2007). This statement represented the interests of the department's economic and political elites, rooted in the region's dominant agro-export and extractive sectors, which together represent more than 80 percent of Santa Cruz's exports. As Zegada (2007, 73) notes, the Cámara Agropecuaria del Oriente (CAO, Agricultural Chamber of the Eastern Lowlands), which represents large-scale agricultural interests such as cattle raising and soy, joined forces with the Cámara de Industria y Comercio (CAINCO, Chamber of Industry and Commerce), which represents industrial and service interests—many of them tied to extractive industries such as mining, oil and gas—in the form of the Comité Cívico pro Santa Cruz, a political-civic association whose primary function is to promote the region's commercial and political interests, in the face of what they represent as the domination of the central government in La Paz. Santa Cruz' autonomy movement makes three central claims: (1) control over police, migration, education, and economic policy; (2) retention of two thirds of all tax revenue generated in the department; and (3) departmental control over natural resources and their exploitation, including the right to negotiate contracts with hydrocarbons and mining firms. These are not minor demands. In 2000, Santa Cruz produced some 42 percent of Bolivia's tax revenue and accounted for more than 40 percent of the country's export earnings (Eaton 2007). Such figures are tightly linked to the region's dependence on export-oriented agribusiness and extractive industries. Between them, soy production and hydrocarbons account for 80 percent of regional exports. As Gustafson (2006) notes, neither generates much in the way of employment or broader economic development. Rather, a small circle of elites tightly maintains both the control of and economic benefit from these sectors.

Despite the fact that this autonomy movement is overwhelmingly tied to the interests of the region's narrow elite, they have succeeded in packaging it as a broad-based, even populist, vision that cuts across class and ethnic divisions, while at the same time cutting formal ties to economic and political elites in La Paz and Cochabamba (Eaton 2007). A particular genius of this movement has been its ability to gain the support of popular sectors and lowland indigenous groups. As Gustafson (2006, 356) points out, lowland elites "increasingly speak of themselves as *mestizos* [as opposed to 'whites'] who share the heritage of lowland native peoples of Santa Cruz. . . . Non-indigenous Cruceños view these peoples as 'our ethnics'" and see them as culturally and racially superior to Andean (Aymara or Quechua) indigenous peoples. Gestures toward lowland indigenous peoples notwithstanding, this is, at heart, a vision of white supremacy that leaves little room for alternative spatial imaginaries on the part of the Guaraní and other groups directly affected by gas extraction (see Perreault 2006; Perreault and Valdivia 2010).

This highly racialized/spatialized vision indicates that the Cruceño autonomy movement, like other autonomy movements in Bolivia, extends far beyond demands for hydrocarbons rents and land rights and incorporates long-standing claims to regional political autonomy, economic self-determination, and profound class-based and ethnic divides both within the region and with the country's Andean west. But the importance of natural resources—and in particular of hydrocarbons—to autonomy claims should not be underestimated. The state's natural gas revenues were some US$1.5 billion in 2007, up from just US$188 million in 2001 (Gustafson 2006). Gas deposits are highly concentrated spatially, with the large majority in Tarija and, to a lesser extent, Santa Cruz. Much of the current dispute has to do with the distribution of gas rents to the various departments. Hydrocarbons-producing departments such as Santa Cruz and Tarija currently receive 11 percent of the direct hydrocarbons tax, divided according to production, a percentage that promoters of the autonomy movement are loathe to give up.[9] Argentina, having limited gas reserves of its own, relies on Bolivian imports. Similarly, the Brazilian state of Mato Grosso, which borders Santa Cruz, is heavily dependent on Bolivian gas, as is the megacity of São Paulo (Gustafson 2011). Currently, Bolivia exports 61 percent of its gas to Brazil, and 9 percent to Argentina (with the remainder consumed internally [Miranda Pacheco 2009]). Thus, for the elites of the gas-producing departments of Tarija and Santa Cruz, who recognize that Bolivia's impoverished population cannot hope to consume at rates comparable to wealthy Brazil and Argentina, there is understandable interest in continuing the current regime of hydrocarbons export.

Conclusion: Nature and Nation in Bolivia

The past is never dead. It's not even past.
WILLIAM FAULKNER, *REQUIEM FOR A NUN*

In this chapter I have examined resource nationalism in contemporary Bolivia. As opposed to the cautionary tone of mainstream resource nationalism literature, written from the perspective (and in the interest) of resource-importing states, I have attempted to present an alternative view. I have argued that understanding resource nationalism—the relationship between nature and nation—involves understanding the place-based histories of resource governance regimes and the ways that resource governance and associated social struggles are territorialized within national space. This, in turn, draws our attention to the ways that historical memory of past resource struggles animate ideas of citizenship and the nation. In Bolivia, natural gas serves as a site of articulation between, and terrain of struggle over, collective identities and national belonging. In this sense, natural gas mediates the relationship between citizens and the nation. And crucially, the nationalist visions formed around natural gas and other resources are animated by long historical memories.

   Writing in the aftermath of the violent 2003 Gas War, a key moment in the process of social upheaval that brought Evo Morales to power, Uruguayan author Eduardo Galeano (2003) noted that in Bolivia, "memory hurts and teaches: natural resources leave without saying goodbye and never return." Historical memory of natural resource exploitation and associated social exclusion runs deep in Bolivia and evokes references to the silver mines of Potosí, which funded the Spanish empire for the better part of two centuries; the loss of the Pacific coast (and its lucrative guano deposits) to Chile in the War of the Pacific; the catastrophe of the Chaco War, retrospectively framed as a defense of hydrocarbons; and the tin mines of Oruro, which for a time made Simón Patiño one of the world's wealthiest men before he and his fortune left for Europe. But as with any historical memory, this is a past imperfect. Partial and selective, these memories nevertheless animate contemporary social movement politics and their claims to natural gas and other resources. Nationalism is, in this sense, inherently both collective and selective, the formation of group identities based on processes of partial remembering and convenient forgetting.

These processes are at work in the rhetoric and policies of Evo Morales and those groups aligned with his Movimiento al Socialismo (MAS, Movement to Socialism) government, who promote an Andean-centered vision of nationalism. They are similarly at work within the Nación Camba and its allies, who promote a starkly different vision of nationalism and the Bolivian nation. As I have argued, the MAS and allied social movements have drawn heavily on collective memories of past resource regimes and associated social marginalization of Andean indigenous peoples. The conceptual reference points for this vision are Aymara and Quechua sacrifices in the Chaco War and the domination of Bolivia's hydrocarbons sector by foreign entities such as Standard and Gulf, at the expense of the masses to whom the nation's natural resources—*patrimonio nacional*—rightfully belong. The territorializing projects of this vision, then, encompass all of Bolivian national space and aim to connect Andean peoples with distant hydrocarbons resources. The Heroes del Chaco, who exemplify this view, are Andean indigenous conscripts who defended the nation's oil and gas fields, and whose actions bestow on their contemporary descendents in La Paz and El Alto a right to those resources. Grupo Willka's mural is, if anything, even more explicit in making this connection, portraying Andean miners and *campesinos* demanding the nationalization of Bolivia's gas, while a pipeline transports it directly from the cracked and bleeding Bolivian earth to the Gotham-like United States.

The Nación Camba and its allies among the elites of Santa Cruz present a contrasting view. Theirs is a regionalist vision, which portrays the Nación Camba as a nation in its own right, ethnically and culturally distinguished from the Andean west by its political progressiveness, economic dynamism, and cultural modernism. In this view, natural gas, like oil, grazing lands, soy, and forests, is integral to regional identity (Gustafson 2011). Far from being natural resources of the Bolivian nation, or *patrimonio nacional*, these resources pertain first and foremost to the region and should benefit above all the departments where they originate. The imagery and rhetoric of the Nación Camba sustain this vision by portraying the region as a land apart — a people and a region oppressed by the central government of La Paz, they seek autonomy and self-direction (Eaton 2007). These forms of regionalism — perhaps the most important terrain of social struggle in Bolivian history (Roca 1979) — easily give rise to popular nationalisms. As Barragán (2009, 93) puts it: "All the ingredients of nationalism are present [in Bolivian regionalism]: distinct geography, different origins and histories, diverse 'races,' leadership and political projects that essentialize each group."

This is not to imply that the autonomy movement of the Nación Camba and its allies in eastern Bolivia can be reduced to a simple claim to hydrocarbons rents, or that the politics of the various autonomy movements in Bolivia are derived automatically or deterministically from resource conflicts. Rather, I wish to argue that natural gas, and the rents derived from its extraction, figure prominently in the various territorializing projects at play in Bolivia, both in the Andean west and the lowland east. Insofar as all these projects are ideologically rooted in the interests of particular social groups, they must be viewed critically. The autonomist vision of the Nación Camba, in particular, serves the interests of the region's economic and political elites, irrespective of their (limited) efforts to legitimate it through cross-class and cross-ethnic alliances (Eaton 2007; Gustafson 2006, 2008). Similarly, the Andeanist vision promoted by groups such as Grupo Willka, and supported in Morales' policies, reflects a particular vision of the Bolivian nation that is not necessarily representative of the Bolivian polity as a whole. Crucially, as with any hegemonic force, the resource nationalisms at play in contemporary Bolivia are not stable and are in need of constant reconstruction. It is within these competing visions that we can glimpse the relations between nature and nation, and the ways that resource governance informs the ongoing process of nation building and citizenship formation in Bolivia.

Notes

1. Examples of state-sponsored territorializing projects are administrative decentralization under *municipalización*, the legal recognition of communal lands as *Tierras Comunitarias de Orígen*, and the establishment of protected areas of oil, gas, and mining concessions. Examples of popular territorializing projects include the various autonomist movements detailed in this chapter or the occupation of lands by Bolivia's landless movement.

2. Small-scale bio-gas digesters, which harvest methane from composting organic matter, are common in China and elsewhere. Such devices do produce natural gas in a usable form on a small scale and use relatively simple technology with little capital

input. Extraction of large quantities of natural gas from below-ground deposits still requires large amounts of capital investment and extremely sophisticated technologies, unavailable to small-scale producers.

3. By the mid-1990s, numerous transnational oil and gas firms were operating in Bolivia, including Argentina's YPF (now Repsol YPF of Spain) and Pluspetrol; Brazil's Petrobras; Total, Fina, and Elf Aquataine of France; Texaco, Shell, Mobil, Maxus, and Enron of the United States; and British-owned BP Amoco (Wu and Pezeshki 1995).

4. The 2006 nationalization law requires YPFB's participation in all phases of hydrocarbons development. However, the technical aspects of exploration and extraction are still largely carried out by transnational firms.

5. See, for instance, the online document "El inmortal Zarate Willka" (http://qolla suyu.indymedia.org/es/2005/01/1514.shtml). Accessed 16 July 2009. See also Zavaleta Mercado (2008).

6. See www.nacioncamba.net/repositorio/mapa.jpg.

7. See, for instance, the document "Quienes Somos," at www.nacioncamba.net /index.php?dir=contenidos&id=1 (go to www.nacioncamba.net and click on the link "Quienes Somos").

8. For a fuller discussion of Bolivian autonomy movements, see Eaton (2007), Gustafson (2006), Molina (2008), Perreault and Green (2013), and Zegada (2007).

9. Because revenues are distributed according to production, Tarija receives US$491 per capita, while more populous Santa Cruz receives just US$46 per capita. Remote, tiny, and resource-poor Pando is subsidized by revenues from hydrocarbons produced in Tarija and Santa Cruz, and thus it receives US$751 per capita—the largest per capita sum in the country.

CHAPTER 4

Rocks, Rangers, and Resistance: Mining and Conservation Frontiers in the Cordillera Huayhuash, Peru

JEFFREY BURY AND TIMOTHY NORRIS

Introduction

The Inca . . . treasury in Cuzco consist[ed] of three chambers of gold, five of silver and one hundred thousand lumps of gold taken from the mines, each one weighing fifty castellanos.[1] In all these provinces there are many mines of gold and silver [that] they get with little trouble.
FRANCISCO XERES, CAJAMARCA, PERU, 1532

On 5 January 1533, Hernando Pizarro set out from the city of Cajamarca on the first European encounter with Incan civilization in Central Peru. The Spaniards had just captured the Inca emperor, Atahualpa, who promised, in a story widely known to history, to pay them a fabulous ransom of gold and silver for his release (Markham 1872). Two months later, the ransom had not yet arrived and rumors were circulating that an Incan army was converging on Cajamarca. Fearing treachery, Francisco Pizarro ordered his brother to march 30 miles south to the city of Huamachuco to hasten the arrival of the ransom and to report on any potential resistance that was being organized. Hernando reported that they pillaged the town, "found a quantity of gold and silver," local people were "tortured" to disclose the whereabouts of the advancing armies, and that he then "resolved to push forward with 14 horsemen and 9 foot soldiers, in order that the Indians might not take heart at the notion that we had retreated" (Markham 1872, 120). Hernando's decision to push forth from Huamachuco led to a three-month journey that covered more than one thousand miles of the Central Andes and established him as one of the very first Europeans to survey the indigenous landscapes of the region. His small party travelled as far as present-day Lima on the coast and com-

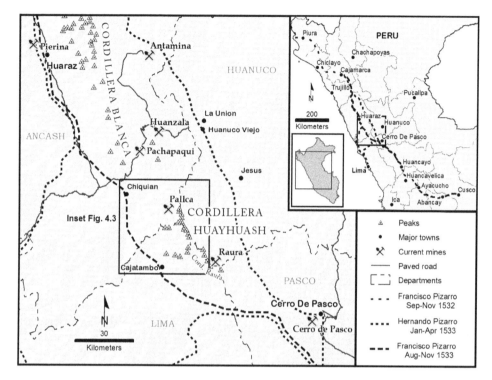

Figure 4.1. Central Peru and Pizarro brothers' routes. Source: Hemming 1970

pleted a full circuit of the Cordillera Huayhuash, a prominent range of mountains that divided the eastern and western Inca road system (see Figure 4.1).

During the expedition, Hernando and his companions noted that "there are mines in many parts" of the country through which they travelled (Markham 1872, 121) and they recorded extraordinary details about local demographics, livelihoods, and infrastructure. They remarked that the Central Peruvian highlands were "populous" (Markham 1872, 121) and that the coastal areas were even more densely settled. They also noted that expansive areas of irrigated crops such as maize and fruits were planted throughout the region and that vast herds of "sheep" (llamas), some of them with "very fine wool" (vicuña), covered the hillsides and high valleys (Markham 1872, 85). As they walked up the Santa River valley (today known as the Callejon de Huaylas), they noted that the land had "abundant supplies of maize and many flocks," that "many villages were in sight," and when they reached "the great town called Huaras," they were given 200 llamas "merely to supply the wants of the Captain and his men" (Markham 1872, 78). The Spaniards were also astonished by the quality of the Incan highways as "such beautiful roads could not in truth be found in Christendom" (Markham 1872, 121). The roads were well paved, bridges of stone or wood crossed every stream, and the expedition marveled that the deep valleys were spanned by incredible rope "bridges of network" (Markham 1872, 121). The largest part of the chronicle of the expedition, however, was reserved for very rigorous accounts of the precious metals that they plundered from every town they encountered. In Pachamac, for instance, one of the largest Incan religious centers outside of Cuzco, Hernando seized 850 pounds of gold and 1500 pounds of silver.[2] As the party crossed a high pass in the Cordillera Huayhuash where the "snow was very deep" (Markham 1872, 85), they encountered the bulk of Atahualpa's ransom en route to Cajamarca. Shortly after his return, Hernando was ordered to return to Spain with the Crown's share of the treasure and to deliver his account of the conquest of the Incan Empire. In the end, according to the records that Hernando personally delivered to the King of Spain astride a vast treasure fleet, Atahuallpa paid a ransom (unsuccessful though it was) of more than 12 tons of gold and 12 tons of silver, which, based on 2010 values, would be more than US$500 million.

Hernando's chronicle of his three-month journey through the Central Andes is historically significant because it is one of the only surviving first-hand accounts of Incan civilization, population, and mining activities in Central Peru at time of the Spanish conquest.[3] It is also another compelling example of the power of frontiers to reconfigure the natural and social order in the name of empire, similar to Turner's (1920) classic treatment of the American frontier. As recent research on frontiers suggests (Tsing 2005; Redclift 2006), frontiers can be thought of as "edges" that separate social and natural processes such as the institutions that govern public and private ownership or violence and the law. These frontiers are where ideological, cultural, and geographic spatial relations are constantly reconfigured and where "competing definitions of sustainability and progress meet and collide" (Redclift 2006, 206). As Tsing (2005, 28) suggests, resource frontiers might also be thought of as waves travelling across landscapes that "disengage nature from local ecologies and livelihoods," which therefore "free up" natural resources for global capitalism and commodity production. In this context, as the vanguard of the advancing Spanish empire, Hernando Pizarro's conquering expedition can be viewed as the "grip of worldly encounter" that led to centuries of colonial expropriation of precious metals from the Western Hemisphere (Tsing 2005). The passing of this extractive wave extinguished the spatial and cultural order of Incan empire in its wake. By the mid-seventeenth century, little was known of pre-conquest mining methods in the Viceroyalty of Peru, and most of the landscapes of the Central Andes featured in Hernando's chronicle were abandoned and the population had disappeared. The crest of this wave was characterized by a turbulent period of contestations between rival versions of civil society, cultural identity, and material control. As such, extractive frontiers can be thought of as places where new scalar relationships and governance structures are forged in response to shifting global forces and where struggles over meaning and materiality occur.

Like every gold rush in history, the extractive wave of the conquest was cyclical in that it only featured a very short period of intense "friction" (Tsing 2005) that was then followed by a long period of diminishing contestation. As history demonstrates, a series of successive waves of these resource frontiers have swept across the Andes in response to political trends, new technologies, capital flows, resource demand, and labor (Thorp and Bertram 1978).[4] The edges of these frontiers have been particularly important as they have often formed the terrain upon which frequently violent struggles have taken place and where local ecologies and livelihoods have been transformed, new forms of governance and patterns of access to resource have emerged, and encounters between cultural forms and identities have occurred.

In this chapter, we argue that the same terrain from which Hernando Pizarro extracted his ransom from the Incas, in particular the Cordillera Huayhuash, is at the edge of several recent extractive frontiers that have been scaling the Central Andean escarpment of Peru from the early 1990s through the 2000s. Indeed, since the end of the civil war and the subsequent restructuring of resource governance throughout the 1990s, the region has become a destination for new forms of global mining and international nature-based tourism. The convergence of these frontiers on the same region has fostered a host of competing economic and environmental imperatives. In this chapter, we first review the relevance of these new frontiers and struggles within current discussions in political ecology research and then briefly review the environmental and social context of the Cordillera Huayhuash. We then outline the recent convergence of mining and conservation frontiers in the region and how this is linked to local struggles over natural resource governance institutions, access to resources, and livelihoods. Finally, we conclude the chapter with a brief discussion of the future of these new frontiers.

Fractious frontiers in political ecology research

The recent acceleration of global capital flows and resource extraction frontiers has created new zones of contestation across the planet and has forged a variety of new spatial linkages between the global economy and local places and between zones of production and consumption (Tsing 2005; Redclift 2006; Bridge 2008; Smith 2008; Bebbington 2009). The edges of these frontiers have created, as Tsing (2005) argues, a heterogeneous array of places where "friction" and encounters across difference are occurring because of articulations among partially hegemonic spatial imaginaries. These zones of contestation along the resource frontier, whether they are due to struggles against dispossession (Harvey 2006; Watts 2009), by the loss of cultural identity and lifeworld (Habermas 1994; Radcliffe and Westwood 1996; Postero 2007), or their social and environmental effects (Bury 2004; Tschakert and Singha 2007; Hilson and Banchirigah 2009), resonate deeply with research themes in the field of political and cultural ecology. In particular, the frontier dynamics of successive waves of extractive production and consumption are closely related to cultural and political ecology research foci such as natural resource control and governance and access to resources.

Political ecology research has generally focused on the political and economic determinants of environmental problems (e.g., Blakie and Brookfield 1987; Peet and Watts 1996). Within this approach, numerous authors have addressed the ways in which access to and control over resources are governed as well as the geographically differentiated effects of governance on social and ecological outcomes (Wolf 1972; Bassett 1988; Hecht and Cockburn 1990; McCarthy 2002; Prudham 2004; Watts 2004c). Drawing on fields ranging from cultural ecology (Geertz 1963; Nietschmann 1973) to political science (Ostrom 1990) and economics (North 1991), this body of work highlights the importance of institutions in the determination of governance and environmental outcomes. The state, the market, and the community can be thought of as the principal governance institutions that are linked by formal and informal rules that constrain and shape human interaction with the environment (Lemos and Agrawal 2006). Much like other recent studies, we focus on the interactions between these institutions in order to illustrate the role of particular institutional actors in shaping political and economic relations during the most recent period of neoliberalization across Latin America (McCarthy and Prudham 2004; Liverman and Vilas 2006). In addition, as many countries in Latin America have begun to adopt "post-neoliberal" governance systems, it is also important to understand how these interactions are affected by the uneven impacts of neoliberalism across Latin America.

Property rights form part of governance institutions and play an important part in determining access to natural resources (Ribot and Peluso 2003). Private property, supported by the coercive power of the state, has been a central element of the global neoliberal agenda since the 1990s (Watts 1994;

Mansfield 2007). As an institutional mechanism, private property allows a very limited range of entitlement possibilities for sustaining livelihoods or enhancing personal capabilities (Sen 1981; Leach, Mearns, and Scoones 1997; Leach, Mearns, and Scoones 1999), yet has been supported as the key solution to avoid environmental degradation and to encourage economic growth (Hardin 1968; de Soto 2000). However, empirical evidence demonstrates that the imposition of centralized private property institutions on existing local land tenure regimes has often tended to exacerbate inequalities or has failed to promote positive environmental management (Scott 1998). Furthermore, studies have shown that institutions can form around non-private property governance mechanisms—generally communal tenure regimes with a blend of locally negotiated usufruct and possession rights and/or collectively managed resource appropriation—that can also lead to sustainable human–environment systems (Ostrom 1990). Despite this recognition, there is still little agreement on how successful sustainable governance institutions form and evolve (Agrawal and Gibson 1999; Dietz, Ostrom, and Stern 2003; Ostrom 2007). Thus far most research has analyzed the governance or conservation of one specific resource (for example, water or forests) across a variety of institutional contexts with a particular focus on tenure regimes. Only very recently has scholarship attempted to analyze multiple resources and user groups in the same geographical location, hence emphasizing a complex of nested institutional arrangements across scales of analysis (Hayes 2007; Brondizio, Ostrom, and Young 2009). We extend the focus of this recent work by focusing on the "vertical" frontiers between a variety of property rights institutions that govern subsurface and surface relations, the tensions between regulations that govern mineral resource claims beneath the ground, and conservation, tourism, and local livelihoods that constitute the surface institutional complex.

Only recently has political ecology research begun to seriously engage non-hydrocarbon subsurface socioenvironmental systems (as noted in Chapter 1 of this volume).[5] The focus of this recent work revolves around the enclosure of subsurface resources (Bury 2005; Bridge 2008), the conflicts generated through this enclosure (Hilson and Yakovleva 2007; Smith 2009; Tschakert 2009), and the inherently transnational nature of negotiating this enclosure (Emel and Huber 2008). The rapid enclosure of resources that is currently taking place highlights the need for new research that analyzes the role that regulatory and land–tenure institutions play in local socioenvironmental outcomes. We address this need, which is also highlighted by Himley (2008), by documenting the practices of neoliberal environmental governance, and through the use of local place-based research methods.

Political ecology has long engaged with the themes of nature conservation and access to and control over natural resources within protected areas. Many protected areas have contentious histories of enclosure (Neumann 1996). Though state-regulated during the twentieth century (Berkes 2007), many of these areas are now dominated by a few transnational nongovernment organizations (Chapin 2004; Adams and Hutton 2007), particularly in developing countries. Relatively recent conservation approaches, such as community-based conservation (CBC) and community-based natural resource management (CBNRM), recognize the difficulties of centralized conservation initiatives and their tendency to result in "paper parks" (Neumann 1998). The local effects of these new forms of conservation are still being discussed—indeed, while some are considered massive funding successes (but dramatic implementation failures) (Sundberg 1998; Blaikie 2005), others have resulted in improved resource stewardship (Hecht and Cockburn 1990; Ostrom and Nagendra 2006; Himley 2009). We engage in these ongoing conversations through our focus on new private conservation areas (PCAs) in the Central Peruvian Andes, in order to illustrate how these new protected areas promote forms of resource governance that are very different from those fostered by extractive industry.

Finally, the convergence of multiple resource governance frontiers in particular places poses new challenges for access to and use of physical and biological resources by different user groups. Neoliberal governance has often promoted a variety of new resource commodification activities to promote economic growth. While these transformations might appear to be coherent at national or global scales of analysis, their confluence in specific locations often results in contradictory prescriptions for resource access and use and therefore conflictual social struggles as new mechanisms of control are negotiated. Our research focuses on the confluence of mining, conservation, and nature-based tourism frontiers in the Cordillera Huayhuash with the goal of illustrating the ways in which these struggles are emerging from recent efforts to commodify the region's physical and biological resources. We also evaluate how resistance to this restructuring of access to resources in the region is "coproducing" the social and environmental systems of the region (Ostrom 1996; Bakker and Bridge 2006).

The findings in this chapter rely on several periods of case study in the Cordillera Huayhuash that began in 2002, utilizing a mix of qualitative techniques such as archival research, household questionnaires, key informant interviews, participant observation, and participatory mapping exercises. Archival research was conducted using governmental and a variety of civil society and NGO sources focused on conservation efforts in the mountain chain. Semistructured questionnaires and unstructured surveys were conducted with more than 20 households from four local communities in 2005 and 2006, focusing on household livelihood activities, resource use, and the impacts of conservation and new ecotourism in the region. In 2011, 172 household questionnaires and over 40 unstructured interviews were conducted in ten local communities, focusing on conservation, mining, and tourism. A convenience sample was utilized for both rounds of interviews and surveys, but households representing a variety of livelihood activities and locations were selected. Key informant interviews were conducted with community representatives, civil society and NGO representatives, governmental agency personnel, and tourists visiting the region. A number of workshops and focus groups with local community members were also conducted to further examine conservation and natural resource management issues. Finally, extensive participant observation related to conservation, natural resource management, and participatory natural resource mapping was conducted throughout the region. One author (Norris) was formally involved in community affairs from 2003 to 2011 and served as an assessor to a local NGO, the Huayhuash Development Center. Finally, in conjunction with extensive data collection efforts at both the national and international scale, new geographic information databases were created to delineate community boundaries, quantify and locate land-use activities, identify areas of conflict both within and between communities, and establish a foundation for future research and conservation activities in the region.

Research context: The Peruvian experiment and the Cordillera Huayhaush

From the 1960s through the 2000s, Peru has oscillated between democratic and authoritarian forms of government. In the early 1960s, an oligarchic government presided over the country, a regime that was followed by more than a decade of military rule from 1969 to 1980 and a brutal civil war from 1980 to 1993, in which nearly 70,000 people perished (TRC 2003). During the 1980s, successive administrations presided over a civil unrest and economic upheaval that led to more than 2,000,000 percent hyperinflation and massive impoverishment of the Peruvian people. Then, in a complete reversal, and through the use of military suppression and a coup d'état, democratic and neoliberal reforms were instituted during the 1990s and 2000s. During this tumultuous history, two enduring issues have profoundly influenced the fate of the country's leaders: Peru's relationship with global capitalism and the governance and exploitation of its abundant natural resources. The gamut of policies

pursued to address these challenges has included isolation and nationalization (1969–1980), hostility and corporatism (1980–1990), and global integration and privatization (1990–2010).[6] Yet despite this diversity of positions,
most either failed, were not fully implemented, or led directly to the downfall
of their architects.[7] In addition, nearly all of the policies pursued by Peru's
leaders, whether they were military dictators or democratically elected presidents, have been deeply divisive for at least part of the country's population
and have frequently resulted in some form of civil unrest.[8] During the most
recent period of global integration and decentralization that began in the
early 1990s, two of the most contentious issues have been the rapid growth of
mineral extraction activities and conservation, both of which are deeply dependent upon international capital flows for growth and the spatial reordering
of natural resource governance. Mining and nature-based tourism—which is
predicated on the conservation of nature and historical monuments—have,
respectively, become the largest and second-largest sectors of Peru's economy.
While not of equal magnitude in terms of the social resistance that they generate, both have become the frontiers of environmental and social change expanding across the country's diverse landscapes and are the fault lines around
which resistance and struggles are emerging.

Beginning in the early 1990s, President Alberto Fujimori initiated a con-
stellation of economic and political reforms to integrate Peru into the rapidly
globalizing international economy and to foster new transnational mineral
investment. This reversal of the Peruvian Experiment of earlier years (e.g.,
Lowenthal 1975) was accomplished through the use of authoritarian measures that included military suppression of the country's long-running civil
war, seizure of all the institutions of the state via an *autogolpe* ("self coup"),
implementation of drastic government spending cuts, "economic shock ther-
apy" for the Peruvian people, and the creation of a new constitution that en-
shrined the principles of private property and land tenure rights (Webb and
Baca 1993; Torero 2001). Drawing on well-developed neoliberal policies informed by the "Washington Consensus" (Williamson 1993) that were being
implemented around the region by international financial institutions such
as the World Bank and the International Monetary Fund (IMF), all sectors
of the Peruvian economy were opened to foreign direct investment (FDI) by
removing restrictions on remittances of profits, dividends, royalties, access to
domestic credit, and acquisition of supplies and technology abroad. In addition, the government offered tax stability packages for foreign investors for
terms of 10 to 15 years and adopted a wide-ranging privatization program that
auctioned off most state-held resource extraction operations. To further allay
investor concerns, a number of bilateral and multilateral investment guar-

antee treaties were ratified. Finally, a new national mining law was adopted
that revised mineral claim procedures and centralized the spatial organization of concessions under a new geographic reference system. This guaranteed national and transnational mining firms exclusive control of the necessary land resources to implement their operations (Bury 2005). The results of
Peru's neoliberal restructuring have been nothing short of revolutionary. The
country is now considered to be one of the most open and liberal countries in
Latin America (IMF 2001) and is deeply woven into transnational mineral
investment capital flows. The country has become a globally ranked mineral
and metals production center. Between 1991 and 2008, transnational mining companies invested more than US$30 billion in the mining sector, which
is now dominated by global mining corporations, and operations with more
than 20,000 hectares account for more than 46 percent of all mining claims.
Minerals now make up 62 percent of Peru's exports, currently more than 10
percent of the country is under active concession, and 89 percent of all of the
area ever claimed for mining has been claimed since 1990. These new operations have been very productive in such a short period of time. Between 1990
and 2009, mineral exports totaled more than US$120 billion (BCR 2009;
Bebbington and Bury 2009; MEM 2010). Comparatively, this is 350 percent
more than all mineral exports from Peru between 1950 and 1990. Rapid increases in mineral production have also resulted in significant increases in royalties and payments to local regions and municipalities because of the decentralization of national mining income (referred to as the *Canon Minero*). This,
in turn, has rescaled governance debates and conflicts over state resources to
local places across the Andes (Eaton 2004).

In conjunction with the end of the civil war and neoliberalization of the
mineral sector, much of Peru's terrain is being reordered through the creation of new conservation governance mechanisms. Like many other developing countries, the country's system of protected areas grew rapidly from the
mid-1990s through the 2000s. As of 2011, more than 15 percent of the country was covered by nationally protected areas, which was one of the great-
est amounts for countries in Latin America (SERNANP 2011). In 1961, the
first national park was created, but successive military governments quickly
increased the size and extent of the country's protected areas in order to enhance national pride, centralize control of the country's resources, and reori-
ent national resource extraction activities towards state-controlled economic
development (Solano 2005a, b). By the end of the 1980s, roughly 6 million
hectares had been classified as conservation areas. In the 1990s, the purpose
of national conservation activities was refashioned, in part, into a new mechanism for fostering international tourism to the country. This occurred in con-

junction with the nearly total elimination of state support for protected area management activities and tourist management and promotion infrastructure (Desforges 2000; Bury 2008a). Finally, during the first period of Fujimori's presidency, a new Natural Resources Management Institute (Instituto Nacional de Recursos Naturales, INRENA) was created to oversee the country's protected areas system. A host of subsequent laws and constitutional provisions were created to transform the institutional context for managing protected areas, and in 2008 a new Ministry of the Environment (Ministerio del Ambiente, MINAM) assumed control of the country's protected areas through the National Service of Natural Protected Areas of the State (Servicio Nacional de Areas Protegidas, SERNANP).

The consequences of this spatial expansion of conservation activities have been as profound as the changes that have taken place in the mining sector. Since 1996, new conservation areas have increased by more than 300 percent and at the end of 2011 cover more than 22 million hectares across more than 100 different areas. In addition, new forms of "private" protected areas have recently been created (including in the Cordillera Huayhuash), which at the end of 2011 included 40 different parks that covered approximately 400,000 hectares (SERNANP 2011). These changes in protected areas governance have created a variety of new spaces for tourism throughout the country. From a low of just over 200,000 visitors in 1992, tourist inflows to Peru increased to 2.6 million people in 2011, and are projected to continue to grow in coming years. In economic terms, tourist-related activities have become the second largest sector in the Peruvian economy. In 2009, international tourism generated US$2.4 billion in receipts. Between 2004 and 2009, the number of international tourists who visited at least one of the national protected areas ranged between 21 and 35 percent of all tourists visiting the country (INEI 2005; MINCETUR 2010). Figure 4.2 illustrates the recent growth of protected areas and international tourism in Peru. Finally, the rapid growth of tourism has increasingly been drawing tourists away from traditional historical tourism areas such as Cuzco. A recent strategic tourism plan for the country highlights these changes as it argues for the creation of a new series of ecotourism-related areas along the northern coast (Huanchaco, Mancora, Trujillo), tropical lowlands (Iquitos, Puerto Maldonado), and highlands (Cajamarca, Huaraz, Lake Titicaca) (MINCETUR 2005).

As mining and conservation have become prominent features of Peru's new political economy during the 1990s and 2000s, their frontiers have not spread evenly across the country. While they might be understood as constituting similar forms of capital seeking new opportunities for accumulation, they represent very different forms of natural resource governance, have dif-

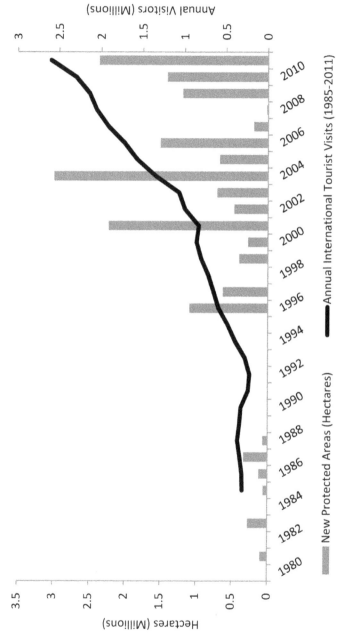

Figure 4.2. Tourism and conservation growth in Peru. Sources: MINCETUR 2012; SERNANP 2011

New Protected Areas (Hectares) ■ Annual International Tourist Visits (1985–2011) ━

ferent implications for local environments and livelihoods, and at the local level they often represent competing and very divisive futures. One area on which these competing frontiers have converged is the Cordillera Huayhuash (pronounced "why wash"), located along the continental divide of the Central Peruvian Andes, 35 kilometers south of Huaraz and 200 kilometers north of Lima (see Figure 4.1). The Huayhuash, one of twenty mountain corridors in the Peruvian Andes, includes the country's second tallest mountain, Yerupajá (6617 meters), as well as 14 other major peaks (6 of these greater than 6,000 meters) (Kolff and Bartle 1998). The range consists of a 30-kilometer north-to-south trending ridge of ice and snow-clad summits. The flanks of the ridge have been corrugated by glacial streams and lakes that have formed precipitous gorges that drain into both the Amazon and Pacific Basins. The range contains more than 50 lakes and 115 glaciers that cover more than 8,000 hectares that have been in recession since at least the early 1930s (Coney 1964; Hidrandina 1988).

The relief of the range, from below 3000 meters up to 6617 meters (in less than 20 horizontal kilometers), has created conditions for a wide variety of climates and ecosystems. Generally, the climate of the region is punctuated by a dry season between April and September and a rainy period between October and March. The high valleys and peaks are dominated by a cold and dry climate, but along the flanks of the range, climatic and biological conditions allow for at least six distinct life zones (TMI 2001). The Cordillera, because it is one of the few tropical mountain chains in the world, is also the location of important, but relatively rare, high mountain ecosystems. Studies have identified more than 1,000 plant species, 62 bird species, and more than a dozen mammal species in the region, including the threatened queñal (*Polylepis* spp.) plant and the rare Andean Condor (*Vultur gryphus*) (Weberbauer 1945; Cerrate de Ferreyra 1979; Fjeldså and Krabbe 1990; Waterton, Smith, and Fjeldså 1996).

Communities in the region are dispersed along the lower flanks of the range, and small settlements extend throughout the high valleys up to 5,000 meters. Below these villages are the larger communities of Cajatambo and Chiquian, which are also the major access points to the range (see Figures 4.1 and 4.3). Three different national administrative units trisect the range, the departments of Ancash, Huanuco, and Lima. Table 4.1 shows that in 2001 an estimated 18,100 people lived in the area (TMI 2001).

The principal economic activity in the region is animal husbandry, with approximately 24,000 head of sheep and 7,800 head of cattle in the area. At lower elevations, smallholder agriculture provides secondary products such as corn, grains, and tubers for local consumption. Some cheese is produced

Table 4.1. Communities in the Cordillera Huayhuash

Community	Population‡	Date of Recognition†	Department	Province	District	Altitude (MASL)
Huayllapa	800	1935	Lima	Cajatambo	Copa	3570
Jesus	6200ʲ	1930	Huanuco	Lauricocha	Jesus	3490
Llamac	900	1938	Ancash	Bolognesi	Pacllon	3230
Pacllon	1400	1941	Ancash	Bolognesi	Pacllon	3520
Pocpa	600	1941	Ancash	Bolognesi	Huasta	3470
Queropalca	1800	1929	Huanuco	Lauricocha	Queropalca	3850
Uramasa	600	1936	Lima	Cajatambo	Cajatambo	3300
Dispersed	5800					

Sources: †MINAG 1998; ‡Estimated from survey responses.
Note: ʲJesus is a large community with a number of *anexos* (smaller settlements) that are recognized only within the community—usually the two *anexos* of Tupac Amaru (approximate population: 400 people) and Quishuarcancha (approximate population: 500 people) are considered as the "communities" in the territory coincidental with the glaciated portion of the Cordillera Huayhuash.

for sale in regional markets as far away as Huanuco and Huaraz (a distance of as much as 100 kilometers) and there is also an internal market for dairy and wool products (e.g., milk, cheese, ponchos, blankets, and minor clothing items). Beginning in the 1990s, people have diversified their economic activities to include the provision of tourist services in the form of guides, donkey drivers, porters, and cooks and the provision of unskilled labor to the mines (Pallca and Raura) on a temporary basis.

Current governance within the communities is based on the Law of Campesino Communities, which was passed in 1987 under the first presidency of Alan García. According to this law, communities are governed by a *junta directiva* (executive officers) who are elected every two years by the *asamblea general* (the constituent body of the community). There are strong stipulations regarding membership in the *asamblea* and how community territories are claimed and defined. The 1987 law states that "the lands of peasant communities . . . are inalienable," though the inalienability was partially undone by the new 1993 Constitution and subsequent legislation culminating in the 1995 Land Titling Law, which allowed the sale of community land under a 66 percent vote of the *asamblea* (GOP 1987; GOP 1995).⁹ The systems of governance created have been described as common property resources (CPRs): the community has closed boundaries, membership is strictly controlled, decisions regarding resource use are made in a collective fashion, information regarding resource use is published in the *asambleas*, and the *asamblea* provides a low-cost conflict resolution mechanism (Pinedo 2000). Yet we also agree with Mayer's (2002) observation that many governance systems in the Andes are semiprivate regimes operating under the guise of common property. Although the community may hold a common property title, the tenure regime within the community is split between private *possesionario* plots (plots held by hereditary or community-ordained possession) at lower elevations near the community and communal grazing areas located in the upper watersheds (Mayer 2002). Communal titles were further weakened in 2008 through a series of presidential decrees that constituted part of the ratification of the free trade agreement with the United States: the vote for the alienation of community land was reduced to 50 percent of community members present at the *asamblea*. This practically removed all barriers for the sale of community territories and resulted in violent conflict across the country. These new regulations were repealed within months (Smith 2008; Bebbington 2009; Smith 2009), yet numerous sales were made before this occurred.

Rocks and resistance: The new mining frontier

Mineral extraction has a long history in the Cordillera Huayhuash that is documented from the time of the conquest. Records from the community of Llamac indicate that there were artisanal mines at the Minapata site during the conquest (Bodenlos and Ericksen 1955; Robles Mendoza 2006; Huaranga 2008). Currently, this site is being worked by the Japanese-owned company Mitsui Mining and Smelting, which acquired a few mining claims in 1964 and then acquired claims to major deposits in 1973 (INGEMMET 2011).[10] On the southern side of the range, Hernando Pizarro noted that a number of mines were present near Cajatambo in 1533. In Huayllapa and Uramasa, silver, copper, and lead were extracted from the Auquimarca hacienda in the eighteenth and nineteenth centuries (Raimondi 2006), a place where two artisanal mines continue to operate to this day. The village of Queropalca was founded as a *campamento minera* (mining camp), where artisanal extractive activities took place for more than one hundred years (Queropalca 2007). However, the most recent expansion of the extractive frontier in the Cordillera Huayhuash has shifted from such small-scale artisanal mining activities to larger transnational operations. This has also been facilitated by the rapid spatial reorganization of subsurface mineral rights since the 1990s, which reshaped resource governance in the region and led to repeated contestation over these new subsurface property rights. Prior to 1990, the total subsurface area claimed in the region totaled just over 3,000 hectares. By the end of

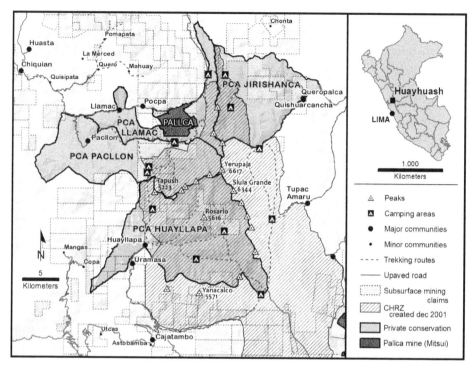

Figure 4.3. Mining and conservation in the Cordillera Huayhuash. Sources: INGEMMET 2011; SERNANP 2011

2001, more than 24,000 hectares were under claim, and by the end of 2008, the number had grown to more than 40,000 hectares, which is a 1,297 percent increase of area claimed in just less than 20 years (INGEMMET 2011) (see Figure 4.3).[11]

The exploitation of the Pallca mine site by Mitsui Mining and Smelting[12] marked the opening of the current mining frontier in the Cordillera Huayhuash (see Figure 4.3). Exploration activities in the region began in 1994 and were accompanied by Mitsui's efforts to negotiate with the community of Llamac for the control of the surface property rights necessary to reach the underground lead, zinc, and silver deposits.[13] Community resistance to the mine was immediate and resulted in claims that the mine would lead to serious environmental degradation and a loss of tourism income. Access roads to the Pallca site were blocked with rocks by some community members, and a series of failed negotiations were mediated by the Ministry of Energy and Mines (Ministerio de Energía y Minas, MEM).[14] In June of 1997, a *servidumbre* (easement) was signed between Llamac and Mitsui, granting the company the necessary surface rights to gain access to subsoil mineral deposits. In return, the communities of Llamac and Pocpa received approximately US$4,000 each, received guarantees that manual labor would be hired by the mine at US$7 per day, and were promised that schools would be improved and an unpaved road constructed between Chiquian and Llamac (see Figure 4.3).[15] Exploration activities continued for another two years, and then on 7 June 1999, mine workers punctured an underground aquifer. The surge of water and material that flowed directly into the Llamac River caused serious particulate pollution that killed most of the fish and threatened the community's drinking water (Kolff 2000). Two days later, the communities of Llamac and Pocpa confronted mine officials at the site, and after negotiations failed, attempted to shut down the mine's generator. In the ensuing struggle, three community members were shot by private police, and of these three, one was seriously injured.

Despite the serious environmental impacts of the punctured aquifer on local communities and the Llamac river, the mine and MEM continued to pressure Llamac to allow Mitsui to expand its operations. Through what has been characterized as *negocio esforzado* (forced negotiation), Llamac "sold" 1500 hectares of their land to the mine on 12 October 1999. However, no monies ever changed hands as a result of this land transaction, and instead a water development project was to be built by the mine that was valued at S/.900,000 (approximately US$250,000).[16] According to the mine the water project eventually cost S/.4,500,000 (approximately US$1.3 million) and various smaller projects were to be supported, including the Club de Madres (Mothers' Club), a new *plaza de armas* (town square), and completion of the road from Chiquian to Llamac, which put the total transaction value close to S/.6,000,000 (approximately US$1.7 million). In any case, resistance to the mine's purchase grew very quickly as a result of conflicts between the company's strict vision of its private property rights and the mixed bundles of usufruct and possession rights held by individual community members. For example, one landowner in Pocpa set a US$100,000 price on his less than one-hectare family plot, owned through possession rights within the community, which was necessary for the road construction project. Although this slowed road construction and exacerbated already tense relations between the communities of Llamac and Pocpa,[17] the mine deployed its superior technical capacity and resources to frustrate the road blockade. Mine engineers designed two new bridges and blasted a new route for the road across a nearly vertical cliff face on the opposite side of the canyon.

In addition to local direct resistance to the mine, a local civic association filed a complaint against Mitsui with the Congressional Commission on Environment, Ecology and the Amazon, arguing that, because of the 1999 puncture incident, levels of cyanide and cadmium were above permissible levels in the Llamac River. The complaint resulted in a request for an environmental impact assessment (EIA) from MEM, but few changes took place in the mine's operations (GOP 2002).[18] In January 2002, Mitsui made a presentation of the EIA in Chiquian (MEM requires this public notification before allowing mineral exploitation activities to begin at any operation). Public outcry accompanied the event and in the following weeks, 96 observations/ critiques of the EIA were formally submitted to INRENA (Business Wire 2003).[19] Despite a host of criticisms and charges that the EIA process had been scarcely democratic (GRADE 2002)—and amidst a series of violent conflicts that the mine had generated between mine personnel and communities—the EIA was approved, and the mine started operations on 19 March 2006, only a few months behind the proposed schedule.

Once the mine began to operate, more organized forms of resistance and negotiation appeared in Llamac. Late in 2006, the community filed a lawsuit against the mine, claiming that the original land sale was unfair because of the failure of the water development project and that the 1999 land purchase did not engage in sufficient public consultation.[20] Mitsui decided to settle out of court: a document subtitled "Peaceful Coexistence" was signed by community leaders and mine representatives in 2008, and Llamac would receive further development projects and two new vehicles (MEM 2008).[21] Nevertheless, after a meeting in May of 2010 between the *junta directiva* of Llamac and the mine's business director, the president of Llamac indicated that the mine was failing to meet parts of the agreement. In addition, conflict and contestation over the boundaries between Llamac and the mine, particularly between usufruct grazing rights and private property, continue to create further friction.

The new extractive frontier has also resulted in a series of struggles over resources in neighboring Huayllapa (see figure 4.3). In the Cordillera Raura, just to the southeast of the Cordillera Huayhuash, the small Peruvian-owned Raura Mining Company has run a polymetallic operation since the 1960s. In 1995, the company bought 3,600 hectares of subsurface mining rights surrounding a mountain called Tapush (see Figure 4.3). The majority of these claims lie across both Huayllapa and Pacllon's titled lands, a situation that allows the mine to choose which community to negotiate with for access rights.[22] In 2007, representatives of the mine first started to visit Huayllapa and offer *turnos* (manual labor in operating the Raura mine) at US$10 per day to young men in the village. Then in 2008, the company began formally negotiating with Huayllapa for access rights to the Tapush claims. At first, there was much resistance to the mining project, largely fueled by Huayllapa's desire to further develop tourism activities and their recent investment in the creation of a PCA in the community. When President García's free-trade presidential decrees came into effect in June 2008, the mine ramped up their negotiating efforts. A contract was signed for exploration rights in August of the same year under a new provision that required a minimum vote of only 50 percent of attending community members in order to engage in land transactions.[23] Just before this deal was closed, however, tension was evident between older and younger men in the village: the older men preferred to turn the mine away, while the younger men were eager to enter into the cash economy of the mine. Even though the decrees were immediately repealed in September, the August contract remains legally binding and the community is still obliged to provide access rights to the mine, even if the majority of the *asamblea* is not in agreement (del Castillo 2009).

The relationship between Huayllapa and the Raura mine has also involved overlapping scales of governance. At the national scale, the Department of Lima (the state) has financed the construction of a new road from Uramasa to Huayllapa. The mine is still negotiating for property rights to build the road from Huayllapa up to the base of Tapush, but because these negotiations have not been completed, it has resorted to airlifting earth movers to the proposed mine site. It also appears that forced negotiating tactics and other incentives are being utilized to secure the remaining property rights that cover both the higher common grazing areas and the lower *possesionario* (occupied) plots. The transnational governance context of the mine is largely due to the fact that a Norwegian company, SN Power, is developing a hydroelectric project that would draw water both from Huayllapa's and Uramasa's watersheds to satisfy the mine's energy needs. This is problematic for local livelihoods that are based on animal husbandry and tourism.

In addition to current conflicts surrounding new extractive operations, a series of potential mining conflicts over access to resources are emerging along the southern flanks of the Cordillera Huayhuash near Uramasa. The Peruvian-owned mining company Minsur recently purchased claims near Rosario (Huayllapa) and Yanacaico (Uramasa), and respondents in Uramasa indicate that exploration activities are already taking place. This has provoked heated debate within the community regarding the supposed negotiation that the mine is obliged to undertake for legal access to the claims, as it appears that the community has not been formally consulted.

Rangers and resistance: The private parks frontier

The edges of the recently arrived conservation frontier in the Cordillera Huayhuash are defined by a state-led protected area effort that is opposed by a number of local conservation initiatives. In December of 2001, the Cordillera Huayhuash was designated by the Peruvian Congress as the Cordillera Huayhuash Reserved Zone (CHRZ) (see Figure 4.3). This was the first step towards creating a national park in the area and was largely promoted by actors from outside of the region interested in biodiversity conservation. When the communities were approached regarding this restructuring of resource governance, the idea was quickly rejected. The nearby imposition of the "fortress conservation" or "Yellowstone model" (Stevens 1997; Neumann 1998) in the Huascaran state-managed protected area (approximately 35 kilometers north of the Huayhuash, in the Cordillera Blanca) was well known in the Huayhuash, and communities rejected the thought of Lima technocrats managing their growing tourism industry. Although the national park would have placed legal restrictions on mining activities, Huayhuash residents considered the possible loss of autonomy to be a worse fate.

Prior to this moment in 2000, new national legislation was implemented that included a "novel legal framework" for PCAs (GOP 2001; Solano 2005a, b).[24] Specifically, the new law outlined a two-step process for titled and registered land to be legally recognized as a PCA: first the owner must write a technical document justifying the need for a conservation area, and second, a conservation plan must be written. Both steps are overseen and approved by INRENA (now SERNANP). Local communities in the Huayhuash chose to utilize this new conservation framework and create PCAs in response to the state-led CHRZ as a mechanism to limit central government interference in the region. They also perceived PCAs (albeit incorrectly) to be a way to prevent future mining activity and to retain sovereignty over their lands.[25] Communities that held the required land title started their efforts in 2002, and four communities gained recognition as a PCA between 2006 and 2009 (see Table 4.2 and Figure 4.3). The three remaining communities cannot develop PCAs because they lack registered land titles for the entire community.

To date, the frontiers created by these two different forms of resource governance—biodiversity conservation versus tourism management—have not erupted in conflict, largely because of the state's soft stance towards the communities.[26] Notwithstanding the PCAs, according to MINAM, the CHRZ still exists and someday the state may reassert its vision of conservation through a state-run protected area. This overlap of state and private conservation areas is unprecedented in Peru, and MINAM officials are reluctant to

Table 4.2. Development of private conservation in the Cordillera Huayhuash

Community	Justifi-cation presented	Approval of justifi-cation	Approx. cost of justifi-cation*	Conser-vation plan completed**	Approx. cost of conser-vation plan*	Approx. total cost*
Huayllapa	Feb 2004	Dec 2005	$10,000	May 2006	$20,000	$30,000
Pacllon	July 2004	Dec 2005	$10,000	May 2006	$10,000	$20,000
Queropalca	Sept 2005	May 2007	$3,000	July 2007	$3,000	$6,000
Llamac	Jan 2006	Jan 2009	$10,000	Sept 2009	$3,000	$13,000

Notes: * The costs presented are all estimates based on conversations, rumor, and gossip.
** These dates are estimates.

predict future outcomes, yet they have repeatedly indicated that the PCAs in the Huayhuash will be given time to grow and that MINAM is dedicated to letting the private conservation policy experiment run its course. At the same time, the new PCA governance regime generates friction among the communities due to unequal access to new tourism resources and between the communities and nonlocal actors that seek to appropriate the natural resources in the region for either tourism or conservation.

The management of entrance fees charged to tourists is one focal point of private conservation governance conflicts in the Huayhuash. In 2005, community leaders met to discuss the growing problem of violent robberies and attacks targeted at trekking groups, some of which resulted in deaths. A decision was reached to charge entrance fees and use the income to pay *rondas campesinas* (an authorized form of armed local police) to patrol the tourist camps. Within one year of the fee implementation, the communities managed to quell the problem and, at the same time, collect a substantial income from the tourists. The cost to each tourist in 2005 was approximately S/.70 (US$20) and has since been increased to S/.135 (US$45) for the entire trekking circuit. It is estimated that more than 3,000 tourists passed through the range in 2009, drawing approximately US$140,000 in entrance fees. Some of this income goes to paying the *rondas campesinas*, and the rest of the fees collected create substantial surplus funds within the communities. All of the communities have invested a few hundred dollars in the construction of latrines and signs at their respective campsites, yet it is difficult to account for a large part of the fee-generated income. Uramasa has invested some of the money in tourism infrastructure and Tupac Amaru has created a conservation fund. In the cases of Huayllapa, Pacllon, and, to a certain degree, Llamac, large portions of the entrance fees were directly appropriated by the environmental professionals who were hired to write the documents necessary for recognition as a PCA (see Table 4.2).

Almost all of the tourism in the Huayhuash is mule-based trekking around a circuit that takes from 8 to 10 days to complete. The donkey rental (US$5 per day—two donkeys per tourist), the management of donkey trains (US$10 per day), and the provision of guide and support services (US$10–100 per day) provide an important alternate source of income in the Huayhuash, yet most of this income is captured by tourist agencies that are not based in the region (Bury 2008a). Prior to the imposition of entrance fees, this situation created tensions between the communities and the tourist agencies. With the advent of the fees, the frustrations within the communities have lessened, but now the tourist agencies complain that they pay fees while receiving little in return. Furthermore, the service-based income that does enter the communities is captured in a highly uneven manner (cf. Auer and Norris 2001; Farriss 2007). This has generated fierce intracommunity competition, and several respondents indicate that donkeys and horses have been killed as an exclusionary competitive strategy.

The root of these intracommunity conflicts is primarily the uneven capture of tourism income across the mountain range. The capture of tourism income is based on the beauty of the entire landscape, which can be classified as an open-access resource: there is no mechanism to limit the number of tourists or agencies that enter the range (lack of excludability), yet increased appropriation and use of the natural resources degrades the overall value of the range (subtractability). As the use of pack animals for tourists completing the circuit increased significantly from 1998 until 2008, researchers and local residents have noted pasture degradation, garbage accumulation, and declining fish populations (Bury 2008a). Nine of the eleven campsites that make up the trekking circuit are located in common grazing areas in the upper watersheds of various communities. These resource–governance overlaps (of campsites, grazing CPRs within each individual community, and the open-access resources across the entire range) generate a host of conflicts over pasture use for livestock and the appropriation of the landscape for tourism activities. These conflicts are the subject of great debate within the communities, yet no solution has thus far been reached.

The landscape that is articulated within the PCAs has also created new opportunities for conservation agencies and environmental groups seeking to protect or manage resources in the region. As noted above, the development of three of the PCAs was a direct source of project income for environmental engineers located in Huaraz and Lima.[27] Another example of these new resource-control and governance activities is related to the queñal forests endemic to the Andes that are popular targets for conservation by international conservation agencies. In 2002 and 2008, Peru signed debt-for-nature swaps with the U.S. government and assumed a commitment to invest over US$40 million in nature conservation (Conservation International 2002; USAID 2009). These two deals were negotiated with the help of Conservation International (CI), the World Wildlife Fund (WWF), and The Nature Conservancy (TNC). In 2009, CI started to direct some of these funds towards queñal conservation in the district of Huasta, on the northern flanks of the Huayhuash. These projects were managed by two medium-sized conservation NGOs, one based in the United States and one in Peru. Although the community of Huasta receives direct benefits in terms of environmental services, capacity building in resource governance, and some paid labor, most of the financial resources remain in the international capital circuit (cf. Chapin 2004). In a similar vein, an independent water-quality study organized by one of the authors in 2010 and 2011 (Norris) spent only approximately 10 percent of the total budget within the communities. The fact that few resources from these projects flow to local communities generates serious questions about who benefits from these conservation activities.[28]

Conclusion: Frontier futures in the Cordillera Huayhuash

The arrival of both mining and conservation frontiers in the Cordillera Huayhuash illustrates a number of key elements related to the political economy of environmental change in the region. First, while Peru adopted apparently uniform and coherent neoliberal reforms beginning in the 1990s and continuing through the 2000s, the consequences of these reforms as they have spread across the Andes have been uneven and often contradictory. As conflicts over governance and access to resources in the region demonstrate, neoliberal change has also resulted in a number of frontier disputes that are creating intense friction and contestation over resource control and governance. The convergence of these resource frontiers might be viewed as a continuation of the "Peruvian Experiment," in that debates about the purpose of different forms of property and social welfare are still active across the country. This is particularly so in the domain of resource governance and access, where the Cordillera Huayhuash case illustrates the coexistence of private property-based environmental communitarianism and hard-rock subsurface neoliberalism in the same small space. These forms of control do not coexist peacefully, however; indeed, resistance and conflict have been escalating across the region. This suggests that the future of this particular set of "experiments" has yet to be resolved and that negotiations over and the coproduction of environmental governance along this frontier will induce everyday and organized resistance (Polanyi 1944; Scott 1985).

The confluence of resource frontiers in the Cordillera Huayhuash also highlights the ways in which mining, conservation, and community resource-access regimes involve very different institutions and access mechanisms. These resource-tenure regimes, including below-ground private property and several above-ground mixed communal and *possesionario* forms of property, overlap across the landscape of the region while at the same time being influenced by a variety of state and international actors. The uneven and uneasy coexistence of these various forms of resource governance illustrates several of the edges around which current resource contestations are focused. While a complex combination of resource tenure and management institutions might emerge as a result of these disputes, it is also possible that vertical tensions between surface and subsurface regimes will, in the end, redefine these institutions. Surface tenure regimes exist largely because of a long history of human interaction. Subsurface tenure regimes, however, present very different potentialities. Mineral exploitation throughout the region could erase most surface-tenure regimes for possibly a very long period, suggesting that the widespread imposition of private mineral rights would be accompanied by the decline or disappearance of other forms of resource management and control.

New resource frontiers in the Cordillera Huayhuash also illustrate the ways in which mineral extraction often fosters social conflict, such as the Mitsui land purchase, Mitsui EIA, or Raura negotiations with Huayllapa. These conflicts are responses to predatory resource-governance structures only interested in capturing resource rents and involving minimal respect of communities' rights to be informed. In addition, new private conservation activities illustrate the ways in which community-led private property-based activities are also transforming the region. While such conservation governance efforts are unique in Peru and certainly warrant more attention in the future, they also illustrate how neoliberal-led governance has fostered new forms of landscape commodification to capture tourism fees and accumulation. The ways in which the environment is packaged and delivered to the global tourism industry, environmental NGOs, and the research community is another set of issues that critical researchers may explore in the future (Brockington and Duffy 2010; Igoe, Neves, and Brockington 2010; Arsel and Büscher 2012).

The effects of new extractive and conservation activities on resource access and governance in the Cordillera Huayhuash also illustrate why these new frontiers should be important focal points for political ecology research. As our findings suggest, the edges of these new frontiers are where the most divisive struggles are taking place and where they have real material consequences for the people of Central Peru. By emphasizing the contingent nature of these conflicts and focusing on the places where these struggles are taking place, research that follows new resource frontiers is capable of speaking to cultural and political ecology research that has been long preoccupied with these violent environments (e.g., Peluso and Watts 2001). In addition, frontier-based research might contribute to emerging debates focused on commodity chains and the complex production of hybrid ecological and social outcomes, for it is often at the frontier where these new relationships are being forged.

Our focus on two competing resource-governance frontiers also raises important questions for the future in terms of future conflicts over natural resource management and opposing visions of development. Our analysis suggests that mining currently takes precedence over private conservation efforts in Peru, but we also recognize that conservation efforts can, in some instances, be sustained in close proximity to mining efforts. In fact, the Peruvian government is intent on facilitating the coexistence of both of these seemingly incompatible land-use designations (for example, see INRENA 2006). The convergence and coexistence of these two antithetical concerns in the Huayhuash raise important research questions for the future expansion of the neoliberal frontier as well. Further research should explore these tensions, particularly because we recognize that the fate of the region currently hangs in the balance as the resource frontier wave washes over the mountain range.

Notes

1. A castellano of gold weight was 4.55 grams, or 0.16 ounce. One hundred thousand castellanos of gold "lumps" would have been 455 kilograms, or roughly 1,000 pounds, of gold (data calculated using Hemming's [1970] figures).

2. Hernando mentions that the Incas denied that there was any gold even after being tortured at Pachamac. After he "made some search" and discovered the gold, he noted that "in the mosque there was found some gold dust, which was left behind when the rest was concealed" (Markham 1872, 123). Based on this account, and other chronicles from Cuzco, the conquistadors argued that the Incas hid vast amounts of gold and silver in undisclosed locations. These suspicions have fueled generations of adventurers and treasure hunters seeking "lost Incan gold" in the Andes.

3. Two written accounts from Hernando's expedition still exist today. Another account was written by Miguel de Estete, who was sent by Francisco Pizarro to account

for the expedition's activities and conquered treasure. Both accounts are included in Francisco Xeres' narrative of the conquest of Peru (Markham 1872). Xeres was Francisco Pizarro's personal secretary and returned to Spain with the first treasure fleet to publish his account in 1534.

4. Note that extractive frontiers are not necessarily mineral. Several of Peru's extractive frontiers were agricultural, whereby a restructuring of governance allowed for extraction of rent (Thorp and Bertram 1978) and in the case of Indonesia wood was the principal resource in the history of extractive frontiers (Tsing 2005).

5. Watt's long-term work in Nigeria clearly engages the hydrocarbon component.

6. For reviews of these periods, see Becker (1983), Thorp (1998), Bury (2005), Bebbington (2009), and Bebbington and Bury (2009).

7. For example, Belaúnde's first administration's failure is widely credited to his concession to Standard Oil's demands, and García's first administration's failure is often credited to his attempt to nationalize the banks.

8. While any thorough explanation for why social resistance is a nearly constant and recurring feature of recent Peruvian politics is beyond the scope of this chapter, it should be noted that deep inequality, extreme poverty, and widespread corruption have also been prevalent features of the recent past.

9. The philosophy behind this and previous legislation from the 1969 agrarian reform aimed to create systems of social property (Harding 1975).

10. Prior to Mitsui's entrance, Bodenlos and Ericksen (1955) note artisanal activity in the 1940s along with a chain of small-scale claims in the area. The history of claims is corroborated by Robles Mendoza (2006).

11. As noted by Bebbington and Bury (2009), only some concessions in the region will likely become active mines. The extent of the concessions, however, is indicative of a number of important issues that include: (i) the types of mining–livelihood–environment relationships that the central government is willing to countenance; (ii) the distribution and location of potential mining activities in relation to other social and environmental factors; and (iii) the predisposition of the mining sector to invest (17297). In addition, the presence of the claim is often enough to introduce uncertainties in local livelihoods that foment resistance (Bebbington et al. 2008b).

12. Mitsui Mining and Smelting is wholly owned by the Japanese conglomerate Mitsui and Co., Ltd. Mitsui and Co. reported close to 4 billion dollars in net profit in 2011 (company website).

13. Although anyone can buy subsurface mineral rights from the central government in Lima, Peruvian law dictates that access rights must be negotiated with the owner of the land that lies above the mining claim. If the owner refuses to negotiate, MEM can call in an arbitrator to negotiate a fair market price that must be accepted. In this sense, a landowner can slow the mine's entrance but cannot put it off indefinitely.

14. According to several accounts, the mine installed a negotiator in the community of Llamac with a bottomless beer fund as a means to gain the community's confidence.

15. Prior to the construction of the new road, travelling to Llamac required a one-day walk from Chiquian. Goods, either for consumption or sale in local markets, were transported with donkeys.

16. The S/.900,000 figure comes from the public record of the purchase and values

the land at approximately \$380/hectare. This valuation is very close to the prices that Antamina (a large neighboring mine) paid in land transactions from 1997 to 1999 in the nearby communities of Huaripampa, Ango Raju de Carhuayoc, and Santa Cruz de Pichiu. These prices were more or less arbitrarily assigned as there was no preexisting land market in which prices were established before the sale (Gil 2009).

17. Conflicts between Llamac and Pocpa have a long history. Relatively recently, violence erupted between the communities when the Santa Cruz *hacienda* was expropriated from its owners prior to the agrarian reform—with the outcome that Llamac received a better deal. However, in this particular case, the purposive obstruction of the road project altered the terms of the deal for road maintenance, as the mine had no access to the lower part of the road, and the maintenance burden fell on Llamac. This created further bitterness between the two communities and tension between both communities and the mine.

18. MEM requires that operating mines monitor water quality downstream from the mine site, yet this information is not made public. It is unlikely that cyanide or cadmium was present in the water, but because of a lack of transparency with the water monitoring, in communities affected by mining activity, levels of confidence are low in the science that is conducted behind closed doors in the mine facilities.

19. Although INRENA has no jurisdiction over the final approval of the EIA (this responsibility lies with MEM), at this time they were responsible to provide their own comments on the EIA, and also a public forum for commenting on the EIA.

20. As with many development projects, the irrigation project was designed by engineers from Lima with little consultation in the community. As a result, the final product does not serve the community's needs—control valves are in the wrong place, the water does not get delivered to the agricultural plots in the community, and the community does not have the capacity to manage/change the water flow in the constructed concrete conduits (Martínez Cano 2003, Robles Mendoza 2006).

21. The community of Pocpa also negotiated for an entire set of new houses that are currently being built by the mine. The row of houses, referred to as "Nuevo Pocpa" by local residents, emerged from a similar set of conflicts with the mine. However, it is unclear whether the funds for the project come directly from Mitsui or from the Canon Minero.

22. In theory, the mine can negotiate with one community and then simply burrow beneath the other community's land.

23. Legislative decree 1015 was signed into law on 28 June 2008 by then president Garcia and was repealed on 21 September 2008. While it was effective, it facilitated the alienation of lands from communities that held communal titles.

24. This legislation was influenced heavily by both the ILO 169 convention from Geneva in 1989 and the biodiversity convention from the Rio Earth Summit in 1992. Peru ratified both of these conventions in 1994 and subsequently developed a new protected-area law, which was adopted in 1997 and implemented in 2001.

25. Although the PCA framework admits the conservation area into the national system of conservation areas and the new Ministry of the Environment will oversee stewardship of any recognized PCA, the governance of community lands, including the negotiation of a sale or easement to a mine, is still under the jurisdiction of the 1995 Land Titling Law.

26. In 2008, there was a well-publicized conflict between INRENA and the com-

munity of Catac over control of the tourism resource located at Pastoruri in the Huascaran national park. In this case, Catac filed a complaint with the Ombudsman Office and won their case. Amongst other reasons, this incident influenced the stance that INRENA (now SERNANP) takes with local communities.

27. The four PCAs developed in the Huayhuash were, at the time of creation, the only PCAs in Peru financed with funds from the communities' internal treasuries. All other PCAs concurrently developed were financed by international donors such as the United Nations Small Grants Program. As an apparent reaction to the excessive costs to the communities in the Huayhuash, new legislation was introduced in 2008 that reduced the necessary documents (and, hence, the financial outlay) for PCA recognition.

28. In the early 2000s, following the 1998 publication of a coffee-table book of the Huayhuash, a similar argument surfaced in the communities: the authors of the book had appropriated the spectacular landscape for their personal gain with no benefit reaching the communities and, furthermore, the communities were never consulted regarding this publication and subsequent use of "their" landscape. For comparison, see similar arguments about the commodification of the "spectacle" of nature (Igoe, Neves, and Brockington 2010).

CHAPTER 5

Water for Gold: Confronting State and Corporate Mining Discourses in Azuay, Ecuador

JENNIFER MOORE AND TERESA VELÁSQUEZ

Believers say, God intentionally put gold next to water as a test for human beings to see whether they would choose life or death. One's left with the impression that we've fallen into temptation and that we're bringing about our own death.
FATHER TEODORO DELGADO, AFTER A TRIP TO THE HEADWATERS
OF THE CHICO RIVER UPSTREAM FROM TENGUEL[1]

Occasional towns break up the otherwise green corridor of banana planta-tions that line the Pan-American Highway demarcating the limits of the rural parish of Tenguel, in the province of Guayas, Ecuador. Producers ship tens of thousands of boxes of the familiar yellow fruit from nearby ports every month. Since the United Fruit Company broke ground in Tenguel in the 1930s, it has been one of the most agriculturally productive areas along Ecua-dor's Pacific coast.[2] However, farmer Lenin Quezada fears that all of this is at risk in exchange for another treasured export: gold.[3]

At night, to the east of Lenin's home, the lights from the mines look like low-set stars along the foothills of the Western Andes in the neighboring county of Camilo Ponce Enríquez. Ongoing small-scale gold extraction has led to the so-called deaths of the Chico and Siete Rivers and transformed the lives of farmers like Lenin. Local fishing and tourism were the first to dry up since their water started running blue-grey from discharges at the mines. But most of all, as a member of one of several small producers' associations in the area, Lenin fears for their farms and access to international markets.

On the other side of the same mountain range, highland dairy farmers such as Manuel Maldonado have heard of Tenguel's plight and are resisting a similar future. Manuel believes that large-scale gold mining at the headwaters of the Irquis and Tarqui Rivers is too much of a risk for small and medium-scale dairy producers like himself, whose farms line the valley in the rural parishes of Tarqui and Victoria del Portete. He is not convinced by promises that Canadian mining companies such as IAMGOLD, a medium-tier gold producer and owner of the Quimsacocha Project in the high *páramo* (wetland) upstream of his community, will be more responsible than small-scale mining operators on the coast.

In this chapter, we examine two cases in which small and large-scale mining jeopardizes the water supply of domestic and international commodity producers. We trace how dairy farmers in Victoria del Portete and export banana farmers in Tenguel adopt similar strategies to defend their water resources. Their use of scientific and legal studies broadens activist tool kits but has limited results given the continued commitment to industrial mining expansion under the ostensibly post-neoliberal, socialist government of Rafael Correa.

Mining and Community Mobilizing Under Post-Neoliberalism: Questions for Political Ecology

The field of critical political ecology examines the intersections between society, politics, and nature (Blaikie and Brookfield 1987; Robbins 2004; Bebbington 2007b). Since the 1990s, political ecologists have demonstrated how indigenous and agrarian communities organize around environmental and cultural discourses to defend their land and livelihood rights (Baviskar 1995; Peet and Watts 1996, 2004; Sawyer 2004). Research in Latin America has focused on how indigenous actors generate alliances with environmental organizations to intervene in national and international politics and protect their access to land and resource rights (Turner 1995; Moog Rodrigues 2004). However, new forms of popular politics are on the rise (Albro 2006; Postero 2007), particularly during a period of rapid extractive-industry expansion that threatens the rights of indigenous and nonindigenous communities (North, Clark, and Patroni 2006; Kuecker 2007). Challenging assumptions that identity is the primary basis for political struggle, this study resonates with the tradition of the political ecology of indigenous social movements but also pushes its boundaries in several ways.

First, while the grassroots organizations that we examine *do* fashion environmental discourses to keep dairy and banana production safe from potentially deadly gold-mining projects, their members are far from anticapitalist, for they are well situated within global commodity networks.[4] The activists come from capitalist family farms and, though some have indigenous roots, they collectively identify themselves as *campesinos*.[5] Though not part of a romantic subaltern class, they play an important role in contesting contemporary forms of capitalism. They articulate a development model distinct from those based on extractive industry and favor what they refer to as a life-sustaining model based upon agricultural activities over a death-inflicting model associated with gold mining. Overall, their defense of life, water, and farming represents understandings of development that are both market-oriented and ethically minded. They call for community access and control over clean water in order to keep small and medium-scale agriculture viable and rural communities healthy.

Second, while it is common for indigenous and agrarian movements to couch their arguments in appeals to indigeneity or cultural resources, the small-scale farmers from the rural parishes of Victoria del Portete and Tenguel discussed in this chapter go against the grain by arguing against mining expansion, using combined strategies of street protest and the production of scientific and legal studies. In the coastal lowlands, activists use water-quality studies produced by municipally contracted biologists to demonstrate high levels of heavy-metal contamination in their rivers. In the highlands, home-grown legal experts investigate violations of legal and constitutional norms in the granting of mineral concessions to a multinational company. In both cases, local activists and their expert counterparts generate knowledge that they believe should be sufficient to shut down mining activity threatening their water supplies. While other, excellent work in political ecology provides accounts of the ways in which the production of scientific and technical knowledge can deepen the effects of neoliberal governing powers (Goldman 2005), in this case we see how small-scale farmers attempt to direct such knowledge toward liberatory ends.[6]

Third, our work assumes a skeptical position with regard to the Citizen's Revolution or "Twenty-First Century Socialism" being implemented by the administration of President Rafael Correa, which purports to enhance the state's capacity to intervene in economic and social policies in the interests of the nation's most marginalized people. A U.S. and Europe-trained economist with little political experience, Correa won the 2006 presidential elections as candidate for the Country Alliance political movement. The middle-class bases of the new movement rejected the conservative political establishment responsible for the implementation of neoliberal policies. Correa promised to increase social investment and "bring an end to the long neoliberal night" (*El Mundo* 2006).[7] Adopting a proposal from the national indigenous movement as one of his first initiatives, the President called a national referendum to ask Ecuadorians if they would like to rewrite the constitution to lay the groundwork for Correa's Twenty-First Century Socialism and declare Ecuador a plurinational country. Although the 1998 constitution was recognized as advancing indigenous cultural and political rights, it was also criticized for opening the door to neoliberal policies.

One of the movement's founders, Alberto Acosta, also an economist but with close ties to indigenous and environmental movements in Ecuador, became Correa's first Minister of Energy and Mines and later President of the Constituent Assembly. He, more than Correa, supported grassroots efforts toward radical change in the mining sector, which culminated on 18 April 2008 when the Assembly decreed a Mining Mandate that suspended all large-scale mining, ordered that the vast majority of mining concessions be reverted to the state, and set a high bar for new mining regulations that would significantly limit large-scale expansion being inaugurated by Canadian mining companies. However, this and other differences with the President led Acosta to resign from the Assembly shortly thereafter. As Acosta parted ways with Correa, Correa's view of mining as an indispensable future source of state revenue and his weak tolerance for social movements—particularly those willing to protest in the streets—grew evident.

Our observations coincide with Ospina Peralta's (2009) assessment that Correa's policy "does not only consist in reducing corporate control over the state, but also that of any association . . . such that subaltern sectors under the Citizen's Revolution are treated similarly to banks, as if they were structurally similar and as if their influence over the state were the same."[8] Similarly, we observe that while the Correa administration implements reforms to strengthen mining legislation and ensure greater economic benefits for the state, it also curbs the influence that social movements may exercise over mining policy. Overall, we find that enhanced state control over the mining sector still weighs in favor of foreign multinationals rather than rural communities. These results concur with Bebbington's analysis (2009) that post-neoliberal governments do not necessarily equate to greater space for social movement participation.

Fourth, we ground our analysis of social movement and post-neoliberal state dynamics on the terrain of mineral extraction. While a growing body of literature draws from a political ecology framework to elucidate questions of power and agency in mining conflicts, it tends to focus on the neoliberal expansion of mining development and thereby analytically separates large-scale mining dynamics from artisanal and small-scale mining (ASM) (e.g. Bebbington, 2007b; North, Clark, and Patroni 2006). Exceptions include analyses that document conflicts between ASM operators and multinational corporations with competing claims to mineral resources (Hilson and Yakovleva, 2007; Tschakert, 2009). Moreover, ASM analyses tend to be situated within studies of the African gold mine sector with some exceptions in the area of environmental contamination and human health in South America from scientific perspectives (e.g., Barbieri, Cournil, and Gardon 2009; Guimaraes et al. 2011; see also Cleary, 1990; and Godoy, 1990). More generally, political ecological writing has said far less about ASM than it has about large-scale mining (Bebbington 2012a). In this chapter we thus help fill that gap in the literature.

Our chapter enriches both the ASM scholarship on Latin America and the literature on large-scale mining dynamics at large. We demonstrate the co-constitution of ASM and large-scale mining by explaining how the vilification of the ASM sector as unruly contaminators (also documented by Tschakert 2009 in Ghana) is deployed by the state to argue for the expansion of large-scale mineral development while obscuring the potential dangers of large-scale mining to the environment and community well-being. In Ecuador, discourses claiming that large-scale mining development is more responsible, sustainable, and hence desirable than ASM were repeated by local and national government officials, becoming a "common-sense" idea (cf. Gramsci 1971) that helped organize public debates over mining. We show how the idea of large-scale mining as more responsible effectively limited legislative reform to annul most mineral concessions in the country, leaving small-scale farmers who mobilized legal and scientific studies to protect their watersheds with little recourse other than public protests for the implementation of their rights.

Methods and Organization of the Chapter

The events that we describe occurred in 2007 and 2008 and were documented by both authors while we lived and carried out field research in Ecuador. Our work was based in the province of Azuay where over a two-year period we followed and analyzed debates over mining expansion. The findings we present were gathered through participant-observation, semistructured interviews with community representatives, municipal authorities, state officials, scientists, and company actors, as well as informal conversations with activists and site visits to Victoria del Portete and Tenguel. We also consulted scientific and legal studies and archival documents and drew from print and radio media reports.

Our chapter is organized as follows. First, we begin by mapping out large-scale and ASM conflicts in Ecuador. Second, we analyze the experience of highland dairy farmers a mere half-year into the administration of President Correa, when they engaged in high-level dialogues and mobilized legal studies to secure the protection of their watersheds in the face of potential mining expansion. Here, we note how the idea that large-scale mining is more responsible than ASM can limit the potential power of farmers' legal studies. Third, we examine how coastal banana growers utilized the results of water-quality studies one year after Correa's inauguration and at the time that a Mining Mandate was decreed nationwide, leading to reforms in the sector. Meanwhile, the state used water-quality studies that demonstrated contamination from ASM as a means of bolstering its arguments that large-scale mining would be more responsible and at the same time limiting banana farmers' demands for the protection of their rivers. We close by drawing the two cases together to show how community arguments that mining should not be allowed upstream of agricultural areas were neutralized by the power of the Ecuadorian state to convert the idea that large-scale mining contaminates less than ASM into widely held "common sense." The final effect of this hegemony has been to contain the participation of small-scale farmers in decisions affecting their lives and livelihoods.

Local mining struggles in a regional framework

The two conflicts we analyze relate to current and future mining operations in the province of Azuay. Azuay is located in the south-central region of Ecuador and is home to some of the most advanced large-scale projects in the country, as well as some of the longest-operating small-scale mines. Our particular points of interest concern present and future mining operations along the western stretch of the province.

The first operation is IAMGOLD's wholly owned Quimsacocha Project, which has indicated resources of 2.1 million ounces of gold (IAMGOLD 2008).[9] Quimsacocha, as we will refer to the project from here on in, is located in the headwaters of the Tarqui and Irquis Rivers, upstream from dairy-producing communities in the rural parishes of Tarqui and Victoria del Portete, within the county of Cuenca.[10] IAMGOLD's mineral concessions of approximately 12,000 hectares overlap in great part with protected areas in the *páramo*. *Páramo* is a high-altitude wetland ecosystem composed of deep cushions of soil and plantlife that act as a sponge to capture and regulate water essential for agriculture and human consumption. Contiguous with Quimsacocha are the makings of a potential mining district with holdings of more than 45,000 hectares belonging to several Canadian-listed junior mining companies.

Our second area of interest is in the far southwest corner of the province in the County of Camilo Ponce Enríquez where artisanal and small-scale mining activities have been taking place since the 1980s. Roughly 70 percent of the surface area of this county is situated within mineral concessions divided north to south into three subdistricts: San Gerardo, Muyuyacu, and Bella Rica (Prefectura Provincial del Azuay 2007). Small-scale mines in Bella Rica have been in production since the early 1980s. Recently, several mines in this area have been sold to foreign investors, principally with Canadian-listed companies looking to expand and optimize their operations. In Muyuyacu, there are various small-scale operations, as well as the exploration-stage open-pit Gaby Project of the Scottsdale, Arizona-based International Minerals Corporation. Gaby encompasses more than 6,000 hectares in mineral concessions and contains measured and indicated reserves of 6.2 million ounces of gold and 284,000 tons of silver. Finally, the northerly subdistrict of San Gerardo was brought into production in the 1990s by a variety of artisanal and small-scale mining operations, currently in conflict with small-scale banana producers living downstream in Tenguel.[11]

This comparative approach not only allows us to analyze extraction in relation to regional dynamics, but it also permits a discussion of small and large-scale mining within the same analytic frame, revealing the ways in which discourses surrounding different types of mining are co-constituted as part of these regional dynamics. While artisanal and small-scale mining have been portrayed in the press and by industry and public authorities as lawless and disastrous to environmental health and human well-being, large-scale mining activity in the hands of multinational corporations is framed as "responsible."[12] We note two ways in which the juxtaposition between large and small-scale mining serves as a discursive strategy to legitimate multinational mining operations.

First, the emphasis on small-scale mining impacts supplants discussion of the risks inherent in large-scale mining activity. Certainly, mining activities in areas such as the county of Camilo Ponce Enríquez *have* been poorly regulated and *have* caused tremendous damage to various watersheds. However, the state moves straight from this observation to the conclusion that multinational miners are more responsible, assuming that their state-of-the-art technology will minimize environmental impacts.[13] This idea, in turn, limits the levels of state and public support that farmers from Victoria del Portete and Tenguel can generate when they call attention to the risks inherent in *any* mining activity, including large-scale mining. Instead, the state appropriates their legal and scientific arguments about the environmental risks associated with mining activity to help advance development of a large-scale mining sector on the grounds that such risks can only be managed through the types of complex, modern technologies to which only this sector has access.

Second, local officials suggest that if large foreign companies are not permitted to continue with their operations, then, despite overlap with sensitive ecosystems and headwaters important for human consumption and agriculture, small-scale miners will invade their lands and make an even bigger mess that will be impossible to control. These officials argue that it will be easier to control one multinational company than a swarm of small-scale miners. While there is indeed evidence that small-scale miners will enter where large-scale miners are operating or have operated,[14] it is not immediately evident that public authorities are any better prepared to deal with multinational mining companies than small-scale operators. Additionally, the perception that large-scale mining is more responsible seems to be a mere echo of recent industry public relations campaigns in which Canadian-listed multinational mining companies have been portrayed as more amenable to addressing civil society concerns, more transparent, more likely to generate local partnerships with communities and states, and more likely to adopt international environmental standards.[15] Yet there is good reason to challenge these representations since mineral exploration companies in Ecuador have already been accused of violence against community activists.[16]

Overall, we view the juxtaposition of small versus large-scale mining as part of a repertoire of discursive practices used by the state and multinational corporations to garner support for their projects and neutralize critique (Benson and Kirsch 2010; Kirsch 2010. See also Sawyer 2003.). As a result, by considering small and large-scale mining struggles in tandem, we upset the facile juxtaposition being made between the two and unravel state discourses promoting large-scale mining. We observe that both types of mining could jeopardize the water supply that serves agrarian communities, suggesting (regardless of the tonnage of earth a mine will move) that its potential effects on community health and livelihoods should be independently assessed and held up to public scrutiny.

Quimsacocha

"My hand will not tremble to suspend IAMGOLD's mining concessions, *compañeros*, it is not a problem."[17] With these words, President Rafael Correa spawned hope among a group of community leaders that the Ecuadorian government would finally intervene on behalf of their rural parishes. The Environmental Defense Committee, comprising small and medium-sized dairy farmers and the Coordinating Committee for Community Water Systems of Azuay (la Unión de Sistemas Comunitarios de Agua Azuay, UNAGUA) representing the water boards of Victoria del Portete and Tarqui, had already spent two years trying to get the state to safeguard their water supply without luck. Correa's election to the presidency seemed promising. During a July 2007 meeting, the newly elected President assured leaders that the government was "on their side" and declared, "We will never let water be contaminated—water is life."[18] In this section we show how *campesino* participation in high-level dialogues led to their disillusionment with the Correa administration. While the state responded to *campesinos'* concerns by creating an environmental conservation area that was off-limits to mining, the decision left *campesino* watersheds unprotected and bolstered the image of the state as being responsive to citizen concerns and IAMGOLD as being a "responsible" corporation.

Redirecting *Campesino* Activism

President Rafael Correa and community leaders met in June 2007 during a series of road blockades against multinational mining companies in the southern and central part of the country. The protests began on 5 June and were led by the National Coordinating Committee for Defense of Life and Sovereignty (Coordinadora Nacional por la Defensa de la Vida y la Soberanía, CNDVS). Approximately 5,000 people from the southern coast, highlands, and lowland Amazonian region participated. The CNDVS, formed only five months earlier, was at that time composed of a loose coalition of indigenous and nonindigenous *campesinos*, social Catholics, health workers, and environmental and human rights nongovernmental organizations. Protesters demanded that the government declare the country free of large-scale mining and place a moratorium on new mining concessions. Not only were the Environmental Defense Committee and UNAGUA active participants in CNDVS, but they also acted as intermediaries between CNDVS leadership and rural communities in Azuay.

After four days of road blockades, then Minister of Energy and Mines (Ministerio de Energía y Minas, MEM) Alberto Acosta visited the focal point of the uprising in Tarqui to smooth over political tensions that could undermine the newly installed government. An advocate of indigenous collective rights, Acosta sympathized with protesters, stating that he "shares their demands because there are more than 4,000 mining concessions that were given without regard for legal or constitutional frameworks" (*El Comer-*

cio 2007). He proposed the formation of a high-level commission to gather evidence about mining concessions such as IAMGOLD's, with the possibility of reverting them back to the state. Openly critical of large-scale, open-pit mining, he also proposed that an emergency decree be emitted to review the mining law and that a national referendum be held over mining (*El Comercio* 2007).

At the cost of breaking with skeptical CNDVS members, UNAGUA leadership opted for state engagement. CNDVS leadership maintained a no-dialogue position and gave the Correa administration fifteen days to suspend concessions, threatening to return to the street on 26 June. Manuel Maldonado, then President of the Environmental Defense Committee, sided with CNDVS. He explained: "We knew that it was a show. We had had two or three conversations with Acosta and it was like a media campaign: that the Constituent Assembly is coming [and it will resolve all the problems in the mining sector]."[19] But, water board leaders were still hopeful about Correa's campaign promises. Rogelio Pauta, former President of the Victoria-Tarqui community water board and affiliate of UNAGUA, recalls that during his presidential campaign Correa had visited Cuenca and declared, "[If] I come to power, mining companies will leave the country."[20] So, at the expense of movement solidarity and betting on presidential authority to resolve their conflict with IAMGOLD, water board leaders agreed to meet the President in Quito in early July.

During the meeting with UNAGUA, Correa affirmed that he would suspend IAMGOLD's concessions but that he needed proof that they overlapped with community water supplies and were obtained inappropriately. Without grounds for the suspension, he anticipated that IAMGOLD "will bring a tremendous lawsuit against us, and will bankrupt the country."[21] Prior to any suspension, he also urged *campesinos* to avoid street protests, warning: "Be wary of feeling desperate or of wanting a quick solution."[22] Street blockades, he indicated, would only "harm a government that's on your side."[23] Correa proposed that a tripartite commission review legal and environmental aspects of IAMGOLD's holdings whose concessions, he said, he would not hesitate to revoke should they find supporting evidence.

UNAUGUA viewed the commission as an opportunity to legitimate their protests in defense of water, participating on the grounds that they would not meet with IAMGOLD and deal only with the government. "Our struggle is not irrational," explained then legal advisor to UNAGUA Carlos Pérez.[24] "We are not violent as the mining companies paint us . . . We accepted the government's proposal to demonstrate [legally] that the communities are in the right and that the government made the mistake, for which it has to respond."[25]

As the commission set about its work, a reduced group of anti-mining activists returned to the street in late June. Provincial Governor Oswaldo Larriva publicly demanded that the demonstrations be brought to an end, but "with respect for the human rights of protesters" (*El Mercurio* 2007). Police repression, however, was reported to be brutal (Moore 2007).[26] Participant accounts suggest police overwhelmed protesters in number and force, using heavy tear gas and anti-riot vehicles (Moore 2007). Maria Zhuño recalls that tear gas hung heavy over the valley, "like fog during the rainy months," and says police threw gas into some homes, nearly asphyxiating children inside.[27] Dozens were reportedly wounded and more than 33 detained and charged.[28]

Mobilizing Expert Knowledge

After a month of intensive research, Carlos Pérez and Hernán Loyola found what they were looking for. They established that IAMGOLD had violated three bodies of law: the 2001 Mining Law, the Environmental Regulation (Reglamento Ambiental) and the 1998 Political Constitution (Pérez and Loyola 2007). The first two violations relate to IAMGOLD's lack of permission to conduct exploratory work near headwaters or in the Yanuncay-Irquis Protected Forest. Both circumstances require special permits before mining titles can be granted. In the first case, Pérez and Loyola found no record that the company had petitioned the National Council of Hydrological Resources for permission to obtain mining titles in areas that would endanger highland lakes and rivers destined for domestic water use, as required by Article 11 of the mining law (Pérez and Loyola 2007). In the second case, they allege that IAMGOLD did not fully follow Article 19 of the environmental regulation for mining activities, which requires mining companies to submit a Preliminary Environmental Impact Assessment (PEIA) and an Environmental Management Plan to an interministerial commission responsible for approving concession titles in protected areas for forests and vegetation. Though IAMGOLD did submit a PEIA, the company did not receive complete approval from the inter-ministerial commission (Pérez and Loyola 2007). On this basis, the legal investigation purports that the National Mining Director's Regional Office violated proper procedure when it approved IAMGOLD's concession titles (Pérez and Loyola 2007).

The report also found IAMGOLD to be in violation of Convention 169 of the International Labour Organization (ILO) and Article 84 of the 1998 Political Constitution that guarantees communities the right to be consulted before commencement of any prospecting or exploration of nonrenewable resources that may affect their environment or culture (Pérez and Loyola 2007). Pérez and Loyola determined that instead of conducting a community-wide consultation, IAMGOLD developed "economic agreements with state functionaries such as mayors, presidents of the local parish government or university rectors, which are not communities, but are instead public officials" (Pérez and Loyola 2007).[29] Pérez and Loyola attached more than 57 notarized testimonies to their report from water board leaders, with thousands of signatures from water users attesting to the fact that they had not been consulted regarding IAMGOLD's exploration plans.

Concurrently, officials from the MEM and the Undersecretary of Environment conducted an investigation to verify *campesino* claims that IAMGOLD's plans for the future gold mine would adversely affect water resources in the *páramo*. The MEM's report affirms the presence of "a *páramo* system that is very important. This ecosystem provides hydrological services that guarantee water quality and quantity" (MEM 2007).[30] It continues: "We observed nine important bodies of water that could be affected by future extractive activities" (MEM 2007).[31] In other words, the inspection verified that mining activity could compromise both rural and urban water supplies.

However, although all parties agreed that mining activity could jeopardize important water resources, their conclusions differed. On one hand, Pérez and Loyola concluded that IAMGOLD's two main concessions, Río Falso and Cerro Casco, should be annulled. On the other hand, although the MEM acknowledged the importance of hydrological resources in the area to downstream communities, they recommended that IAMGOLD renounce only 3,000 hectares of its concessions that would conserve water resources serving the city of Cuenca. The report did not mention IAMGOLD's lack of permits from the National Council on Hydrological Resources nor did it provide maps or data to substantiate why certain areas rather than others should be prioritized for protection. In other words, UNAGUA's efforts to legitimize community concerns were, for the most part, in vain since it is not clear that they were even considered in the state's decision concerning Quimsacocha.

The Fallacies of "Responsible" Mining

On 14 November 2007, the MEM announced that the state would oblige IAMGOLD to cede 3,200 hectares in mining concessions to the state for the conservation of lakes and community water supplies. The MEM called this a first step and said it would continue investigations toward conservation of additional water resources in the area (*El Mercurio* 2008a). Cuenca's municipal water company (Empresa Municipal de Telecomunicaciones, Agua Potable, Alcantarillado y Saneamiento, ETAPA), charged with conservation of the 3,200 hectares, called the announcement "an unprecedented decision" (*El Mercurio* 2008b).[32] But water board leaders gave the announcement a decidedly different epithet. "It was a farce," says Rogelio Pauta, "a lie."[33] The landmark decision left water board leaders feeling deceived and betrayed.

The 3,200 hectares would not protect important tributaries of the Irquis and Tarqui rivers that supply about 2,000 people from Victoria del Portete and Tarqui with irrigation and drinking water and that coincide with confirmed gold deposits. Instead, they pertain to a watershed serving the city of Cuenca and the suburban parish of Baños and are in an area where mineralization is not believed to exist. The decision reinforced asymmetrical relations between the city and countryside that have marked Victoria del Portete and Tarqui's relationship to Cuenca for decades by protecting the city's water supply but not the countryside's. The incident "indisputably generated total distrust" of the President, says Carlos Pérez.[34] Such distrust, however, was only among community members and activists. More widely, in Cuenca and beyond, the decision, though a loss for water board leaders, would generate support for the government and IAMGOLD alike.

For state authorities, the declaration was evidence of revolutionary changes taking place. In January, during a public ceremony to sign over the area to ETAPA, then Minister of Mines and Petroleum Galo Chiriboga stated that the agreement marked a "before" and an "after" (*El Mercurio* 2008b). Without referring to irregularities found in the granting of IAMGOLD's concessions, he described "a 'before' full of corruption and decisions absolutely contrary to community interests," in contrast to an "after" in which the state has "rescued water resources, which are the right of all people, from the hands of a private company."[35] Chiriboga added, "Correa's government of the Citizen's Revolution could not allow that a strategic good of this kind be maintained in the hands of a private company" (*El Mercurio* 2008b).[36] In this way, the government distanced itself from the neoliberalism of the past.

IAMGOLD also took advantage of the decision and quickly emitted a press release to celebrate itself as a socially and environmentally conscious corporation. "Giving back the small portion of our concessions was done to send a clear message," stated IAMGOLD President and CEO Joseph Conway in a press release. "IAMGOLD is committed to preserve and protect the environment. It was the right thing to do" (IAMGOLD 2007). The press release, published one day after the government announcement, mentioned that the area flagged for conservation would safeguard the water supply of surrounding communities. It also assuaged investor fears that the decision would impact upon future profits: "The land contains no prospects and will in no way affect the eventual operation there" (IAMGOLD 2007). The company further asserted that the area was never destined for mining. "We had determined, by our own initiative, that the area be a natural reserve," said the leader of IAMGOLD's community relations team, noting that they were "establishing a scientific monitoring station in the area."[37]

As a result, the symbolic conservation of water resources in the *páramo* upheld an image of a "revolutionary" state while furthering the notion that large-scale mining is compatible with environmental conservation.[38] It also aided the representation of IAMGOLD as a "responsible" mining company, a corporate oxymoron, sensu Benson and Kirsch (2010), in which "idioms of ethics, health and environmentalism and corporate responsibility conceal the contradictions of capitalism" in attempts to manage and neutralize critique of their practices. By turning the conservation of the *páramo* into a media spectacle, the state deflected attention away from the UNAGUA study, which alleged that IAMGOLD acted irresponsibly in a context in which legal and democratic procedures had been violated. Thus, while the state *appeared* to respond to *campesino* concerns, *in practice* the 3,200 hectares conceded did not address the risk that *campesino* water resources might be contaminated nor respond to the evidence that IAMGOLD had gained title to its concessions inappropriately.

As we will see in the following section on Tenguel, representations of "responsible" multinational mining companies also help generate support for contentious projects such as IAMGOLD's among key decision-makers through its juxtaposition with small-scale mining. Local officials echo what the environmental manager at the municipal water company, Margarita Salamea, has said. Despite her concerns over the possible impacts of large-scale mining in the *páramo*, she indicates that if left with the alternative of small-scale operators, she would elect large-scale mining: "Companies assure us that they will not contaminate. But when we read their documents, we get worried. They say that they will use the best technology, but they don't explain what [technology] they will use."[39] However, she fears that if projects like IAMGOLD's are not developed, artisanal miners who lack "culture, education, and technical knowledge" will invade and contaminate the area.[40] As a result, she concludes that it would be "easier to regulate one company, rather than two hundred" small-scale miners.[41] Such existing logic within local state institutions isolates *campesino* struggles in the area, leaving them with few strategic allies.

Tenguel

Only a few months after Chiriboga announced the reversion of 3,200 hectares from IAMGOLD, then President of the National Constituent Assembly Alberto Acosta christened another "historic"[42] moment that raised the hopes of farmers from Tenguel fighting heavy metal contamination of their rivers from small-scale mining. The assembly's Mining Mandate passed on 18 April 2008 and would bring an end to "the free-for-all" in the mining sector, said Acosta.[43] For Tenguel's Assembly for the Defense of Our Rivers (Asamblea para la Defensa de Nuestros Ríos, APDNR), Article 3 of the Mandate was key: "Declare extinct without economic compensation mining concessions granted within protected natural areas, protected forests and buffer zones defined by the competent authority, and those that affect springs and water sources."[44]

Similar to rural water board members in Azuay who sought to put community claims into legal terms, these small producers believed that scientific studies would be the best way to bring attention to the environmental and health risks associated with mining activity. Composed primarily of small banana and cacao producers, many of whom are members of international fair trade or organic producers' associations, the APDNR sought to end contamination from upstream small-scale mining and have the headwaters of the Tenguel River declared off-limits to mining. Toward this end, they used preexisting contacts within the Municipality of Guayaquil to finance water, soil, and sediment studies that proved heavy metal contamination of their four rivers.[45]

This section shows how APDNR's scientific studies also had limited results. Although Ministry of Mines and Petroleum (Ministerio de Minas y Petróleo, MMP) functionaries acknowledged that poor mining practices in the San Gerardo subdistrict were causing contamination, the state also appropriated *campesino* claims in ways that the activists never intended: to champion the virtues of large-scale mining.

Subversive Science

Armed with their first scientific study, released on 4 April 2008,[46] APDNR lobbied the National Constituent Assembly. "It is essential to use the scientific method to demonstrate [what we're saying],"[47] says President of APDNR Lenin Quezada. Before getting involved with APDNR, Quezada participated in an epidemiological study that is part of an international lawsuit against Monsanto and other multinationals regarding allegedly mislabeled pesticides used on large banana plantations.[48] As a result, he came to believe that scientific evidence is the best way to back claims against powerful actors.[49]

Preliminary testing results for heavy metals in the Chico, Gala, Tenguel, and Siete Rivers were alarming. The study revealed high levels of heavy metals such as mercury, arsenic, copper, vanadium, and cobalt in all four rivers.[50] It also provided evidence for what APDNR wanted to demonstrate: small-scale miners in the subdistrict of San Gerardo in the county of Camilo Ponce Enríquez were responsible for the "deaths" of the Chico and lower Gala Rivers. Contamination of the Chico River, which flows into the lower Gala River where the two meet near the eastern limit of Tenguel, dates back to around 2001 when local residents captured a massive fish kill on video.[51] The Siete River, which courses along the southern limit of the parish, was deemed "severely contaminated"[52] and considered "dead"[53] by the mid-1990s as a result of mining in the Bella Rica sector, the southern subdistrict of Ponce Enríquez. As a result, despite a natural abundance of water on the coastal plains, these farmers fear for their lives and livelihoods because of growing water scarcity due to contamination.

Quezada observes that banana production has fallen dramatically for small-scale farmers like him who have to irrigate with contaminated waters and cannot afford to drill deep water wells. He says this has led to a reconcentration of agricultural lands in the hands of a few.[54] For her part, APDNR secretary Carmen Rodríguez emphasizes health concerns. Women and children who still wash laundry or bathe in the rivers are known to suffer from skin outbreaks. This activist also questions whether incidents of cancer might be connected to mining-related contamination.[55]

Based upon this study that begins to "ratify what is going on,"[56] APDNR wanted the government to take action and hoped to obtain support from the National Constituent Assembly. Having helped organize Correa's campaign in Tenguel, Quezada was hopeful. "We are part of this dream, this revolution," he insists.[57] In addition to the application of the Mining Mandate, they want the state to help clean up their rivers and to declare the Tenguel River an ecological reserve and off-limits to mining. Declaration of a no-go zone in the Tenguel watershed is of particular importance given that it is the main source of drinking water for about 15,000 inhabitants and provides irrigation water for about 30,000 hectares of cultivated land.[58] The release of the Mining Mandate raised expectations that their demands could become a reality.

Political Allies and the Promise of Quick Change

Then Guayas Assembly Member Martha Roldós from the Ethics and Democracy Network political party (Red Ética y Democracia, RED) is an important ally of APDNR. She helped facilitate meetings for APDNR in Montecristi and introduced them to other sympathetic assembly members such as Alberto Acosta. Roldós became motivated to support APDNR members in late 2007 when she met them and visited mines in the upper area of Ponce Enríquez: "When you see a crystalline river flowing along and then something indescribable in smell, color, and appearance joins the river from which point on the river is dead, one becomes indignant. Then to see *campesinos* who have invested in organic banana and cacao production discover that it's not worth anything because the government has let their water become poisoned . . . one can't be the same again."[59] For Roldós, approving the Mining Mandate was the high point of what the constituent assembly could offer such communities.

The Mandate overrode the limitations of the current mining law at the time, which only permitted the state to annul mining concessions on the basis of nonpayment of conservation patent fees by ordering the MMP to revoke concessions for various reasons including impacts on watersheds. Three days after it was passed, Roldós wrote to then Minister of Mines and Petroleum Galo Chiriboga, attaching a copy of the water, soil, and sediment study conducted by the Municipality of Guayaquil. She asked that he apply the Mining Mandate to concessions contaminating the four rivers in Tenguel and requested that the Tenguel and Siete Rivers be declared an ecological reserve. As a result of her petition and additional pressure from Acosta,[60] Minister Chiriboga visited Tenguel on 13 May 2008. This was an important achievement. "It was the first time a Minister had ever come to Tenguel," says Carmen Rodríguez.[61] However, rather than provide a clear remedy for Tenguel, Chiriboga's visit would once again help set the Correa administration apart from past governments that had ignored Tenguel's plight and strengthen the case for large-scale mining.

Chiriboga's visit began with a tour of mining sites followed by a meeting with Tengueleños in the central plaza of the parish center, where he noted "a state of abandon" in the area after 20 years of neglect by past governments" (*La Voz del Pueblo* 2008).[62] Affirming his own government's commitment to change, he said, "The lives mining has taken don't have a price. If miners want to work, they have to respect water, health, agriculture, and livestock . . . This government is not anti-mining, but it will never permit abuses from mining operators" (*La Voz del Pueblo* 2008).[63] He urged affected communities to be patient, given the time required to bring about improvements, and promised a new project between the Municipality of Ponce Enríquez and the University of Guayaquil to "recover and remediate a good part of the environmental damage affecting the rivers."[64] Shortly after Chiriboga's visit, the MMP also suspended mining operations in about 2,000 hectares of mineral concessions in the area of San Gerardo.[65] The suspension was a temporary achievement, but Chiriboga never mentioned the Mining Mandate.

Instead, Chiriboga's plan once again reinforced state and industry campaigns to promote the case for large-scale mining. Chiriboga's morning agenda illustrated this for the press. He visited two mines in Bella Rica, the southern subdistrict of Ponce Enríquez. The first revealed an overflowing tailings pond spilling untreated waters directly into the river (*La Voz del Pueblo* 2008). The second showed a mine "in perfect order with everything in its right place" as a result of "million dollar investments" (*La Voz del Pueblo* 2008).[66] President Correa articulated a similar message to the press around the same time, outlining an even clearer dichotomy between large and small operations that he would later repeat over and over during his weekly radio addresses. "It's paradoxical," he said, "but big mining companies generate less environmental impact than small-scale ones, we can't let ourselves be deceived."[67]

Small-scale operators in the area of San Gerardo would also off-load certain responsibility for environmental damage onto even smaller miners. Immediately following release of the Mining Mandate, the press reported that mineral concession holders in Ponce Enríquez are "conscious of damage that mining has caused to nature" (*El Nacional de Machala* 2008),[68] insisting that at least a few title holders are taking measures to mitigate such negative impacts. A month later, mine operators from the San Gerardo subdistrict would also initiate an agreement with the Municipality of Ponce Enríquez, outlining a series of proposed improvements.[69] However, the press added that "informal miners" or unorganized artisanal miners who "don't have any environmental plan and who aren't controlled by any law" complicate solutions for contamination downstream and "also need to do their part" (*El Nacional de Machala* 2008).[70]

With the responsibility for contamination shifted onto the smallest mining operators, any consideration about what further mining expansion might mean in the headwaters of Tenguel's rivers was overlooked. Specifically, there was silence on the presence already of multinational mining companies in the headwaters of the Tenguel River, which APDNR proposes should be protected. A variety of mining companies and associations are active in this area, including the Toronto and Zurich-listed International Minerals Corporation (IMC), which has a prefeasibility study for an open-pit gold and copper mine with measured and indicated resources of 6.2 million ounces of gold and 284,000 tonnes of copper.[71] APDNR's proposal that one watershed should be off-limits to mining would also not get much of a hearing during government meetings that followed.

The Less-Than-Revolutionary Reality

In the same way that the Mining Mandate was allowed to slide quietly under the carpet, so too was APDNR's proposal to have the headwaters of the Tenguel River protected. We have found only one reference to this proposal, in a report prepared for the Municipality of Guayaquil by one of their technicians who attended a strategy meeting that the Ministry of Environment held in early July 2008 to address Tenguel's dilemma.[72] The Ministry's Environmental and Social Reparation Planning group (Plan de Reparación Ambiental y Social, PRAS) reviewed the document that Martha Roldós sent to Minister Chiriboga in late April 2008, along with inspection documents from mining authorities dating back to 2006. With regard to the suggested ecological reserve, concern was raised about poor definition of protected forests in the area, "which would be a problem with regard to this request."[73] But after this, the issue of the proposed reserve disappears from public record. It is interesting to note, however, that regional mining authorities present at the meeting did reveal various obstacles they face in implementing environmental controls in the area, such as "insecurity, kidnappings, and lack of personnel ([they only have] one delegate responsible for three provinces)."[74] One might reasonably argue that these limitations might themselves be a potential reason to consider placing limits on mining expansion.

The report, however, did make a number of recommendations that seem to form the basis for gradual efforts to address Tenguel's situation, although not always in articulation with ongoing efforts by APDNR. Recommendations included that the Municipality of Guayaquil should continue with its monitoring activities and that the legal investigation it was initiating at this time against San Gerardo mine operators for environmental infractions under the criminal code should be pursued. It also suggested that better coordination between regional municipalities could help improve environmental management in the area and that international funding should be sought for remediation efforts. Finally, it proposed that various processing plants operating along the headwaters of the Chico River in San Gerardo might be relocated in a single area. This latter proposal, now referred to as an "Industrial Park," seems to be a key strategy that the state is pursuing, despite the fact that it appears to be leading toward further conflict with communities.[75]

In contrast, more immediate measures that were hoped to bring about change in Tenguel proved lackluster. Less than six weeks after mines in San Gerardo were suspended, the process of lifting the suspension began. In early July 2008, Undersecretary of Environmental Protection Lucy Ruiz partially lifted the suspension in response to reports that some laid-off workers had taken up panning for gold.[76] With artisanal miners perceived to be the biggest culprits, Ruiz wrote that this "could become a new source of contamination given that this activity uses mercury to separate gold from the sands."[77] Therefore, with the desire to put miners back to work on larger operations, and although improvements such as the installation of filtering tanks and tailings pond liners were not yet completed, Ruiz recommended that suspended mines resume their activities while processing plants remained closed. The full suspension was lifted on 29 August.[78]

Finally, it was also revealed in September 2008 that Chiriboga's promise to establish a remediation project with the University of Guayaquil was little more than words. When the Rural Parish Council of Tenguel asked about the project, the Rector of the university replied in writing and stated, "No such agreement exists."[79]

As a result, the devastation of small-scale mining would continue to serve as a model for bad practices and everything that large-scale extraction is not, while APDNR became increasingly disillusioned with the ineffective Mining Mandate and the Minister's disingenuous promises to complete the remediation project. In a letter to the Mayor of Guayaquil, Jaime Nebot, on 20 August 2008, the APDNR expressed its concern that the suspension had been lifted "without taking into account the petitions of the people of Tenguel and the offers of the Minister of Mines and Petroleum Galo Chiriboga . . . in which he affirmed that the Ministry would undertake a study with the University of Guayaquil to reduce the high indices of contamination [in the rivers]."[80] The APDNR did, however, continue to receive support from the Municipality to fund further scientific studies with which they would continue pressuring state institutions, while also seeking legal routes through which to hold mine operators and possibly the government to account.

Nonetheless, the ongoing activism of the APDNR has also been greatly complicated by the presence of mercenaries in Tenguel believed to be operating under directions from mine operators in San Gerardo. From August 2008 until the time of writing, Carmen Rodríguez has been under state protection as a result of intimidation, including several death threats that activists interpret as warnings that she should desist from her work in defense of health and water rights. Indeed, Rodríguez recalls that early on in her involvement in efforts to defend Tenguel's rivers, one of the miners she knew "said to not get too involved because around here they silence people."[81] Indignant, she comments, "The only crime I have committed is to defend our water and to try to prevent that people keep dying from cancer as a result of mining activities."[82] APDNR President Lenin Quezada has also reported receiving threats and has been robbed three times since he became involved in activism.[83] But he will not back down. "Sometimes life throws you a challenge," he says. "I could stay quiet, or simply not do anything. But it's worse knowing the monstrosities that are going on and to not get involved."[84]

An Obvious Choice for Azuay Province?

"Azuay could be sitting on the largest gold deposit in the world and live off that tremendous wealth, but for the capricious whims of a few who would prohibit these riches from being removed. [They say] that mining will contaminate water resources! These are lies, myths, fixations that do not stand up to even the most basic analysis. There can be mining that does not contaminate. . . . [But] they become even more absurd [when they say]: 'No to large-scale mining, yes to small-scale mining!' Small-scale mining is the most polluting means of mining because it is artisanal and unruly."
PRESIDENT CORREA, DURING HIS WEEKLY NATIONAL RADIO ADDRESS, 18 OCTOBER 2008[85]

During various other public addresses such as that quoted above, generously smattered with insults against anti-mining activists, Correa has repeatedly insisted that large-scale mining is more environmentally sound than small-scale operations and that it could be the panacea for Ecuador's development woes under his administration's management. In fact, ever since the National Constituent Assembly passed the Mining Mandate to "get its house in order,"[86] Correa has been the most prominent pro-mining spokesperson at the national level, largely relieving Canadian companies of the need for extensive public relations campaigns. He further insists that Ecuador will not repeat its history with oil, which after more than 40 years has not alleviated poverty, but rather has impoverished communities in the Northern Amazon.[87] In lieu of debating continued dependency on extractive industries, reforms to strengthen the state's role in regulating multinational miners have taken center stage. Ultimately, left with a choice between "responsible" large-scale mining and "devastating" small-scale mining, the former becomes the obvious option. However, containing an issue of considerable public interest to a decision between "the lesser of two evils"[88] has serious consequences for *campesino* organizations questioning the compatibility of mining activity in their headwaters with the future of their lives and livelihoods.

Seeing themselves as part of the same struggle, highland and coastal farmers view agriculture as another productive activity that contributes to the economic life of their communities and the country, and they therefore prioritize the security of their water supply. They would frame Ecuador's mining debate as a question of whether mining expansion should occur in fragile ecosystems. But despite having expanded their strategies to include legal and scientific studies as a way to lobby the new government administration for change, promises have been broken and their concerns ruled out. Overall, their hopes of making headway under the presumably post-neoliberal government of Rafael Correa have not been realized. Rather, their concerns have been appropriated by the state and industry to promote "responsible" large-scale mining, albeit under somewhat stronger legislation. Returning to the streets to assert their claims, however, has led to insults, repression, and the threat of serious criminal charges, resulting in fewer active participants. As a result, Correa's style of governance has generated a crisis in activist strategies.

On the one hand, Correa has pleaded with communities to refrain from holding demonstrations at a time when his government is still consolidating power. He has threatened, as when he spoke with water board leaders, that if they don't follow his advice "a neoliberal government will come and privatize" resources.[89] On the other hand, as we have shown in this paper, if they use less confrontational strategies of activism, mobilizing studies, and participating in dialogues—while they may get acknowledged—they are still not heard. Ospina Peralta (2009) interprets this dilemma as a crisis in representation. He points out that "the state has closed its doors to organized sectors without offering them any change" and observes that reforms taking place as part of the Citizen's Revolution ironically leave few channels for subaltern groups who continue to be discriminated against when they express their demands. For the most part, all that they are promised, he says, "is that their petitions, duly delivered to secretaries in public offices and stamped with the date and transaction number will be considered in due time" (Ospina Peralta 2009).[90]

As a result, although the left platform on which Correa was elected *did* bring with it social justice–minded people such as Alberto Acosta, who *did* take initial steps toward more fundamental reforms such as the Mining Mandate, Correa's agenda has meant that such reforms have been applied selectively at best. Meanwhile, the government has not wavered in its commitment to corporate interests. So although the state revoked nearly 2,000 mineral concessions under the Mining Mandate, almost halving the area slated for potential mineral development,[91] major projects such as IAMGOLD's remain largely untouched, and mining expansion in the headwaters of the Tenguel River continues mostly undisturbed apart from intermittent suspensions. As a result, *campesino* activists feel that Correa's Twenty-First Century Socialism is rebuilding the nation at the expense of their rights. The rights being struggled for by the *campesinos* discussed in this chapter are not, however, best understood through some of the more normative political ecologies of indigenous and rural movements. In Tenguel and Victoria del Portete, *campesinos* are struggling for rights to market oriented livelihoods, rights to be heard, rights to access and produce technical information, and rights to clean and secure water. The challenge facing them now is how to rethink their strategies and reorganize their bases of support in order to pressure the government to bring about these rights in a context in which an ostensibly progressive government portrays their demands and struggles as conservative, anti-modern, and ultimately opposed to Twenty-First Century Socialism.

Notes

1. LA TV Program, part of a special documentary series about contamination from small-scale mining in the area of Tenguel, produced by Fernando Ehlers, broadcast May 2008. Original quote: "La gente creyente dice que Dios a propósito puso el oro junto al agua como una prueba para el ser humano a ver que escojan, la vida o la muerte. Da la impresión de que caímos en la tentación y está haciéndonos la muerte."
2. For a fascinating account of the history of Tenguel and the United Fruit Company, see Striffler 2002.
3. The name *Lenin Quezada* is a pseudonym. Throughout the text we have used pseudonyms except in the case of public figures.
4. They are not homogenous producers, but vary in number of hectares, technical expertise, access to markets, and access to clean irrigation water. Thus we follow critical approaches to the concept of *community*, which acknowledge that communities are stratified by capitalist relations of production, as well as gender and ethnic/racial difference, and that not all members participate equally in the construction and benefits of the term *community*. See, for instance, Joseph 2002.
5. However, in late 2009, *campesinos* would begin to embrace their indigenous an-

cestry during mobilizations related to the controversial water law reforms proposed by the Correa administration.

6. We understand *campesinos'* use of legal and scientific reason and their appeals for water rights as an engaged "universal," as described by Tsing (2005: 9), who suggests that universals are implicated in "both imperial schemes to control the world and liberatory mobilizations for justice and empowerment." We focus on the latter. See also Hardt and Negri (2000).

7. Original quote: "salir de la larga noche neoliberal."

8. Original quote: "no consiste solamente en reducir el control empresarial sobre el Estado, sino de cualquier gremio . . . los sectores subalternos, tratados por la *revolución ciudadana* igual que la banca, como si fueran estructuralmente similares y como si sus efectos sobre el Estado fueran los mismos."

9. IAMGOLD is in the process of negotiating the sale of its Ecuadorian subsidiary to INV Metals, but intends to assume a 45 percent interest in INV Metals with representation on its board of directors. See http://www.invmetals.com/s/News Releases.asp?ReportID=542565&_Type=News&_Title=INV-Metals-Announces -Amendments-To-Quimsacocha-Acquisition.

10. The *páramos* of Quimacocha provide approximately 150,000 people from the countryside and from the city of Cuenca with water: 130,000 in the city (Interview with Margarita Salamea, former Environmental Manager for the municipal water agency, [16 February 2009]) and roughly 20,000 in the countryside (Personal communication, Rogelia Pauta, [13 October 2009]). However, this number is anticipated to increase. The municipal Water for the Future program, cofinanced by the Inter-American Bank, will expand potable water services from the Quimsacocha watersheds to growing suburban and rural areas of Cuenca (Interview with Carlos Ordoñez, former Director of Potable Water for the municipal water agency, 16 February 2009).

11. As early as 1997, the conflict between miners and farmers was foreseen, when the national mining program, financed with a technical assistance loan from the World Bank, carried out a study of mining in Ponce Enríquez: "In the near future, [the contamination of watersheds] could substantially affect populated areas and other productive activities, particularly shrimp farmers, as a result of the risks of contamination with mercury. The possible conflicts related to environmental impacts caused by mining appear latent. But they could be unleashed in the near future if the current levels of contamination persist." Original Spanish quote: "En un futuro cercano, pueden afectar sustancialmente a centros poblados (contaminación de las fuentes de agua) y a las otras actividades productivas, particularmente las camaroneras, por los riesgos de contaminación con mercurio. Los posible conflictos derivados de los impactos ambientales ocasionados por la minería permancen latentes. Pueden desatarse en un futuro próximo si siguen los actuales niveles de contaminación ambiental" (Carvajal and Rivadeneira 1997).

12. Hilson and Yakovleva (2007) also discuss how stereotyping of small-scale miners as "a menace" in Ghana serves World Bank, state, and industry efforts to promote large-scale mining expansion.

13. For example, Rafael Correa, National Radio Address, 18 October 2008. Also see "La minería en el Ecuador: Una fuente de esperanza," a comic produced by the Secretaria de Pueblos, Movimientos Sociales y Participación Ciudadana.

14. See Acción Ecológica and Friends of the Earth (1999), "Ecuador no sera un país minero," which documents this occurring in the area of Podocarpus National Park following exploration by ECUANOR, a Norwegian company. See also Hentschel, Hruschka, and Priester (2002), "Global Report on Artisanal & Small-Scale Mining," commissioned by the MMSD project.

15. Such a campaign was particularly prominent in Ecuador before President Correa became such a vocal advocate of Canadian multinational miners. The company Corriente Resources spearheaded this campaign at the national level using the slogan "Trato Justo" ("Fair Deal"). See, for instance, "Sustainable Mining Framework: 10 Principles," used by members of the International Council on Mining and Metals (ICMM). Available on the ICMM website: www.icmm.com.

16. In the case of Corriente Resources and Ascendant Copper (now Copper Mesa Mining), serious human rights violations were reported in relationship to their operations in March 2007 by a series of human rights and environmental organizations. See "Informe sobre la situación de las personas y pueblos afectados por las actividades mineras y petroleras en el Ecuador," presented to the Interamerican Human Rights Commission at their 127th Period of Ordinary Sessions on 2 March 2007 by the Center for Economic and Social Rights (Centro de Derechos Economicos y Sociales, CDES), the Ecumenical Commission on Human Rights (Comisión Ecumenica de Derechos Humanso, CEDHU), the Intag Defense and Conservation Organization (Defensa y Conservacion de Intag, DECOIN), and Acción Ecológica. Canada has also been criticized for not properly regulating the activities of its extractive industry companies abroad, leading to human rights violations that go unaddressed (see One World 2007). In 2009, three villagers from Intag, Ecuador, launched a lawsuit against the Toronto Stock Exchange and Copper Mesa Corporation, urging legal reforms in Canada. See related documents here: http://www.ramirezversuscoppermesa.com/index.html.

17. Recording from meeting with President Correa, June 2007. Original quote reads: "a mi no me tiembla la mano para suspender la concesión de IAMGOLD, compañeros, no hay problema."

18. Recording from meeting with President Correa, July 2007. Original quotes read: "convénzanse que tienen un gobierno que esta a su lado," and "no permitiremos jamás que se contamine el agua—el agua es vida."

19. Interview, Manuel Maldonado, 24 May 2009. Original quote reads: "Porque ya sabíamos el montaje que había hecho. Ya teníamos unos dos, tres acercamientos con Alberto Acosta, posteriormente con el gobierno. . . . Siempre era la campaña mediática. Que la constituyente viene . . . y ellos iban a regular."

20. Interview, Rogelio Pauta, 22 March 2009. Original quote reads: "El [Correa] dijo, 'compañeros yo entro en el poder, se van las mineras del país. No, las mineras no entrarán.'"

21. Recording from meeting with President Correa, 4 July 2007. Original quotes read: "Que pasa si se suspende IAMGOLD, y me muestra que si tiene estudio ambiental, que si hay consulta previa . . . y nos ponen tremenda demanda y quiebra el país."

22. Recording from meeting with President Correa, 4 July 2007. Original quote reads: "cuidado por esa desesperación de remediar las cosas ya, rápida . . ."

23. Recording from meeting with President Correa, 4 July 2007. Original quote reads: "perjudican un gobierno que está a su lado."

24. Interview, Carlos Pérez, 17 July 2008. Original quote reads: "no es nuestro interés la defensa loca."

25. Interview, Carlos Pérez, 17 July 2008. Original quote reads: "No somos violentos como muchos de las empresas mineras nos pintan . . . sino, recogemos la propuesta del gobierno de formar parte la comisión, y ahí vis-a-vis, frente a frente con los documentos evidenciar donde estar las violaciones y probar que estuvo mal. La falla no es de la comunidades, la falla es del ejecutivo. Y el ejecutivo tendrá que dar su respuesta al país de porque ellos fallaron."

26. Correa started a smear campaign against the CNDVS even before the second round of protests in July. During his meeting with water board leaders, Correa referred to the National Coordinating Committee as an "extremely infantile" group of radicals and cautioned water board leaders, "Be careful not to be manipulated by people who have nothing better to do, like the [CNDVS]. Those people do great harm through their radicalism." Original Spanish quote: "cuidado no nos dejemos manejar por tipos que no tienen nada que hacer como la Coordinadora Nacional para la Defensa de la Vida. Esa gente hace mucho daño con ese radicalismo, yo le diría, extremamente infantil."

27. Interview, Maria Zhuño, 28 May 2009.

28. Constituent Assembly, "Informe Definitivo de Mayoría sobre Amnistías a Personas Involucradas en Hechos Acaecidos en el Cantón Chillanes, Provincia de Bolívar; en el Paro Nacional Minero y Casos de Criminalización por Defender la Territorialidad, Derechos Colectivos y de los Pueblos," 11 July 2008.

29. Original quote: "vía suscripción de convenios económicos, por parte de funcionarios estatales como alcaldes, presidentes de juntas parroquiales o rectores de universidades, ellos no son comunidad, son autoridades o funcionarios públicos."

30. Original quote reads: "existe un sistema lacustre de páramo muy importante ya que este ecosistema ofrece servicios hidrológicos que garantizan la calidad y cantidad de agua."

For a recent declaration on the importance of the *páramo* ecosystem, see the 2009 Loja Declaration from the Second World Congress on *Páramo*, 21–25 June 2009, Ecuador. Specifically, recommendation number ten of the declaration states: "In the interest of the common good, mining should be excluded from the *páramo* in all of its forms taking into consideration the context, legal framework and sovereignty of each country." Available at http://www.paramo.org/files/Declaración%20de%20Loja%20 sobre%20los%20Paramos%202009%20_Final_.pdf.

31. Original quote reads: "Se observa que cerca de nueve cuerpos importantes de agua podrían ser afectados por eventuales actividades de explotación."

32. Original quote reads: "fue calificada por el funcionario [de ETAPA] como un 'hecho sin precedentes'."

33. Interview, Rogelio Pauta, 22 March 2009. Original quote: "los 3,200 hectáreas fue una farsa, una mentira."

34. Interview, Carlos Pérez, 17 July 2008. Original quote: "Esas experiencias llenas de enormes frustraciones, decepción . . . la palabra de el es la ley . . . eso indiscutablemente crea total desconfianza."

35. Original quote reads: "Hoy marcamos un antes y un después en materia minera: un antes lleno de corrupción, de decisiones absolutamente contrarias a los intereses de

nuestras comunidades. Hemos rescatado de las manos privadas de una organización empresarial el agua que es el derecho de todo su pueblo, de toda su comunidad."

36. Original quote: "No podía el gobierno de la revolución ciudadana, de Rafael Correa, que un bien estratégico de esta naturaleza siguiera en poder de una empresa privada."

37. Interview, IAMGOLD Community Relations Manager, 29 November 2007.

38. We refer to the 3,200 hectares as a "symbolic" conservation of water resources because at the time that this chapter was written, the state had yet to hand over the land titles to ETAPA for conservation.

39. Interview, Margarita Salamea, 9 February 2009. Original quote: "Ellos aseguran al, creo al, el cien por ciento que no van a contaminar pero cuando hemos leído sus documentos si nos ha preocupado. [Ellos dicen] vamos a poner la máxima tecnología. ¿Cuál tecnología? Entonces no nos responden a algunas cosas."

40. Interview, Margarita Salamea, 9 February 2009. Original quote: "la experiencia nuestra con minería artesanal es que son gente sin cultura, sin educación y que lo hace sin ningún conocimiento técnico."

41. Interview, Margarita Salamea, 9 February 2009. Original quote: "más fácil regular a uno que a doscientos es mi punto de vista personal."

42. National Constituent Assembly, Boletin 883, Sala de Prensa José Peralta, Ciudad Alfaro, "La votación fue nominativa por disposición del presidente Alberto Acosta," 18 April 2008.

43. National Constituent Assembly, Boletin 883.

44. National Constituent Assembly, Montecristi, 18 April 2008, Mandato Constituyente No. 6, Articulo 3: "Se declara la extinción sin compensación económica alguna de las concesiones mineras otorgadas al interior de areas naturales protegidas, bosques protectores y zonas de amortiguamiento definidas por la autoridad competente, y aquellas que afectan nacimientos y fuentes de agua."

45. Tenguel is also the most southerly rural parish of the County of Guayaquil. Even though it is separated from the country's most populated city by an intervening county, Guayaquil is its corresponding municipality.

46. Municipalidad de Guayaquil DMA-CA-2008-309, "Oficio No. AG-2007-40572 del 3 de Diciembre 2007 Informe Monitoreo de los Ríos, Canal, Suelo y Aguas de Pozos de la Parroquia de Tenguel," signed by Eng. Jorge Narvaez Ochoa Coordinador de Gestión Ambiental and Eng. Francesca Escala Benites Asesor Técnico de Gestión Ambiental, 4 April 2008.

47. Interview, Lenin Quezada, 20 May 2009. Original quote: "Hay que demostrar usando el método científico."

48. *El Expreso de Guayaquil*, "Discapacidad, la cara oculta de las fumigaciones en Los Ríos" and "Trabajadores contra las multinacionales," 4 January 2009.

49. Interview, Lenin Quezada, 20 May 2009.

50. Municipalidad de Guayaquil DMA-CA-2008-309, "Oficio No. AG-2007-40572 del 3 de Diciembre 2007 Informe Monitoreo de los Ríos, Canal, Suelo y Aguas de Pozos de la Parroquia de Tenguel," signed by Eng. Jorge Narvaez Ochoa Coordinador de Gestión Ambiental and Eng. Francesca Escala Benites Asesor Técnico de Gestión Ambiental, 4 April 2008.

51. Video and testimonies, visit to San Rafael, 20 May 2009.

52. MMSD, "La Pequeña Minería en el Ecuador," Fabián Sandoval, October 2001, citing Ministerio de Energía y Minas del Ecuador (1999), "Monitoreo ambiental de las áreas mineras en el sur del Ecuador 1996–1998, PRODEMINCA," Quito; Original table p17: "Grado de impacto sobre recursos hídricos calificado como 'severo'."

53. PRODEMINCA, "Perspectiva Socioeconómico de la Pequeña Minería y la Minería Artesanal: estudio de caso de Nambija y Ponce Enríquez," by Sociólogo Miguel Carvajal and Eng Agronomist José Rivadeneira, May 1997, p11.

54. Interview, Lenin Quezada, 20 May 2009.

55. Diario Correo, "Protesta ambientalista se cumplió a medias," 3 April 2008.

56. Teresa Velásquez, field notes, 19 November 2008. Original quote: "Queremos ratificar como va esto y demostrarlo al gobierno para que sepa q[ue] realmente esta pasando con estas comunidades, somos mas de diez mil habitantes. No se pueden descuidar la parte de la salud."

57. Interview, Lenin Quezada, 30 January 2009. Original quote: "Somos parte de este sueño, de esta revolución."

58. *Horizonte*, "Comisión de inspección hizo recorrido aguas de Río Tenguel envenenadas por mineros," 15 February 2008

59. Interview, Martha Roldós, 18 March 2009. Original quote: "Cuando ves un rió cayendo cristalino y luego se cae una cosa indescriptible por el olor y color y aparencia y en adelante el rió esta muerto, se quede con una indignación. Ve los campesinos que se han (des)forzado por invertir en hacer producción orgánico de banano y cacao, y luego descubrir que no les sirve para nada porque el gobierno permitio que se envenene el agua. Entonces ese fue una experiencia, y no podía ser lo mismo."

60. Interview, Martha Roldós, 14 February 2009.

61. Interview, Carmen Rodríguez, 6 March 2009. Original quote: "Estaba bien la gente porque tuvimos primera vez en la vida que llego un ministro a Tenguel."

62. Original quote: "Es evidente el abandono."

63. Original quote: "Las vidas que la minería ha tomado no tiene precio y si los mineros quieren trabajar, tienen que respetar el agua, la salud, la agricultura, y la ganadería de la sociedad circundante . . . el Gobierno no es anti-minería, pero jamás permitirá abuso por parte de los mineros."

64. *Horizonte*, "En el río San Rafael vio la magnitud de la contaminación de las aguas," May 2008. Original quote: "para recuperar y remediar buena parte de los danos ambientales ocurridos en los ríos."

65. Memorando No. 082 DINAMI-ALM-2008, signed by Dr. Santiago Correa Toscar, 19 May 2008; includes the concessions Bella Gala, Papercorp, Pinglio 1, Quebrada Fría, and Pato.

Memorando No. 199-DEREPA-AZY-2008, signed by Eng. Gonzalo Quezada the Regional Delegate for Environmental Protection in Azuay Province, 2 July 2008; adds that Barranco Colorado and Paralelas are also among those suspended.

66. Original quote: "se pudo observar una inversión millonaria y la aplicación de tecnología en donde todo se encontraba en perfecto orden y cada cosa en su lugar."

67. Gobierno Nacional de La República del Ecuador, "Correa: Sí a la minería, pero con responsabilidad social, ambiental y económica," 23 April 2008. Original quote: "Resulta paradójico, pero las grandes minerías generan menor impacto ambiental que las pequeñas, no nos dejemos engañar compañeros."

68. Original quote: "Los concesionarios están consciente del daño que se le ha causado a la naturaleza."

69. *Horizonte*, "Se firmó convenio entre el municipio y concesionarios mineros," 15 June 2008.

70. Original quotes: "mineros informales," "no tienen ningún plan ambiental, no están bajo ninguna ley," and "quienes deben poner su parte."

71. Estimated total gold production based upon agitation leach method. See International Minerals Corporation, "NI 43–101 Technical Report on the Preliminary Feasibility Study for the Gaby Gold Project, Ecuador," 26 March 2008.

72. Municipalidad de Guayaquil, Memorando DMA-CA-2008–886, No. 4, September 2008, from Eng. Francesca Escala B. Asesor Técnico de Gestión Ambiental, "Informe de actividades realizadas en el Ministerio del Ambiente (PRAS)."

73. Memorando DMA-CA-2008–886, No. 4, p. 3. Original quote: "se tocó el caso de Pucará donde no están definidas las limitaciones del bosque protector por lo que sería un problema respecto a lo solicitado."

74. Memorando DMA-CA-2008–886, No. 4, p. 3. Original quote: "problemas como: inseguridad, secuestro, falta de personal (un delegado para tres provincias)."

75. Interview, Representative of the Environmental Unit from Ponce Enríquez, 21 May 2009.

This becomes an important theme in 2009. See letters from APDNR to the Minister of Environment, Oficio #139-APDNR, 4 June 2009, and to the Minister of Mines and Petroleum, Oficio #140-APDNR, 29 June 2009, in this regard.

76. Memorando No. 199-DEREPA-AZY-2008, signed by Eng. Gonzalo Quezada the Regional Delegate for Environmental Protection in Azuay Province, 2 July 2008; mentions that Barranco Colorado and Paralelas are among those suspended. Memorando 1555-SPA-DINAPAM, "Solicita levantar suspensión de actividades," signed by the Undersecretary of Environmental Protection Lucy Ruiz M., 3 July 2008.

77. Memorando 1555-SPA-DINAPAM. Original quote: "lo que puede convertirse en nuevos focos de contaminación debido a que en esta actividad se utiliza el mercurio para separar el metal aurífero de las arenas."

78. Memorando No. 204-DINAMI-ALM-2008, "Suspensión de actividades," signed by Dr. Santiago Correa Toscano, Quito, 29 August 2009 (dated 2009, but should read 2008).

79. Universidad de Guayaquil Oficio No. 456-R-2008, letter to Presidente Julio Simbala de la Junta Parroquial de Tenguel, signed by Dr. Carlos Cedeño Navarrete, Guayaquil, 13 October 2008. Original quote: "no existe un convenio en los términos por ustedes indicados."

80. Asamblea Pro-Defensa de Nuestros Rios Gala-Chico-Tenguel-Siete, Oficio No. 095 P-APDNR, addressed to Sr. Abg. Jaime Nebot Saadi, signed by Lenin Quezada, Carmen Rodríguez, and Pascual Valdivieso Presidente del Comité Pro Mejoras del Recinto San Rafael, Tenguel, 20 August 2008. Original quote: "ha levantado dicha suspensión sin tomar en cuenta las peticiones del pueblo de Tenguel y el ofrecimiento del Ministro de Energía y Minas, Galo Chiriboga . . . donde afirmo que el Ministerio a su cargo realizaria un estudio con la Universidad de Guayaquil, con el fin de reducir el existente alto índice de contaminación."

81. Interview, Carmen Rodríguez, 5 March 2009. Original quote: "el Chiquito me

advirtió que no me mete mucho porque aqui callen a la gente. Claro que también los trabajadores también lo decían. Que no te mete, mucho, igual dije no me va a pasar nada. Siempre esto mantenía. No me va a pasar nada."

82. Denuncia, addressed to Señor Agente Fiscal de lo Penal de Guayas, signed by Carmen Rodríguez, 8 April 2008. Original quote: "el único delito que he cometido es defender las aguas y prevenir que se sigan muriendo la gente con cancer por culpa de las concesiones mineras."

83. Teresa Velásquez, field notes, Tenguel, 19 November 2008.

84. Interview, Lenin Quezada, 30 January 2009. Original quote: "A veces la vida te pone un reto y quedarme callado sería bueno. No hacer nada también sería bueno, pero lo mas malo es saber que están haciendo monstruosidades y no intervenir."

85. National Radio Address, President Rafael Correa, 18 October 2008. Original quote: "Azuay puede estar sentado en la reserva del oro más grande del mundo y vivir de esa tremenda riqueza y por capricho de unos cuantos, no podemos sacar esa riqueza. '¡Que contamina las fuentes de agua!' Esas son mentiras. No resiste el menor análisis. Puede haber minería que no contamine fuentes de agua . . . Incluso se llega a mayores absurdos. 'No gran-minería pero sí a pequeña minería!' Sepan Uds. que la mas contaminadora es la pequeña minería, porque es artesanal, desordenada, etc."

86. Corriente Resources News Release, "Corriente and Other Mining Companies Meet with President Correa and Top Officials: Correa Says Responsible Mining Will Go Ahead in Ecuador," 25 April 2008.

87. National Radio Address, President Rafael Correa, 11 October 2008.

88. Interview, Margarita Salamea, 9 February 2009.

89. Recording from meeting with President Correa, 4 July 2007. Original quote reads: "Cuidado por esa desesperación de remediar las cosas ya, rápida . . . perjudican un gobierno que esta a su lado, perdemos la asamblea y viene un gobierno neoliberal que les va a privatizar el agua."

90. Original quote: "el gobierno cierra las puertas del Estado a los sectores organizados y no les ofrece nada a cambio . . . Solamente les promete que sus peticiones, debidamente entregadas en las secretarías de las oficinas públicas, con el sello de la fecha y el número de trámite en la solapa, serán consideradas a su debido tiempo."

91. Correspondence from Alberto Acosta, 2 October 2008.

CHAPTER 6

Territorial Transformations in El Pangui, Ecuador: Understanding How Mining Conflict Affects Territorial Dynamics, Social Mobilization, and Daily Life

XIMENA S. WARNAARS

Introduction

The lush green mountain range of the Cordillera del Cóndor lies in the very southeast of Ecuador. With its valleys and steep cliffs covered by the dense cloud forest air, the Cordillera has become host to mines of various forms and guises. In the 1990s, these mountains were covered in landmines placed by the military during the war with Peru. Today, in these same mountains, transnational companies seek to develop mines in order to extract gold and copper on both sides of the border. The arrival in the early 2000s of large-scale mining projects owned by the Canadian companies Corriente Resources and Kinross-Aurelian has triggered resistance among local populations. Social and armed political conflicts are once again becoming part of everyday life for people living along the Cordillera.[1]

In this chapter I seek to understand the ongoing social transformations in the parish of El Pangui in Zamora Chinchipe province that are, I argue, a result of increased mining conflict and social mobilization. I examine the effects of these mining projects on preexisting territorial dynamics and the influence of these territorial dynamics on the ways in which mining investments are contested. I am particularly interested in those less-visible dimensions of environmental struggle that are embedded in the routines of daily life, as well as in the ways in which the memory and history of territorialization and settlement influence social movement organizing. I suggest that at the heart of territorial dynamics one finds differing understandings of, and meanings apportioned to, nature–society relationships that over time have contributed to a layering of conflicts in the Cordillera del Cóndor.

The editors of this volume call for a deeper engagement with the subsoil because of its immense power in and significance for societal and territorial transformations. In this chapter I reiterate that call by presenting a case study[2] in which the presence of subsoil mineral deposits has set in motion a range of transformations. The case is particularly interesting from the perspective of a political ecology of the subsoil because the minerals in question have not yet crossed the earthly boundary in any material sense, to interact with human practice or the global economy. Symbolically, however, they have long since crossed this boundary and, in the process, have triggered profound societal transformations. Following a brief conceptual discussion, I introduce the region of southeast Ecuador and my methodological approach to studying mining conflicts. On that basis, I then analyze the ways in which conflicts over extraction, territorial change, and everyday life have become mutually constitutive in and around El Pangui, discussing implications for political ecologies of social movement activity around the subsoil.

Literature Review

Studies of struggles over natural resources have drawn attention to a range of issues: the causes of these social conflicts and the socioenvironmental impacts of extractive industry (Geddicks 1993; Ballard and Banks 2003, 19; Bury 2004); the ways in which people seek environmental justice (Tsing 2000; Perreault 2006; Bebbington 2007b); the relationships among extractive industry, environment, livelihoods, and institutional change (Bebbington and Bury 2009); and the bearing of indigeneity and identity politics on extraction (Ali 2003; Sawyer 2004; Kirsch 2006). While the argument of this chapter is located in these traditions, my particular concern is to push their boundaries forward. In particular, I seek to show (1) the ways in which struggles and social movements around mining are themselves artifacts of prior and ongoing processes of territorialization as much as they are shapers of territory, (2) the importance of memory, popular ontologies, and everyday practices in determining how mining and territorial dynamics affect each other, and (3) that territory—its identity, its control, its physiognomy, its meaning—is constituted at the interface of the territorializing projects of mining companies and local populations. In the following three subsections, I explore some of the ideas that underlie this analysis, relating them to other currents of thought within the broad fields of political ecology and social movement studies.

Environmental Struggles and Struggles Over Meaning

Political ecologists understand that conflicts involving the environment are as much about meaning as they are about land and resources (Peet and Watts 2004). Here, values and beliefs can shape people's identities and mobilize actions, such that cultural meanings become constitutive forces. As Donald Moore argues, "struggles over land and environmental resources are simultaneously struggles over cultural meaning" (Moore 1996, 127). While there are many different meanings at the core of environmental struggles, in this work I focus on two main realms. First, struggles involve the various and often-contradictory views of "nature" and natural resource use held by people in El Pangui. These views have had an important role in processes of territorialization, settlement, investment, and nation building and the impact of these processes on the environment. Put in other terms, contrasting ontological assumptions about the world and nature play a significant role in social conflict and environmental change. At the same time, nature itself also has a certain level of agency and exerts influence over humans, society, and territorialization processes (Morse and Stocking 1995; Mitchell 2002; Raffles 2002; Rubenstein 2004; Kosek 2006). Indeed, Ecuador's new Constitution of 2008 gives rights to Nature and deploys the indigenous concept of *Sumak Kawsay*, which appeals for a development model that gives specific attention to the role of Nature.

The second area of meanings relates to how people experience, remember, and understand conflict. In the canton El Pangui, land has long been disputed and highly politicized. Prior to the arrival of the mining company, the town and various communities in the canton had already witnessed many struggles and conflicts over land ownership, rights, demarcation, and natural resource use. These struggles are a product of a long history of the coming and going of different actors, as well as of the boom and bust cycles of natural resource-based frontier capitalism. These disputes over land and resources affect how social actors relate to each other and to their environment, becoming part of mundane activities and daily life in ways that are hidden from view. I suggest that memories of previous conflicts can be significant for the ways in which current mining conflicts are experienced and understood, and that they can motivate human actions and social mobilization.

Territorialization and Cosmographies

The concept of territorialization used here rests upon definitions of human territoriality that I borrow from Paul Little's (2001) political ecology of Amazonian territorial disputes. Little defines human territoriality as "the collective effort of a social group to identify with, occupy, use, and establish control over the specific parcel of their biophysical environment that serves as their homeland or territory" (Little 2001, 4). He builds his definition on Robert Sack's notion of human territoriality as "the attempt by an individual or group to affect, influence, or control people, phenomena, and relationships, by delimiting and asserting control over a geographic area" (Sack 1986, 19). In these definitions, territories are considered as both processes and products.

However, as this case study shows, territories are not fixed and finished products of human endeavor. Rather, territories are continuous processes in which both humans' and nature's agencies play a role. They are constantly being produced, contested, negotiated, and demarcated. While Ecuador's war with Peru brought an end to decades of boundary disputes between the two nations, other frictions over the enclosure of a given territory continue among inhabitants of El Pangui. These disputes are currently taking violent forms as the mining companies try to assert control over a certain biophysical space.

Brogden and Greenberg (2003) describe territorialization as being the "historical product of contestation and negotiation for access and control over natural resources among competing groups, interest and classes" (Brogden and Greenberg 2003, 291). Conflicts, they argue, develop not only on the ground, but also in political arenas, where people with different interests seek to influence or gain control over agencies, laws, or regulations that govern natural resources. This theme is also present in the work of Little, who describes contestation over territory as being due to a clash of different "cosmographies," which he defines as "collective, historically contingent identities, ideologies, and environmental knowledge systems developed by a social group to establish and maintain a human territory" (Little 2001, 5). In these "clashes," different interest groups exert power and push for the hegemony of their cosmography on the basis of which they then make territorial claims. The result is a layering of conflicts and territorial disputes as new actors, each with their distinct cosmographies, arrive in a region and seek to forge a new territory in areas with inhabitants who have already established territories.

I maintain that implicit within the "cosmographies" of different social actors are different understandings of and engagements with nature that influence the processes of human territorialization. Little suggests that Amazonia has been impacted by a history of colonization, development, and

environmental cosmographies leading to different patterns of human territorialization, shaping the settings within which contemporary social mobilizations take form.

Social Movements, Networks, and Identity

Social movements have the ability to challenge dominant powers by accentu-
ating other sets of values in pursuit of alternative forms or models of development (Bebbington 2007b). Bebbington et al. (2008b) argue that social mobilization in the mining context can be understood as "a response to the threats
that particular forms of economic development present, or are perceived as
presenting, to the security and integrity of livelihoods and to the ability of a
population in a given territory to control what it views as its own resources"
(6). The case study presented in this chapter allows us to witness the process
through which a social movement manages alliances and networks and strategically constructs discourses and identities, all set on the stage of a particular
set of territorial dynamics.

Mining-related social movements in Ecuador appeal strategically to existing collective identities while also constructing new ones through the articulation of discourses that range from sovereignty, land rights, indigeneity,
environment, democracy, and participation to the rights to employment and
development. Movement strength and cohesion seems to derive from a strong
identity in "which members are aware of sharing a number of cultural and
sociopolitical commitments and attributes" (Bebbington, Abramovay, and
Chiriboga 2008, 14). That said, any given collective identity ought not be
understood as a stable, unified form of solidarity since this would overstate
the extent to which values and individual identities are shared (Jordan 2005).
Indeed, the experience in El Pangui shows how identity, whether individual
or collective, is constantly negotiated, activated, or constructed through the
production of meaning (Foweraker 1995).

Identity construction plays a delicate role in the configuration and reconfiguration of alliances and networks. In the canton El Pangui, as a result of
territorialization and settlement processes, key strategic social and political
relationships have been established in relation to land—its acquisition, colonization, titling, and varied uses. This is reflected, for instance, in the important
role of the Salesian Missionaries in the management of indigenous land in
the absence of the state, civil society mobilization (mainly of *colonos*) through
cooperatives and ecological initiatives to gain land,[3] ecological organizations
interested in teaming up with indigenous communities to establish conser-

vation parks, and illicit land trafficking. Since the arrival of mining projects, social mobilization has strengthened some of these alliances, put other ones to the test, and built new networks and relationships. Some *colonos* seek alliances with indigenous communities, and some indigenous leaders seek alliances with artisanal and small-scale miners to fight a "common enemy," even though prior to the mining conflict these alliances might not have been so straightforward. In yet other cases, previous alliances or simple everyday relationships among indigenous communities — or *colono* and indigenous families — break down when the rising price of land drives individuals to sell lands to the mining companies and so upset the dynamics of family or communal property. Alliances and networks that have been forged through the historical processes of territorialization and settlement therefore change as mining induces new axes of conflict and new territorial dynamics. The larger point here is that while social movements may have internal contradictions or "blurred zones" (Rubin 1998) that affect movement organizing, movement dynamics are also an artifact of the extent to which existing and prior territorialization processes themselves affect alliances, resources, and local politics.

Mining and Social Conflict in Southeastern Ecuador

Located in the provinces of Morona Santiago (cantons Limon Indanza, San Juan Bosco, and Gualaquiza) and Zamora Chinchipe (cantons El Pangui, Yantzaza, Centinella del Cóndor, and Nangartiza) along the border with Peru, the Cordillera del Cóndor is part of the Tropical Andes Hotspot that runs from Colombia to Chile, one of the richest biodiversity zones on Earth (Mittermeir et al. 2004). Running along the border of Ecuador and Peru, it is known as the Conservation Corridor of Abiseo-Cóndor-Kutuku and covers 13 million hectares. The area, however, is also rich in minerals (Figure 6.1). Ecuador's southeastern "copper belt" extends over a 20 × 80 kilometer area and is considered by the mining industry as one of the only undeveloped copper districts available in the world today.[4] In Zamora Chinchipe, south of this copper belt, is a "buried system of gold."[5] In the cantons of Yantzaza and Zamora, there is small-scale alluvial and tunnel mining of gold deposits that are most likely connected to the underground gold system of the Cordillera del Cóndor. The canton of El Pangui is located within and adjacent to mining concessions held by the Canadian companies Corriente Resources and Kinross Gold.

Corriente has four known copper and copper-gold deposits targeted by two projects, the Mirador Project in the parish of El Pangui and the Panantza-

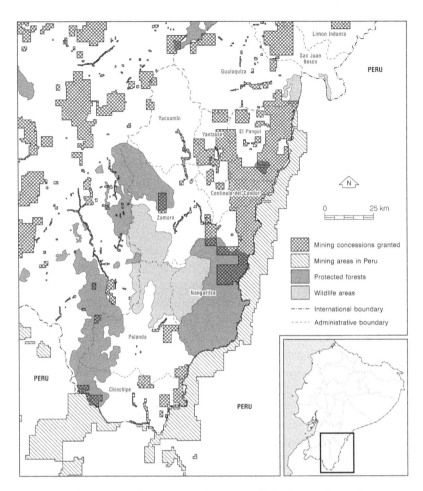

Figure 6.1. Mining concessions, protected forests, and wildlife areas in southeast Ecuador. Courtesy of Acción Ecológica

San Carlos Project in the adjacent province of Morona Santiago. The Mirador project has a measured and indicated amount of 11 billion tons of copper, and the Panantza–San Carlos project has an inferred 6.7 billion tons of copper. Kinross's gold and silver project—previously known as Fruta del Norte and now called the Cóndor Project—consists of 38 mining concessions totalling approximately 95,000 hectares across four parishes, including El Pangui. The Cóndor Project consists of a total measured and indicated amount of 13.7 million ounces of gold and 22.4 million ounces of silver.[6] All projects are in the exploration stage, and the companies have the permits that Ecuador's new Mining Law requires for them to move forward.[7] Kinross Gold has experience in exploration and production in other countries and is advancing with their project in Ecuador. Corriente, on the other hand, is mainly an exploration company and, after looking for a buyer since 2008 for all their Ecuador projects, eventually sold to a Chinese state-owned mining conglomerate in May 2010. All projects began with exploration work around the year 2000, although it was not until the end of 2006 that mining conflicts became visible and violent.

People in the Amazon in Ecuador, as in other countries in Latin America, have experienced many conflicts over land and resources. However, the current mining struggle is new to the Ecuadorian Amazon; indeed, the scale, intensity, and speed with which it is growing is striking. For an area that had previously not had any large-scale mining conflicts prior to 2005, the mining conflict in El Pangui—as well as other towns along Ecuador's southeastern border—involved increased protests, armed confrontations, burning of campsites, physical abuse, and progressive militarization towards the close of 2006. The first set of grievances and actions took place in the province of Morona Santiago over a much-questioned hydroelectric energy project that had direct links with the Corriente mining projects. The actions, meetings, and mobilizations in Morona had a significant impact on the development of the mining conflict in El Pangui (and in southern Ecuador, in general). They inspired people to build shared networks and resources, having cultivated a common sense of perceived threat.[8] Unlike the important indigenous mobilizations of prior periods (Bebbington et al. 1992; Perreault 2002; Andolina 2003; Van-Cott 2005; Yashar 2005)—including those over oil (Sawyer 2004)—ecologists, small-scale miners, indigenous people, farmers, cattle growers, men and women of all ages, the church, and some universities all seemed to be speaking with the same "voice" in these struggles over mining.

In El Pangui, the conflict became violent and militarized in the first few days of December 2006. Following three days of meetings and marches, open confrontation occurred, pitching a large group of people from El Pangui and Gualaquiza against company personnel and paramilitaries. The most violent actions, which involved human rights abuses, kidnapping, paramilitary intervention, and physical abuse, took place in Tundayme near the campsite of the Mirador project and a few kilometers from a military post.[9] Following negotiations, the Ministry of Mines and Petroleum (Ministerio de Minas y Petróleo, MMP) ostensibly suspended all of Corriente's mining activities in both provinces, though the suspension was never fully implemented.

Subsequent to this suspension, there have been other violent confrontations, but none were as severe as those of the first few days of December 2006. Throughout these confrontations, a range of discourses are being used to frame arguments and enroll supporters. Patriotic discourses once fabricated and used during the war are mobilized to tap into a memory and sentiment of sovereignty over "our" natural resources. Ecological discourses are cast by various groups (e.g., indigenous people, small-scale miners, farmers, cattle raisers, or loggers) to resist large-scale mining on environmental grounds. These discourses also sustain an argument about "the people's" right to choose the model of development they want. Constructions of collective identity are fostered to further strengthen group formation and mobilization. Meanwhile, those who mobilize in favor of large-scale mining also build discourses that similarly argue that the people have the right to choose a model of development—arguing that people would choose large-scale mining if they were properly informed about its modern technologies and the benefits it could bring, rather than being fed disinformation by their leaders.

For its part, the government of Rafael Correa vociferously promotes Corriente and Kinross, heralding them as the most important large-scale mining projects in Ecuador and ones that will establish the modern socially and environmentally responsible mining industry that the country needs in order to bring about economic development to fill gaps in an economy dependent on depleting oil reserves. On 15 March 2008, Correa stated in his weekly radio program that "at this moment the largest copper reserves in the world are in Chile. The initial studies tell us that we have larger reserves than Chile. We could become the principal exporters of copper in the world. . . . [R]esponsible mining in the country could become the future of our country and open the doors to come out of underdevelopment. . . . We cannot sit like beggars on a mountain of gold."[10]

Territorial Dynamics of El Pangui Settlement

People of the Ecuadorian Amazon have experienced many processes of settlement and territorialization: *mestizos* and highland *campesinos* have sought its pastures and "empty" lands, oil companies and government have sought its hydrocarbon wealth, and the military has attempted to establish "live frontiers" as a strategy in its border wars and disputes with Peru. The establishment of Salesian, Fransiscan, Jesuit, and later Evangelical missions also became an important part of "taming" the Amazon and of making the area inhabitable (Báez, Ospina, and Ramón 2004).

Settlement took place more systematically in the second half of the twentieth century through government colonization programs and the Agrarian Reform of 1964, which paved the way for mestizos and highland people to inhabit the Amazon. It was not uncommon for indigenous peoples to be cheated into selling their lands, signing over communal deeds under the effects of alcohol. The loss of land has meant drastic changes in the lifestyle of the Shuar, the primary indigenous group of the region. As a collateral effect of promoting "settlement" of the Amazon, these government programs and agrarian reforms also created conditions for land speculation and accumulation. Land acquisition came to be seen as a business in itself, and land trafficking became increasingly significant (Báez, Ospina, and Ramón 2004).

In the 1980s, in addition to the search for available agricultural land, in Zamora Chinchipe a gold rush occurred in the area of Nambija, south of El Pangui. Indeed, many of the *colonos* currently living in El Pangui are former small-scale mine workers who moved there following a devastating accident in Nambija in which more than 300 miners perished under a landslide.[11] On arriving in El Pangui, these farmers-turned-miners returned to farming. Today, these *colonos* with prior (or in some cases, ongoing) ties to ASM are one of the strongest groups resisting large-scale mining companies in the province either because of their knowledge of the harmful effects of mining, their painful memories of mining, or their desire to protect their ASM interests. Still others have become ardent proponents of an ecological discourse calling for an alternative form of development. As one informant said, when asked why he rejected mining: "We are no longer miners, we are ecologists."[12]

Economy and Natural Resource Use

The Cordillera del Cóndor has vast areas that have been transformed by the chaotic and unorganized expansion of animal husbandry and subsistence farming. Most land, however, is dedicated to subsistence farming and grain production for cattle. Meanwhile, agricultural products that could be transformed or processed in Zamora Chinchipe, thus promoting an internal market, are imported from the neighboring provinces of Loja and Azuay.[13] According to the Integrated System of Social Indicators of the Ministry of Social Development Coordination, the Amazonian provinces overall have the lowest total gross agricultural production per hectare cultivated in the country.[14]

Around El Pangui, large areas are deforested in order to make way for pasture lands, and the thin layer of rich soil nutrients that once covered the jungle floors is being depleted as a consequence of clearing more and more land. Some anti-mining actors are aware of the environmentally devastating effects of their animal husbandry and happily express that they are becoming more ecologically minded—strategically incorporating a new identity—since they do leave some trees when they clear grasslands. Ironically, it is in part thanks to the entrance of mining projects that these actors have revalorized their agricultural activities and begun to reflect (albeit minimally) on the physical impacts that their activities have on the environment. Nevertheless their ideal vision for the future is shot through with discourses of development and progress that imagine an ever-expanding agricultural frontier coupled with industrialization. While taking a walk on the lands of a young *colono*, he explained to me: "I am saving to build a proper pig pen and have each pig lined up in individual corrals over there [pointing]. I already have the design! Then I want to get one of those automated milking systems for my cows, so I can produce more, and [chuckling] so I don't have to wake up so early to milk them."[15]

Shuar use of land and resources is just as complex. For instance, in the critique of the idea of the "ecological noble savage," Redford (1991) argues that as indigenous people become more acculturated and their traditional lands more populated by mestizos, they also begin to exploit the Amazonian forests in much the same way as do their mestizo neighbors. The process of acculturation is not only a result of an imposed education system controlled by missionaries, but also a combination of forced sedentary lifestyles in which groups of families have been reorganized, grouped into centers, and exposed to and adopted monetary and market-based economies (Descola 1985; Taylor 1985). This is evident in land use in El Pangui, as well as in neighboring cantons. Previously, indigenous communities used land for horticultural activities but have slowly substituted these activities to clear land, plant pastures, and acquire cattle. However, in spite of these trends, the Shuar tend to reforest their lands, cultivate former garden crops such as coffee and cacao as cash crops, and thus maintain more biologically diverse landscapes than do their mestizo neighbors (Rudel, Bates, and Machinguiashi 2002).

While acculturation and the adoption of new practices mean that Shuar and *colono* production systems do not appear substantially different, land use clashes continue as a result of different modes of understanding nature. For instance, *colonos* value water sources in productive (and reproductive) terms, a value reflected in the price of land, while Shuar see water sources, such as the waterfalls where the Spirit of Arutam dwells, as spiritually important for the survival of the Shuar culture. In addition, Shuar cosmology considers the environment as multidimensional and part of a pluriverse, where humans and nature are intrinsically connected. On more than one occasion, Shuar spiritual leaders have expressed concern that mining will disturb the delicate balance of local ecosystems and water cycles and that this will have repercussions in the continued existence of their people: "Arutam is angry, the environment cannot continue to be destroyed like this, we need to care for it . . . he [Arutam] is going to come and teach us a lesson, why else do you think this [meaning the mining conflict] is happening?"[16]

War, Peace Parks, and a Mountain of Gold

In addition to the confrontations and struggles that occur among social groups and over the physical and cultural boundaries that define them, the region has experienced violent national border disputes with its southern neighbor Peru, with wars fought in 1941, 1981, and 1995. The 1941 war was temporarily resolved by the Protocol of Peace, Friendship, and Boundaries signed in Río de Janeiro in 1945. However, hostilities resumed that eventually lead the Ecuadorian government to demand the annulment of the Río protocol. Although these wars can be understood as a consequence of each nation's interest in expanding their sovereign territories and controlling space, locally it was believed that the wars had a great deal to do with the regional presence of minerals, such as gold, copper, and even uranium. The ex-president of Peru, Fernando Belaúnde, once stated in 1995: "It is not true that the disputed area contains oil. But there is a mountain of Gold."[17]

The most recent, and apparently final, Peace Accord between Peru and Ecuador was signed in Brasília in 1998 and sought to promote peace through development of the border region, transport integration between the two countries, and promote free trade across the frontier. The Accord makes specific mention of the promotion of mining,[18] as well as the creation of a transboundary protected area on both sides of the border. However, the creation of such "Parks for Peace" has not halted mining interests from advancing within the conservation areas. On the contrary, in Ecuador (notwithstanding Nature's new constitutional rights), the president has the power to declare a mining project in the public interest even if it is located within a conservation park or reserve, or on indigenous lands. A very similar situation occurs on the Peruvian side of the border (Figure 6.1.), where mining concessions have also increased and the government uses faculties similar to Correa's in order to allow international mining projects to operate close to the frontier, on the grounds that they are in the national interest. Indeed, the terms of the Peace Accord would appear to have become functional for the mining industry, as government institutions responsible for implementing the Accord prioritize mining activities along the border.

Postwar Pangui

The local population in El Pangui is quite aware that their settlement, serving as a "live border," was part of a military strategy to protect national boundaries against the constant threat of Peruvian invasion. Furthermore, many Shuar participated vigorously in the war, in part to demonstrate their commitment to Ecuador and so counteract national discourses that considered indigenous people's claim to land as a threat to national sovereignty. Having actively protected their sovereign lands, many people, both Shuar and *colono*, now feel betrayed by the national government when the same lands are being "sold off to a new foreign invader." The promotion of mining by the national governments, in both countries, instills resentment among the population that fought in the war or offered to go and live in border towns to be part of the "live border" military strategy.

Memories of the war are still alive among the local population, particularly in women who remember feeding and supporting the troops. During interviews, this memory was repeatedly called upon by women as they expressed their frustrations with the mining conflict, since the same troopers they fed during the war are today security guards for the mining company and, in their words, point their guns in the "wrong" direction. Although the company claims to need the security forces to protect them from vandals and violent protestors, for those who lived through the war with Peru, such as the El Pangui movement leader Rodrigo Aucay, the use of armed security guards is a clear sign that they are in the midst of another armed conflict.

Disputing Territory, Meaning, and Movements

The core questions addressed in this chapter are *How has conflict over mining transformed territorial dynamics?* and *How do these territorial dynamics then influence social mobilization* (or, in the language of this book, *subterranean struggles*)? My fieldwork revealed changes in territorial dynamics in five main domains. These changes are analyzed in the following sections, reflecting the themes noted earlier in the opening conceptual discussion of this chapter.

1. Environmental Struggles and Struggles Over Meanings

First, conflicts involving the environment are about both land *and* meaning (Peet and Watts 2004); that is, symbolic struggles affect material transformations. In El Pangui, mining conflict has brought about changes in the meanings that are ascribed to conflict, as well as physical changes in the Cordillera. The meanings associated with land disputes during settlement processes, with the wars with Peru, and with contemporary mining in the same geographical area are quite different. Key words (e.g., *sovereignty*) in one conflict continue to resonate in subsequent conflicts, though with different significance. While the war left its marks on the physical geography of the region, with trenches and land mines, mining will leave its own marks. And while the Cordillera evokes memories of violence and international armed conflict, today it is just as likely to conjure up images of the physical force associated with mining conflicts.

During one trip on the way to the mining camp, four women that accompanied me sat in the back of the truck and talked about the confrontation with the paramilitaries during the mining conflict in 2006. They also pointed to the mountain range in the distance where the war was fought, and they made jokes about the Peruvians and how silly they were: "They just sat there like hens and our men shot them from the trees." They laughed and joked that if their husbands do not behave they will place them in the trenches that are still here from the war. I didn't pry into their stories, as it seemed their jokes were probably hiding deeper scars and pain. At times I could not follow the conversation as they passed back and forth from memories of the war to the mining conflict, from a far past to a recent one, all conjured by the same mountains, trees, roads, and rivers. When we arrived at the bridge over the Zamora River, we got out and walked, retracing the steps of the confrontation in December 2006. They pointed to the place where they stood, scared, watching the paramilitaries approach them. We stopped where they got down on their knees to pray for the violence to stop. We paused at the place where a group of protestors were beaten and kidnapped. My beautiful view of the lush green Ecuadorian Amazon turned eerie.[19]

Processes of resignification also occur at a much more local scale, as in land disputes between neighbors. In one case, I witnessed a longstanding disagreement over boundaries, as I would regularly accompany one family to their lands to give water to their cows, and each time their neighbors had physically moved the boundary fences, causing a great deal of annoyance and frustration. The family I accompanied explained that the renewed boundary disagreement arose because of the two parties' different stances on mining. This disagreement could no longer be resolved in neighborly conversation but was exacerbated into legal actions to fix the land limits. In addition to situations like these, the way the company has acquired land, the rise in land trafficking, and the revival of land disputes and confrontations between landowners, such as the one narrated, all point to old conflicts acquiring new meanings.

One day I was invited to attend the wedding of a young Shuar couple who were being wed by a mestizo priest in the Salesian Mission of Bomboiza,[20] located about 10 km north of El Pangui. Directly after the ceremony, as we walked out of the church, with its daunting wooden architecture, the priest and an anti-mining leader murmured about a forced eviction that occurred the night before; a Shuar home located adjacent to a Shuar neighbourhood known to be pro-mining had been burned down to the ground. They walked slowly, distancing themselves from the crowd and speaking in a low voice. I was intrigued by the story but followed the crowd and left in a caravan of trucks to the wedding dinner. We passed by the still smoky wooden rubble and I received no more explanation than that the evicted family had invaded the lands of the mission and were relatives of an important pro-mining Shuar leader. A few days later I visited Shuar friends in Gualaquiza, where I would regularly eat their delicious *ayampacos*. I asked if they knew about the burned home and was told that the lands had been ceded to the Shuar family by the priest previously in charge of the mission, which legitimized their presence and use of the lands. He explained that the new priest didn't recognize this apparent "gift" because he considered the lands Mission property. What had appeared to be a land issue only between neighbors, more notably between a Shuar family and the mission, was reinterpreted in terms of mining stances, with more people, unrelated to the dispute but active in the mining issue, feeling compelled to take part. Territorial conflicts and land disputes like these may not be new in El Pangui, but the ways in which they are interpreted, and the sociopolitical resonance of these different interpretations, most certainly are new and have been permanently inflected by the rise of mining in the region.

2. Routinization of Territorial Conflict

This brings me to my second point. In El Pangui, territorial conflict has, to a certain degree, become a routinized part of daily life. Daily activities, such as buying groceries at the neighbor's food store, using the internet services from the man across the road, choosing which taxi to take, or which hotel to stay in, all depend on whether "they are with us or not." Of course, allegiances change, and a taxi not taken one month may well be taken the next. What is more continuous, however, is that the calculations underlying such choices are always informed by where people stand vis-à-vis the mining question. Reflecting this routinization, conflict has become embedded in cultural practices and government institutions. In particular, since the violent confrontation in the first few days of December 2006, social relationships, as well as local politics, are assessed in terms of one's stance on mining.

The mining issue is present in town activities such as Carnival or the street march celebration of the "cantonization" of El Pangui. Every February, on-lookers at the march tell their stories of the open confrontation between "us" and "them" that had happened in previous years, as they wait to see if anything will happen *this* year. At the elementary school, name-calling, class debates, and small brawls have occurred between children of parents with different views on mining. One of my most prized informants and a fieldwork assistant was an 8-year-old boy who was son to a prominent anti-mining leader. I met him almost every day after school, and we hung out in his family's store while I waited for the adults to free up time for an interview. One day he was upset and told me he had a fight at school. With his head down but gaining courage to talk, he said: "They called me an anti-miner and that my father was brainwashed by the NGOs! But I answered them! I told them off and made them quiet! I said they were traitors, selling our patrimony [*vende-patria*] and wanted to live in contamination!"[21]

Such exchanges of "insults" reminded me of the competing discourses of candidates in local elections. All the candidates for the local elections of 2009 necessarily had mining on their manifestos. Candidates' positions on mining were heard for weeks from loudspeakers and bus radios. While the promotional song of the Pachakutik indigenous political party waxed lyrical about "defending life and the environment . . . large-scale mining has no place here," the promotional song of the opposing Movimiento al Socialismo (MAS, Movement for Socialism) party chanted: "More work! More construction! More mining!"[22]

3. Territorialization and Cosmographies

I aimed to examine how mining projects might be affecting preexisting territorial dynamics, in a context in which the new actor (the company) arrives to an area that already has a tense and complex history in relation to land, natural resources, and conflict. My third point is I found that land ownership, distribution, and resource allocation have been changing drastically since the mining projects began, in ways and at scales not seen before. Almost the entire canton has been divided into mining lots held in concession, mostly by Corriente Resources. The company has been buying progressively more land from individuals and families that are within or on the border of their concessions. This has impacted the geography of land ownership and territorial control, leading the company to become the sole owner of almost half the district of Tundayme.[23] If we consider the historical processes of territorialization in El

Pangui as having been characterized by the struggles for (or the denial of) access to resources, these changes in land ownership also affect people's understandings of rights, property, land, and resource use. Prior to the arrival of the company, *colonos* had established control, and later ownership, of lands that had previously belonged to the Shuar, pushing them farther into the jungle. The *colonos* justified this change on the grounds that, as citizens, they had the right to access and purchase lands that they considered empty. Once the company arrived and started to acquire land, these same *colonos* have lost the same lands that they had fought to make theirs, either because they sold them to the company or they were expropriated. Resentful of this process, *colonos* claim that the foreign company should not have rights to lands or access to resources that are Ecuadorian. This is laden with an extra layer of resentment toward the national government that promotes the mining projects, since both *colono* and Shuar fought to protect these same lands from Peruvian invasion during the war and are now told to make way for a company that many consider "new invaders." In a further ironic twist, having once rejected historical Shuar claims to land, a group of *colonos* have now sought out an alliance with the Shuar from Machinantza Alto, which is located within the area of the mine's concession. As part of their effort to halt mining activities to prevent the company from further purchasing lands, these *colonos* have encouraged the Shuar to claim title to their ancestral lands on the basis of the very same indigenous rights arguments that the *colonos* had previously dismissed.

Earlier I described environmental struggles as resulting from the superimposition of contrasting "cosmographies," expressed in El Pangui through the idiom of "development models." Existing differences in cosmographies and the social tensions that derive from dissimilar ideas about how land *should* be used seem to have been played down or minimized since the mining conflict began. Instead, it appears to have become more significant to emphasize agricultural activities *in general*, regardless of whether there are differences over how to use land or which form of production is more "sustainable" or "ecological." The concern is to build a more embracing anti-mining argument that says people in El Pangui, both Shuar and *colono*, choose agriculture above mining and that these two activities cannot coexist. In this case, existing tensions between people are strategically minimized, even if they may continue to exist as latent tensions or prejudices. This suggests that since the mining conflict began, differences have been more strategically negotiated in pursuit of a convergence among the differing cosmographies that exist among the region's social groups. This convergence is expressed through local political agendas which espouse an alternative development model that is ecological, is sustainable, respects nature, is in line with *Sumak Kawsay*, includes indigenous peoples, fosters long-term employment generation, and, as such, is opposed to mining.

4. Social Movement, Identity, and Networks

Fourth, social movements around mining activities do not map neatly onto prior identity or interest-based movements, such as the indigenous movement, or organizations of artisanal miners. As we have seen, the mining projects affect a wide array of people, and consequently any social mobilization (in rejection as well as in favor of mining) includes this array of "identities." This is reflected in the fact that a variety of preexisting and new organizations have become involved in mobilizing around mining issues. These include, for instance, ASM associations, local government, environmental nongovernmental organizations (NGOs), indigenous organizations, and the Catholic Church.

5. Changing Networks, Coalitions, and Identities

Lastly, the conflict has brought about the emergence of new networks and coalitions and the rupture of others. In earlier sections, I gave a glimpse of the relationships that have emerged and developed over time among different actors in El Pangui in relation to their shared or conflicting interests in land, settlement, and territorialization. Since the arrival of the mining companies, new and quite distinct coalitions have been formed. In some cases, this has happened among such unlikely allies as small-scale miners and environmentalists, who otherwise have contradicting land use interests; or between *colonos* and Shuar, who have shared prior tensions in relation to land ownership. At the same time, other coalitions have broken down, such as those between small and large-scale miners. Previously, these groups were on the same front in support of mining. Over time, however, they became increasingly divided as the national government began to give ever more preference to large-scale projects.[24] New divisions have also emerged *within* groups, organizations, communities, and families. One father shared in an interview that he did not know what to do anymore with his son, because since he started working for the company they have fights and his family is divided: "I ask him: what are you doing? Is there a future there? They just use you. The youth don't want to work the land, they want it easy, they don't want to wake up early anymore to help with the cows or work the land. Who am I going to give my land to [*heredar*] when I die? He is just going to sell it! One day, when the company doesn't need him anymore, he will understand and then he will have nothing. At least we have land, it is ours, we work it, we eat from it, and we are independent."[25]

Another example is that prior alliances of environmentalist and indigenous organizations ruptured when indigenous leaders considered some environmentalists too "company friendly." Meanwhile, within the anti-mining movement, a relatively small and radical group broke ties with the remaining organizations on the grounds that their version of militancy was the only legitimate avenue for action.[26] Furthermore, the arrival of the company has increased interest in acquiring land and may have (inadvertently) encouraged illicit land trafficking, an activity that itself has induced the emergence of new coalitions. While specific coalitions emerge or unravel, the more general point in El Pangui is that, in an area where land and territory have long been objects of dispute and layers of conflict have built up over time, the creation and demise of coalitions can be a volatile process.

These shifts in coalitions go hand in hand with shifts in identities and the emergence of new discourses on environment and development. The effects of identity construction in this sense are multiple, particularly when collective identity is coupled with local politics around mining. The prefect of the province Zamora Chinchipe, who is a person of Saraguro indigenous identity and a key figure in the anti-mining movement, incorporated a small-scale mining identity and discourse into his electoral platform in 2009, strategically symbolizing the new alliance between indigenous groups and small-scale miners. Meanwhile, many of the *colonos* who had once been miners or continue to have ties with small-scale mining have incorporated an environmentalist discourse in order to legitimize their "green politics" and so to establish coalitions with environmental organizations. Indeed, this was the electoral strategy of another prominent anti-mining leader in El Pangui, himself a former small-scale miner. In a sense, identity construction can facilitate the emergence of new coalitions, justify breaking old alliances, foster the adoption of new discourses, and serve to legitimize new positions. Identity is thus shaped by interaction in various social locations such that individual identities and collective ones are mutually constitutive (Alavrez, Dagnino, and Escobar 1998). Furthermore, the political positions and potential alliances linked to identity claims are framed by the mining conflict in ways that are not uniform. The identity of *being Shuar*, for instance, is mobilized and given meaning in ways that legitimize quite different positions in the struggle over mining. In some instances, *being Shuar* is used as an argument for defending ancestral land rights and so rejecting mining; in other cases, *being Shuar* is tied to the principle of having the right to choose one's own model of development and so having the right to support the option for mining.

Conclusion

As my fieldwork came to an end, I took a look back from the bus and saw the same scene that had met me on my first arrival in El Pangui: people outside the municipal building smoking their cigarettes, the vendor with his wheelbarrow full of fresh fish, and ladies sitting in front of the town's only beauty salon watching passersby. In the distance stood the green Cordillera topped with hovering clouds and, beyond it, Peru. At first glance, the scene revealed neither the conflict that is part of everyday life nor the mining project that is being developed amidst the Cordillera. However, significant changes and transformations are certainly taking place in El Pangui.

Throughout this chapter, I have attempted to show how the arrival of mining projects is affecting territorial dynamics in El Pangui. Conflict over mining is affecting everyday life and is given new meanings that set it aside from previous land disputes and territorial struggles. The social mobilization in response to mining has built upon these same dynamics, though it too is undergoing transformation as mining conflict influences coalitions, identity, and movement organization. Because of these transformations, it is important to get inside social movements to better understand the whole range of motivations, interests, and meanings at play. In addition, people's own logic regarding the relationship between environment and humans may give further insight as to the reasons why and the ways in which differently located people respond to mining conflicts as they do.

I have also aimed to demonstrate that mining conflicts are far from straightforward. They are not simply about two opposed groups fighting over whether mining activities should go ahead. Territories and the environment, like human relationships and social movements, have complex histories. Indeed, these complexities are as present in the mining question as they are in any other aspect of social life in El Pangui. Understanding mining conflicts, like digging for minerals, therefore requires sorting carefully through the many layers and levels in which different parts of the ore are dispersed. I have tried to suggest elements of a framework that might help in such a task.

The chapter has argued that conflict over the environment is, in fact, *constitutive of* territory. The ways in which people view nature, resources, and the physical environment influence settlement patterns and processes as much as do development visions and models. However, the environment also plays a role. The physical geography of the Cordillera del Cóndor, with its mineral deposits, its biodiversity, its areas of particular ecological sensitivity, and its environmental conditions apt for agriculture, feeds back into various forms of territorial dynamics and the axes of social conflict that constitute part of these dynamics.

If the past is any indication, the current conflict in El Pangui is likely to affect future dynamics and development options for the territory. If the large-scale mining projects go forward, the changes described here will most likely persist, intensify, and play a significant role in further territorial transformation. Daily routines, government policies, and forms of social protest and mobilization will also continue to unfold in ways affected by the subsoil and the different ways in which it passes into social life aboveground.

Notes

1. Corriente Resources and its subsidiary Ecuacorriente (ECSA) were bought in early 2010 by CRCC-Tongguan Investment Co. Ltd., a jointly owned direct subsidiary of Tongling Nonferrous Metals Group Holdings Co., Ltd. and China Railway Construction Corporation Limited.

2. Fieldwork started in September of 2008 and lasted until July of the following year. I had bases in the city of Cuenca, Azuay province (see Chapter 5 by Moore and Velásquez) and in El Pangui. The field research was carried out using ethnographic methods. I used firsthand observation and daily participation and conducted different types of interviewing methods, ranging from casual conversations to structured interviews. I collected data and reviewed archives from local municipalities, libraries, and schools in El Pangui and Gualaquiza, as well as in other government institutions and NGOs in the cities of Zamora, Loja, and Quito. The first four months were dedicated to: travelling throughout Ecuador; interviewing key actors, organizations, and government institutions; participating in forums, workshops, and meetings; visiting the sites of the proposed mining projects; participating in actions and protests; and conducting group interviews in affected communities. Towards the end of January, I moved permanently to El Pangui and associated mainly with *colonos* and Shuar peoples who had "neutral" or critical views of mining, though on occasion I engaged with individuals who worked in the companies or supported mining activities. As my fieldwork period coincided with local, regional, and national elections, for about six weeks I accompanied key candidates in their political electoral campaigns. I spoke regularly with local government in the cantons of El Pangui, Yantzaza, and Gualaquiza and, when travel permitted, in Limon Indanza. In spite of my efforts, I was not successful in securing interviews with key actors in the company, the church of El Pangui, the police, the military, or leaders in favor of mining.

3. *Colonos* are people who have moved into the area from other parts of Ecuador.

4. See www.corriente.com.

5. TNM's Mining Persons of the Year: Aurelian's Anderson, Barron, Leary, *The Northern Miner*, Dec. 4 2008.

6. See www.kinross.com.

7. The new Mining Law was passed in January 2009 and its regulations in September 2009. The Law was issued almost a year after the passage of the Mining Mandate that was supposed to have halted all mining activities, reverted all concessions to the state, and put in place a review of contracts. Much to the dismay of environmentalists appealing for the Mandate, it was not carried out in full. The anti-mining movement demanded that the government carry out the Mandate and opposed (rather violently, in some parts of the country) the Mining Law for various reasons, including legal contradictions with the Constitution.

8. By threat, I mean the perception that mining activities and the development of the projects would bring about socioenvironmental impacts, increased conflict, breakdown of livelihoods, and so on.

9. These allegations come from varied sources collected during my fieldwork, although some information also comes from my own visit to Gualaquiza and El Pangui in January of 2007, prior to my PhD studies. The sources range from documents, interviews, statements, reports, audiovisual material, and press releases in the months of December 2006 and January 2007 from Provincial Police Comando of Zamora Chinchipe, Comité de Defensa de Naturaleza, Salud y Vida del Pangui, Federacion Shuar del Pangui, Confederación de las Nacionalidades Indígenas de la Amazonia Ecuatoriana (CONFENIAE, Confederation of Indigenous Nationalities of the Ecuadorian Amazon), Coordinadora Campesina Popular, Acción Ecológica, Ecumenical Human Rights Commission, regional and national press, Municipality of El Pangui, Municipality of Gualaquiza, Ministry of Defense, Observatorio de Conflictos Mineros America Latina, and Mining Watch Canada. For a report of the case see: "Informe sobre la situación de las personas y pueblos afectados por las actividades mineras y petroleras en el Ecuador," presented to the Inter-American Commission on Human Rights, 2 March 2007, available at www.cidh.org.

10. "Message by the President to the Legislative Commission in his second year of government," 15 Jan 2009, http://www.elciudadano.gov.ec/info2008.pdf.

11. "Mineros habían convertido montaña de Nambija en colmena," 11 mayo 1993, Explored: Archivo digital de noticias desde 1994, http://www.explored.com .ec/noticias-ecuador/mineros-habian-convertido-montana-de-nambija-en-col mena-41936.html (accessed 4 May 2010).

12. Field note recording, group interview in El Pangui, 20 March 2009.

13. The current prefect of Zamora Chinchipe province, Salvador Quishpe, is a key actor in the anti-mining movement. As one of the discourses against mining is the promotion of agricultural activities, Quishpe and the indigenous political party Pachakutik envision the province as a producer and manufacturer of agricultural products. The idea behind this is that it would break the dependence with the export market in Loja, strengthen the agricultural sector of the province, and thus strengthen the argument/position against large-scale mining.

14. "Informe Social 2003, Desarrollo Social y Pobreza en el Ecuador 1990–2001," Capítulo 11, Productividad agrícola y pobreza rural. SIISE. (http://www.siise.gov.ec /Publicaciones/2infl1.pdf).

15. Field notes during a visit to the farmlands of a *colono* family in El Pangui, November 2008.

16. Field note recording, group interview in El Pangui, 20 March 2009.

17. In "Una Guerra en El Cenepa: Un Cerro de Oro," *Revista Vistazo*, 2 February 1995, page 11.

18. See "Acuerdo amplio Ecuatoriano-Peruano de integración fronteriza, desarrollo y vecindad", Anexo 5 under the Project of the Program D of the Bi-National Ecuador-Peru, as well as http://www.planbinacional.gov.ec.

19. Field notes during visit to Tundayme and ECSA campsite, November 10 2009.

20. The Salesian Mission of Bomboiza was and still is of particular importance for colonisation and settlement of the Ecuadorian Amazon. They were officially in charge of mediating land issues in the name of the indigenous people to the extent that the Ecuadorian government assigned them official faculty in the 1960's to settle land disputes and land distribution in the area.

21. Fieldwork notes for Edison Aucay.

22. The MAS party candidate for mayor of El Pangui, Luis Portilla, won the elections in 2009. Members of the MAS party favor mining, arguing that it will be good for economic development as long as companies abide by Ecuadorian laws and local and national government carry out their role in controlling the activity.

23. This point was made by the NGO ArcoIris in a workshop given on 15 May 2009. Supporting this argument are the following data that I collected from the Municipality of El Pangui: there are 21 registered land purchases in the year 2004, totalling 177,950 hectares (this includes two purchases in 2001 and one in 2002); in 2005, 12 purchases of 758 hectares are registered; and in 2006, 26 purchases of 1,250 hectares are registered.

24. One example of the preference for large-scale mining by the national government is the growing interest in eradicating small-scale and artisanal mining with the argument that it is an illegal and highly contaminating activity, more so than large-scale mining. On 15 September 2010, the national government sent about 1,500 military to Paquisha, just south of El Pangui, to forcefully evict small-scale miners located within their large-scale mining concessions owned by Kinross-Aurelian, directly south of the Corriente Resources project. No regard was paid for miners who held legal concessions or were landowners (see *Ecuador Times* 2010).

25. Field note recording, San Marcos, 8 May 2009.

26. The Coordinadora Nacional por la Defensa de la Vida y la Soberanía (CNDVS) had originally grouped all organizations and activists of the anti-mining movement in January 2007, but then later broke ties with almost all of the founding organizations.

CHAPTER 7

Hydrocarbon Conflicts and Indigenous Peoples in the Peruvian Amazon: Mobilization and Negotiation Along the Río Corrientes

ANTHONY BEBBINGTON AND MARTIN SCURRAH

The Peruvian Amazon was the scene of significant mobilization and violence during the 2000s, with concerns over extractive industries at the very heart of these conflicts. As indigenous people and others have questioned the Peruvian government's efforts to expand the hydrocarbon frontier, perhaps their most frequent point of reference has been the experience of oil extraction in the region of the Río Corrientes (Corrientes River) in the Northeast Peruvian Amazon. The history of Río Corrientes shows how petroleum production activities can generate social and environmental abuses in an isolated area where government agencies are barely present and offer little oversight of the extractive process (see also Chapter 9 in this volume, by Postigo, Montoya, and Young). At the same time, the case illuminates the conditions under which such abuses can catalyze conflict and shows how an affected population can develop organizations, strategies, and alliances that allow it to combine resistance and negotiation in its efforts to contain the extractive frontier. In this instance, as we discuss, such resistance and negotiation ultimately led to a shift in relationships between the population, business, and the state, and brought *parts* of this state more directly into the regulation of extractive activity, with effects that reach beyond the specificities of the case.

In political ecology terms, the experience in Río Corrientes is a case of a renewable natural resource-dependent way of life being undermined by the expansion of activities that form part of an integrated, energy-intensive system that extracts subterranean resources that have no relevance or value for local livelihood strategies. The extraction and transport of this subsoil resource involves the dispossession of territory, the presence of a company that assumes many of the functions and privileges of government, and the despoilation of critical natural assets as a result of oil and waste water spills that contaminate the soil, ground, and surface water, with severe consequences for human health (cf. Santiago 2006). At the same time, this is a case that reveals how, beyond any politics of resistance and opposition, social movements may also identify and engage with more progressive elements of the state in ways that can generate positive change in the regulation of extractive industries, even within neoliberal-extractivist contexts. This is important, as it draws attention to the possibilities of progressive change even within the constraints of a relatively authoritarian form of neoliberalism such as that which characterized Peru between 2005 and 2010. The experience also shows that parts of the state apparatus that do not necessarily share the ruling regime's commitments to such forms of neoliberalism can themselves become active players in these processes of change. This in turn challenges political ecologists to assume quite nuanced approaches to both movements and the state, to avoid over-easily apportioning taken-for-granted motivations to these institutionalized actors, and to pursue research strategies that explore and understand the slippages within both states and movements.

In this chapter we trace the history of oil extraction in the region and describe the slow process of organization that occurred among the local and national indigenous populations as they responded to this extractive activity. The largest section of the chapter is dedicated to a discussion of how the conflicts around Río Corrientes intensified during the 2000s, as well as their culmination in a series of direct actions that forced both government and company to negotiate with the indigenous population. This negotiation and its results are considered in some detail. In the final section we analyze the experience, identifying factors that made this negotiation possible and arguing that the case offers important empirical, conceptual, and normative insights into the broader issues raised by struggles over the subsoil in South America.

The material we present was collected between 2007 and 2009 as part of a larger project on social movements and poverty. The project as a whole involved 138 key informant interviews, of which roughly 50 were directly relevant to this case study. (Some other interviews were also relevant in providing context to the case, even when the primary topic was not related to Río Corrientes.) Interviews were conducted (all in Spanish) with informants from the indigenous movement, the petroleum sector, the state, NGOs, and researchers. In particular, much time was spent with informants working in the Human Rights Ombudsman's office who played key roles in the Río Corrientes case, as becomes clear later in the chapter. In addition, we conducted an exhaustive review of secondary material and press reports in order to reconstruct the timeline of the conflict. Finally, we presented the material in a

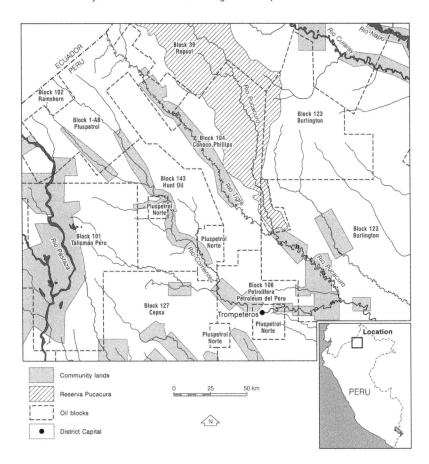

Figure 7.1. Community lands and oil blocks in the Corrientes basin

series of workshops at which actors involved in the case were present (as well as others who were not). These workshops served to clarify uncertainties in the research as well as identify areas in which interpretations diverged, both among actors and between them and us. It also merits note that each of us have longer-standing relationships either with the case or with the Ombudsman's office because of other work in which we have been involved as researchers or, in Scurrah's case, as former South American Regional Director for Oxfam America.

The Case

Oil and Indigenous Organization Along Río Corrientes

Río Corrientes originates in Ecuador, flowing southward until it empties into the Amazon River southwest of the city of Iquitos. The area is inhabited principally by the Achuar people, although there are also small groups of Kichua and Urarina Indians (see Figure 7.1). The communities are organized into two federations: the Federation of Native Communities of Río Corrientes (Federación de Comunidades Nativas del Río Corrientes, FECONACO), founded in 1991, whose members hail from 30 communities, mostly from Upper Río Corrientes; and the Federation of Indigenous People of the Lower and Upper Río Corrientes (Federación de Pueblos Indígenas del Bajo y Alto Corrientes, FEPIBAC), founded in 2003, with members from 18 communities, mostly from Lower Río Corrientes. The two federations are affiliated to two different national indigenous organizations, respectively: the Inter-ethnic Association for the Development of the Peruvian Jungle (Asociación Inter-étnica de Desarrollo de la Selva Peruana, AIDESEP) and the Confederation of Amazonian Nationalities of Peru (Confederación de Nacionalidades de la Amazonía Peruana, CONAP). AIDESEP is the older of these two organizations, while CONAP is generally felt to have the more conciliatory position in relation to modernization and state-led development (Chirif 2010a).

Though they were founded in the 1990s, the origins of these organizations can be traced back to 1970 when the state-owned company PetroPeru began exploratory drilling on Block 8–8X, a concession granted by the Ministry of Energy and Mines (Ministerio de Energía y Minas, MINEM) on the territories of the Achuar, Kichua, and Urarina indigenous peoples. In mid-1971, the Peruvian government signed an oil exploration and extraction contract with the Occidental Petroleum Company, authorizing it to begin exploration and exploitation operations on Block 1AB, located on a remote section of the Río Corrientes Basin inhabited by the Achuar.

Under Peruvian law, which follows the Roman legal tradition, both sub-surface (e.g., oil) and certain surface (e.g., forest) resources belong to the state. Under the Native Communities Act of 1974 (modified in 1978), indigenous communities were granted property titles to the areas they occupied for housing and gardens, but were only granted concessions that gave them access to use the forests and streams on which they depended for hunting and gathering. Thus, in a purely legal sense, the granting of oil and gas concessions to private companies was not seen as interfering with indigenous rights. Likewise, because communities were granted territory as a concession, not as property, the oil company was also able (with government support) to lay out seismic lines,[1] establish drilling platforms, and construct pipelines across these territories.

By the mid-1970s, Occidental Petroleum Corporation had begun large-scale production, converting its installations in the Río Corrientes basin into the largest oil fields in Peru, pumping more than 40 percent of the nation's oil. Occidental continued exploring and scaled up production, drilling 144 wells from 1978 to 1982, 129 of which were productive (La Torre López and Huertas 1999, 54). From 1972 to 1990, Occidental conducted seven seismic explorations on Block 1AB, employing a total 10,712 kilometers of open trails for the purpose of producing seismic lines (La Torre López and Huertas 1999, 51), transforming Block 1AB into what the government's National Office for Natural Resource Assessment described as the "most polluted region in the country" (ONERN 1984). The Peruvian state's response to this situation was both muted and contradictory. On the one hand, the government adopted an Environmental and Natural Resources Code (Legislative Decree 613) in 1990, which constituted the country's first systematic effort to define a general framework for environmental protection (Calle and Pulgar-Vidal 2006). Yet it also passed legislation that created conditions for further socioenvironmental conflict, such as the 1993 Hydrocarbon Act (Law 26221), which granted companies concessions for up to 30 years for oil exploration and up to 40 years for natural gas (Finer and Orta-Martínez 2010).

Indeed, during the 1990s there was increasing local protest over the socioenvironmental impacts of Occidental, and a series of oil spill-related complaints were filed as pipelines ruptured in both 1994 and 1996. Meanwhile, more than an estimated 85,000 barrels of produced water were being dumped each day into Río Corrientes from Occidental's Block 1AB and PetroPeru's Block 8–8X, leading to critical concentrations of chlorides and other environmental damage (La Torre López and Huertas 1999, 55).[2] In 1996, the mayor of the Trompeteros District filed charges with the Ministry of Justice against Occidental and PetroPeru. FECONACO requested that a special commission be formed to carry out an environmental audit and evaluate the degree of contamination of Río Corrientes (Lu 2009, 29). Yet the Ministry of Energy and Mines ultimately concluded that emissions fell within maximum allowable limits (Lu 2009, 30). The company's Complementary Environmental Plan (CEP) never explicitly broached the local population's situation or the need to restore the human habitat, solve the social problems generated by its activities, or reinject produced waters into the ground rather than pour them into the river.

When Occidental expanded its operations and acquired neighboring Block 64 in 1995, the Achuar communities complained about "the serious contamination of the environment, the water, and the resources the communities depend upon" in adjacent Blocks 1AB and 8 (EarthRights International, Racimos de Ungurahui, and Amazon Watch 2007, 16). That same year, AIDESEP's Regional Organization in Iquitos (Organización Regional de Aidesep Iquitos, ORAI) engaged the services of an environmental NGO to analyze water samples taken from the region. Results showed elevated levels of acid, salt, temperature, and electric conductivity, and it was concluded that the water was unfit for human consumption and could be harmful to plants and animals (La Torre López and Huertas 1999, 60). Indeed, by the 1990s human health impacts of oil became progressively more apparent. The head of Villa Trompeteros's health center in 1995 declared that community residents were suffering serious health problems on account of endemic diseases, poor nutrition, low levels of resistance, and environmental contamination. Among the mestizo population, there were cases of AIDS and the number of malaria cases had increased by 70 percent between February and October 1995 (La Torre López and Huertas 1999, 65). In response, the Ministry of Health dispatched a commission to visit the area, which concluded that communities along the Corrientes and Tigre rivers required improved health services.

Articulating Protest Across Scales

In 1995, a small group of professionals — mostly lawyers — created the nongovernmental organization (NGO) Racimos de Ungurahui to advise AIDESEP. Racimos's president, Lily La Torre, made contact with FECONACO the following year when she was asked to present a series of lectures on the rights of indigenous communities. In interviews she expressed her shock at the control and intimidation exercised by the company, with support from the authorities, over the communities. The company accused FECONACO leaders of stealing, which led to their incarceration and the weakening of the organization. A local teacher, who was an outspoken critic of the company, was also threatened and forced to leave the area. Racimos's president was herself accused of being a terrorist and a spy for Ecuador and was later obliged to clarify her position with representatives of the Ministry of Defense in Lima.[3]

The corporate scene shifted after the Argentinean oil company Pluspetrol won the bid for Block 8 in 1996 and acquired Occidental's rights to Block 1AB in 2000. According to Pluspetrol representatives,[4] the company did not expect to find such high levels of environmental damage. In 2002, Lily La Torre started to work once again with the FECONACO leadership to elaborate strategic demands to present to Pluspetrol and the Peruvian government, as well as legal action against Occidental. While the ensuing dialogue with Pluspetrol representatives led to a document in which Pluspetrol spoke vaguely of reinjecting produced waters, no specific timetable was laid out, and FECONACO's leaders soon concluded that Pluspetrol had no intention of keeping its promises. In November 2005, FECONACO declared that it would allow no further oil operations in its territory:

> This grave situation of continued and accumulated contamination and the flagrant violation of national environmental legislation, human rights, indigenous rights, and international environmental treaties that Peru has ratified have been persistently condemned by our organizations. Furthermore, these facts have been recently recognized by the Peruvian Congress's Commission on the Amazon and Indigenous Affairs, by Loreto's regional government, by the Ministry of Health's Environmental Office [Spanish DIGESA], and by the Energy Regulatory Commission [Spanish OSINERG] yet sanctions are not being enforced . . .[5]
>
> It is only recently, and because of our demands, that the company, Pluspetrol, operator of both blocks, has begun to inject into the subsoil a small part of the produced waters—it did not do so in the past because of the lenience of the MINEM, whose norms do not require such reinjection. For 35 years, our river has had 1.1 million barrels of these poisonous waters dumped into it on a daily basis. This is equivalent to approximately 10,000 tons of salt and 3 tons of barium per day, not counting impacts from multiple crude oil spills over large areas of our lands, the cultural impacts, and the damage to lives, property, human health, and a healthy environment.
>
> Therefore, we feel that we are within our legitimate rights to defend our remaining healthy territory and resources, and for that reason we, the communities of the Río Corrientes Basin, unanimously declare that we will not accept further oil company operations in our territory. (FECONACO 2005)[6]

With support from Racimos and AIDESEP, the federation's leaders met with the Minister of Health in 2005 and managed to convince her to order a study of the human health situation in the oil company's area of influence. This study would include the testing of district residents' blood samples for cadmium and lead levels by specialists from the National Health Institute's Centre for Occupational and Environmental Health Protection (CENSOPAS-INS) (Lu 2009). While the Ministry of Health was carrying out these water quality and human health studies, FECONACO and its allies also organized an international mission to perform a nongovernmental analysis of the situation along Río Corrientes (Earth Rights International, Racimos de Ungurahui, and Amazon Watch 2007, 7). Their goals were twofold: (1) to apply pressure on the Ministry of Health by collecting data that might validate (or invalidate) the results of the official study; and (2) to collect data for a lawsuit that the group was preparing to file in the state of California against Occidental for compensation for harming the health of the affected population of the Río Corrientes Basin. The lawsuit was finally admitted for trial in Los Angeles by the federal court of appeals on 6 December 2010.

During the early months of 2006, there were signs that Ministry of Health officials were alarmed by what they had discovered and were attempting to bury the report or delay its publication. However, the results were leaked, prompting FECONACO and its allies to push even harder for the report's formal publication. In exercising this pressure, FECONACO requested assistance from the Ombudsman's Office, which sent an official letter to the Ministry of Health demanding that the report be published.[7] Report results, which were finally released at the end of March 2006 on the Ministry of Health's webpage, showed that nearly 99 percent of people tested had blood cadmium levels that exceeded the maximum allowable limits, 66 percent of 2–17 year olds had blood lead levels that exceeded maximum allowable limits, and that levels were deemed dangerous to health in 13 percent of the cases (Ministerio de Salud 2006; Lu 2009, 33–35; Orta Martínez et al. 2007, 6). The report became an invaluable tool for the campaign designed to force the government and the company to take action to solve the problem.

FECONACO's leadership, now armed with evidence from an official report and with support from its allies, launched an advocacy campaign directed at the Ombudsman's Office, the Ministry of Health, and the Congress. Because the García administration was soon to take over the reins of government, the initial campaign strategy focused on the media in an attempt to influence public opinion, including a documentary and a news program broadcast on television in August 2006.[8] Several news stories in the international media concerning the case were also reprinted or reported on by the national media in Peru. In this context, FECONACO leaders travelled to Lima in August to meet with representatives from the new government and, in response to the Minister's instructions to the Deputy Minister that Pluspetrol be asked to fund a health program and his promise to create a high-level Multisectoral Commission to be officially installed in Iquitos on 26 September, made two explicit requests: (1) that an official resolution, whether from the President or a minister, be issued as a means of formalizing the commitments made, and (2) that money be allocated in the budget to carry out those commitments. They agreed to meet again a month later in Iquitos, once the resolution had been issued.

On 26 September 2006, authorities (*apus*) from different communities and leaders from FECONACO, ORAI, and AIDESEP marched from the campus of the local university to the offices where the meeting was scheduled to take place. The high-level commission, however, never arrived. Faced with the indignation of both indigenous people and the citizens of Iquitos, the minister quickly issued the resolution to create the Commission and dispatched a delegation to the city the following week, on 4 October. Tensions emerged again when members of the Commission announced that they would meet in the Prefecture; FECONACO declared this an insult, given that the invitation had been to meet in FECONACO's offices. In response, the Commission members nominally conceded by moving the meeting to the local bishop's offices. Meanwhile, Pluspetrol flew CONAP's president in from Lima and arranged for FEPIBAC's representatives to be transported to Iquitos so that they could participate in the meeting, although neither had taken part in any of the prior negotiations. In the face of all these maneuverings and disagreements, the meeting never took place and the delegation returned to Lima (Chirif 2006).

From Struggle to Negotiation: The Dorissa Accord

The Accord on Paper

During the days after the failed meeting, FECONACO, community leaders, and their advisors discussed their options and decided to seize control of Pluspetrol's installations. Though this was the first time that an Amazonian indigenous organization had used such a negotiating strategy, the reasoning was that experience thus far had shown that only a dramatic show of force would convince the government to listen to their demands. In addition, they had support from a range of international and national allies, including some within the government itself.[9] At dawn on 10 October 2006, the communities seized the installations at Blocks 1AB and 8, shutting down half of Peru's total national oil production. The company had underestimated the degree of frustration in the indigenous population and was caught completely off guard.[10] The seizure proceeded altogether peacefully, as the on-site workers did not resist and were later helicoptered out by the company. AIDESEP issued a declaration from Lima indicating that FECONACO's act was not an isolated and spontaneous one but rather that of an organization forming part of the national Amazonian indigenous movement, which supported its cause:

The *apus* of the Achuar communities firmly decided to retake control of their territories, blocking access to the oil wells, demanding that the company withdraw from their territories and halt all its production activities there. Faithful to its principles and objectives as leader of the indigenous movement, AIDESEP appealed to government authorities, the Ombudswoman, and civil society as a whole to sit down with the Achuar people to find an immediate solution to these issues which have the potential to lead to serious confrontations that nobody wishes to see. (AIDESEP 2006)

Within two days the government sent a delegation, with logistical support from Pluspetrol. The delegation sought to negotiate an agreement before any of the communities' advisors, who lacked the resources available to Pluspetrol, could be present. When Lily La Torre did arrive, she met with federation leaders and the *apus* to analyze the agreement. Together they decided to propose amendments in the face of a series of irregularities in how the agreement had been drawn up:[11] it had been drafted under pressure by company officials; it did not contain all of the agreements reached by the parties; it attached no deadlines or durations to the agreements made; it did not recognize the communities' decision to reject any new oil concession on their lands; and finally, it had been read only in Spanish, without being translated into Achuar, and had been signed at night by flashlight. In response, the proposal sent on behalf of the communities included, among other items: (1) a pronouncement that they would not endorse new oil concessions on their lands; (2) provisions for carrying out the reinjection of produced waters; (3) time schedules and mechanisms describing how decisions would be made, and oversight exercised, in the health and comprehensive development programs Pluspetrol had agreed to support; (4) a temporary "emergency" food program; (5) provision of potable water; (6) remediation of environmental liabilities and damages; and (7) incorporation of the indigenous people into the government's national basic health scheme (FECONACO 2006).

The government reacted immediately, launching a media campaign to discredit FECONACO and its advisors. Among other things it was claimed that the demand for no further hydrocarbon concessions was an imposition of Racimos and other outsiders, though the demand had, in fact, been raised and supported at FECONACO's annual general meeting earlier in 2005. In the process, as AIDESEP sought assistance from *its* allies in the press, the media became a battleground in the struggle to define how this standoff should be interpreted. AIDESEP also approached the Ombudswoman, who during a press conference responded to Prime Minister del Castillo by explaining that she did not agree with him and believed that the Achuar "did not initiate the conflict." Furthermore, she stated that since 2005, her office had been informing the government of the elevated levels of water pollution in Río Corrientes as a result of the dumping practices of Pluspetrol.[12] She refuted the accusations of violence and recommended that the government renegotiate the agreement. The Prime Minister responded by requesting her intervention.[13]

Representatives from the Ombudsman's Office and Lily La Torre were helicoptered in by Pluspetrol to inform the population about the government's response, to attempt to reestablish the people's trust in the government, to open up a space for dialogue, and to promote the revision of the Accord. Due in large part to the intervention of the Ombudsman's Office, the three parties (FECONACO, the government, and the company) met to renegotiate the agreement on 22–23 October 2006. The Ombudsman's representatives acted as observers and facilitators, while the bulk of the negotiations were handled by MINEM Deputy Minister Pedro Gamio and Lily La Torre. Once again, and in the presence of armed indigenous men and police ready to retake the installations, the negotiations were rushed and the negotiators had to make agreements without having time to consult with authorities in Lima. The resulting Dorissa Accord stated that:

(1) Pluspetrol would reinject produced waters from Blocks 1AB and 8 into the subsoil.

(2) Pluspetrol would pay 40,169,986 soles (ca. US$14.4 million) over a 10-year period to fund a comprehensive health plan that would be directed by the Ministry of Health's regional office through the Río Corrientes Comprehensive Health Plan Special Project (Proyecto Especial Plan Integral de Salud del Corrientes, PEPISCO).

(3) Loreto's Regional Government would construct and equip a small hospital in Villa Trompeteros with funds from Pluspetrol.

(4) The national basic health service (Seguro Integral de Salud, SIS) would be extended to include indigenous communities.

(5) Loreto's Regional Government would be in charge of preparing and executing a comprehensive development plan (Programa Integral de Desarrollo, PID) in the river basin for an amount of 11 million soles (ca. US$3.94 million).

(6) Pluspetrol would pay the rental of a motorboat for one year, after which the Regional Government would provide a new one as part of the PID.

(7) The national food program (Programa Nacional de Asistencia

Alimentaria, PRONAA) would provide temporary food aid for one year to communities while their natural resource base was being repaired and regenerated.

(8) Pluspetrol would repair and renovate the potable water system.

(9) FECONACO and DIGESA would jointly monitor water quality. FECONACO and Pluspetrol would monitor the remediation of damages.

(10) Pluspetrol and PetroPeru would remediate Block 8.

(11) The Ombudsman's Office and the FECONACO-affiliated communities, in coordination with relevant government offices and Pluspetrol, would supervise compliance with the Accord.

FECONACO celebrated the Accord as a "victory": "We have achieved agreements to begin to avoid the contamination of our rivers, streams, land, and lakes, to guarantee our nutrition, and to meet the health needs of our children. The state has pledged to share 5 percent of the oil tax with the communities located within the oil company's area of influence . . . however, and most important, we have taken a giant step towards having our dignity restored, gaining the respect our indigenous communities so rightly deserve, and realizing our historic desire for self-determination" (FECONACO 2006). Of course, how far this really was a "victory" depended on the translation of these agreements into practices. We discuss this translation in the following section with a focus on three areas: environmental monitoring, health, and the development plan.

The Accord in Practice: Implementation and Regulation

Environmental monitoring. Four years after the Dorissa Accord, Pluspetrol had complied with the reinjection of produced waters into the subsurface and had concluded its environmental remediation of Block 1AB, though not of Block 8 (FECONACO 2009; Quarles 2009). Though the reinjection of produced waters marked a significant "victory," it is also important to recognize that this merely brought operations up to some sort of minimal good practice. Other serious environmental problems remained and were now being detected by a raft of monitoring initiatives put in place by different actors as they sought to ensure that the environmental effects of extraction were being regulated in ways that met their particular concerns.

The Dorissa Accord contemplated a joint environmental monitoring system between Pluspetrol and FECONACO in representation of the affected communities. However, FECONACO declined to participate and so instead, there was joint monitoring by Pluspetrol and FEPIBAC, FECONACO's rival and Pluspetrol's ally. In addition, Pluspetrol's compliance with its environmental obligations was being monitored by the recently created state agency which was charged with officially certifying compliance (Organismo Supervisor de Energía y Minería, OSINERGMIN). For its part, FECONACO was carrying out regular environmental monitoring with the support of international and national NGOs (World Wildlife Fund [WWF] and Shinai, respectively). Indeed, by February 2010, the federation was referring to "the persistence of a problematic environmental situation in the Corrientes region" and "the presence of numerous and repeated oil spills throughout the region." Since 2006, 58 oil spills had been recorded, of which 42 were "of great importance." Meanwhile, for its part, a surface water study by the regional health authority (Dirección Regional de Salud, DIRESA) had found high levels of hydrocarbons, in some cases more than ten times internationally accepted limits (FECONACO 2009, 1).

Although the creation of the semiautonomous OSINERGMIN meant that the Ministry had gained some credibility in its ability to monitor company compliance with environmental obligations, FECONACO was not yet persuaded, given the long history of lax state regulation and supervision and the recent experience with leaks in the Camisea natural gas pipeline (Ross 2009). Consequently, FECONACO and its allies Racimos and Shinai requested an independent evaluation of the remediation efforts in the affected areas of Block 1AB (conducted by the U.S.-based NGO E-Tech International, which had also conducted critical assessments in Camisea). This evaluation revealed serious deficiencies in how remediation work had been designed and conducted. The study also concluded that the remediation standards used were below international and even MINEM standards and that the environmental conditions failed to meet the minimum levels required by MINEM (Quarles 2009, 2–7). Given that OSINERGMIN had already classified these areas as "remediated," E-Tech's work cast doubt upon the Pluspetrol-supervised remediation efforts and the quality of OSINERGMIN's supervision and certification. Indeed, the very existence of so many parallel and competing monitoring efforts plainly illustrates the level of mutual distrust in the state as a neutral defender of the environment or the public interest. The lack of effective mechanisms to negotiate or resolve these differences in measurement and interpretation has left environmental remediation as a pending issue.[14]

The struggle to control the health program. The health project (PEPISCO) that grew out of the Dorissa Accord was extensive and covered toxicological monitoring, nutrition, health services strengthening, and health worker training.[15]

Indeed, DIRESA had never before put a similar project into action, and its annual budget was equal to one third of its budget for the entire Loreto region. In March 2007, Pluspetrol transferred funds for the first year of activities. Implementation was slow since DIRESA was unprepared for such a large responsibility; the regional government was disorganized and its personnel lacked training. The project languished in its first two years, and by October 2008, FECONACO began to request that the funds be managed directly by the project or by an independent contractor. However, both DIRESA and the Ombudsman's Office opposed such a move.

Meanwhile these health initiatives became caught up in the longer-standing tensions between FECONACO and FEPIBAC. While FECONACO leaders dominated PEPISCO's board, FEPIBAC began demanding equal representation and accusing the Board of misuse of funds (*La Verdad* 2009). On 31 August 2009, about 150 members of FEPIBAC surrounded the Villa Trompeteros health center and demanded they be represented on the PEPISCO board. Yet despite these difficulties, by 2010—nearly four years after the Dorissa Accord had entered into force—DIRESA was still in charge of the project, the Villa Trompeteros hospital was under construction, more health workers and doctors had been hired, community members were being trained as health promoters, and the project had made an agreement with a Swedish university for support for blood testing and health monitoring. This success reflected three factors: the constant pressure by both the Ombudsman's Office and FECONACO; the reappointment of PEPISCO's first Director, who together with FECONACO had prepared the original proposal presented during the Dorissa negotiations; and the cooptation of FEPIBAC's representatives who, though unsuccessful in the elections to PEPISCO's board, had been invited to attend meetings as observers.

Development. If achievement of the Accord's environmental and health components was at best "partial," progress on the commitments to foster socioeconomic development initiatives was *minimal.* After a year spent "developing" without community participation, the regional government discovered that it could not satisfy the central government's fiscal and capacity criteria necessary to make the investments identified in the plan. Communities and federations had even less chance of satisfying these criteria.[16] By 2010, the plan was still not being implemented and the regional government had not even developed the terms of reference for a bidding process to construct the promised riverboat. Having lost their patience, FECONACO's leaders publicly requested that the Ombudswoman take up the issue.[17]

Interpretations of this situation varied widely. Some, such as the Multisectoral Commission of the Corrientes, Tigre, and Pastaza River Basins, established prior to the Dorissa Accord and led by MINEM's representative, argued that the president of the regional government had blocked implementation. For their part, other officials in MINEM argued that a fall in oil prices had left the regional government without the royalty funds to cover its share of the investment. Meanwhile, the Ombudsman's Office argued that the problem was a lack of financial and professional capacity in the regional government. Whatever the case, although the conflict had brought *parts* of the state into geographical and institutional domains in which the latter had been previously inactive, it also revealed the incapacities and ostensible treacheries of other parts of the state. In the words of AIDESEP leader and former FECONACO president, Henderson Rengifo: "The Loreto regional government is languishing. It has done absolutely nothing. This shows once again how our national, regional, and local government leaders do not accomplish anything. They do nothing for the people."[18] Expressing similar sentiments another FECONACO leader said quite bluntly: "We came to the conclusion that the regional government has no policy for working with indigenous people."[19]

Partly in response to this inaction, and also in an attempt to continue combining negotiation and pressure, FECONACO and Racimos presented an urgent action motion before the United Nations Committee for the Elimination of Racial Discrimination (CERD) in 2008. Through the motion they sought measures to protect the rights of the Achuar people. In a letter addressed to the Government of Peru dated 7 March 2009, the Committee expressed "its concern about the contamination and environmental degradation derived from oil industry activities on indigenous territories in Peru and for their impact on the health and traditional ways of life of these peoples." The Committee requested information from the government about the communities affected by hydrocarbon activities and about new concessions in the area, with a view to studying what was happening. It also requested information about legislation relevant to the right of indigenous peoples to participate and be consulted, the monitoring of environmental impacts, and the concrete application of such legislation (Coordinadora Nacional de Radio 2009).

Interpreting Corrientes

One theme running through this case has been that the struggle to control and remedy the impacts of oil extraction on indigenous communities is part and parcel of the struggle of indigenous movements to redefine the nature of their relations with the state (cf. Sawyer and Gomez 2008). This struggle has been a process in which indigenous groups have sought to make themselves and their concerns visible to the state (and society) and to bring particular sorts of state practices into their territories, particularly practices of regulation and social service provision. This has involved steady, cumulative processes of organization and alliance building, moments of direct action, sustained periods of negotiation, and joint initiatives with those parts of the state that have been—for reasons of mission and commitment—supportive of indigenous peoples' rights. In this section we elaborate and reflect on some of these patterns.

Subterranean Strategies and the Struggle for State Formation

While the catalyst of conflict in Río Corrientes was private sector abuse and environmental irresponsibility, much of the ensuing struggle was over the state. For the indigenous leadership and their advisors, the ultimate goal was to force the Peruvian government to regulate private enterprise in ways that guaranteed human rights. In assuming this position, indigenous organizations and their allies defined the conflict not only as a struggle to obtain redress for past damages and ensure improved future behavior by the company, but also as a struggle to convince the state, in its many dimensions, to recognize indigenous people as citizens and so to respect and protect their rights by controlling and regulating company activities.

This focus on the state was also a strategic choice. Indeed, the FECONACO and AIDESEP leadership felt that direct negotiation with Pluspetrol would ultimately fail because the company would be able to use its affinity with the rival federation FEPIBAC (and CONAP nationally) to turn any such negotiation to its advantage. Framing the problem as one of "the state and human rights" rather than of "the company and compensation" avoided this risk. Furthermore, as it happened, this focus on ensuring that the state guarantee rights also enabled the subsequent convergence of interests with the Office of the Ombudswoman.

Engaging the state, however, taxed the movement's capacities and perseverance in the extreme. MINEM's authoritarian, legalistic, and technocratic style and identification with Pluspetrol's interests led it to seek to drive wedges between communities and FECONACO, AIDESEP, and their non-governmental allies. Indeed, MINEM consistently favored a relationship with the more conciliatory FEPIBAC and CONAP, a position that was also promoted by the government's National Institute for the Development of Andean, Amazonian, and AfroPeruvian Peoples (Instituto Nacional de Desarrollo de Pueblos Andinos, Amazónicos y Afroperuano; INDEPA) within the context of the environmental and health programs. Meanwhile, the movement's engagements with the regional government were deeply frustrating, as they encountered a newly elected regional President loath to honor the commitments made by the outgoing administration, and a bureaucracy lacking the capacity or resources to deliver on these commitments anyway.

"Bringing the state back in" (Evans, Rueschemeyer, and Skocpol 1985) and demanding that it enhance its capacities to regulate and deliver services at the extractive frontier was, therefore, anything but straightforward—and indeed, this helps to explain why, in so many cases, local populations ultimately opt to negotiate for direct compensation from the company rather than for institutional change in the state. That said, FECONACO found much more scope to work with the regional health authority, DIRESA, and the Ombudsman's Office, in each of whom they encountered both greater technical capacity *and* sensitivity regarding the intercultural and rights-based dimensions of the relationship between the state, oil industry, and indigenous peoples. Indeed, the explicit mission of the Ombudsman's Office was to protect and generate respect for the rights of citizens—especially the most vulnerable—in their relations with the state, and to reform national government so it would conform to the rule of law and the formal codification of human rights in Peru.

The Ombudsman's Office is part of the state but depends on Congress rather than the Presidency. This gives it an important degree of political autonomy and legitimacy. With this autonomy in hand, it was able, in stark contrast with other state agencies, to coproduce norms and agreements with the indigenous movement and other actors. It was, furthermore, peopled by a group of professionals—mainly competent lawyers—who were committed to a democratic state and the rule of law based upon respect for human rights. More specifically, as it became involved in implementing the Dorissa Accord, the Office hired a forestry engineer to assist in the process. This combination of technical and legal expertise, coupled with a willingness to take risks, proved critical in opening up some space for negotiating with other parts of government and the state.

The crucial point is that FECONACO, AIDESEP, and their allies shared an important agenda with the Ombudsman's Office: one of fostering institutional reforms in the state that would increase its propensity and capacity to protect and enhance human rights. Though they differed on questions of direct action, this broader convergence enabled an affinity that allowed FECONACO, AIDESEP, and their allies to share strategies. This served as a counterpoint to those other parts of the state that sought to protect and sustain institutional arrangements favoring extraction of the subsoil and pa-tronage relationships between the state, the company, and the local popula-tion. The reality of this struggle between competing visions of the state and its role ensured that the movement could not succeed completely in its effort at "bringing the state back in," though neither was the outcome in Río Corrien-tes one of pure failure. The Accord was signed, environmental monitoring was conducted and broadened, produced waters were reinjected, and health care provision improved. Progress on development investment was, conversely, far more muted, as the capacity and the lack of political commitment of the re-gional government challenged even the skills of those in the Ombudsman's Office. However, in a modest but real way, progressive elements of state for-mation occurred in Río Corrientes as a result of prior struggle, contemporary negotiation, and the particular capacities and state–society convergences that characterized this case.

Conflict, Negotiation, and Institutional Capacities

The development of events in the Río Corrientes case followed a clear path:

(1) Affected communities organized themselves.

(2) Evidence of social and environmental impacts was gathered.

(3) Attempts were made, without success, to initiate a dialogue with authorities.

(4) The local population occupied company facilities as a means of exerting pressure.

(5) Negotiations were carried out.

(6) Implementation and enforcement of the Accord began.

The sequence of events was a blending of organization, research, mobiliza-tion, advocacy, negotiation, and monitoring. Each part demanded different capacities and skills. While social movements sometimes prefer to achieve their objectives through mobilization and protest aimed at forcing the ca-pitulation of their adversary, it is rare that governments or companies merely concede without passing first through a process of negotiation; indeed, many activists consider reaching that stage a major achievement. In Río Corrientes, FECONACO achieved just this, passing from direct action to negotiations and obtaining a series of implementable commitments.

The negotiations were a result of the persistence of FECONACO and its allies in making their demands, and in this sense the occupation of the company's facilities was a means of applying pressure rather than an objective in and of itself. Nevertheless, the chain of events created a situation in which actually managing to negotiate was difficult. First, the positions of the parties had become particularly polarized, because one side had insisted and the other had resisted for such a long period of time. Secondly, negotiations took place in a tense setting in which the indigenous people had taken control of the company's facilities and security forces were threatening to retake them. Third, the remote location in which negotiations occurred meant that advisors could not be consulted and information was not available. And finally, negotiators were under pressure to find rapid agreements in the face of potential violence *and* of a company concerned about lost revenue while oil was not being pumped.

The first round of negotiations produced a settlement that was so general that it was ultimately not in the interests of the population. This was a consequence of (1) the lack of experience and knowhow of FECONACO's leaders and community *apus*, (2) the absence of some of their advisors, especially those from Racimos, (3) the bad faith of the government negotiators who were simply seeking an agreement to meet their and the company's interests,[20] and (4) the absence of third parties to act as facilitators or observers. Had the initial Accord been the final agreement, there is good reason to believe that there would have been a return to direct action and mobilization, probably accompanied by greater levels of violence and polarization, as has happened in other conflicts around the country (Caballero Martín and Cabrera Espinoza 2008; Caballero Martín 2009). The fact that a second round of negotiations took place was due first to the insistence of a FECONACO advisor, and second, to the Ombudsman's decision to make this case an emblematic one and to persuade the Prime Minister to return to the negotiation table. According to some within the Ombudsman's Office, this posture was itself a contingent effect of the fact that the Ombudswoman had recently assumed her position and so was in search of a case that would help project her position and authority. Indeed, when the second version of the agreement was reached after two days of intense negotiation, it was not only tighter, but also included an unexpected pledge by the Ombudsman's Office to accompany FECONACO in monitoring its implementation.

The case also demonstrates a second pattern. While movements might mobilize people, organizations, and resources to influence policies and decisions that are of interest to them, movements often lose momentum once their participants proclaim "victory" and return to their everyday activities. As a result, it becomes difficult for movement leaders and their allies to maintain the motivation and pressure for monitoring the decisions and commitments that have been made, not least because this phase of a negotiated settlement requires tasks that are detailed, are long term, are often boring, and sometimes demand a certain level of professional and technical knowhow. Furthermore, movements often stand at a great disadvantage when monitoring compliance because members are not familiar with the details of administrative and legal procedures, are not fully trained to handle their technical aspects, are typically elected, work with little or no pay, and hence are unable to dedicate the time needed to monitor the situation fully and permanently.[21]

In this instance, the Ombudsman's Office compensated for some of these limitations. In the face of inertia, resistance, and bad practice in other parts of the state, staff of the Ombudsman's Office attended dozens of meetings, wrote numerous official letters, made public condemnations of what was happening, organized press conferences, and used all other means at its disposal to persuade, motivate, goad, prod, threaten, and force the different government agencies to take the necessary measures to implement the Accord. In this process, the Office had to move beyond the classic definition of its role, which is to ensure that individual and community rights are not compromised by government policy and action. In this instance, the Office intervened directly in state activities so as to motivate and to assist government officials to find ways around the obstacles blocking the implementation of the Dorissa Accord. In the face of a regional government bogged down by its internal procedures, the Office proposed solutions to its administrative and organizational difficulties. And when there were inadequate public funds for the comprehensive development program, the Ombudswoman identified surplus money in oil tax revenues.

When the Ombudswoman made the decision to play an active role in monitoring and enabling the implementation of the Accord, she ran the risk of overstepping her role and responsibilities and of taking on functions that were proper to officials in the Executive branch. We have already noted that some of the calculations at play in assuming this role may have been political as well as ethical, but regardless of the motivation, the experience had an important pedagogic role: it allowed the Ombudswoman and her Office to see the problems and obstacles within the state that limit implementation of agreements in other conflicts in which the Office was involved, to understand how and why state practices were generating conflict and citizen complaints, and to begin visualizing the importance of a government reform process as a means to end the recurring cycles of social conflict that have characterized Peru in general, and the extractive sector in particular (Bebbington 2007b; Caballero Martín 2009).[22]

In short, two lessons were learned from this process. The FECONACO leadership learned that it was necessary to maintain the commitment of its membership and the strength of its alliances in order to ensure that the victory won as a result of its struggle and negotiations did not become pyrrhic during the long and complex implementation stage. The Ombudsman's Office learned that the abuse of citizens' rights by the state was a combined effect of political will and institutional capacity, and that producing a less conflictive and more democratic Peru would, therefore, require attention to both of these dimensions.

Conclusions: Río Corrientes as an Emblematic Struggle

In the debates over extractive industry, democracy, and development in Peru, much is made of so-called "emblematic cases" (*casos emblematicos*). These cases are emblematic in the sense that a series of critical issues come together in ways that illustrate the essence of the *problematique* of extractive industries, while also illuminating means of moving beyond the dead ends and polarizations that so frequently characterize conflicts over extraction. The experiences in Río Corrientes have become one such emblematic case. Thus, when national indigenous leaders spoke during Amazon-wide mobilizations in 2008 and 2009, they frequently referred to Río Corrientes as an example of how fossil fuel exploitation, extractive industries, and the expansion of capitalism throughout the region threatened their way of life and even their survival as indigenous people. In the same vein, the documented environmental and human health impacts of Pluspetrol's activities in the Río Corrientes area are used by researchers as a tangible and proven example of the threats that extractive industry presents to indigenous people in general (Orta Martínez et al. 2007). Meanwhile, the Ombudsman's Office views the case as emblematic in that it is a clear-cut instance in which the government's own documentation demonstrated violation of indigenous peoples' rights as a consequence of the state's own action and inaction, and in which parts of the state *knew* that this was occurring and still did not respond. Indeed, the case was deemed so emblematic by the Ombundsman's Office that this was the only time it had agreed to mediate a negotiation process and monitor compliance with agreements drawn up among government, companies, and citizens. For their part, political commentators have referred to this as an example of indigenous peoples' capacity and willingness to react to a situation and coordinate their organizations' and allies' efforts in order to consolidate their movement and effect change. Finally, the experience culminating in the Dorissa Accord and its aftermath has also been viewed as a demonstration that conflict *can* lay the basis for negotiated settlements in which the local population makes a genuine gain, the state becomes more involved as a regulatory body, and the population is still nonetheless able to continue exercising political pressure when the need arises.

In addition to being *politically* emblematic, Río Corrientes is also a *conceptually* emblematic experience. First, it reveals, in sharp detail, not only the ways in which extractive industry transforms territorial dynamics and human well-being, but also that subterranean struggle can, in turn, shift the nature of the relationship between extraction and environment—in this instance, by shifting practices of governance. Second, it demonstrates how and why conflicts over extraction are never only local, and that the resources mobilized in these conflicts are at once international, national, and subnational. Third, the case is a call to recognize the multifaceted nature of the state, even in its relationships to neoliberalism. The actions and role of the Ombudsman's office, as well as of parts of the Ministry of Health, demonstrate that the convergences between state practices and neoliberal commitments need not be complete, and that elements of the state can work in ways that counter the normative commitments to neoliberalism that other parts of the state apparatus reveal. This does not deny the important neoliberal and capitalist commitments within the Peruvian state (witness MINEM's identification with the interests of Pluspetrol). It does, however, suggest the importance of recognizing that this relationship varies across different parts of the state. Fourth, and perhaps most importantly, the experience shows the importance of not fetishizing struggle and conflict. This is a case in which direct action and formal negotiation are each parts of the repertoire of tactics used by a social movement and can coexist and be used simultaneously by different parts of the movement.

There is a further important lesson to be drawn from this case, which is not simply that "the devil is in the details," but rather, that details have causal effects. In this instance, the specificities of the negotiating process have had material implications for subsequent events and for what, in the final instance, a process of struggle was able to achieve. Had the first Accord not been overturned, subsequent levels of conflict, patterns of environmental remediation, and health care would likely have been quite different from what has actually occurred. And this would not have happened had not particular advisors and allies been involved and been so persistent. The same point applies to various themes in this case: the tensions between FECONACO and FEPIBAC, the choice of staff in the Ombudsman's Office, the timing of the change in the Presidency in the regional government, and so on. The general point is that in tracing these political ecologies of extraction, tracking details such as these matters greatly to the causal accounts that are given.

Finally, this case should perhaps be seen as *normatively* emblematic. More than any other case discussed in this book, Río Corrientes makes clear that there is no endpoint in the struggle to protect human rights and well-being in the face of extractive industry. On the one hand, the case shows that even when the situation is desperate, there is room to make significant gains in the fields of human and environmental rights. On the other hand, it also reveals that those gains are never assured because they can always be undermined or reversed. In that sense, the case demonstrates that in the pursuit of human development, there will always be a critical role for subterranean struggle.

Acknowledgments

This research was funded by a research grant (Grant Number RES 167-25-0170) from the UK Economic and Social Research Council through a program cofinanced by the UK Department for International Development. The authors thank Alberto Chirif, Lucila Pautrat, and Lily La Torre for comments on an earlier version of the chapter. Although we have taken their comments into account upon revising the chapter, we assume responsibility for the opinions expressed. We also thank Wendy Pinedo and Nick Scarle for their help with Figure 7.1.

Notes

1. These are lines along which explosives are detonated as part of the exploration process.

2. *Produced water* refers to water extracted with oil and then discharged into the environment. It often has high temperatures and dissolved salts and heavy metals such as barium, cadmium, arsenic, and lead that make it highly toxic for human health and damaging to the environment. One of the achievements of the indigenous struggle was to persuade the oil company to reinject this water into the oil reservoir, a technique often employed to force oil out of reservoirs nearing depletion.

3. Here we draw on interviews.

4. Interviews with Roberto Ramallo and Marisol Rodríguez Vargas, 31 March 2009.

5. The latter is now called OSINERGMIN (Energy and Mining Regulatory Commission).

6. See http://www.servindi.org/actualidad/164/164.

7. On the Ombudswoman's Office and its role, see Leys (2010) and Pegram (2008).

8. See "Documental: Una muerte en Sion, explotación del territorio Achuar," http://lamula.pe/2009/06/documental-una-muerte-en-sion-explotacin-del-territorio-achuar/.

9. Here we draw on interviews with different indigenous leaders.

10. Interviews with Roberto Ramallo and Marisol Rodríguez Vargas, 31 March 2009.

11. Personal communication from Lily La Torre, 17 December 2009.

12. See *La República*, Wednesday, 28 October 2006, http://www.larepublica.com .pe/component/option,com_contentant/task,view/id,128112/Itemid,0/.

13. In January 2013 the former Ombudswoman, Dr. Beatriz Merino, was elected president of the Peruvian Hydrocarbon Society (Sociedad Nacional de Hidrocarburos, SNH), representing some 16 companies. At SNH's launch, she called for public policies promoting hydrocarbons and a redesign of state institutions to establish an efficient regulatory framework. She also affirmed hydrocarbon companies' support for the law of prior consultation and emphasized the importance of dialogue and participation. ("Beatriz . . ." March 11, 2013, http://www.actualidadambiental.pe/?p=18283.)

14. In April 2012 regulations were issued for the implementation of the 2011 law of prior consultation of indigenous peoples as required by ILO Convention 169. However, a coalition of indigenous organizations in the Pastaza, Corrientes, and Tigre basins impacted by hydrocarbon operations made remediation of past environmental damage a condition for participating in this mechanism. Despite four government reports documenting damage to human health and the environment, it was not until such damage was shown on national television that a state of environmental emergency was declared. ("Entidades . . ." Feb. 27, 2013, http://www.servindi.org /actualidad/83244; "Perú: Declaran . . ." March 26, 2013, http://www.servindi.org /actualidad/84680.)

15. The plan was prepared by DIRESA and FECONACO together.

16. Peru's Ministry of Economy and Finance (Ministerio de Economía y Finanzas, MEF) designed the National Public Investment System (Sistema Nacional de Inversión Pública, SNIP), whose purpose is to optimize the use of public resources allocated to investment by promoting the development of a "culture of projects." There is a series of requirements for investment plan preparation as well as a special methodology that demands that those in charge of drafting the projects have a certain level of education and training.

17. See http://diariolaregion.com/web/2010/08/09/sobre-incumplimiento-del -acta-de-dorissa/.

18. Interview with Henderson Rengifo (former FECONACO president), 14 July 2009.

19. Interview with Petronila Chumpi (another FECONACO leader), 28 March 2009.

20. In this regard, it is worth noting that MINEM Vice-Minister Pedro Gamio was a former employee of Repsol and Chevron.

21. If there are few or no extrinsic rewards (such as pay) for social movement participants, intrinsic rewards are sought. These are more available during the excitement of a campaign and less prevalent during the process of implementation. The reverse tends to be the case for state and company functionaries. Campaigns are seen as potential threats and nuisances (i.e., negative intrinsic rewards) while the tedium of implementation is compensated for by monetary compensation and associated extrinsic rewards.

22. Some of these lessons are reflected in the design and strategies of the National Office for Dialogue and Sustainability (Oficina Nacional de Diálogo y Sostenibilidad, ONDS) created in the Prime Minister's Department (Presidencia del Consejo de Ministros, PCM) in 2012 to prevent, manage and transform conflicts.

CHAPTER 8

Synergistic Impacts of Gas and Mining Development in Bolivia's Chiquitanía: The Significance of Analytical Scale

DERRICK HINDERY

Introduction

This chapter sets out to contribute to the growing body of literature on the political ecology of extractive industries by analyzing synergistic environmental and social impacts arising from gas and mining development in Bolivia's eastern lowlands. I use the term *synergistic* to refer to impacts generated by linkages between different forms of resource exploitation, particularly natural gas development, mining, logging, ranching, and hunting. Synergistic impacts are produced by chain reactions occurring at multiple scales within and beyond what Bury and Bebbington (Chapter 2 in this volume) describe as the *extractive complex*. I also use the term more broadly to show how such reactions are, in part, an outgrowth of neoliberal policies, financing, and foreign direct investment (FDI). I argue that in analyzing the consequences of extractive activities, it is critical to ensure that the scale of inquiry transcends single projects, instead considering synergies produced across the extractive complex at a regional level and beyond, and taking into account Latin America's geopolitical economy and economic geography.

In this chapter I focus on the Don Mario gold mine, enabled by Enron and Shell's Cuiabá natural gas pipeline. Linking political and economic dimensions of extraction with impacts revealed or measured through interviews, documents, satellite imagery, and field observations, I respond to calls to seriously address both the *politics* and *ecology* within political ecology (see Chapter 1 in this volume, and Bebbington and Batterbury 2001). Data gathered by the author reveals relationships between neoliberal economic policies, foreign direct investment in mining and gas development, and impacts on indigenous communities, the Chiquitano Forest, and Pantanal Wetlands. Such links have been made elsewhere, in other contexts. In Peru, a variety of neoliberal reforms paved the way for foreign mining investment under Fujimori (Bury 2005), and later under Garcia. Bebbington (2009) has described how in the Peruvian Amazon, Garcia's administration has promoted natural resource-based economic growth by formalizing private property rights and attracting foreign capital in the mining and hydrocarbons sectors. Bury and Norris (Chapter 4 in this volume) explore links to resource conflicts in the Cordillera Huayhuash, Peru. Elsewhere, I have demonstrated how in the hydrocarbons sector, World Bank-funded capitalization (i.e., partial privatization) of Bolivia's state oil company facilitated the entrance of multinational oil corporations such as Enron and Shell, generating significant impacts to the aforementioned ecoregions and indigenous peoples (Hindery 2004, 2013).

Yet, as Bebbington (2009) suggests, governments from across the political spectrum are pursuing extractive models of development throughout Latin America. In Bolivia, an extraction-oriented, developmentalist mindset continues, despite the country's leftward political turn and increased recognition of indigenous rights. Increased revenues are being spent on social programs, but "the human and political costs of such a development strategy can also be significant" (Bebbington 2009, 14). In this context, Latin America's "Open Veins" (Galeano 1970), which have exported primary commodities under exploitative conditions for five centuries, appear to be bleeding increasing amounts of minerals and hydrocarbons regardless of political bent. In the Amazon Basin, various interconnected infrastructure projects—what Soltani and Osborne (1997) have called "arteries for global trade"—have drastically expanded such development, creating new geographies of extraction as economic globalization has taken hold in the region.

Existing literature related to the hydrocarbons sector in Bolivia has primarily focused on the political economy of natural gas and oil in relation to dynamics of social change (Webber 2008) and conflict over distribution of revenues (Kohl and Farthing 2006; Postero 2007; Schroeder 2007). In addition, Kaup (2008) has shown how Bolivia's social movements have used natural gas to both secure and disrupt processes of capital accumulation, affecting the state's ability to regulate the sector financially. With few exceptions (see Chapter 10 in the volume by Bebbington et al.) related research has made important theoretical and empirical contributions, but it does not focus on the consequences of natural gas development on indigenous communities and sensitive ecosystems. In this chapter I seek to do so, giving particular attention to the case of the gas-fired Don Mario gold mine.

Case Background

Although the Cuiabá pipeline crosses both the Chiquitano Forest and Pantanal Wetlands, the discussion here is limited to impacts on the Chiquitano Forest, where the Don Mario mine is located. The Chiquitano Forest has been recognized as globally outstanding with respect to biological distinctiveness (Dinerstein et al. 1995). In the 1990s, a Conservation International Rapid Assessment Program team concluded that the area "may well be the largest remaining tract of relatively undisturbed tall dry forest in the Neotropics, if not the entire world" (Parker et al. 1993).

In 1999, GasOriente Boliviano, a subsidiary of energy corporations Enron (subsequently Ashmore/AEI) and Shell, built the Cuiabá pipeline from Rio San Miguel, Bolivia, to Cuiabá, Brazil, bisecting the middle of the Chiquitano Forest and Pantanal Wetlands. In June 1999, the U.S. export financier, the Overseas Private Investment Corporation (OPIC), provided Board approval for a US$200 million loan to Enron for the pipeline, though by February 2002 OPIC had cancelled the loan and distanced itself from the project. Nonetheless, Enron officials noted that OPIC Board approval had in and of itself provided the "green light" for the commencement of construction through the Chiquitano Forest, rather than around it, along existing roads—the alternative that had been proposed by indigenous and environmental groups (Hindery 2013). Company representatives rejected the proposed alternative route on economic grounds, arguing that they would incur cost overruns and needed to construct the pipeline during the dry season of 1999. They stated that the Brazilian government could fine them US$1 million per day if the pipeline was not functioning by 1 March 2000. Vice-Minister of Sustainable Development Neisa Roca stated she wanted the pipeline to be built along the alternative route but that the Vice-President's Office instructed her to issue the environmental license for the route bisecting the forest (see Figure 8.1). Although company rhetoric highlighted potential fines as the reason the controversial route was preferred, the evidence outlined below suggests Enron and Shell conspired with Empresa Minera Paititi S.A. (EMIPA) to route the pipeline through the forest in order to supply gas to the Don Mario mine.

Mineral concessions at the Don Mario mine are held by EMIPA, a Bolivian subsidiary of Canadian company Orvana Minerals Corporation (Orvana Minerals Corporation 2009). Orvana has interests in three projects located in the Don Mario district, which comprises 70,100 hectares of contiguous concessions and a permanent workforce of 221 employees as of September 2009. According to Orvana's website and annual information forms, since 2002 the company has constructed and managed the Don Mario gold

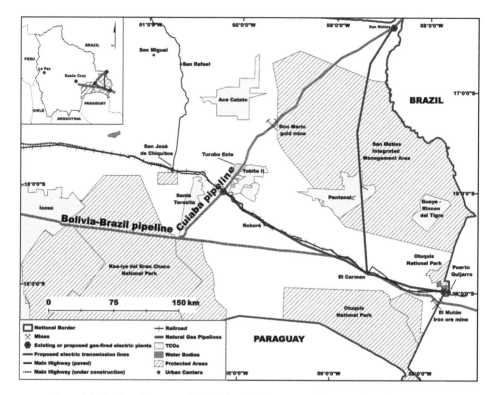

Figure 8.1. Pipelines in eastern Bolivia. Credit: Map prepared by Daniel Redo

mine. Commercial production of the lower mineralized zone (LMZ) began in July 2003 and generated significant cash flow until it was depleted in late 2009. During this period 420,000 ounces of gold were recovered. The company's revenue in 2009 was US$56 million. The company has been mining the lower-grade, adjacent Las Tojas gold deposit (14 km north of the Don Mario mine) since 2009, which was expected to produce gold until mid-2010 (for an estimated 27,000 ounces). In addition, Orvana began copper, gold, and silver production at a third deposit, the upper mineralized zone (UMZ), in 2011, soon after Las Tojas was depleted, and anticipates mining to continue through 2019. Since the latter two projects are smaller in scale and just beginning, in this chapter I focus only on the principal Don Mario deposit in the LMZ.

Links Between the Cuiabá Pipeline and Don Mario Mine

In September 2002, Orvana issued a press release stating that its wholly owned subsidiary, EMIPA, had purchased the Don Mario concession, gold mill plant, and equipment from Compañía Minera del Sur (COMSUR) and planned to build a natural gas-fired plant for the generation of electrical power (Orvana Minerals Corporation 2002). Since I knew the only source of gas near the Don Mario mine was the Cuiabá pipeline, I informed Chiquitano indigenous organizations and traveled to the mine in September 2002 with indigenous representatives and a delegation of nongovernmental organizations (NGOs). We discovered and documented EMIPA excavating a trench for a 4 km pipeline from the Cuiabá pipeline to the Don Mario mine, as well as a gas outtake valve located precisely where the Cuiabá pipeline passes by the mine. Neither the original environmental impact study (EIS) nor the supplemental environmental impact study (SEIA) for the Cuiabá pipeline contemplated the installation of gas outtakes or the construction of this 4 km lateral pipeline. Thus, all of the social and environmental impacts associated with the reactivation of the Don Mario mine can in part be indirectly attributed to the Cuiabá pipeline, which enabled this reactivation in 2003 through the provision of gas for the mine's gas-fired power plant and for smelting dore[1] in the process plant. In turn, the EIS for the main Bolivia-Brazil pipeline, which supplies gas to the Cuiabá pipeline, was also inadequate in its analysis of secondary impacts and, in particular, failed to candidly illustrate the extent to which it would trigger increased extraction and construction of additional pipelines that feed into it or are supplied by it, including the Cuiabá, YABOG, and GASYRG pipelines. With regards to the main pipeline, the only reference made along these lines was a response given during a consultation meeting in which consultants indicated that it would be technically possible for gas to be provided to local towns but that the project did not include such valves (Dames and Moore 1996). Nor did the EIS disclose how the pipeline might supply mines such as the Don Mario mine and El Mutún[2] mine.

Despite these issues, in July 2002 the Vice-Minister of Sustainable Development and Planning, Hernan Cabrera, and the Interim Superintendent of Hydrocarbons, Delfin Pozo Jimenez, granted licenses for this lateral spur pipeline connecting the Cuiabá pipeline to the mine (Ministerio de Desarrollo Sostenible y Planificación 2002). The mine's original environmental license was granted by former Vice-Minister of Sustainable Development Neisa Roca in 1999, the same year that the environmental license for the Cuiabá pipeline was granted. The manner in which these licenses were obtained was not transparent, and Chiquitano communities and representatives were not informed about them. News articles published at the time of the mine's reactivation in 2003 confirm the importance of the Cuiabá pipeline: "Don Mario's feasibility has been enhanced by the routing of the Cuiabá gas pipeline, through which Bolivia exports natural gas to Brazil and which passes close to the property . . . 'A four-inch or six-inch pipeline will be enough [to pump gas] for power generation and eventually for heating, as was the case with Puquio Norte,' the Comibol official said." (Business News Americas 2003).

In 2002, 2006, and 2008, I conducted interviews with representatives from EMIPA and Enron and Shell's subsidiary Transredes about the relationship between the Cuiabá pipeline and Don Mario Mine. Representatives from both companies admitted that during construction of the pipeline, Enron and Shell had left a valve behind precisely where it passes by the mine so that the mine could tap gas from the pipeline in the future (Figure 8.2). This fact was neither mentioned in the pipeline's EISs nor conveyed to stakeholders. Furthermore, a careful examination of the Cuiabá pipeline's route demonstrates that the pipeline cuts through a relatively intact and expansive stretch of Chiquitano forest between San José de Chiquitos and San Matías, yet it veers approximately 15 km to the northwest toward the Don Mario mine, located within this relatively intact stretch of forest, rather than following a straight route directly between the two urban centers (Figure 8.1). In part, the pipeline meanders in order to follow terrain that was most suitable for construction, but such deviations only appear to vary 5 km laterally at most.

The Role of Exiled President Gonzalo Sánchez De Lozada in Relation to the Don Mario Mine and Cuiabá Pipeline

To fully understand the relationship between the Cuiabá pipeline and Don Mario Mine, it is necessary to understand the role of former President Sánchez de Lozada and the World Bank's International Finance Corporation (IFC). The Orvana press release referred to above not only stated that EMIPA planned to build a natural gas-fired plant, but also boasted that former Bolivian President Gonzalo Sánchez de Lozada, who now lives in exile in the United States,[3] had been appointed Chairman of the Board of Directors. On 11 January 2002, Sinchi Wayra S.A.—which, at the time, was an indirect subsidiary of Sánchez de Lozada's own COMSUR—acquired a 52.5 percent controlling interest in Orvana for US$4 million and initiated work on the LMZ of the Don Mario mine (Orvana Minerals Corporation 2003, 2009). Thus, COMSUR, which Sánchez de Lozada founded in 1962,

Figure 8.2. Gas outtake valve where the Cuiabá pipeline crosses the Don Mario mine. Photo: Derrick Hindery, 2 September 2008

effectively took control of Orvana. COMSUR appears to have secured an exceptionally good deal, as the US$4-million-transaction occurred during a period when the gold industry was depressed and Orvana lacked capital (Orvana Minerals Corporation 2003). Orvana laid off employees, and between 28 February 2001 and 11 January 2002 did not have paid employees, instead relying on the Board of Directors and Corporate Secretary to perform all management duties. Under the transaction agreement, COMSUR also arranged financing for the gas-fired plant. In February 2002, COMSUR financed EMIPA's US$8 million purchase of the gold mill plant and equipment from COMSUR's Puquio Norte open-pit gold mine. Thus, COMSUR simply transferred its equipment from Puquio Norte to Don Mario (Business News Americas 2003).

During Sánchez de Lozada's brief second presidency, 2002–2003, his stake in COMSUR was held in trust, until the end of his term (Beltrán 2003). During his first term, 1993–1997, he had championed the implementation of neoliberal economic reforms and had capitalized[4] five nationalized state enterprises, including the state mining company, COMIBOL. Indeed, he had a vested interest in capitalization of COMIBOL, as COMSUR acquired a number of mines that were sold under capitalization (Conaghan, Malloy, and Abugattas 1990). For example, in 1999 Empresa Metalurgico Vinto, the world's fourth largest tin smelter, was sold to British company Allied Deals, which was in turn purchased by COMSUR (Kosich 2008). In what began to look like a corporate shell game for avoiding liability or taxes, subsequently, in 2005, COMSUR sold Vinto to Glencore for US$90 million, but Glencore's Bolivian subsidiary is merely Sinchi Wayra, an indirect subsidiary of COMSUR until 2005. After March 2005, COMSUR undertook corporate reorganization, transferring all common shares held by Sinchi Wayra, along with a debenture of Orvana in the amount of approximately US$90 million (the same amount as Vinto) to Fabulosa Mines Limited, a wholly owned subsidiary of COMSUR (Orvana Minerals Corporation 2009).

Bolivian President Evo Morales forcefully declared that all of Sánchez de Lozada's companies must return to the state:

> "The Vinto Mining Complex was created in 1971 and acquired in 2005 by Glencore from ex-President Gonzalo Sánchez de Lozada (2002–2003) as part of the transfer of shares from Compañía Minera del Sur (Comsur). Glencore, through its affiliate Sinchi Wayra, paid the ex-President approximately 200 million dollars for 62 percent of Comsur's shares and an additional 90 million for Vinto. Vinto was transferred to private hands 'for the price of a dead hen' and in a fraudulent manner in the decade of the nineties,

claimed the President [Morales]. 'The ex-President Gonzalo Sánchez de Lozada took possession of this company. I want to say and warn that all of those companies that were Goni's[5] must return to the Bolivian State." (Bolpress 2007)

Morales nationalized Vinto in 2007 and subsequently also nationalized Glencore's Colquiri mine in 2012 (Nuthall and Dyson 2012). Sánchez de Lozada was also linked to the Cuiabá pipeline, as his administration capitalized state oil company YPFB in 1997, which was partially acquired by Enron, Shell, and other multinational oil corporations. Since that time there has been considerable controversy regarding Sánchez de Lozada's interest in capitalization, which has been the subject of investigation by Bolivia's Chamber of Deputies (Cámara de Diputados). For instance, Sánchez de Lozada signed the original contract with Enron in 1994 during the Summit of the Americas in Miami, which gave Enron exclusive rights to construction of pipelines in Bolivia and guaranteed annual returns of 18.5 percent on investments (Petropress 2000). Congressional deputy Andrés Soliz Rada, who was a member of the Investigatory Commission for the Enron case, stated that Sánchez de Lozada had requested permission from Congress to travel to the summit but never mentioned signing a contract with Enron. The controversy continues through to the time of this writing. In April 2009, Bolivia's Supreme Court requested that Congress decide whether legal action should be taken against Sánchez de Lozada, former Vice President Victor Hugo Cardenas, various former ministers, and former legal representatives of Enron for crimes related to the signing of contracts with Enron (Los Tiempos 2009). In 2008, the Morales administration formally requested the United States to extradite Sánchez de Lozada and two of his former ministers for charges associated with the 2003 Gas War, including homicide, torture, and crimes against freedom of the press (The Democracy Center 2009). At the time of this writing, the United States had not responded to the government's request (Human Rights Watch 2012).

Gas export data for the Cuiabá pipeline also reveal a compelling link between the pipeline and the Don Mario mine. Individuals I interviewed from Enron and Shell's subsidiaries, Ashmore, and NGOs stated that since construction ended the Cuiabá pipeline has largely not been exporting gas to the endpoint of the pipeline, the 480 MW gas-fired power plant in Cuiabá, Brazil. In January 2009, an Ashmore spokesperson told me that the power plant operated with gas from the pipeline for some time, but then ceased to function because of gas shortages. Ashmore's website states that its Brazilian subsidiary Empresa Productora de Energía Ltda (EPE), the operator of the

Cuiabá gas-fired power plant, has not operated since August 2007 because of lack of gas supply.[6] Data from YPFB and Ashmore's Brazilian subsidiary Gas-Ocidente do Mato Grosso Ltda (GOM) confirm there has been insufficient supply. An official I interviewed at YPFB in 2008 stated this was because the volume of gas that had been committed for export through the Bolivia–Brazil pipeline did not leave sufficient gas for export to Cuiabá. Data from GOM show that although the Cuiabá pipeline was scheduled to deliver 403 million cubic meters to the Cuiabá power plant in 2008, only 9 million cubic meters were actually delivered (excluding data for November 2008, which are absent) (GasOcidente 2010).

The shortage of gas supply to the Cuiabá plant raises an important question. Since Enron and Shell justified the Cuiabá pipeline project based on its potential to supply gas to the Cuiabá plant, then why has the Don Mario mine always received gas since its reactivation in 2003, while the Cuiabá plant has not? Although it is difficult to determine underlying motive(s), the entire body of evidence outlined above suggests that for some reason(s), since 2003 provision of gas to the Don Mario mine was clearly prioritized over exporting it to the Cuiabá plant. This itself suggests the importance of the relationship between the pipeline and the mine and also supports the argument that rather than follow alternative routes, the pipeline bisected the forest precisely so that it could pass by the mine. In fact, despite the fact that the Cuiabá pipeline supplied no gas in 2009 (GasOcidente 2010) — 293 million cubic meters were supposed to have been delivered — Orvana's 2009 Annual Information Report notes that the company was awaiting the government's signature of a new contract to supply the Don Mario mine with gas: "As a result of legislation passed by the Bolivian Congress, the Company was required to negotiate a new natural gas supply contract with a government-owned entity. The Company has signed a new contract for natural gas and is awaiting the signature of the government. The new contract was effective from September 17, 2008 and is not expected to have a material impact on the Company's costs" (Orvana Minerals Corporation 2009, 34).

In 2010 EMIPA and the government signed the contract, which will not expire until 2016 (Orvana Minerals Corporation 2010). This is significant in that the contract was negotiated with the Morales administration, which renegotiated contracts with various multinational oil corporations since "nationalization" began in 2006. Although the terms of this particular contract are not publically available, the fact that EMIPA was able to renegotiate a contract in which the government authorized provision of gas to the privately owned mine suggests that the Morales administration continued to prioritize economic growth based on extractive industries. As noted in Chapters 1 and 3 of this volume, extraction was central in the politics that led to the election of Morales. Morales' party, The Movement for Socialism (MAS), has clearly argued that the state needs to promote extraction in order to generate surplus for redistribution, especially to historically marginalized groups. Presumably the new contract between EMIPA and the government will increase the amount of revenue generated for the government and decrease EMIPA's share.

Involvement of the World Bank Group's IFC in the Don Mario Mine

The private-sector investment and loan arm of the World Bank Group, the IFC, held 11.1 percent equity in COMSUR (Compliance Advisor/Ombudsman 2003, 19). In June 2003, the regional indigenous organization Coordinadora de Pueblos Étnicos de Santa Cruz (CPESC) therefore submitted a formal complaint to the Office of the Compliance Advisor/Ombudsman (CAO) of the International Finance Corporation about the Don Mario mine. The letter cited concern about lack of consultation and timely provision of adequate information about the project, the absence of a compensation program for indigenous peoples, potential social and environmental impacts, and a flawed EIS (CPESC 2003). It called upon the World Bank to terminate financing, requested compensation, and asked for sanctions to be imposed based upon violations of the Bolivian Environmental Law, International Labor Organization Convention 169, and World Bank operational guidelines regarding indigenous peoples, the environment, and project supervision. In response, the CAO undertook a 10 day long investigation, which included visits to the mine, visits to affected Chiquitano communities, and meetings with the NGO Colectivo de Estudios Aplicados al Desarrollo Social (CEADES, Collective for Applied Social Development Studies), IFC's Bolivia office, the Ministry of Sustainable Development, and the Defensoría del Pueblo (the Bolivian Ombudsman's office). The compliance audit, which was completed in June 2004, recommended that the IFC develop a transparent and predictable complaint resolution, form strategic partnerships to help improve COMSUR's social and environmental performance, and deepen public consultation. However, a report produced by Chiquitano indigenous organizations in 2005 noted various examples of lack of compliance with the CAO's recommendations, including the fact that COMSUR continued to fail to share information openly and transparently (PC TURUBO et al. 2005).

Issues Related to the Indigenous Peoples Development Plan

Although EMIPA obtained environmental licenses from the Bolivian government to operate the mine and 4 km pipeline, the company did not obtain free, prior, and informed consent from affected communities and did not offer a compensation program, which was a violation of Article 15 of the Mining Code and International Labor Organization Convention 169 (ratified as *Ley 1257* [Law 1257] in Bolivia). Also, given the World Bank IFC's interest in the mine, the lack of development of a compensation program at the inception of the project violated World Bank Operational Directive 4.20 (subsequently replaced by OP 4.10), which requires implementation of an indigenous peoples development plan prepared in tandem with the development of a project. A subsequent audit by the IFC's CAO found that COMSUR's consultations for the EIS did not meet a standard that the CAO considered should be acceptable to the IFC (Compliance Advisor/Ombudsman 2003). Community members from one community requested that COMSUR finance an educational project, potable water, and a soccer field, but the company rejected their proposal. At first, the company did not accept that five Chiquitano communities closest to the mine were indigenous (OICH and CEADES 2005). In response to these issues and deficiencies noted in the EIS,[7] communities living near the mine mobilized in conjunction with CEADES, pressuring EMIPA and the IFC to develop a comprehensive compensation program through letters, press outreach, and negotiations. During this period, Chiquitano indigenous organizations denounced company attempts to donate diesel and offer employment to leaders (OICH and CEADES 2005). The former, along with CEADES, highlighted links between exiled President Sanchez de Lozada, party politics, the IFC, and the mine to garner media attention. Thus, as with the cases outlined in Perrault and Bebbington et al.'s chapters in this volume (Chapters 3 and 10 respectively), extraction is intimately tied to political struggle. In 2006, three years after the mine had begun to operate, the company agreed to finance a five year long, US$620,000 compensation program, the Indigenous Peoples Development Plan, or PDI. Some community members were concerned that the amount was significantly lower than the US$3.6 million that an independent consultant had recommended. One individual perceived compensation to be inequitable in relation to the mine's overall profits: "For me what the mine is providing is very little because the mine profits enough in one day, yet just gives us a crumb."[8] In addition, there were complaints that the program compensated only five communities in the vicinity of the mine, but not those located farther away that could be affected indirectly.

The PDI consisted of a variety of community development projects, including educational support, sanitation, purchasing of community goods and services, organizational strengthening, environmental monitoring, agriculture (yucca, maize, vegetables, sugarcane, pasture), cattle raising, pig farming, fish farming, beekeeping, and carpentry. Interviews conducted in 2006 and 2008 reveal mixed reactions about the program, but in general many community members were more content with it than they were with the PDI for the Cuiabá pipeline. However, a number of problems were reported. One regional Chiquitano leader commented that the program was systemically flawed because it was not developed in a bottom-up manner, based on needs identified by the communities, but rather was based on needs identified by the mine's consultants. Some community members elaborated on this point, stating that the cattle project was the only successful community development initiative because of greater community buy-in and experience with cattle raising. In general PDI participants noted a lack of technical support and follow-through. One individual alleged that the pig farming project failed because it was imposed by the company and lacked technical and veterinary support. Community members stated that a fish farm failed because the soil was acidic, the fish were not fit for the local environment, and the embankment of the fishpond ruptured during heavy rains. Fish were reportedly Pacú (*Colossoma macropomum*) brought from the Chapare region. Similarly, the beekeeping project reportedly failed because the bees were not native.

Reports noting future expansion of the mine raised concern amongst affected communities that once again they might not be consulted or compensated if they did not engage in acts of pressure. Orvana's 2009 Annual Information Form details the need to update the existing environmental permit for the Don Mario mine because of the projected installation of a sulfuric acid plant to leach ore from the oxide and transition zones of the anticipated UMZ project. An EIS is being prepared by a Bolivian consulting company, but it does not appear that Chiquitano communities have been informed thus far. In fact, the Annual Information Form states that the study will include the "design of a strategic community information plan in order to minimize any negative perception the community might have in relation with the project." This statement contravenes various Bolivian and international laws regarding consultation and free, prior, and informed consent.

Environmental Impacts

Deforestation at the Mine and Along Access Roads

At the Don Mario mine, forest was cleared for the mine, fresh water reservoir, 4 km lateral pipeline, workers camp, processing plant, airstrip, and tailings pond. The largest patch of clearing was for the tailings pond, which amounted to approximately 47 hectares (Figure 8.3). Thus, forest clearing exceeded the 36 hectares authorized by the San Jose de Chiquitos Forest Operation Unit of the Santa Cruz government's Superintendencia Forestal in 2002 (Superintendencia Forestal 2002). In this administrative resolution, the agency charged Bs 68,664 for the timber extracted from the clearing, reportedly in accordance with the Forestry Law (*Ley Forestal 1700*). In 2005, the mine again requested permission for forest clearing, for 85,548 hectares, which nearly totaled the entire size of the Don Mario district. Curiously, the Superintendencia Forestal authorized the clearing, and only charged Bs 68,664 (Superintendencia Forestal 2005). Why such a vast amount was authorized is unclear. Community members allude to rampant corruption at the agency. Despite this authorization, a preliminary analysis of May 2004 SPOT satellite imagery shows that only approximately 150 hectares were deforested in the district.

It appears that deforestation along the road to the mine is considerably greater than that which occurred at the mine itself. Although the road to the mine was originally built for logging, mining exploration, and a limited amount of production that occurred prior to the mine's major reactivation in 2003, during construction of the Cuiabá pipeline (1999–2000), Enron and Shell's consortium GasOriente Boliviano maintained and restored the road. In addition, a 2008 interview confirmed that EMIPA improved the road between the mine and Taperas since then.

The EIS for the bi-oceanic highway notes that the stretch of Chiquitano Forest located in the vicinity of the Don Mario mine (the north-central Chiquitanía) has been historically isolated because of a lack of transitable roads, but recently, because of various private initiatives, including the mine, Cuiabá pipeline, and logging, the area is becoming less isolated (Consorcio Prime Engenharia, Museo Noel Kempff Mercado, and Asociación Potlatch 2000, 4.13.2.). Moreover, secondary logging roads and the Don Mario mine road have accelerated logging and deforestation in the region.

"Until very recently, the only access [to the Chiquitano Forest ecoregion] was a rustic road between San Juan de Chiquitos and Candelaria del Río Mercedes, which is used to herd cattle from ranches in the Pantanal of San Matías, to bring them to the railroad near Taperas. Recently, forestry companies have established various secondary roads, and, together with the Don Mario mine, have significantly improved the southern sector of this road, including the construction of a bridge over Río Tucavaca. The construction of the Cuiabá pipeline also represents another new incursion into this zone of pristine forests. Until recently, the level of deforestation in this sector was nearly nil, but in 1999 a ranch established to the north of the Community of San Juan deforested approximately 10,000 hectares. Evidently, the investor has not undertaken studies or permits required by the Superintendencias Agraria and Forestal, and currently is the object of legal action." (Consorcio Prime Engenharia, Museo Noel Kempff Mercado, and Asociación Potlatch 2000, 10.2.3.3.)

While it is unclear exactly which ranch this excerpt refers to, preliminary analysis of May 2004 SPOT satellite imagery and 2002 Landsat imagery appears to show that at least 1,500 hectares had been deforested along the road for one or more ranches to the south of the ranch outlined in red, depicted in Figure 8.3. Since these are the only two areas of significant clearing along the road to the mine, it is likely that the excerpt refers to the ranch(es) to the south. With regards to the ranch outlined in red, the amount of forest cleared is approximately 890 hectares. Based on analysis of the imagery previously noted, clearing appears to have occurred after 2002, when the mine was being reactivated, and when the road was improved further. There is at least one additional access road leading to the west of this clearing, but the transitability of the road appears to be inferior to that of the mine road. Thus, this clearing can be associated with mine reactivation, which was enabled by gas supply from the Cuiabá pipeline. This finding refutes IFC's statement that clearing along the access road to Don Mario is thought to be largely unrelated to the

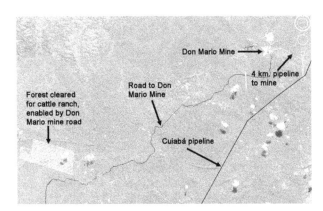

Figure 8.3.
Satellite image of Don Mario mine, gas pipeline, and forest clearance

mine (Compliance Advisor/Ombudsman 2004, 3). However, it does appear that clearing for the ranch(es) to the south of the 890 ha ranch, along the mine road, occurred prior to 2003. Nonetheless, this clearing is still likely associated with prior exploitation of the mine, as it occurs along the mine road.

Logging and Hunting

Authorized and unauthorized logging in the vicinity of the mine has occurred at the mine itself, along the road between the mine and the bi-oceanic highway, along the Cuiabá pipeline right-of-way (ROW), and at cattle ranches accessible by the mine road (Figure 8.3). Logging is the principal commercial activity in the area, with concessions to two companies with sawmills at San Juan and Buena Vista, the communities closest to the mine.

Based on interviews and field observation, lack of reforestation and afforestation of the Cuiabá pipeline ROW in the vicinity of the mine, which was required by the EIS, coupled with inadequate or nonexistent barriers where the pipeline crosses roads or private properties, facilitated entrance of unauthorized loggers, hunters, and livestock. This finding is consistent with Dourojeanni, Barandiarán, and Dourojeanni's (2009) claim that although moderate deforestation is typically associated with construction of pipeline ROWs, subsequent agricultural clearing, logging, and hunting along them can ensue. Some community members and mine officials have also alleged that narcotraffickers and biopirates have used the ROW. In 2002, Chiquitano community members stated that workers from the Don Mario mine had entered the pipeline ROW to hunt and log. Soil degradation has resulted because of forest clearing for the ROW and entrance of livestock. Grasses and other combustible vegetation have proliferated, increasing fire risk. Burnt sections of the ROW were observed near Ipias. These impacts violate section 8.10 of the pipeline's EIS (Erosion Control and Revegetation Plan), the environmental license, and the Plan of Corrected Measures issued by the Ministry of Sustainable Development in 2003. On-site observations in 2006 and 2008 revealed that the ROW for the 4 km lateral pipeline to the mine had been afforested significantly better than the Cuiabá pipeline (near the pipeline juncture), but there was a maintenance road cutting down the middle of the 4 km ROW, which I drove along with mine employees.

In August 2006, a resident of San Jose de Chiquitos told me he worked clearing forest at a cattle ranch located along the road to the mine. He said the ranch is just a veneer, and that massive illegal logging occurs there. In addition, he noted that hunting occurs in the area too, around pools of water. The individual also reported an abundance of animals, including tapir, jaguar, pumas, deer, foxes, and monkeys. An unauthorized logger I interviewed in August 2007 stated that he sells logs to a Brazilian mill located along the mine road. He said that increasing numbers of unauthorized loggers were coming from Brazil in order to avoid stricter environmental laws and enforcement. Unauthorized Brazilian loggers were observed in August 2006. One Chiquitano community member expressed concern that rural electrification along the mine road, enabled by electricity supplied by the Ipias gas-fired power plant (which uses gas from the Cuiabá pipeline) was increasing the capacity of sawmills and associated logging. Community accounts suggest that EMIPA partly financed this electrification.

In 2008, Chiquitano community members living in the vicinity of the mine suggested that EMIPA should finance checkpoints to curtail illegal logging along the mining road. However, a representative from the mine commented that the company had supported one checkpoint, which was dismantled shortly after it was erected, and stated that some Chiquitano community members had discouraged such posts, suggesting they were implicated in logging. He stated that in March 2008 the mine submitted a formal complaint to the Forestry Superintendent that several community members had logged Bolivian Rosewood (*Machaerium scleroxylon*). There are differences of opinion amongst community members with respect to logging and checkpoints. One individual claimed that the company simply lost the political will to follow through with the idea after the checkpoint was dismantled, which he lamented because he viewed it as an effective means to reduce not only logging, but also hunting, narcotrafficking, and biopiracy. The same community member reported that unauthorized loggers had dismantled the control post. Yet a local Chiquitano leader said that one of the original arguments for the creation of the PDI was to discourage community members from unauthorized logging, through the creation of alternative community development projects. A number of other Chiquitano community members attested that some community members were involved in logging.

Issues Related to the Tailings Pond

According to mine staff interviewed in 2006, the tailings pond was engineered to withstand a 500 year flood and is lined with an impermeable 1.5 mm high density polyethylene (HDPE) membrane barrier. However, neither the canal surrounding the tailings pond nor the area in between the canal and the tailings pond is lined. Tailings pipes sit in a trench lined with HDPE, but the trench is only approximately 0.3 m deep. In addition, there is no retaining wall lined with an impermeable barrier around the perimeter of the

pond. A number of Chiquitano community members and indigenous organizations alleged the tailings pond overflowed on 13 December 2004 (OICH
and CEADES 2005), but mining officials dismissed this, claiming that only
the freshwater reservoir overflowed during the 2004–2005 rainy season. Indigenous leaders complained they were not allowed to inspect the mine until
two months after the event, when they observed the company expanding the
tailings pond, which was not specified in the EIS. They were able to inspect
only the tailings pond, but not the settling tank. They further claimed that
the company's own reports showed that in 2004 the amount of precipitation
that fell exceeded what the tailing pond could withstand, according to the
EIS. The company's reluctance to heed the Chiquitanos' request is inconsis-
tent with the CAO's recommendation that the company respond to community concerns through improved dialogue and outreach (Compliance Advisor/
Ombudsman 2004). An independent investigation has not been conducted to
corroborate either of these claims.

Impact on wildlife is also of concern, given the high levels of biodiversity
present in the Chiquitano Forest and immediately adjacent Pantanal Wetlands, a few kilometers from the mine. EMIPA notes the following numbers
of species in the area: 33 mammals, 106 birds, 23 reptiles, 14 amphibians, and
22 fish (e.g., tapirs, anteaters, capybaras, toucans, and turtles). The company
states that it protects wildlife by training workers and posting signs that prohibit hunting, fishing, logging, burning, and wildlife trade. Birds are scared
off from landing on the tailings pond with a siren and firecrackers. Company
Powerpoint presentations and reports (Orvana Minerals Corporation 2009)
allege that fences have been built around the pond, but none were observed
(Figure 8.4). Community members claim to have seen wildlife entering the
pond. These observations and those detailed previously with respect to hunting are contrary to statements made in an IFC publication entitled "A Guide
to Biodiversity for the Private Sector," which uses the mine as a hallmark example of how private sector companies have met the challenges of biodiversity
management (IFC 2006). It applauds the mine's "biodiversity management
actions" of banning hunting and of fencing off the tailings facility.

EMIPA only monitors water contamination (e.g., by arsenic, cyanide, cadmium, lead, manganese) at two wells located next to the tailings pond. However, the wells do not adequately cover the entire perimeter of the pond, tailings pipes, processing plant, and chemical storage areas. The wells are located
at the north end, below the tailings dam (Figure 8.4). Whether or not the
pond is stable is another concern. The pond was built on fill material in accordance with an engineering study, but it appears that it could be prone to
slippage due to inadequate drainage.

Figure 8.4. Don Mario Mine tailing pond; note high density polyethylene membrane, animal siren, and mine in background. Photo: Derrick Hindery, 5 August 2006

A regional Chiquitano leader emphatically stressed the need for an independent commission to investigate potential contamination and conduct sampling of groundwater, surface water, soil, plants, and animals. Another community member expressed concerned about how tailings will be managed after the mine closes. According to a 2009 report, Orvana anticipates expanding its tailings dam facilities, including conducting a stability analysis and raising of the dam to accommodate continued production (Orvana Minerals Corporation 2009). The report also states that when mining is complete, residual cyanide will be naturally destroyed through exposure to sunlight and oxygen and that the saturated tailings will be capped, causing remaining cyanide to precipitate out as stable iron isotopes, such that there would be no danger even if the liner eventually failed. However, there is no analysis of the environmental fate or remediation of other contaminants.

Besides concern about contamination stemming from the tailings ponds and other facilities at the mine, community members expressed concern that hazardous chemicals could spill from speeding mine vehicles, and that the contingency plan is insufficient since it can take up to two hours for staff from the mine to reach the community. One community member vehemently complained that company vehicles traveled up to 120 kph through his community, suggesting they should be required to reduce their speed to 30 kph, build speed bumps, and cross the community using a peripheral road. He reported an incident in which a child found a barrel that fell off a company vehicle in his community that was leaking an acidic substance that produced a vapor cloud. Company representatives claimed this was merely carbonated water. Although neither claim could be corroborated, a review of substances authorized by the Ministerio de Gobierno and the Ministerio de Desarrollo Sostenible y Planificación shows the following substances were authorized for transport: sodium cyanide, ammonium nitrate and other explosives, sulfuric acid, hydrochloric acid, sodium hydroxide, potassium hydroxide, calcium hydroxide, calcium oxide, quicklime, diesel, heavy oils and lubricants, acetone, nitric acid, sodium borate, sodium carbonate, silver nitrate, lead oxide, silica, gasoline, and natural gas (Ministerio de Desarrollo Sostenible y Planificación 2003; Ministerio de Gobierno 2002).

Water Supply Issues

Groundwater at the Don Mario district is scarce, and surface water is only present during the rainy season. Consequently, the mine built a freshwater dike to store water. Staff claim the reservoir is positive because it attracts wildlife, yet no studies have been undertaken to corroborate this, or to determine environmental impacts such as whether the building of the reservoir has led to increased exposure to toxins associated with the mine (e.g., through fugitive dust emissions or contact with the tailings pond).

Future Expansion

As mentioned previously, EMIPA began mining the adjacent lower-grade Las Tojas gold deposit in 2009. It expects to mine the UMZ from 2010 through 2019. Existing infrastructure at the Don Mario mine will be used, which includes facilities dependent on gas from the Cuiabá pipeline. Hence, all impacts of these expansion projects will be cumulative and associated impacts of the Cuiabá pipeline, none of which were mentioned in the pipeline's EIS.

Synergies with the Bi-Oceanic Highway and Initiative for the Integration of Regional Infrastructure in South America (IIRSA)

In much of this chapter I have addressed synergistic impacts of the Don Mario mine associated with the Cuiabá pipeline and, to a lesser extent, the Bolivia–Brazil pipeline. Other projects underway or planned in the region will likely exacerbate these impacts. The bi-oceanic highway, financed by the Inter-American Development Bank, will probably have the most significant repercussions, as discussed in the project's EIS:

> The gold is already exploited in Puquio Norte (San Ramón) and the estimated longevity of the mine is 7 years, meaning that the highway does not represent a potential benefit since the mineral is to be exhausted before the highway is completed. The same could occur with the Don Mario mine, which already benefits from the proximity of the [Cuiabá] pipeline, and which will benefit substantially from the highway, since its principal road link will be with the city of San José. (Consorcio Prime Engenharia, Museo Noel Kempff Mercado, and Asociación Potlatch 2000, 10.2–6)

The nongovernmental organization CEADES and Chiquitano Indigenous Organization (OICH) have made similar observations:

> The most noteworthy impacts caused by activities related to the highway are the following: New mining companies that will cause additional social and environmental impacts in the area . . . Moreover, mining companies are already operating in the Chiquitanía, causing significant social and environmental impacts, such as Mutún and the Don Mario mine. The highway will accelerate the impact of these mines, attracting colonists and facilitating transport of contaminated materials." (Organización Indígena Chiquitana et al. 2007, 101)

Although beyond the scope of this chapter, it is worthwhile noting that synergies will likely occur with planned and existing projects promoted by the Initiative for the Integration of Regional Infrastructure in South America (IIRSA),[9] including industrial waterways, railroads, and roads that will connect to the bi-oceanic highway, thereby facilitating export of minerals from the Don Mario mine.

Discussion and Conclusions: Can't See the "Forest" (Synergistic and Cumulative Impacts) for the "Trees" (Project-Level Impacts)

Synergistic and cumulative impacts examined in relation to the Don Mario gold mine suggest that the scale of analysis undertaken in project EISs bears heavily on the extent to which such impacts are or are not addressed. EISs are required to address cumulative and associated impacts but do not always do so for a variety of reasons, ranging from competence of consultants to difficulties predicting impacts. Dourojeanni, Barandiarán, and Dourojeanni (2009, 129) have elaborated on the latter point in relation to infrastructure projects planned for the Peruvian Amazon: "Environmental, social and economic impacts of each one of the infrastructure projects and use of proposed resources combines and produces synergies in a variety of ways that is not always predictable, and in this case are multiplicative and potentially as serious or more serious than in isolation."

Building on what Bebbington and Bury allude to in Chapter 1 of this volume, projects such as the Don Mario gold mine and Cuiabá pipeline are part of a broader reorganization of Latin America's geopolitical economy and economic geography. Although these projects predate IIRSA, they will likely interact with and amplify impacts associated with IIRSA projects (e.g., gold from the Don Mario mine could be exported along the bi-oceanic highway).

The conspiracy between Enron, Shell, and EMIPA, as detailed in this chapter, reveals that scale of analysis may be intentionally obfuscated. The case of the Don Mario mine is particularly disturbing, as the evidence assembled in this chapter shows that Enron and Shell intentionally left a valve behind precisely where the Cuiabá pipeline passed by the mine. It suggests the companies knew that gas would be extracted from the pipeline yet did not disclose this information in the EIS. From a political ecology framework, it is clear that powerful political and economic interests (namely the oil and mining corporations mentioned in this chapter), financed and perhaps condoned by international financiers, concealed synergistic impacts. Given that the mine's operation is directly dependent on gas from the pipeline, impacts related to the mine are cumulative, associated, and synergistic impacts of the pipeline. As production in the LMZ ceases and production in Las Tojas and the UMZ initiates, impacts resulting from such expansion will also be linked to the pipeline.

More broadly, besides synergistic impacts resulting from the Don Mario mine and Cuiabá pipeline, there were significant synergies between neoliberal economic policies and mining and gas development in the region. Capitalization of the state oil and mining companies, YPFB and COMIBOL, triggered a wave of foreign investment that led to unprecedented impacts on the Chiquitano Forest, Pantanal Wetlands, and Chiquitano indigenous communities affected by the Don Mario mine, enabled by gas from the Cuiabá and Bolivia–Brazil pipelines. In turn, this investment (as well as capitalization) was enabled and amplified by financing from a number of international financial institutions. Although the US$200 million loan from U.S. government agency OPIC triggered construction of the Cuiabá pipeline through the Chiquitano Forest and Pantanal Wetlands, OPIC claimed to have no responsibility in addressing ongoing impacts of the pipeline, since it cancelled the loan in 2002, after Enron's bankruptcy and in the wake of controversial impacts caused by the pipeline.

Similarly, the IFC's financing of COMSUR's operations at the Don Mario mine, through its 11.1 percent equity interest, would suggest shared responsibility with respect to resolving the issues outlined in this chapter. IFC's assessment report on the mine had the stated objectives of resolving the Chiquitanos' complaint and leveraging COMSUR to take corrective action, but evidence presented in this chapter suggests that such goals have not all been met. While some evidence suggests that the IFC financing enhanced EMIPA's mining practices and compliance with domestic and international laws, for the most part the IFC seems to have shirked its responsibility ever since COMSUR ceased to be its client in 2005, despite the persistence of ongoing issues. More broadly, World Bank support for capitalization and modifications of policies, laws, and regulations in the 1990s was paramount in encouraging Enron, Shell, and other oil corporations to invest in the Cuiabá and Bolivia–Brazil gas pipelines (World Bank 1994a, 1994b, 1994c, 2000), which enabled reactivation of the Don Mario mine. It appears that the World Bank has discounted these synergies. The same can be said of international financial institutions that financed the Bolivia–Brazil pipeline, which feeds the Cuiabá pipeline, namely the Inter-American Development Bank, World Bank, Andean Development Corporation (CAF), European Investment Bank, Export-Import Bank of Japan (JEXIM), and Banco Nacional de Desenvolvimento Económico e Social (BNDES).

In July 2004, on the World Bank Group's 60th birthday and at the close of the bank's Extractive Industries Review, approximately 100 indigenous people from 22 communities affected by COMSUR's operations in the south of Potosí marched with Chiquitano community members affected by the company's Puquio Norte and Don Mario gold mines. They held banners stating "COMSUR + World Bank make more poverty" and "COMSUR and World Bank: No to the violation of human rights," demanding compensation for social and environmental damage.[10] Under the administration of Evo

Morales, with the adoption of a New Constitution, old laws and regulations are being modified or scrapped, with many overtures towards the enhancement of provisions relating to indigenous peoples' rights and environmental protection. Some changes were already made in the 2005 Hydrocarbons Law and the 2007 Supreme Decree No. 29033, regulating consultation and decentralized participation of indigenous peoples and *campesinos* in hydrocarbons activities (CEJIS 2008). The 1997 Mining Code (*Ley 1777*), created under the neoliberal administration of Sánchez de Lozada, remains to be modified and still has many elements that contravene International Labor Organization Convention 169 (adopted as *Ley 1257* in Bolivia) (CEADES 2006). Although such legal and regulatory changes hold promise for environmental protection and indigenous peoples' rights, it remains to be seen how they will be implemented and whether they will keep the underlying engines of development in check. Thus far, evidence from the notorious TIPNIS conflict as well as extraction in the Chaco and the Bolivian Amazon suggest limited progress on the ground (Hindery 2013).

Notes

1. Dore is unrefined gold alloy that still needs additional processing to become pure metal.

2. El Mutún is reputedly the world's largest iron ore deposit and is located to the east of the department of Santa Cruz. The Indian steel company Jindal currently has the contract to develop the deposit. The El Mutún project is comprised of both mining activities and an associated smelter and would, if realized, become the largest investment by Indian capital in Latin America.

3. In October 2003, Sánchez de Lozada was ousted from Bolivia during the "Gas War" and currently lives in exile in the United States.

4. Capitalization entails the creation of joint ventures. It differs from privatization in that the money gained from the sale of the state company does not go to the state but, rather, stays with the company to finance future investment (Ewing and Goldmark 1994). Through "capitalization," the Bolivian government sold 50 percent of the equity in the state oil company, YPFB, to various multinational oil corporations, including Enron.

5. *Goni* is a nickname for Sánchez de Lozada.

6. See http://www.aeienergy.com/?id=216.

7. Chiquitano indigenous organizations elaborated a report detailing many violations of the EIS and various domestic and international laws (OICH and CEADES 2005). For instance, the report alleges that the EIS does not even consider impacts to the Pantanal Wetlands, which are located several kilometers downstream from the mine.

8. Interview conducted by the author.

9. The IIRSA is a regional initiative to develop transport, energy, and communi-

cations infrastructure, with participation from twelve South American countries, including Bolivia. See http://www.iirsa.org/index_ENG.asp?CodIdioma=ENG.

10. Action on World Bank's 60th Birthday, July 2004, CEE Bankwatch Network, Friends of the Earth International, Jubilee USA Network, Oilwatch International, Rios Vivos Coalition, Sustainable Energy and Economy Network, 50 Years is Enough Network, http://www.foei.org/en/what-we-do/mining/global/extractive-industries -review/j22.html.

CHAPTER 9

Natural Resources in the Subsoil and Social Conflicts on the Surface: Perspectives on Peru's Subsurface Political Ecology

JULIO C. POSTIGO, MARIANA MONTOYA,
AND KENNETH R. YOUNG

Introduction

It is commonly understood that subsurface natural resources such as minerals and petroleum are owned, controlled, and utilized in ways that are fundamentally different than other kinds of natural resources found on the Earth's surface at the same location. In most countries, the state owns the subsoil and can designate exploration and exploitation rights to other entities such as private companies, sometimes in spite of incompatibility with surface land use and the wishes of land users. This dichotomy of access and of usage rights may lead to conflicts between land users and the state, and potentially between sustainable land uses and extraction of nonrenewable resources. While local land use systems have more potential to be managed in ways that through appropriate agricultural, pastoral, or forest-extraction practices are sensitive to environmental conditions, the removal of mineral and hydrocarbon resources often proceeds despite environmental and other concerns.

The term *critical zone* as used in the earth sciences refers to a cross-section of the uppermost part of the Earth's surface, including the groundwater, soil, vegetation, and the boundary (lowermost) layer of the atmosphere (Anderson, Bales, and Duffy 2008; deB. Richter and Mobley 2009). It has been highlighted for special research and funding attention because it includes processes that have typically been separated by the formal academic disciplines, namely hydrology, soil science, vegetation ecology, and the atmospheric sciences.[1] Previously, there was no research framework for tying together studies on all the fluxes of energy, nutrients, and water that pass from the air into the soil and then into groundwater. We propose that such a focus would enrich political ecology's engagement with the subsurface. In particular, it would connect the study of social and economic power relations with geomorphic and hydrologic process.

Furthermore, we propose that the key to understanding many recent and ongoing social conflicts is through the consideration of the ways that sub-surface rights differ from and complicate surface land rights. We use the in-sights of a nascent subsurface political ecology (see Chapter 1 of this volume), combined with critical zone concerns, to examine several case examples from places in Peru where we have done fieldwork and research on the social and ecological dimensions of resource use and environmental change. We intend these cases to be illustrative of broader patterns and processes found in other parts of the world, such as the importance of social mobilizations and the continuing relevance of the "resource curse," wherein places with many natu-ral resources, ironically, are among the poorest and most negatively affected by activities associated with those very same resources (Atkinson and Hamilton 2003; Davis and Tilton 2005; Stevens and Dietsche 2008). In a review article, Bridge (2004a) developed four major themes that characterize research on these topics: there are important physical and chemical consequences of ex-traction; both socioeconomic costs and benefits of commodity production should be considered in evaluations; there are inherent asymmetries in power among the stakeholders; and there is, therefore, a need to project political ecology into a broader discourse about social and ecological relations through examining the subsurface.

Social and environmental conflicts about lands located above mineral re-sources are current affairs metaphorically resting upon the foundations of more than five centuries of resource extraction in Peru (Thorp and Bertram 1978; Lockhart and Schwartz 1983; Elliott 2007; Postigo 2010), often to the detriment not only of local peoples, but also of the socioeconomic devel-opment of the country (Defensoría del Pueblo 2007; CooperAcción 2010). That these are fundamental concerns, not just the outcome of particular his-torical processes in Peru, is seen through examples in which resource abun-dance "increases the likelihood that countries will experience negative eco-nomic, political and social outcomes" (Rosser 2006). Hence, resource-rich nations grow slower than resource-poor ones (Sachs and Warner 1995) and the places in those countries with the most metals and minerals are often the most contaminated and least benefited in terms of sustainable develop-ment (Ross 1999; Rosser 2006). They may be prone to civil unrest and weak democracies (Le Billon 2001). In Gavin Bridge's (2004a) words, these are "contested terrains."

To help outline the dimensions of a subsurface political ecology, four vignettes are here presented respectively of mines, the complications of also

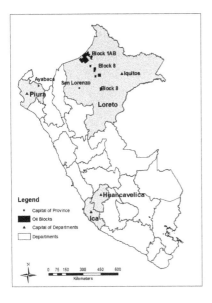

Figure 9.1. Locations in Peru mentioned in this chapter

considering water rights, the changes caused by the exploration for hydrocarbon resources, and the environmental and social implications of the extraction of petroleum. (See Figure 9.1 for locations of places mentioned in the text.) The first vignette is set in the humid mountains of northernmost Peru, in a part of Piura that has been the scene of conflicts between local people who depend on farming for their livelihoods and the state, which is promoting the establishment of a "mining district." The second vignette is set in central Peru and explores the highland–lowland connections that link the natural resources found in the highlands of Huancavelica with a new agricultural frontier created using government subsidies in the coastal deserts of Ica. The third vignette is set in the lower part of the Pastaza River in the Peruvian Amazon, in a lowland rainforest area thought to have subsoil hydrocarbon resources. This case describes ways in which petroleum exploration has threatened and hurt the Kandozi. The fourth vignette is set in the Pastaza River and nearby Corrientes River, areas that have experienced four decades of oil extraction. In particular, the effects on the Achuar are described, a case also explored in Chapter 8 of this volume by Bebbington and Scurrah. Each vignette demonstrates the power of social actors operating at national and international levels who prioritize the use of geological resources. However, local groups of farmers in the highlands and forest-dwelling indigenous people of the lowlands have, at times, been able to paralyze those efforts through mobilization, networking, and engaging public opinion.

Vignette 1: Mines, Metals, and Minerals

Social conflict related to subsurface resources is epitomized by the mobilizations, protests, and violence associated with the Río Blanco mining development in northern Peru, on the border with Ecuador. Local interests in agriculture collided with national and international desires for subsurface resources. This particular copper and molybdenum project is located in humid mountain areas, with steep slopes used for agricultural fields or grazing, or with patches of cloud forest. Following earlier protests, in April 2004 and again in July 2005, several thousand people from Ayabaca and from nearby Segunda y Cajas mobilized and marched for a couple of days over rough terrain to protest in front of the guarded entrance to the land claimed by the company (Figure 9.2). On each occasion they were met with violence from members of the national police and other security forces commonly employed by mining companies for short-term service (Bebbington et al. 2007b).

If the goal was to smooth the way for further exploration and exploitation in the area, then this was a counterproductive means to address local concerns about land rights and possible contamination. Entryways into the area were blocked by the now-motivated and organized local people, who began to network with nongovernmental organizations (NGOs) with experience in helping similar communities affected by mining. The personnel preparing the exploration phase of the project resorted to taking in supplies and visitors by helicopter, as they were not permitted entry by land. The British company tasked with the exploration work, Monterrico Metals, eventually sold the rights to a larger company, the Chinese Zijin Mining Group, which would then carry out the investment and construction required for the exploitation phase, planned to include a large open-pit mine dug to below the water table. In late 2007, local organizations convened a referendum in which the mining was rejected. The current situation is one in which the Peruvian state continues to promote the development of a mining district in the area; local people continue to resist through various nonviolent means; the operations of the mining company have been temporarily blocked, as its environmental impact assessment was judged inadequate; and NGOs continue to be involved in aspects of the social mobilization and networking, and in regards the environmental concerns.

To some extent, it is the nature of ancient geological patterns and processes that define the scope and location of these conflicts. The mineral deposit in this case is of a size and quality that warrant international interest for investing in an area with very poor infrastructure. If it were buried deeper underground or were smaller in size, then presumably it would not be of such

Figure 9.2. Fortified guard station at entrance to contested lands claimed by the mining company in northern Peru. This was the site of social protests by local people and violence by police and security agents contracted by the mine. Photo: Kenneth R. Young

interest. The Peruvian government was, and continues to be, willing to offer substantial incentives to encourage investment.

The proposed extraction would result in many environmental risks, including slope instability, habitat fragmentation, and negative effects on water quality. The original vegetation of the highest peaks is a very humid tropical alpine ecosystem, called *páramo* in the northern Andes, while the mountain slopes have humid to pluvial montane forests, depending on the degree of exposure to humid air masses from the Amazon basin. Rainfall is higher than normal in occasional El Niño years, when extra humidity also comes from the nearby Pacific Ocean. The steep slopes would erode when deforested, the native plants and animals would potentially lose critical habitat, and the high rainfall would carry contaminants through surface and groundwater flows. Transboundary concerns are also apparent, as contaminated waters would be entering the headwaters of the Amazon basin, with at least some risk of environmental degradation affecting the people and ecosystems downstream. The proposed mining district borders with Ecuador, so concerns about possible effects on water quality, habitat fragmentation, and erosion and mass wasting would all have an international dimension. In principle, the government of Ecuador or entities interested in neotropical biodiversity conservation would be dismayed by these economic development plans, which would seem to benefit Peru but could only hurt Ecuador and reduce the regional connectivity of wildlife habitat. The biodiversity value of a site with these characteristics in this part of the tropics is high, not only because the cloud forests and *páramos* are species rich, but also because endemism (the degree of uniqueness of the biota) is also known to be high (Renjifo et al. 1997; Young et al. 2002; Pennington et al. 2010). Often overlooked is that additional unique agrobiodiversity is contained within the land-use systems of the zone.

The local farmers have many crop varieties adapted to local conditions, and the harvesting of native plants with traditional medicinal uses is highly valued by local people. That said, what probably motivated much of the social resistance was their interest in controlling the fate of their lands, based on our conversations in the respective communities in 2007. Despite the odds, the mobilization was successful in blocking unwanted development. The mine proposed by this particular company and the mining district planned by the government would occupy areas considered part of the communities and districts and could reduce their value for agriculture. Even though considerable political pressure was brought to bear on the local people—significant economic incentives have been offered, and violence or threats of violence have been reported—there still is little local interest in allowing the establishment of mining in the area.

Vignette 2: Groundwater—Into the Critical Zone

Our groundwater resource example combines earth science perspectives with subsurface natural resources. It comes from Huancavelica, a department located in the south-central Andes of Peru. Today this is the poorest part of the country (FONCODES 2006), notwithstanding its long historical importance for mining. Not only does Huancavelica epitomize predictions of the resource curse, but newly valuable natural resources also continue to hinder its development and prosperity. Huancavelica has recently become the origin of yet another valuable resource, namely water diverted from the highlands (along with water from other sources) to irrigate intensive industrial agriculture on the arid Pacific coast (Figure 9.3).

Resting above the largest mercury deposit in the Americas, Huancavelica

Figure 9.3. Agricultural lands created in the deserts of Ica with water originating in the Andes Mountains. Photo: Julio C. Postigo

was one of Spanish America's main sources of this metal, which was highly in demand for its use in amalgamation, the separation of silver from silver ore (Bakewell 1984b; Nriagu 1993). In fact, the history of mining in Huancavelica can be said to span 3,400 years, given that cinnabar, the ore form of mercury, was turned into a red pigment that was utilized as body paint and to cover gold objects of the Andean elites for several millennia (Cooke, Wolfe, and Hobbs 2009). Amalgamation was a technological adoption from Mexico (Fisher 1977; Bakewell 1984b) that replaced smelting when surface ores rich in silver were depleted; it was needed to exploit lower grades of ore (Nriagu 1993; Abbott and Wolfe 2003). Its use in the late 1500s motivated mercury mining at scales large enough to supply silver mines such as Potosí, in what is now Bolivia, and Cerro de Pasco, in Peru (Fisher 1977; Nriagu 1993; Cooke et al. 2009). By the nineteenth century, mining in Huancavelica had become less commercially important and was typically informal, with multiple artisanal miners carrying out small-scale operations that supplied silver mines in Huancavelica and Junín into the early decades of the 1900s (Contreras and Diaz 2007). The mining legacy in today's Huancavelica is most often in the form of abandoned mines, tailings, and poverty (Álvarez et al. 2008), although recent rises in commodity prices and the presence of newly exposed peaks once covered by glaciers are driving some new operations.

The topography of the Huancavelica highlands is that of a plateau interspersed with large lakes amongst higher mountain ranges, some of which were glaciated until the 1990s, when glacial retreat became common (Postigo, Young, and Crews 2008). Community lands are found at elevations ranging between 3,800 and 5,200 meters above sea level and covered with dry tropical alpine vegetation. There are diverse combinations of puna grassland, native pastures, and wetlands often dominated by mosaics of cushion plants. The peasants' main livelihood activity is herding flocks of alpaca, llama, and sheep. The wetlands are particularly important for alpaca, as the dominant plants are highly desirable as forage.

The land tenure system is characterized by the common property of grazing lands. The number of livestock and access to pasture and wetlands through household usufructary rights are key elements for the livelihoods and the productive systems of these communities (Orlove and Custred 1980; Orlove 1982; Browman 1990). Pasturelands are mainly located on poor soils and are either dependent on highly seasonal rainfall or else are bog wetlands that are maintained by groundwater inflow. Additional livelihood strategies include fishing for introduced trout and small-scale fish farming. More recently, a large-scale trout farming operation has been established in a highland lake by a joint venture between local people and larger-scale investors (Hepworth et al. 2010). Hence, water plays a crucial role in this landscape, shaping livelihood and vegetation patterns, as well as human occupation.

It is the presence of this water that has created the current access dilemmas affecting local people in Huancavelica. Downhill, at the base of the Andes on the Pacific coast, the department of Ica has become one of Peru's new agro-export frontiers. Agricultural demand for water from the Huancavelica highlands is great, and surface waters have been diverted towards Ica. In addition, the farms in Ica use well water from the water tables of the coastal valleys that originated as groundwater flow from the high Andes, in this case from Huancavelica. In a recent study analyzing water governance in the Ica-Huancavelica basin, Hepworth et al. (2010) (see also Oré 2005; Oré et al. 2009) found that the headwaters of the Pampas River, which drain an area of 392 square kilometers, were diverted from the Amazon basin to the Pacific by a 58 kilometer long system of channels (with a flow capacity of 15 cubic meters per second) and tunnels that act to transfer to the Ica basin 120 million cubic meters per year of the Pampas River's water plus the outflows of highland lakes—Choclococha, Orcoccocha, and Ccaracocha, all located in Pilpichaca district, Huaytará province. Lake Choclococha was dammed to increase its volume so that water can be conveyed to Ica during the highland rainy season that lasts from November through March. Though the infrastructure was originally constructed to provide water for the cultivation of cotton in the Ica valley, it has also become a critical source of irrigation water for the entire valley, specifically for the large agro-exporters in the hyper-arid desert of Ica. In doing so, the channel runs across highland community lands, picking up water from all the streams and rivers flowing from upstream, thereby diverting water from the farming communities of Carhuancho, Choclococha, Santa Ines, Llillinta, and Pilpichaca (Hepworth et al. 2010). The channel's design and operation give only token attention to environmental flows: there are but two flow gates along the channel and no institutions in place to monitor flow and needs in the entire basin. The system is incapable of allocating water on an equitable basis, leaving the highland people with a small fraction of the diverted water (Hepworth et al. 2010).

This engineered design expresses the goal of several different national administrations in Peru to favor agriculturalists over herders, mestizos over indigenous groups, the coast over the mountains, the export-led economy over the subsistence economy, and large-scale agribusiness over smallholders (Eguren 2006; Álvarez et al. 2008). Consequently, highland pastures are being degraded and wetlands are shrinking because of the effects of the water transfer. These conditions notwithstanding, highland communities are often not allowed to enlarge or create pastures through simple irrigation systems. In addition, several mines currently operating in the area, along with the old abandoned mining sites, generate water pollution with toxic metals; cadmium and copper exposures are higher than World Health Organization standards (Hepworth et al. 2010). Finally, poverty levels are high in Huancavelica while people are now also affected by climate change, which is the major driver of transformation of the formerly glaciated peaks, as is true elsewhere in the tropical Andes (Körner et al. 2005; Barry 2006; Thompson et al. 2006; Magrin et al. 2007). The cumulative effects and their feedbacks could undermine household adaptive capacity and jeopardize community-level resiliency (Postigo 2010).

Social mobilizations and protests have been relatively muted in Huancavelica so far. Although a planned 74 kilometer extension of the channel to bring another 60 million cubic meters into the Ica Valley was rejected by the community of Carhuancho, this action did not stop the project. Then, in 2007, the project was paralyzed when the Latin American Water Tribunal ruled in favor of the community, which was receiving technical support from a local NGO (Campese et al. 2007; CEPES 2007; Hepworth et al. 2010). The

Ica valley itself has been an area of conflict because the increasing demand of water from agro-exporters drives an unsustainable exploitation, lowering the water table and leaving dry wells—in addition to increased inequality.

Vignette 3: Hydrocarbon Exploration

Since the 1970s, Peru has sold rights for the exploration and exploitation of its oil and natural gas reserves. In recent years, concessions have proliferated with many implications for land rights and social conflict (Finer and Orta-Martínez 2010; see also Chapter 2 in this volume). In 1974, only 3 blocks had been granted for exploitation and 17 were under exploration. By 2009, there were 19 contracts for exploitation and 68 for exploration. As of October 2010, these concessions included 3 contracts for exploitation (Blocks 1AB, 8, and 67) covering 7813.07 square kilometers and 28 contracts for exploration covering 183,117.24 square kilometers in the Marañon sedimentary basin of the northern Peruvian Amazon alone.[2]

Peru can be subdivided into eighteen sedimentary basins, which are the areas with potential for hosting hydrocarbon reserves. The Marañon basin is the largest and was the first subjected to exploitation in the 1970s. However, as in the other basins, the surface ecology of the Marañon basin is important. It hosts the world's largest humid tropical alluvial fan (a so-called megafan), which encompasses 60,000 square kilometers, of which approximately 54,000 square kilometers are in Peru, and is situated on the eastern catchment of the Amazon River basin, draining from the Ecuadorian Andes into the Peruvian northwestern Amazon (Räsänen et al. 1992). The history of the past 10 million years and characteristics of remote areas in the Andes continue to influence the ecology of the Amazon River through landforms and chemicals weathered into streams (Roddaz et al. 2005; McClain and Naiman 2008). In addition, this area combines Andean rivers carrying changing pulses of volcanoclastic sediment loads with Amazon-origin black-water rivers. Together they create—on the surface—a patchy living matrix of forests and wetlands that favors the development of diverse ecosystems and habitats that support the existence of a rich flora and fauna (Puhakka et al. 1992). However, these same geological processes have subsurface consequences, giving rise to the resource-rich Marañon sedimentary basin. It has been producing petroleum since 1970 from the fields in Block 1-AB and Block 8, and more recently from Block 67, with initial reserves of 729 MMbo (million barrels of oil), 320 MMbo, and 250 MMbo, respectively (Karoon Gas Australia Ltd 2010).

Granting petroleum concessions without informing or having local communities' consent was and is the modus operandi of the Peruvian Government (Chirif 2010b). Consequently, these concessions create contested spaces (sensu Bridge 2004a), especially in an area such as the Abanico del Pastaza, which is populated by nine different indigenous groups with approximately 20,000 inhabitants who rely on natural resources for their livelihoods (García 2007; Soto, Montoya, and Flores 2010). One of these groups is the Kandozi, whose territory was entered by The Occidental Petroleum Corporation (OXY) in 1993 without their permission. The Kandozi are located in the lower portion of the Pastaza River basin in northern Peru near the town of San Lorenzo. Their lands encompass some 9,116 square kilometers of tropical forest with seasonally flooded areas and lakes. The historical isolation of the Kandozi has left them vulnerable to many diseases, the worst case of which has been a continuing hepatitis epidemic.

The Kandozi believe that the dramatic increase of hepatitis in 1996 was due to the entrance of OXY's staff into their territory in 1994, after the Peruvian Government (in 1993) granted the 9,000 square kilometer Block 4 to the corporation (Surralles 2007). This concession overlapped with much of the Kandozi territory. It was only when OXY entered the Chapuli River area to begin drilling an exploratory well that the local communities learned about the company (Figure 9.4). The Kandozi wrote a formal letter to the government expressing their opposition to petroleum exploration. They expressed concern about the potential for contamination of the rivers and Lake Rimachi. However, OXY did not stop drilling, and their personnel continued to enter Kandozi territory. The results of the exploration were negative and OXY stopped its activities in the basin in 1995 (Figure 9.4). Nevertheless, the first symptoms of Hepatitis B and D began to appear only shortly after they left (Surralles 2007).

Hepatitis has been devastating for the Kandozi population, not only because of the number of dead, but also because of the depression and fear that it has caused among the people. In 2000, the average incidence rate for Hepatitis B in the area was 52.2/1000 inhabitants, and 106.3/1000 among 15–44 year olds. While the epidemic extended to surrounding areas, 92 percent of the cases were Kandozi people (UNICEF 2005). In 2003, the Ministry of Health declared in an official report that the district of Pastaza, and the Kandozi territory in particular, had the highest risk for hepatitis in Peru. That same year, UNICEF Peru, together with the Ministry of Health, began a vaccination program for the Kandozi in an attempt to save newborns from infection with hepatitis (García 2007). This effort was delayed by cultural and logistical difficulties and lack of interest from the government. People continue to die from this illness (SERVINDI 2010a, 2010b) caused by the pres-

Figure 9.4. Capped exploration oil well left by OXY on Kandozi lands in the Chapuli River area. Although deemed unsuccessful for further development by the petroleum company, this drilling process opened the Kandozi to an ongoing health crisis. Photo: Kenneth R. Young

ence of an oil company for just one year, and yet triggering consequences that will last for decades.

Consistently, the Kandozi have manifested their rejection of the oil companies and have defended their territory (Postigo and Montoya 2009; Montoya 2010). Nonetheless, in 2009 the Peruvian government granted the Canadian company Karoon a concession (Block 144) and exploration rights on lands that overlap the Kandozi territory. If this company finds oil and decides to start operations in the area (the plan is to start drilling in April 2013), this will generate conflicts again between the Kandozi and the outsiders who seek to extract natural resources from the subsoil.

Vignette 4: Petroleum Exploitation

While the cases of Piura and the Kandozi show just how much disruption can be caused when the subsoil is explored, most social and environmental impacts occur when subsoil resources are extracted. Although the Kandozi are suffering from aftereffects of OXY's exploration activities, overall they still have a healthy environment that can provide them with natural resources such as game and fish (Anderson et al. 2009; Montoya 2010). However, this is not the situation for other indigenous groups living in the Abanico del Pastaza, such as the Achuar (Goldman, La Torre López, and Ramos 2007). The Achuar are a Jivaro population of approximately 15,000 living in Ecuador and Peru (La Torre López and Napolitano 2007) who continue to rely on natural resources for their livelihoods; indeed, this part of the Amazon is among the most biodiverse areas on the planet (Brooks et al. 2006; Grenyer et al. 2006; Barthlott et al. 2007). Yet, the entire Achuar ancestral territory in Peru is now underlain by petroleum concessions, and that portion of their territory in the area of the Corrientes River, occupied by 4,000 Achuar, has been completely concessioned off since 1970 (Orta-Martínez et al. 2007). These concessions—Blocks 1AB and 8—were the first petroleum operations in Peru and at their peak accounted for 65 percent of national production (Finer and Orta-Martínez 2010).

Blocks 1AB and 8 are located in the upper sections of the Pastaza basin in Peru and in the headwaters of the Tigre and Corrientes Rivers. In these areas, the level of contamination is alarming (Finer and Orta-Martínez 2010) and has seriously affected public health (Dirección de Ecología y Protección del Ambiente 2006; Orta Martínez et al. 2007). An environmental evaluation published by the Ministry of Energy and Mining (MEM 1998) recorded high concentrations of contaminants (oil and fats, hydrocarbons, lead, and chlorides) in all rivers affected by these production waters (Orta-Martínez et al. 2007). Until 2008, the production waters (La Torre López and Napolitano 2007) from these two blocks, containing hydrocarbon residuals, heavy metals, radioactive elements, and high concentrations of salts, were released directly into these rivers and nearby streams. More than 95 percent of the 1,118,174 barrels of toxic production waters produced daily were entering the Pastaza, Tigre, and Corrientes Rivers.[3]

A large (yet undocumented) number of oil spills have occurred since OXY first started drilling in Block 1AB in 1971. By 1984, the environmental government agency had declared the area as one of the most damaged environments in the country (Finer and Orta-Martínez 2010). More recent data show that 78 oil spills occurred between 2006 and 2010.[4] Another report released from the government in 2004, in this case from the regulatory body for energy investment (Organismo Supervisor de Energía, OSINERG), reported the presence of extensive deforested areas with the visible presence of oil spills (Finer and Orta-Martínez 2010). Furthermore, the MEM's earlier report in

1998 also revealed that natural gas flares were releasing hydrogen sulfide concentrations that were four times higher than permissible levels. The dumping of drilling mud from 348 wells was estimated to have contaminated 52.2 hectares, in addition to more than 300 hectares found polluted with barium (Orta Martínez et al. 2007). Thus, the petroleum-induced impacts in the Abanico del Pastaza have caused continual stresses since 1971. The Achuar and all their natural resources—water, fauna, and soils—have been exposed to toxic substances that have been responsible not only for the disruption of livelihood systems, but are also associated with human health risks.

For many years, the Achuar people report that they have suffered from what were, for them, health problems of unknown origin. Many children, young people, and adults have died without any apparent cause. The Achuar hold the oil companies (Petro Peru and OXY in the past and Pluspetrol at present) responsible for the pollution of their territory; the apparent degradation of natural resources, such as safe drinking water and fish; and the indirect and sometimes unexplainable consequences. Although the Achuar have suffered from mysterious fatal illnesses since the 1980s, it was only in 2005 that a governmental body for occupational health and environmental protection (Centro Nacional de Salud Ocupacional y Protección del Ambiente para la Salud, CENSOPAS) officially accepted that people in the Corrientes River area were exposed to toxic contamination. CENSOPAS's study reported that 66.2 percent of the blood samples of 74 children (2–17 years in age) had excessive lead levels and that 79.2 percent of the adults sampled had lead levels of 10–19.9 micrograms (Dirección de Ecología y Protección del Ambiente 2006). This report also tested cadmium in blood and found that 89.65 percent of blood samples from the children and 99.2 percent of those from adults exceeded the maximum permissible level (Dirección de Ecología y Protección del Ambiente 2006; Orta Martínez et al. 2007).

Confirmation of this severe health situation in the Corrientes River area caused indignation, fear, and frustration among the Achuar because they were facing a seemingly irreversible situation. This 2005 report was also viewed by these communities (and others) as a confirmation of the violation of fundamental human rights by the Peruvian government since the 1970s. This perception aggravated the situation between the Achuar and the government and with Pluspetrol, who were negotiating compensatory agreements. Initially these agreements contemplated amenities such as the construction of health posts or schools. However, after the results of blood samples became public, the Achuar began to also demand that measures be taken to stop oil spills and to reinject production waters into the wells (Scurrah, Bielich, and Bebbington 2010). Although Pluspetrol now reinjects one hundred percent of the production waters of Block 1AB and is in the process of reinjecting the waters from Block 8 (which should significantly reduce the point sources of pollution), many of the effects are still visible, measurable, and will likely be long lasting.

Notwithstanding all these health and environmental impacts, the Peruvian government leased 6 new concessions between 2004 and 2007—partially on Achuar territory (Finer and Orta-Martínez 2010). In October 2010, Peru-Petro leased 25 new concessions at the national level, with 12 located in the Marañon sedimentary basin. One of the twelve blocks (Block 185) is in the Corrientes-Tigre Rivers area, underlying the Achuar and Kichwa territories, and another two (Blocks 166, 186) overlap the Kandozi territory (PeruPetro 2010). The national indigenous organization Asociación Interétnica de Desarrollo de la Selva Peruana (AIDESEP) has publicly questioned whether the government acted appropriately in regards to both national and global concerns, but has received no response to date.[5]

Conclusions

Peru's economy has long been based upon the export of natural resources such as minerals, hydrocarbon, rubber, guano, and timber (Thorp and Bertram 1978; Klarén 2000; Postigo 2010). This economic model renders the country's economy dependent not only on the revenues from exploitation of its natural resources, but also on global demands located far beyond its control. Thus a global economic process has become a driver of the domestic economy and a source of transformations in local social-ecological systems (Bridge 2004a). Furthermore, this dependency engenders an economy vulnerable to transnational companies (Beck 2005) and to countries that demand exported natural resources, which can then heavily influence commodity prices and trade flows.

The four vignettes presented here show different dimensions of the impacts of global demand on local and national social and natural systems. National laws and regulations have been modified to ease private investment (Otto 1997; Naito, Remy, and Williams 2001; Bebbington and Bury 2009) and to weaken the rights of indigenous and local populations to control their land, water, and resources both above and below the ground (Warhurst and Bridge 1997; Downey and Strife 2010). Environmental authorities have typically been powerless to enforce the law in these cases. In addition, the regulation and monitoring of the use of key resources such as water and land are vested with each productive sector in Peru, reinforcing the tendency for overuse or misuse.

It was 500 years ago that diseases caused millions of deaths (Sánchez-

Albornoz 1984; Cook and Lovell 1992) as European colonial powers arrived and began exploiting the natural resources of the "New World" (Lockhart and Schwartz 1983; Denevan 1992a). Although the particulars are different, the vignettes presented in this chapter show that local people in Peru are still being subjected to health and economic risks as access to what lies beneath their lands is sold to the highest bidder. There is little evidence in these vignettes to contradict the expectations of a "resource curse" paradigm that has given resource-rich places little lasting benefit from the extraction of those resources. Nonetheless, the reasons behind that relationship are not clear and the proposals to provide solutions or mitigation are often controversial. For example, Luong and Weinthal (2006) suggest that the critical feature is the actual structure of ownership of the mineral resource in question, depending on the type of private ownership and the degree of state control. Others suggest that it is, instead, institutional types and characteristics that determine outcomes (Mehlum, Moene, and Torvik 2006; Robinson, Torvik, and Verdier 2006), or that the spatiality of the resource matters, with concentrated resource types associated with more negative consequences for human welfare (Bulte, Damania, and Deacon 2005). As a possible solution, Sandbu (2006) offers a scheme to transfer some of the wealth back to the general population of a resource-rich country. In the case of the recent events in Peru described in this chapter, the reality is that it has been protests of local people that have provided impetus for change, rather than progressive national policies. The interactions connecting global capital and local resources are set amidst trade agreements (Beck 2005) and within the evolution of neoliberal reforms (Bridge 2004c). Yet the resource curse in the case of our vignettes is also played out at a subnational level, for example with industrial farmers in Ica gaining at the expense of herders in Huancavelica, or with the capital Lima deciding the fate of lands, human health, and ecosystems in the Pastaza River basin.

There is no doubt that political ecology offers analytical tools for examining these kinds of power relations among the contested terrains of subsurface resource disputes (Blaikie and Brookfield 1987; Rocheleau and Edmunds 1997; Watts 2005). Walker (2005) pointed out the need to better connect political ecology's social science and historical perspectives with additional insights from the ecological (and biogeographical) sciences, and as well as with politics itself (Walker 2007). All of the vignettes point to important biodiversity values found among the natural and utilized landscapes, which are intimately associated with habitat for species and the functioning of ecosystems and agroecosystems. For moving political ecology into the subsoil, it will also be necessary to add expertise from the geological, hydrological, and geomorphological sciences.

In each of these vignettes, the geological particulars were important to consider. The history and confluence of geological processes work to control and determine location, access, and ultimate value of the mineral and hydrocarbon resources involved. Given recent interest in blending the earth sciences into research paradigms that can address flows through the planet's critical zone (National Research Council 2001), it would not overstate the case to suggest that political ecology should also include these insights within human-environment studies. Amundson et al. (2007) and Brantley, Goldhaber, and Ragnarsdottir (2007) conclude that this would require cross-scalar approaches and novel disciplinary linkages among, for example, researchers of lithology, topography, chemical weathering, climate, and ecological disturbances. More recently, Rasmussen et al. (2009) and Wagener et al. (2010) have examined the implications of this more inclusive paradigm for the study of hydrology and landform evolution. However, none of these scholars have included social science perspectives within critical zone studies. The subsurface realm is particularly challenging to address, as so many of the relevant physical and chemical processes are cryptic or cannot be measured directly. A critical zone approach to subsurface political ecology would undoubtedly require new academic structures wherein geohydrologists interact with social scientists. It is likely that the particulars of human use of and impact upon landscapes will not only have consequences for the findings of critical zone researchers, but in fact the causality behind those land-use patterns and land cover changes will also reside within human decision making and behavior.

Social mobilization is often the only tool available for local people as a counterweight to the state–business coalitions that are motivated by the international prices of commodities and fomented by the institutions promoting neoliberalism and open markets (Bridge 2004c; Harvey 2005; Perreault and Valdivia 2010). Furthermore, social mobilizations express: the clash of cultures; uneven power relations between companies and local populations; different development models and economic goals pursued, on one side, by long-term residents and, on the other, by investors and governments; and finally, the lack of institutions and government agencies mediating between market and society (Bebbington and Bury 2009; Postigo and Montoya 2009). People who live among contaminated sites—and must daily travel through old mine tailings or along decrepit pipelines—are not easily convinced that either the state or a private company would be contemplating development plans that will be socially and environmentally responsible. People observ-

ing state-sponsored violence in person or through the media will not be re-
ceptive to outside interventions. Although the resistance shown by spontaneous protestors and networking activists is often surprisingly effective in
Peru given the asymmetries of power that exist, there are many additional
structural changes that could be pursued by local people and by their allies
working at other levels.

As seen in the four vignettes set in Peru, laws and governmental resources,
such as incentives, are often used at the country level to benefit particular
companies rather than promoting development plans controlled by local
people. A subterranean political ecology paradigm that adds Earth's critical zone to these concerns would allow approaches such that water resources
and an assortment of edaphic, hydrological, and geological processes could
be used to inform the further study of power relations, land security, environmental concerns, and basic human rights. Programmatically, these elements
add significant new dimensions to the topics typically addressed by political
ecology. This might require team-based approaches to examining the coupled
human–natural systems. This should be done while also acknowledging the
value of historical approaches, recognizing that many of the current protests
echo resource issues that have affected local people for centuries.

Notes

1. See http://criticalzone.org.
2. See http://www.perupetro.com.pe.
3. See notes to Chapter 7 by Bebbington and Scurrah for a description of production waters.
4. See www.servindi.org/actualidad/27691.
5. Letter from AIDESEP to the Minister of Energy and Mining (de la Jara Basombrío and Pizango Chota 2010).

CHAPTER 10

Anatomies of Conflict: Social Mobilization and New Political Ecologies of the Andes

ANTHONY BEBBINGTON, DENISE HUMPHREYS
BEBBINGTON, LEONITH HINOJOSA,
MARÍA-LUISA BURNEO, AND JEFFREY BURY

In this chapter, we discuss findings from a large-scale comparative research program studying the relationships between socioenvironmental conflicts, territorial dynamics, and development in areas affected by the expansion of extractive industry investment in Bolivia, Ecuador, and Peru. The program was prompted by investment trends, discussed in this volume, and more so by the increasing levels of rural conflict in the region. The apparent ubiquity of these conflicts demanded interpretations that go beyond individual cases to seek patterns, recognize relationships among cases, and ultimately tie together an analysis of socioenvironmental conflict with an interpretation of the political economy of development in the Andes.

In the first phase of the program we asked if and how social movement activity affected the relationships between territorial dynamics and extractive industry, by comparing the cases of Cajamarca, Peru, and Cotacachi, Ecuador.[1] That comparison identified various ways in which movements had influenced these relationships, depending on the timing of movement activity relative to the project cycle of the extractive enterprise, the extent to which movements used direct action, and, most importantly, the ability of movements to bridge social differences within regional society and to build collaborative relationships with subnational government (Bebbington et al. 2007c, 2008b). However, in order to make more general statements, it was necessary to elaborate these ideas on the basis of a larger sample of more varied cases. A second phase of the program therefore included a wider range of experiences drawn from both the mining and hydrocarbons sectors, and located across highland and lowland environments of all three Andean countries. Some of these cases have been the subject of Chapters 5, 6, and 7 in this collection. In the current chapter we read across this broader body of research in order to develop a comparative interpretation of extractive-industry conflicts in the region.

The chapter proceeds as follows. First, we discuss the design and conduct of the research. Second, we offer an interpretation of the intersections between the political economy of extractive industry and rural livelihoods that we then use to help interpret the divergent forms of mobilization that occur around extraction. Third, we close with a discussion of these mobilizations and claims that appear to motivate them, and we suggest that these mobilizations constitute calls for greater and more ordered forms of state practice in the regulation of the extractive sector, demands for more responsive and responsible company practices, and a determination on the part of rural populations to be heard, to be considered as citizens and be part of decisions about national development.

Debating Conflict: On Research Design and Research Opportunity

The formal title given to the research project on which we report was "Conflicts over the Countryside."[2] The title conveyed a double meaning: that conflicts were becoming ever more widely dispersed across the Andean and Amazonian countryside, and that underlying these conflicts were divergences over the sort of future countryside that different social groups wanted to build. Grappling with these ideas demanded a research design that would accommodate both breadth (to address this wide range of conflictive environments) and depth (to analyze ideas and visions underlying and driving this conflict). This also meant that it was necessary to conduct both an in-depth, qualitative *and* quantitative study of a spread of case studies, and to conduct this research over an extended period of time in order to experience firsthand how the dynamics of conflict evolved. This could only be done by working through a network of researchers functioning as a loose yet self-identified team. Several of the authors conducted their PhD research in the process (Denise Humphreys Bebbington, Ximena Warnaars, Teresa Velásquez), another combined research with her work in investigative journalism (Jennifer Moore), while others linked the research to their nongovernmental organization (NGO) activism (María Luisa Burneo and Guido Cortez). The emphases and regional spread of cases are summarized in Table 10.1.

For several members of the team, the boundary between research, activism, and public engagement was a relatively porous one. For Humphreys Bebbington, Moore, and Warnaars, the move from activism to research reflected a desire to conduct more systematic analyses of the phenomena that they

Table 10.1. Case studies and contributors

	Peru	Bolivia	Ecuador
Mining sector:	*Cajamarca* Bebbington, Burneo, Bury, Humphreys Bebbington, 2005–2010 *Piura* Bebbington, Burneo, 2006–2010	*Oruro* Hinojosa, 2007–2009	*Cotacachi* Bebbington, Muñoz, 2005 *Zamora Chinchipe* Warnaars, 2008–2010 *Azuay* Moore, Velásquez, Bebbington, 2007–2010
Oil and gas sectors:	*Río Corrientes/ Loreto* Scurrah, Bielich, Bebbington, 2008–2009	*Tarija 1* Humphreys Bebbington, Bebbington, 2007–2010 *Tarija 2* Hinojosa, Cortez, Chumacero, 2009–2010	

had been encountering in their activist work. At the same time, their prior activism eased access to the cases that they studied—access which otherwise would not have been so straightforward (or even possible), given the sensitivity of the issues at stake and the high levels of distrust surrounding these conflicts. This traffic between research and activism continued throughout the research as other activists and journalists approached members of the team to discuss the issues being studied and, at times, to request involvement in particular cases. For instance, the research in Piura began as a collaboration between Bebbington and the Peru Support Group, a UK-based human rights organization that wanted to explore apparent human and environmental rights issues surrounding a mining project involving a UK company. This collaboration had the advantage of opening up many avenues of inquiry and interviews that otherwise would have been very difficult to secure. However, it also positioned the research in the eyes of the industry and authorities as being motivated by a critical view of mining (Bebbington 2007b). Third, as the research progressed, it drew attention in ways that opened up further possibilities for public and political debate of the issues raised. The work in Piura became the basis for three public debates with representatives of the company, and the basis for two press briefings. In Ecuador, the research led to an invitation from a working group within the national Constituent Assembly to present findings to a public consultation held as part of the Assembly's preparation of text on extractive industries. On another occasion, an invitation came from the International Finance Corporation to participate in a panel debate with industry representatives and journalists.

The more general point is that the research ultimately took on a life of its own. This created opportunities to gain insights that otherwise would not have been available to us. However, it also meant that while we worked across a range of cases, initially with a similar protocol in mind, the final case research was not perfectly comparable. This was all the more so because, in the course of the program, additional resources were generated for some of the cases (Piura, Tarija, and Cajamarca), but not all of them.[3] Consequently, as we read across these different cases, it is important to bear in mind that some of them are far fuller than others and, in some regards, exercise more influence on the interpretations that we are able to offer.

Political Ecologies of Livelihood and Extraction

Remapping for extraction

Since the early 1990s, Latin America has been the terrain of a new phase of expanded investment in mining, oil, and gas sectors (see Chapters 1 and 2, this volume). Three broad factors drive this expansion: increasing global demand (particularly from China and India, but also Brazil and other large emerging economies) coupled with price increases that make even low-grade and complicated ores financially attractive; technological changes that allow the extraction of such dispersed ores, as well as of hard-to-access hydrocarbon reserves; and policy and institutional changes that have provided favorable tax, royalty, and regulatory environments for investors (Bridge 2004c).[4] This latter point is even recognized by industry itself. Regarding Peru, the International Council for Mining and Metals (ICCM) notes that "legislation created an extremely attractive investment regime for large multinational companies" (ICMM 2007, 9).

This is not the first time such a mix of factors has fostered expanded extraction in the Andes: as Gil Montero (2011) and others note, mining expansion in the southern Andes during the seventeenth century also reflected favorable policies on labor (*mita*), increasing demand (in Europe), and technological changes (the use of mercury amalgams). However, the sheer economic and geographical scale of the late twentieth-century variant of these changes *is* different, and it has led to expanded investment both in traditional regions of extraction as well as in new frontiers, with no modern history of large-scale extraction.[5] This is true *among* as well as *within* countries. Thus investment has moved both to "traditional" extractive economies (e.g., Chile and Peru for mining, Peru and Ecuador for hydrocarbons) and to countries with no such history (e.g., mining in Ecuador or El Salvador, hydrocarbons across Central America). Meanwhile, within the Andean countries, investment has gone not only to traditional mining regions (e.g., Potosí, Oruro, Cerro de Pasco) and hydrocarbon frontiers (e.g., Loreto, Tarija, Pastaza), but also to new ones. The period since the late 1990s has, thus, seen important mining interest in Piura and Ayacucho in Peru, in Santa Cruz in Bolivia, and in the Cordillera del Condor of Peru and Ecuador, as well as new hydrocarbon frontiers opening up in the altiplano of Peru, the northern lowlands of Bolivia, and the southeastern lowlands of Ecuador. In this process, the presumed association of mining with the highlands, and of hydrocarbons with the tropical lowlands, is breaking down, with both forms of extraction now being found across the full transect of Coast-Andes-Amazon.

The geographical manifestations of this process are various. By the end of the 2000s, experts estimated that some 55 percent of Peru's highland peasant communities were affected by mining concessions, and that between 2002 and 2008, the area of these concessions had increased by 77.4 percent, from 7,045,000 to 13,224,000 hectares.[6] Meanwhile, between 2004 and 2008 the proportion of Peru's Amazon basin covered by hydrocarbon concessions increased from 14 to more than 70 percent, with concessions overlapping protected areas, indigenous territories, and lands reserved for indigenous peoples (Smith 2009). While in Ecuador the area affected by mining concessions was far less, at around 10 percent,[7] this was still remarkable given that the country has no significant mining history at all; meanwhile, some 65 percent of its Amazon basin is concessioned or available for concession for hydrocarbon activity (Finer et al. 2008). Fifty-five percent of Bolivia's surface is deemed available for hydrocarbon exploration (Humphreys Bebbington 2010).

These patterns underlie the claim that this new round of extraction has done nothing less than rewrite the political ecology of the Andes (Bebbington 2009). This rewriting—or maybe more precisely, remapping—has been produced from centers of power where particular visions of resource-led growth (from government) and resource-based entrepreneurial strategies (from companies) have driven an effort to order national landscapes so that they can more easily be made functional to such visions and strategies. These mappings intersect, overlap, and clash with territorial and livelihood dynamics in ways that further suggest a fundamental reworking of the political ecology of the region.

It is worth noting that this process of granting concessions generates overlaps and disarticulations in more than land use and governance. It also produces overlaps among different state-led projects. While central government grants concessions in ways that reflect both its own geographical imagination of national development as well as a certain blindness to actually existing complexities (cf. Scott 1998), the geographies it produces overlap with those pursued by subnational authorities seeking everything from economic-ecological zonation and land use planning, as in Cajamarca, Peru, to enhanced regional autonomy, as in Tarija, Bolivia. In addition to the uncertainties produced by concessions (see below), these overlapping and often conflicting state projects also produce uncertainty for local populations.

Uncertainty and Dispossession

One interpretation of these concession maps is that they reflect elite visions of how national space should be ordered so that the contents of its subsoil might be brought into national economic and political life in ways that can enhance accumulation and foster economic development. The dominance of the concession also reveals how deeply extraction is embedded in these countries; constitutions claim the subsoil for the nation, and states are under the obligation to exploit natural resources to create wealth. While details vary depending on national legislation, concessions (or contracts, in the case of Bolivia) give rights to their holders to explore the subsoil in search of minerals, oil, and gas. To gain access to this subsoil, concession holders still have to negotiate with owners of surface rights, with the nature of this negotiation varying depending on the details of national laws. Accessing the subsoil is not straightforward, though in most instances concession holders have been supported by national authorities in this process. Concession holders also enjoy, de jure or de facto, the knowledge that they have privileged rights to convert any resource discoveries into a project for extraction.

Another, and by no means mutually exclusive, interpretation of these maps departs from their *effects* and the ways in which they are interpreted by the populations who occupy the territories that have been mapped for extraction. This approach leads us to view such cartographies of concession as representing geographies of real and perceived uncertainty, instability, and threat, though the depth of such perception varies among different populations. There is no local participation prior to the designation of areas for concession, and as a result, oftentimes the residents first learn of a concession when the geologists begin exploration or when companies come to initiate negotiations over access to the surface rights in areas to be explored. In other instances, changes occur without populations knowing that they are related to extractive industry. In particular, on acquiring concessions, companies recruit or create subsidiary companies to begin purchasing land in the areas in which they intend to begin exploration. Thus an early change signaled by concession maps can be found in the shifting dynamics of land markets. Land begins to change hands and prices increase, though to levels which do not reflect the real value of the land to the extractive enterprise (Kamphuis 2010).

If shifts in land markets may trigger some sense of uncertainty, this is all the more so when populations realize that these changes are because their land has been concessioned for exploration and, above all, when they learn that exploration has indeed found minerals beneath their communities. At this point, people's sense of the future changes forever. Whether they welcome or reject the idea of extraction—we encounter both sentiments in all of our cases, as well as a range of "in-between" feelings—there is a growing sense that the future of their physical and social landscapes will look nothing like the past. In the words of Miguel Castro of Tarija, some begin to "wake up every day dreaming of gas." Others worry every day about their future access to the land, water, and social assets on which they have traditionally based their livelihoods—and as Bury's work in Cajamarca shows (Bury 2004, 2007), they are right to do so, for extraction often accompanies significant changes in rural people's asset bases. Yet others, particularly lowland indigenous groups, worry whether their aspirations to recover their territory and to enhance their autonomy will be compromised by the arrival of the extractive frontier—and again, they are right to do so, for attempts to gain territory have been compromised when hydrocarbons have been found (Smith 2009; Humphreys Bebbington 2010).

While asset loss begins in the exploration phase, through the operation of land markets and companies, it becomes more apparent when an exploration project is successfully converted into an exploitation project. At this point, cartographies of exploitation become geographies of real and perceived dispossession. Part of this dispossession involves the resources that are central to the sustenance of rural livelihoods: land, water, and forests. The amount of land to which people lose access varied across our cases depending on the sector (mining consumes more land than does hydrocarbon extraction), the scale of particular projects, and the number of projects in a given region. In some

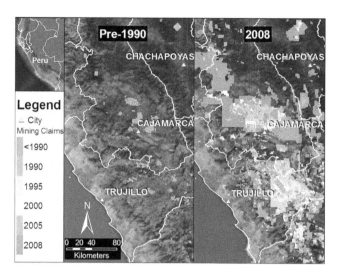

Figure 10.1. Map of concessions in Cajamarca, Peru

regions, such as Cajamarca, Peru, the number of projects being pursued—or imagined—has led to a rapid increase in area affected by concessions, such that most of the south-central part of the department where population is concentrated is under concession (Figure 10.1). Indeed, in Cajamarca, whole communities have lost access to pastures, and many families have also lost land for agriculture. The effects of this have been varied, ranging from intensification on remaining land to migration (Bury 2004; Bebbington et al. 2007c). In many instances, payments received for land have been lost over a period of several years, leaving rural households decapitalized (Bury 2007). Even though the Río Blanco project is still only at the stage of exploration in Piura, families have still lost access to grazing land as well as to the right of access over lands that they and their animals had previously traversed (Bebbington et al. 2007b). Conversely, while Repsol, Petrobras, and British Gas operations in Tarija have not required much land dispossession from indigenous populations in the Chaco, the presence of hydrocarbons *has* meant that the Guaraní and Weenhayek peoples have not been able to effectively consolidate their territorial land claims, frustrating their long-held desire to restore ancestral lands and achieve greater autonomy (Humphreys Bebbington 2010).

Across all our cases, we found that residents worried about the actual or potential loss of water resources that extractive industry might imply, either through absolute reduction in availability or decline in water quality. When concessions are mapped onto watersheds, the reasons for such concerns become clear. By 2008, 15 of Peru's largest rivers had 25 percent or more of their basins under concession (Bebbington and Bury 2009), and in some watersheds this figure is far higher. Figure 10.2 shows the percentage of six different watersheds in south-central Cajamarca that are directly affected by concessions, with more than 40 percent of three basins under concession. Indeed, in 2004, Cajamarca's population mobilized to prevent Minera Yanacocha from expanding its operations into a mountainside considered to be the primary source of both community and urban water (Bebbington et al. 2008c), and during 2011–2012, the department was again convulsed by mobilizations concerned, inter alia, about the potential effects of a new mega-mining project (Minas Conga) on water resources for the Celendín province in the region of Cajamarca. In Tarija, Guaraní organizations have been particularly concerned about the potential loss of water supply from protected areas slated to be explored for hydrocarbons by Petrobras and Petroandina (Humphreys Bebbington 2012b), while a sense of being dispossessed of water runs through community and urban concerns in Azuay (see Chapter 5, this volume, by Moore and Velásquez).

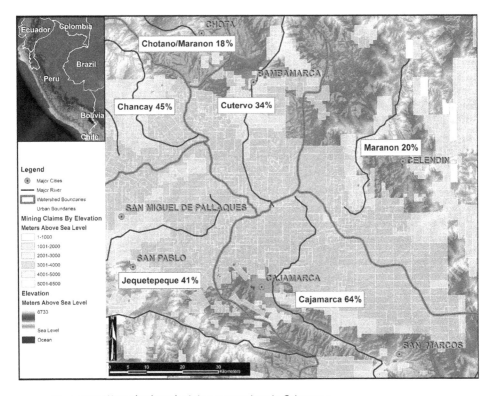

Figure 10.2. Watersheds and mining concessions in Cajamarca

The dispossessions at stake are not, however, only of land and water (Harvey 2003). A recurrent theme in interviews is the sense of being dispossessed of a way of living. Protesting outside a consultation event held as part of the Constituent Assembly process in Ecuador, residents of Intag and Cotacachi held a banner declaring, "We want to live in a healthy environment and in peace," a concern paralleling that of those residents described by Ximena Waarnars in Chapter 6, who lament the extent to which mining conflicts colonize everyday interactions in Zamora Chinchipe. This loss of ways of living is coupled with the loss of landscapes of meaning. In an interview with a woman who lives adjacent to the Yanacocha mine in Peru, what she primarily conveyed was the sense that looking out of their home was no longer the same: the familiar peak was now gone, ground down into tailings, and the night sky was now never dark, permanently illuminated by the mine's lighting.

The loss of ways of living is closely related to another dispossession: of the ability to control space. Material indications of this dispossession are the presence of fences and armed guards on lands formerly governed by community organizations, even when these guards are sometimes hired from the communities themselves. More symbolic indications are the everyday visibility of others—workers, professionals, drivers—living and working in former community spaces. Over the course of the research program, one of the most striking indications of this loss of control came from the area of Itika Guasu, a historic Guaraní area in Tarija that sits on top of one of Latin America's largest gas fields, the Campo Margarita. While the Guaraní of Itika Guasu have assumed a relatively hard line in their negotiations with Repsol, the operator of Campo Margarita, the everyday landscape speaks of the extent to which Repsol orders its space. Tracks in Itika Guasu were built by Repsol and connect its wells and installations, while gas pipelines cut straight lines through the low forest of the Chaco. Along these tracks are road signs each bearing the logo of Repsol—rather than of any local or government authority—that mark the names of, and the distance to, different Guaraní settlements (Figure 10.3). Not so very many miles away, Petrobras does the same in its San Alberto field. As much as marking distance and direction, these signs mark the authority to order landscape: an authority that no longer lies within Guaraní society.[8]

Strategies of Dispossession

This complex of dispossession (of assets, cultures, powers of government, and latent exchange value) is recurrent across our cases. The strategies through

Figure 10.3. Repsol road sign in Itika Guasu

which dispossession is effected are also strikingly convergent. Some of these strategies, of course, have hinged on the use of brute force, and there have been armed confrontations and/or deaths at most of our sites. Some of this use of violence has involved the armed institutions of the state coupled with the criminalization of protest, while other acts have been the work of extra-legal armed groups and individuals. While such use of violence is repugnant, perhaps more important in terms of their overall effect on resources access are other eminently legal and routine strategies of dispossession. Several such strategies are particularly significant.

Discursive strategies of dispossession are used equally by the executive branch, extractive industry companies, and the epistemic communities that surround the extractive sector. Central to these strategies are three devices: the framing of development, the definition of countries as naturally predisposed for extraction, and the counterposition of productive extraction against unproductive or impoverished alternatives. These devices clearly reinforce each other.

Quotations from the presidents of Bolivia, Ecuador, and Peru throughout this volume give a good indication of how development is framed so as to lay the base for dispossession. This framing casts development as a process in which economic growth and technological modernization must precede the generation of surpluses that can then be used for social investment and productive diversification. Note, for instance, the quotations of Evo Morales and Alvaro García Linera (respectively, President and Vice-President of Bolivia):

> What, then, is Bolivia going to live off if some NGOs say "Amazonia without oil"? . . . They are saying, in other words, that the Bolivian people ought not have money, that there should be neither IDH [Impuesto Directo de Hidrocarburos, a direct tax on hydrocarbons used to fund government investments] nor royalties, and also that there should be no Juancito Pinto, Renta Dignidad nor Juana Azurduy [cash transfer and social programs]. (Morales 2009)

> Of course there will be a tension between social-state logic and a sustainable use of nature, and the social-state needs to generate economic surpluses that are the state's responsibility . . . combined with the right of a people to the land is the right of the state, of the state led by the indigenous-popular and *campesino* movement, to superimpose the greater collective interest of all the peoples. And that is how we are going to go forward. . . .
>
> You need to produce on a large scale, to implement processes of expansive industrialization that provide you with a social surplus that can be redistributed and support other processes of *campesino*, communitarian and small-scale modernization.
>
> ÁLVARO GARCÍA LINERA, 2009[9]

These framings of development strategy in the public sphere become coupled with the notion that the "natural" route to such "development as accumulation then redistribution" is through the extraction of natural resources. Peru, for instance, is consistently framed by government, the industry, and its supporters as having the natural vocation to be a "*país minero*" (a "mining country"), while in Ecuador, Rafael Correa argued back in 2008 that "it's absurd to be sitting on top of hundreds of thousands of millions of dollars, and to say no to mining because of romanticisms, stories, obsessions, or who knows what."[10] While activists seek to counter that Peru is not a "mining country," but rather a "megadiverse, multiethnic" country, their considerably less pithy framings gain far less traction.

A further component of such discursive strategies is making clear that not only do these countries have a natural vocation for extraction, but that this also gives a privileged pathway towards modernity. Here framings peddle in easy dichotomies such as that between the modernity of mining and the primitivism and poverty of indigenous and high-altitude communities. The other argument made with increasing assertiveness, and in the face of arguments about the risks that mines hold for water supply, is that mining is, in fact, a highly efficient user of water while agriculture is not.[11] Yanacocha has gone a step further, arguing that mines can produce water through restoring old pits as reservoirs. These arguments are systematically conveyed through radio, the press, and publicly available informational materials from the mine.

While this suite of arguments do not *effect* dispossession, they do important work in creating the conditions of its possibility. They seek to fix in political and public imagination a certain notion of how to achieve development and of the purportedly commonsense reasons why extraction is an obvious means of putting this development strategy into effect. They legitimize extraction's claims on space, and the surface and subsurface within that space.

This framing and fixing has to be accompanied by strategies that make possible the actual acquisition of space and resources. We note three of these. First, and most important, are strategies of legislation. One blatant example was Alan García's use of special temporary powers that he was given by Congress in order to pass legislation that would allow Peru to conform to terms in the Free Trade Agreement with the United States, in order to pass legislation that would facilitate private acquisition of and investment on community-held lands (Bebbington 2012a). Another example is the frequent use of presidential powers to declare mining projects in the national interest, thus allowing them to go ahead. These powers have been used to allow foreign-owned companies to operate close to national borders (as in both the Piura and Zamora cases), as well as to fast-track projects and thus abbreviate lengthy environmental reviews and approval processes (as the Morales administration did for hydrocarbons projects in Norte La Paz). Another significant (though less-visible) example occurred during the final drafting of the new constitution in Ecuador. Discussions of whether the constitution would recognize International Labor Organization (ILO) Convention 169 to give indigenous people the right to free, prior, and informed *consent* occurred into the very last hours of the preparation of the text of the Constitution in Montecristi in the coastal lowlands. While the Constituent Assembly should have been the elected body preparing this text, according to persons present in those final negotiations, President Correa intervened directly by telephone in those discussions with a view to watering down any rights to consent given to communities. The flip side of weakening powers of consent is, of course, to increase the powers of dispossession of those actors who would otherwise have to secure this consent.

There are of course many other examples of the use of legislation to effect dispossession and of the process through which this legislation is molded by interested parties. The direct intervention of embassies in these processes is repeatedly commented on, especially that of the Canadian Embassy. The then Sub-Secretary for Environment in Ecuador referred to the Canadian Ambassador as no more than a representative for the Canadian mining sector in Ecuador, and later rumors abounded regarding the embassy's influence on new mining legislation in Ecuador. Meanwhile in Peru, a direct intervention by the Canadian Ministry of Foreign Affairs in 2005 led to the withdrawal of Canadian nongovernmental funding to Peruvian legal defense NGOs working with communities in extraction-affected areas.

Alongside such discursive and legislative strategies of dispossession sits the use of market mechanisms. Some of these operate through payments to acquire land or rights of use. The use of compensation as a market exchange (cash for land, cash for water, cash for damages) can also be seen as a strategy for effecting dispossession, and Corporate Social Responsibility (CSR) programs are used in a somewhat similar vein. Again, these are not direct instruments of dispossession. However, their role in making dispossession seem both palatable and profitable for populations should not be underestimated, especially if we include the special community development funds that a number of companies have established as part of their agreements with communities within the notion of social responsibility programs. In an extreme case, such as Michiquillay in Cajamarca, such funds run to more than US$200 million. The other function, or at least *effect*, of social responsibility programs is to create clientelisms within local populations, building a basis of support for companies that is critical at the moment that votes are taken and community-level debates framed. These relationships play important roles in laying the bases that subsequently make dispossession more possible.

Opportunities and Their Unevenness

While extraction enacts a broad set of dispossessions, it also generates a range of opportunities. Indeed, much protest around the extractive sector is oriented towards securing or enhancing such opportunities. These opportunities are, however, unevenly distributed. Discourse around new projects frequently emphasizes the employment benefits that they will bring. In truth, however, the medium to long-term direct employment effects of modern extractive industry are few, as capital has increasingly substituted for labor, for reasons both of efficiency and safety.[12] Medium to long-term fixed-employment opportunities are concentrated in skilled sectors. These workers are not drawn from communities, but rather from farther afield and sometimes from abroad, and while some companies in our cases attempt to develop local skilled labor, little of this comes from the most local populations. The geographical effects of this employment generation vary, though in each instance they generate disquiet. In some instances, labor lives in camps on the mine site or gas and oil fields, separate from local centers, triggering dissatisfaction at its failure to dynamize local economies through its spending. This disquiet is felt not only in communities or small towns. In Tarija, for instance, once the exploratory phase is completed much of the skilled and highly paid labor commutes between the gas fields and the city of Santa Cruz, largely bypassing the economy of the Chaco and the city of Tarija. Conversely, when this skilled labor resides locally, as is the case in Cajamarca, its purchasing power leads to price inflation, particularly in the property market, as well as an increasing segmentation among local consumers between those mine workers who consume certain services (e.g., high-end restaurants) and a local middle-class population who cannot. Some analysts suggest that annoyance at this segmentation has motivated middle-class mobilization and anti-mine sentiments in Cajamarca (Gorriti 2004).

At a community level, employment opportunities are concentrated during the construction phase, with more limited options during the operational phase. These opportunities privilege men over women, and typically younger men over older men. More difficult still is that in negotiations with communities, companies often guarantee a certain number of jobs per community, and then communities have to find ways of allocating these jobs, generally on a rotating basis, making for complex intracommunity negotiations as well as producing frustration that few jobs become full-time.

Another set of opportunities, much touted in claims about responsible mining, are those generated by company social responsibility and community development programs. This is an area in which companies' learning curves have been steep in all of our cases, though certain challenges remain that, in some sense, are inherent to the point-source nature of extractive activity. In Cajamarca, for instance, early community relations work by Yanacocha involved, at the admission of their own community development teams, making bilateral agreements with those individuals and communities that it was necessary to placate (e.g., if they threatened protest) or secure the acquiescence of in order for mining activity and expansion to continue. This strategy merely encouraged other local actors to demand benefits of one sort or another, at the same time generating its own tensions because, while many agreements were made by community development team staff, many were not honored and the company actually had no sense of how many outstanding agreements it had. In addition, the company began to recognize that rather than catalyze development, the benefits being handed out were generating further inequalities within and among communities—between those who received and those who did not.[13] From 2005 onwards, the company had to rethink its community development strategy entirely, leading to a new strategy that was based on an explicit distance-decay function. That is, opportunities would be concentrated in those communities immediately adjacent to the mine, would be less intensive in communities located somewhat farther from the mine, and absent elsewhere.

In some cases, the funds associated with community development initiatives become very significant. For instance, when Anglo-American created its enormous development fund in Michiquillay, this in turn induced political maneuvering within the two communities, itself refracted through prior landholding structures and competition and distrust between different sectors of the community (Burneo and Chaparro 2010).[14] A further difficulty it triggered within communities was debate on who would be eligible to vote on the project and the use of these funds. Particularly uncertain was the extent to which community members who had migrated and taken up urban residence in the city of Cajamarca or farther afield were eligible to vote.

Somewhat different opportunities are those created for local service providers. Extractive industry sites—mines more so than wells—require a range of services provided in bulk, such as mechanical support and maintenance for vehicles, food supply, clothing for workers, and simple building materials. While companies source many of these services nonlocally in order to guarantee quality, others *are* sourced locally. Indeed, in response to social conflict a number of companies have sought to increase their local sourcing, as in Cajamarca (Bebbington et al. 2007c). In addition, during construction and periods of mine expansion, companies recruit labor through local companies that organize work gangs. This allows companies to reduce transaction costs and also, because such labor is employed by the contractor, the company is not responsible for worker benefits.

In addition to the specific jobs created, this mode of hiring services creates particular opportunities for local capital and is associated with the emergence of new business both in regional urban centers and in communities where, for instance, labor-recruiting companies become consolidated. This, in turn, fosters new forms of differentiation and relationships of power in the local and regional economies, as well as constant maneuvering to win subcontracts with the extractive industry company.

The most significant financial opportunity created by the extractive economy derives from the tax and royalties paid by companies. The amount of such payment hinges on national tax and royalty rates as well as specific agreements through which government may have given companies favorable tax and royalty conditions in order to encourage them to invest. The geographical distribution of these payments likewise hinges on legislation that varies across the region. In some instances (as in Chile), central government controls these income streams, whereas in others, as in Peru and Bolivia, significant proportions are redistributed to the regions in which extraction occurs, with further formulae determining how these resources are distributed spatially within these regions.[15]

The resources generated in this way are very large, and in fiscal systems that redistribute tax and royalties back to the regions of extraction, this leads to very significant inequalities among regions regarding the revenue they control. Thus in 2007 in Peru, about 67 percent of all "canon" transfers (i.e., tax-related transfers) and 52 percent of all fiscal transfers were concentrated in just 6 of the country's 25 regions and among just 16 percent of the population (Arellano-Yanguas 2012). Meanwhile in 2008 in Bolivia, the department of Tarija was producing 70 percent of Bolivia's natural gas and receiving 35 percent of the country's entire decentralized budget (Humphreys Bebbington 2010). This geographical concentration of opportunities has been an important component in regionalist politics and unrest in Bolivia as other regions and the central government have sought to gain greater shares of these tax and royalty revenues (Humphreys Bebbington and Bebbington 2010). This same concentration has also prompted the government to expand extraction in other departments with a view to increasing the royalty and tax revenue that they would receive. Indeed it appeared that this sort of reasoning underlaid the argument by Bolivia's Vice-President Alvaro García Linera when he said in August 2009, "Is it mandatory to get gas and oil from the Amazon of North La Paz? Yes. Why? Because we have to balance the economic structures of Bolivian society, because the rapid development of Tarija with 90 percent of the gas is going to generate imbalances in the long run. It is necessary, accordingly, to balance in the long term between the territorialities of the state."

In some instances (e.g., Peru) these geographical inequalities also play out at the municipal level, as some municipalities receive far larger transfers than do others. In particular, municipalities located most closely to and most directly affected by projects receive transfers on a scale that completely distorts municipal budgets and provides amounts of money that are very difficult for these authorities to spend, or at least spend well. The arrival of such resources also profoundly transforms local politics as different movements and interest groups jostle, electorally and extra-electorally, in order to gain access to and control over the allocation of these resources.

What emerges from these complexes of dispossession and opportunity is how profoundly and inevitably unequal and unequalizing they are in their effects. We see inequalities *between* territories deriving from both geological differences and fiscal arrangements that produce geographic unevenness in redistribution. And we see inequalities *within* territories in which the new inequalities of power that accompany the arrival of extractive industry lead to new inequalities in exposure to uncertainty and vulnerability, access to resources and labor markets, participation in service provision markets, access to community development interventions, and more. These inequalities are themselves produced by a set of inequities among companies, governments, and communities to frame meanings of development, influence policy, access mass media, mobilize and use science, and divine the nature and value of the subsoil. Meanwhile, local differences in patterns of dispossession, risk, and opportunity are themselves produced by interacting axes of social, spatial, gendered, and institutionalized inequities.

Responses to the Uneven Political Ecologies of Dispossession and Opportunity

These combined and uneven complexes of dispossession and opportunity help explain the high and growing levels of social conflict that have been part of the expansion of extractive industry across much of Latin America. They also caution against singular explanations of this conflict. In the following paragraphs we argue that mobilization and conflict have been driven by a range of motivations, grievances, and incentives. This also suggests that the juxtaposition of "greed or grievance" in explanations of conflicts around extraction (Collier and Hoeffler 2004, 2005; see Caballero 2011 for Peru) is an unhelpful simplification.[16]

Across our case studies, we find one set of protests and conflicts that are best understood as responses to uncertainty and perceived risk. These conflicts manifest themselves subsequent to the granting of concessions to conduct exploration but prior to exploitation. In many instances, these happen before any actual exploitation has occurred. This would be the case, for instance, in Piura and each of the Ecuadorian cases. In other cases, such protests may occur when an existing extractive enterprise seeks to expand its operations in ways that are perceived to generate threats to nearby populations. The most significant example of this would be the massive mobilizations that united both rural and urban populations in Cajamarca when Minera Yanacocha sought to begin exploration in a mountain known as Cerro Quilish, a zone that had long been considered the primary source of water for the city of Cajamarca as well as adjacent communities. This mobilization ultimately led Yanacocha to abandon exploration, though it still suggests that it will extract gold from Quilish in the future.

People's fear of loss is a recurrent theme in these protests, along with frustration at not having been consulted about the prospect of extraction in the territories that they occupy. These fears about loss of ways of living and healthy environments are prominent in such protests, but perhaps most prominent of all are fears about water. Water is such an omnipresent theme in these conflicts because so many mining concessions are located in headwaters of rivers, because hydrocarbon extraction has such a history of water pollution throughout the Amazon, and because the highlands and coasts of the region are already water-constrained environments. Indeed, arguments between different interests in these conflicts as to whether mining will affect water quantity and quality, and whether it does so more or less than agriculture and urbanization, are far from resolved and constitute perhaps the principal domain of struggle over the definition of hegemonic ideas in debates over extraction in the region.

A second group of protests hinge less on risk and more on concerns that extraction has become, or will be, a source of dispossession. Again the motivations are varied in such conflicts. Some reflect concern over loss of access to resources that sustain livelihood or components of livelihood. Others reflect a desire not to lose political authority over certain space, and others a concern over loss of relative autonomy in governing space, particularly among indigenous populations.

A third set of conflicts is quite different and reflects demands for opportunities — or a fear that opportunities will be lost. Thus again, across our cases we have seen instances in which mobilizations have been led by mine workers or populations hoping that extraction will directly or indirectly generate employment. This has occurred, for instance, in Cajamarca, Tarija, Zamora, and Intag. Opponents to mining typically label such mobilizations as having been orchestrated by interests linked to extractive industry, but this strikes us as unhelpful and also as casting protestors as relative automatons willing to go to the streets in return for small incentives. In many areas in which extraction is being proposed, employment is a genuine concern, especially among younger adults.

Somewhat more nefarious are those mobilizations in which orchestrators are facilitated by local and regional capitalists demanding contracts. Again, we would avoid casting the men and women who actually protest as mere pawns in the demands of others; and so in such protests, there is a convergence of demands for employment and contracts. However, there is evidence to suggest that a number of protests have been facilitated by contractors who have lost business with extractive industry companies and who, in essence, use conflict as a way of forcing these companies to recruit their services. Companies involved in labor provision are perhaps the best able to use this tactic.

Last are those mobilizations that are facilitated by politically interested actors. In some cases these actors are motivated by their own political or rent-seeking activities, and they use arguments over extraction as ways of challenging political opponents, strengthening their own parties' bases, or securing their own privileged access to companies and/or government. In other cases it may be elected authorities themselves who help orchestrate protest. Once again, however, we would insist that these authorities and interest groups do not have total power to instrumentalize their constituents, and so such mobilizations reflect grievances and demands that are felt by these populations as well as the maneuvers of authorities. The opportunities sought by such authorities have been of various types. In some instances, authorities (and candidates) appear to view an active assumption of a particular stance vis-à-vis extraction as enhancing their electoral prospects. Increasingly significant, however, are mobilizations that seek to increase the revenue that subnational authorities and populations derive from extraction (Arellano-Yanguas 2012; Humphreys Bebbington and Bebbington 2010).

One striking example of this phenomenon was the conflict in 2009 between the southern Peruvian regions of Tacna and Moquegua, each an important producer of copper (Arellano-Yanguas 2012). In this instance, the copper is produced by the company Southern Peru Copper, using ore drawn from the two departments. Fiscal transfers back to the departments had been based on the volume of ore extracted, such that Moquegua received 22 percent and Tacna received 78 percent of the transfers, based on Southern Peru's tax payments. However, the ore in Moquegua is much richer than Tacna's, and in fact more than three quarters of the final copper produced came from Moquegua. The region thus organized massive street protests demanding increased transfers and culminating in a violent standoff between protestors from the two regions. When central government finally yielded and agreed to increase transfers to Moquegua, the Tacna authorities complained bitterly and protests resumed. These mobilizations also involved municipal authorities and municipal populations. Indeed, transfers to the regions had become so large that in a number of municipalities the bulk of the population was employed by the municipal government using funds generated by tax transfers. Both the authorities and the population feared for their political influence and jobs, respectively, if transfers were to be reduced (Arellano-Yanguas 2012).

A second example from Tarija reflects how both regional and national political authorities can each facilitate conflicts in ways that converge with their broader political objectives. The bulk of Tarija's gas comes from the Gran Chaco province of the department and, by law, 45 percent of the transfers of gas revenue to Tarija are earmarked for the Gran Chaco, 15 percent to each of its three municipalities. These funds, however, passed through the departmental government, who would only release them if the Gran Chaco proposed uses of the money that converged with Tarija's priorities and investment criteria. While tension over this influence of the departmental government had existed for a number of years, it became accentuated in 2008 in a context of wider political conflict between the central government and the lowland departments of Bolivia. In the midst of this conflict, the central government sought an alliance with the authorities of the Gran Chaco, who were far from natural allies of the governing party, offering them a referendum on whether they should receive financial payments directly from central government and manage them autonomously of Tarija. Not surprisingly, they voted "yes." For the central government, this response to the conflict became functional to the goal of weakening departmental authority in Tarija, and for the Gran Chaco it allowed them to achieve the autonomy that they sought.

Conclusions

To return to the question that motivated the research reported on here, there can be no doubt that processes of social mobilization have influenced the political economy of extraction. Even if some mobilizations do not achieve their goals—be these to block extractive industry, to secure its unencumbered expansion, or to negotiate the terms on which companies as well as state and local populations interact—the dynamics surrounding extraction have changed profoundly throughout the region as a result of social protest. There are many indicators of such change. It is now very rare that a mining, oil, or gas-related project might proceed without significant public debate of its merits, shortcomings, and potential interactions with environment and development. The place of extractive industry within the national economy and development models has become a topic of political debate, manifest in electoral campaigns, newspaper editorials, and television current affairs shows. It has largely been the efforts of communities and movements that have placed the topic in the public sphere. Policy instruments for environmental regulation, the use and management of fiscal revenue, consultation with affected populations, and land use planning have changed and/or become the object of far greater public discussion than was previously the case. And many extractive industry companies, particularly the larger transnational companies, have had to expand and rethink their approaches to corporate responsibility, community engagement, and image management. Finally, among the cases included in our research, there are instances in which large-scale investments have either been blocked (as in Cotacachi and Piura) or considerably rethought (as in Cajamarca and Tarija) as a consequence of protest. It would be very difficult to claim that all these changes would have occurred in the ways that they did had there not been such sustained community and social movement activity questioning the forms being taken by the extractive economy.

That said, social mobilization continues. This would seem to suggest that, when seen from the position of movements, not enough has changed. Moreover, in a context in which the expansion of concessions and extraction has continued, and contentious projects continue to receive government support, the leitmotif of some mobilizations has changed. If earlier mobilization had more focused concerns such as water, contamination, and rents, some protests, especially those in Peru, appear to increasingly adopt positions that are simply opposed to large-scale extractive industry in general. Indeed, in June 2011, protests against mining in the department of Puno in the southern altiplano of Peru were on such a scale that, for a few days at least, it appeared that they would prevent voting in presidential elections.[17] While certain voices interpreted these protests as artifacts of political manipulation, and evidently such manipulation was indeed present—reflecting, inter alia, conflicts between regional government and other local authorities—it is less easy to explain away such large-scale mobilization purely in terms of special interests. The same applies to yet more recent mass protests in Cajamarca over the Minas Conga project near Celendín. For while some *mobilizers* might have special interests, we cannot presume that *the mobilized* protest on such a mass scale simply because they are willing to risk their own lives and limbs in order to support the special interests of others. Given the costs and risks of protest, it is reasonable to assume that something else motivates their decision to take to the streets. Indeed, the protests in Puno were significant because, even if they began as a protest over one particular mine, they soon morphed into a call for rescinding all mining concessions in the department. For example, the area under mining concessions in Puno increased by 279 percent between 2002 and 2010 (CooperAcción 2011).[18] This was not necessarily a generalized call for a Puno without mining. It was, though, a call to start over and to find different modes and criteria for planning and making decisions about how extractive industry should unfold in a region, even if this was not the issue at the moment of the more localized onset of the protest. There were echoes here of similar observations that Bonnie Campbell (2003, 2006, 2008) has made in Africa—namely that the problem with mining policy is that it is a policy for *mining* and not policy for the *relationship between mining and development*. There were also echoes of other demands increasingly heard across the region—whether in Zamora Chinchipe, Ecuador (governed by Salvador Quispe of the left-of-center Pachakutik party); Tarija, Bolivia (when it was controlled by Mario Cossio's right of center alliance); or Arequipa, Peru (when controlled by Manuel Guillén's regionalist government)—for a considerably enhanced role for local authorities and local plans in the determination of policies on extractive industry expansion.

One interpretation of the protests in Puno, and of several of the others covered in our cases, is that these movements and struggles are demanding what institutional economists might call changes in "the rules of the game." In this sense, these movements and the struggles in which they engage are primarily reformist. In some cases, of course, movements *are* staunchly against mining. In Piura, for example, there is a clear sense that the *rondas campesinas* (literally "peasant rounds," a particular form of rural social organization) simply do not want mining. Parts of the protest movement in Zamora seem equally opposed to mining. In other instances, however, this seems not to be the case. In Tarija, we have a very strong sense that neither the Guaraní nor the Weenhayek are completely opposed to gas extraction. What they appear to want is greater respect for their territory and livelihoods, a greater share in the benefits, and a greater say in the processes that affect them. Likewise in Cajamarca, while some groups are categorically opposed to the expansion of mining in certain watersheds, few imagine or demand a Cajamarca with no mining. Meanwhile in Oruro, long a mining region, protests at the time of the closure of the Inti Raymi mine were not protests against *mining* but protests demanding more stringent environmental compensation for resources lost and social compensation for jobs lost (Leonith Hinojosa per. comm. 2009).

The new "rules" that these protests demand are not all the same. Some demands emphasize issues of free, prior, and informed consent. Some emphasize the rules governing fiscal redistribution and transfers. Some demand changes in tax rates and royalties. Some demand different systems for granting concessions. Some, most perhaps, simply demand more participatory planning. At one level, then, these protests might be seen as a popular pushback against what James Scott (1998) deems the centralized, simplifying, and authoritarian ways of "seeing" that characterize the high modern state's mode of making the countryside legible, in order to govern it in ways that suit these centralized agendas (also cf. Neumann 2004). There is something to this argument, but it would also be unhelpful to frame these struggles as counterposing an adaptive, everyday *mêtis* of indigenous knowledge and practice against a hyperrational, modern form of landscape ordering whose practice is embodied in the state. Indeed, these movements seem also to be demanding order and planning; there is nothing here that is especially antirational or antimodern.

This call for regulatory order is particularly apparent in the recurrent demands from movement organizations that any expansion of mining and hydrocarbon activity should only occur *subsequent to* a *prior* process of ecological and economic zoning that would seek to characterize the most appropriate land uses in different areas. This zoning process would then be followed by a process of *ordenamiento territorial* (OT, territorial planning), which would take the results of the zoning exercise and convert them into land use plans that would be binding and would, therefore, structure any subsequent geographies of investment, be these in mining, hydrocarbons, house building, commercial agriculture, or other domains. This is clearly a call for order, and it is perhaps for this reason that some critical scholars of development have viewed OT instead as an instrument that allows the state to organize space in such a way as to allow extraction and, through this particular way of encountering nature, to foster processes of state formation that are not in the interests of local populations, as Asher and Ojeda (2009) argue for the case of state–Afrocolombian relations in Colombia. While Asher and Ojeda allow for some reworking of OT processes as a result of Afrocolombian organization and participation, the pattern in the cases we considered suggests that movement organizations and activists are far less ambivalent and skeptical of OT and instead see it (as do some regional authorities) as a means of fostering enhanced participation and engaging extractive industry companies in new sorts of conversation about development. Where one might be more skeptical is in the political feasibility of OT in contexts where the interests at stake are substantially different and where asymmetries of power are immense—for it is one thing to have a set of landscape characterizations, and quite another to turn these into rules that will permit the favored land uses of some stakeholders and forbid those favored by other stakeholders.

Putting these (albeit vital) questions of political feasibility aside, the more general point we wish to make is that in these calls for order and ordering (albeit in a different register, with different criteria), movements and protestors are above all demanding a particular sort of state, probably one that is actually more "state-like" and more Weberian than the actually existing states that they have to deal with. They are demanding state practices based on a fuller sense of science (incorporating ecology, hydrology, agronomy, and forestry as well as geology), on a more routinized set of practices—that is, a bureaucratic approach to planning that reduces the scope for discretionary decisions—and on a more clearly and openly articulated set of criteria than those currently used in government discourses. By the same token, these are demands to be better protected by their state, and for a state that is less allied with industry and elite interests and more oriented towards the defense of citizenship rights.[19] If one of the primary effects of the expansion of the extractive frontier is, as we have argued, to create uncertainty, then in some respect these demands are for state forms and state practices that would reduce uncertainty. And by the same token, if the extractive economy of the last fifteen years has been one that enacted a range of economic, cultural, political, and environmental dispossessions, in some sense the demand here is for a state that would guard against some of that dispossession while simultaneously facilitating local forms of creativity by regulating environmental protection, charging more taxes and royalties, and taking back the powers of governance that have been delegated to companies. Indeed, a recurrent theme in these mobilizations is that the only viable way of confronting dispossession in the long run is through the state. The subterranean struggles discussed here, then, are far from being romantically subaltern. Instead, the alternatives they appear to envision are, for the most part, modern, rational, and economically pragmatic while being based on fairness and greater recognition of the right to diversity.

Notes

1. Territorial dynamics were taken to refer to the relationships between political economy, institutional arrangements, and everyday practices within given territories. These relationships might be manifest in everything from land use, production practices, and regional politics to livelihoods and daily routines.

2. This project was supported by the Economic and Social Research Council of the United Kingdom, Grant Number RES-051-27-0191.

3. Resources in Piura came from the Peru Support Group, in Tarija from Centro Latinoamericano para el Desarrollo Rural (RIMISP, Latin American Center for Rural Development) and the International Development Research Centre, and in Cajamarca from the time of Jeffrey Bury.

4. Of course there are variations on this theme. Following the elections of Evo Morales in Bolivia and Rafael Correa in Ecuador, some companies would say that investment conditions have not been optimum.

5. We specify "modern" because in some of the apparently new mining frontiers, there is evidence of pre-colonial extraction and/or of more recent artisanal extraction.

6. Estimations by Jose de Echave and colleagues at CooperAcción.

7. Presentation in Berlin by Jorge Jurado, former Subsecretary for Mines (in 2007) and ambassador to Germany (in 2011).

8. *Capitánes* is the denomination for political authorities in Guaraní (and Ween-hayek) communities in the Bolivian Chaco.

9. Interview with Álvaro García Linera, "Entrevista a Alvaro García Linera, Le Monde Diplomatique, agosto de 2009," *International Journal of Socialist Renewal*, 2009. English translation, "Bolivia's vice-president defends MAS government's record," available at Links, www.links.org.au/node/1241.

10. Rafael Correa, interview, Cadena Radial, 11 October 2008.

11. Various companies in Peru have dedicated significant resources to elaborating this argument, among them Yanacocha, Southern Peru Copper Corporation, and Anglo-American-Quellaveco.

12. The exception is artisanal or small-scale mining (ASM), in which labor substitutes for technology and capital.

13. This paragraph draws on interviews with staff and managers of the community development team at Yanacocha between 2005 and 2009.

14. It must be noted that these are large communities.

15. This is particularly true for gas-related tax revenue in Bolivia.

16. These approaches are ones that understand the linkages between conflict and extraction as ones generated either by a desire for profit and accumulation—that can come from gaining access to and control of rents, or direct control of the extractive process, in particular in cases of gem mining—or conversely by more deeply seated sociopolitical grievances that find expression through conflicts over extractive industry.

17. This did not happen, in the end, and the elections proceeded.

18. See the bulletin *Actualidad Minera del Perú*, No. 145, May 2011, page 1.

19. Indeed, it is for this reason that the Defensoría del Pueblo has such legitimacy in Peru, because it is viewed as the one part of the state apparatus that does seek to protect citizens' rights when other parts of the state do not respect these rights.

CHAPTER 11

Conclusions

ANTHONY BEBBINGTON, JEFFREY BURY,
AND EMILY GALLAGHER

In Chapter 1 of this book we made several strong claims regarding the relationships between the subsoil and Latin American political economy as well as the relationships between the subsoil and political ecology. We argued that since the early 1990s, the extraction of subsoil resources in Latin America has taken on forms that are fundamentally different from those of earlier periods, notwithstanding the long histories of mining and hydrocarbon investment within which contemporary extraction is rooted. We also claimed that extraction has become central to the region's more general political economy. At the same time, we argued that a close look at extraction in Latin America would support the claim that the subsoil has a special significance for political ecology, one that has thus far been undervalued.

Ultimately, we believe that these claims have been amply demonstrated. The purpose of this concluding chapter is to support this assertion. First, we summarize why it is fitting to talk of "new geographies of extraction." We point to newness in simple spatial form, the ways in which extraction bundles nature and society, the socio-spatial processes that produce these geographies, the nature of struggle that surrounds contemporary extraction, and the imagined and material frontiers produced by the expansion of extractive industry. As we make these points, we also note different ways in which the authors demonstrate the centrality of extraction to contemporary processes of territorial, national, and continental transformation. Second, we summarize how and why the chapter contents, taken as a whole, suggest interesting avenues for political ecology. In particular, they draw attention to the importance of material flows across frontiers and boundaries. They also reiterate but complicate the significance of the state and social struggle to political ecology. While the state is a prominent actor in all cases discussed in the chapters, it has many faces that do not always look in the same direction. And while the authors consistently reveal causal interactions between struggle and extraction, they are not quite as consistent in endorsing any easy association of struggle with notions of subaltern or progressive alternatives. Indeed, the authors challenge scholars to be nuanced in how they speak of and categorize struggle and conflict. Third, on the basis of these arguments, we identify areas for further research in the political ecology of extraction.

New Geographies of Latin American Extraction and Transformation

Caveats on Novelty

When presenting versions of several of these chapters, we have often been asked very directly, "So what's new? Latin America has a long history of struggles over access to resources and control over rents; isn't this just more of the same?"[1] The question makes a serious point: it is easy to overstate novelty and lose sight of the historical continuities that should be part of any explanation of the phenomena being framed as new. And indeed, history looms large in many of the chapters in this book. The case of Bolivian struggles over gas (Chapter 3 by Perreault) shows how contemporary politics around natural gas in Bolivia have to be understood in terms of historical memories of war, long-standing regional and racial inequalities, and prior separatist tendencies in the eastern lowlands. In a similar vein, the dynamics in northeast Peruvian Amazonia (Chapter 7 by Bebbington and Scurrah, and Chapter 9 by Postigo, Montoya, and Young) suggest that the intensity of struggle over pollution in the region only makes sense when seen in terms of four decades of oil development and the more or less systematic undervaluation of indigenous rights and bodies throughout that whole period (see also Smith 2009). Meanwhile, the evocative discussion of El Pangui's new mining frontier in southeast Ecuador (Chapter 6 by Warnaars) shows how the dynamics and fault lines of contemporary protest find part of their explanation in a long-sedimented history of different constructions of territory and conflicts over land in the region. In a slightly different register, the experience in Cordillera Huayhuash (Chapter 4 by Bury and Norris) shows the histories that can keep certain territories off the map of extractive investment flows—in this case, because the conflict of Peru's long civil war had made the area relatively inaccessible to mining companies.

These examples make clear that many of the dynamics of the current round of expanded investment in the extractive sector intersect with territorialized and national histories that are either real or imagined and almost always deep.

Indeed, Postigo, Montoya, and Young (Chapter 9) write of social and environmental conflicts "resting upon the foundations of more than five centuries of resource extraction in Peru." Political ecologies of extraction must be ever cognizant of this sedimentation. This, however, does not mean that what lies on the top of these layers cannot itself be simultaneously embedded *and* fundamentally new. In the following sections we argue that this is what is revealed in these chapters.

In a similar vein, one might ask whether there is anything specifically Latin American to the dynamics analyzed in this book. In the opening chapters we noted that the recent surge of extraction is related to global processes, and that countries beyond Latin America are also witnessing an upsurge in investment in the extractive economy. So this collection is not an exercise in Latin American exceptionalism. However, there has been a particular convergence of policy, political, and geological conditions that has made the region particularly interesting to extractive industry (see Chapter 2). These new investment flows articulate with histories and sociopolitical formations that are particular to the continent, and in the process produce new and specific geographies.

Space and Scales, Flows and Velocities

As we noted in Chapters 1 and 2, the "new extraction" has opened up new spaces to the economy of large-scale mining and hydrocarbons. In some cases, these new spaces are whole countries (e.g., large-scale mining in Ecuador or hydrocarbons in Nicaragua), while in other cases they are regions within countries (e.g., hydrocarbon lots in the altiplano of Peru and Bolivia, or hard rock mining in the Sierra Nevada of Colombia). In several of the chapters, authors have focused specifically on these new "territories of extraction" (Humphreys Bebbington 2010): southeast lowland Ecuador (Chapter 6 by Warnaars), the southern highlands of Ecuador (Chapter 5 by Moore and Velásquez), and the highlands of Piura (Chapter 10 by Bebbington et al.) and the Cordillera Huayhuash, both in Peru (Chapter 4 by Bury and Norris). In each case, the analyses demonstrate how this new extraction has transformed the dynamics and everyday life of these territories as well as the national politics of the countries in which they are located.

In several chapters, authors have also made clear that these new investments in extractive industries are part of a larger, and also new, "complex" of activities that form a network of infrastructure and built environments that has been developed across Latin America in order to seek out, extract, and transport minerals, hydrocarbons, energy, and water. In Chapter 2 we made this point with respect to a regional scale, while several authors note how it takes form subnationally. Hindery's discussion in Chapter 8 is especially important in this regard because, beyond the apparent insider dealing, corruption, and lack of transparency surrounding the extractive economy in Santa Cruz, his painstaking inspection of official papers and pipeline construction sites reveals how investments in extractive industry are not imagined in isolation, even when their feasibility and environmental impact statements are considered on a project-by-project basis. Indeed, one of the benefits of this collection is that while each chapter reveals the complexity of individual cases, when taken as a whole, the chapter authors suggest that something much larger is going on, namely a regional transformation of which the dynamics reported in these different chapters are parts. This regional transformation may not be perfectly tuned, and it has certainly gone through its own moments of rupture and crisis, but it is *regional*, and it is being imagined and engineered as such by companies, consultants, finance capital, governments, and international organizations. For instance, discussing a proposed gas pipeline for the south of Peru, one of its promoters, Alfredo Barnechea (2012), comments: "The final pipeline was going to circulate in the midst of many large mining projects (Las Bambas and Southern's concessions), providing them with energy while feeding gas to several power stations (beginning with one in Quillabamba that, once connected to Machhu Picchu, would be lined to the national electricity network)."[2] Thus, while Perreault very rightly alerts us to the importance of understanding the intersections between gas and the imagined geographies of both Evo Morales's Movement for Socialism (Movimiento al Socialismo, MAS) and the conservative Nación Camba, it is equally vital to get a handle on the geographies that are imagined by national elites, multilateral technocrats working in bodies such as the Inter-American Development Bank (IDB) and the Latin American Energy Organization (Organización Latinoamericana de Energía, OLADE), the strategic planners of extractive industry companies, and public and private investors. When these actors imagine geographies, they tend to think in terms of national and supranational transformations, not individual projects.

The immense scale at which these transformations are occurring is evident in other respects, related above all to the technologies at play and the risks at stake. The current round of extraction mobilizes a new suite of technologies whose potential effects are both uneven and novel. In the mineral sector, open pit mining delivers unprecedented forms of landscape transformation: mountains "chopped down," gaping holes opened, whole systems of surface hydrology destroyed or relocated. Conversely in the hydrocarbon sector, new extraction technologies being deployed in remote areas of the Amazon Basin or to access oil and gas in "tight" shales near water resources and super-deep salt domes pose tremendous risks to the environment. In comparison with the underground shafts and oil derricks of the past, the visible and invisible landscape changes associated with open pit mines costing hundreds of millions or billions of dollars, or of pipelines crossing half continents, are of a new order, even when much new hydrocarbon extraction technology seeks to reduce the scope of physical landscape change (e.g., by avoiding associated road construction and working "offshore" sites). These scales of transformation also evoke a sense of the new scales of uncertainty and risk that were explored, above all, in Chapter 10. As suggested in several chapters, these new scales of risk are interpreted through the lens of historical comparisons, leading companies to argue that communities overestimate risk and do not recognize the advances of modern technology. So history and memory are again central to how people make sense of contemporary extraction, but they are making sense of scales and practices that are most definitely new.

These new geographies of extraction have involved the reworking of material and financial flows as much as of spaces and landscapes. Gas taken from the Peruvian jungle, liquefied and frozen on the Peruvian coast, and shipped to Mexico to be thawed and then distributed to other countries represents a substantially new material flow that has articulated, in both real and imagined form, a range of investments in gas in the western half of South America. New material flows are just as significant within countries. Pipelines crisscross territories carrying not only hydrocarbons, but in some instances also ore in slurry form, pumped from mine sites to coastal installations. Meanwhile the new flows of ore, waste rock, construction materials, and so on, which continue to depend on road traffic, transform lived environments as the dust, noise, hazards, and congestion associated with vehicle movements fundamentally change everyday life in ways that resonate with Warnaars' description of El Pangui.

The increasingly substantial investments of Chinese, Brazilian, and Indian capital in mining and hydrocarbon extraction, as noted in Chapters 2 and 10, reflect new flows of capital and future flows of minerals across the Pacific. That said, capital from Brazil, Russia, India, China, and South Africa (BRICS) is not the only new flow reworking the region. Canadian companies have become much more significant sources of investment in the region (North, Patroni, and Clark 2006), and the days when the United States was the extractive hegemon are changing. This is especially so for the case of hard rock mining, notwithstanding the fact that the main investor in Latin America's largest gold mine—Yanacocha in Peru, discussed in Chapter 10—is registered in the United States. Canadian companies are preparing to move glaciers from high mountain peaks at the Pascua-Lama project in Chile, have invested more than US$9 billion in Peru, are claimed to be implicated in human rights abuses surrounding the Marlin mine in Guatemala, and are suing the government of El Salvador under the provisions of the Central American Free Trade Agreement (CAFTA) (Barrick 2010; MEM 2011). Meanwhile, Canadian technical and political assistance has been linked to the Ministerio de Energía y Minas (MINEM, Ministry of Energy and Mines) in Peru, and observers are convinced that Canada influenced the drafting of new mining legislation in Honduras and Ecuador. Indeed, Canadian investment looms large in Chapters 5, 6, 8, and 10. Similarly in the hydrocarbons sector, while the United States continues to be an important player, Spain and Brazil (each featured in Chapters 3 and 10), and Argentina (Chapters 9 and 10) also emerge as critical sources of investment and players in hydrocarbon politics. Indeed, while the shifting spaces of extraction in South America may be considered the surface manifestation of the new extractive economy, it is the reconfigurations of investment networks, actors, and flows that produce these new spaces.

Another aspect of these "new" extractive geographies is the pace at which changes in investment, exploration, and extraction activities have taken place. In Chapter 2 we illustrated the magnitude and relative scale of transformations over the past two decades of this "super cycle." We also focused on the rapid and increasing rate of these changes, a phenomenon also highlighted by several of the authors in this collection. As demonstrated in Chapters 5 and 6, gold and copper exploration has surged since 2000 in Ecuador. Similarly, a recurring theme is that between 1990 and 2007 in Peru, more mining claims were granted for exploration than during the previous two centuries. This pattern of sudden and rapid change has been further intensified in the post-2000 period as international capital has flowed into the Amazon Basin in search of new gas and oil deposits, across the Argentinian grasslands in search of shale gas that can be released through hydraulic fracturing ("fracking"), and along the Central American isthmus in search of new mineral deposits. As the data from Chapter 2 indicate, since 2000 the aggregate rate of extraction of most minerals more than doubled in South America, natural gas and petroleum production increased by several hundreds of percent in Bolivia and Mexico, shale gas reserves increased by hundreds of years for Argentina, Mexico, and Brazil, and foreign direct investment in extraction increased by *tens of thousands of percent* in many of the smaller countries in the region, such as El Salvador.

The other unique aspect of this "new" period of extractive activities is that the pace of change has become increasingly volatile. While extractive cycles have always been prone to "boom" and "bust" periods, the significant and nearly continuous growth of international capital that fostered rapid increases in mineral and hydrocarbons production across the region in the 1990s has been much less stable in the post-2000 period. This instability was exacerbated by two global economic crises (in 2000 and 2008) that stretched from Wall Street to the pits and pumps of Latin America's new extractive landscapes. These economic crises also included massive and unprecedented infusions of currencies into the global monetary system from the developed world's various bank rescue programs (Troubled Asset Relief Programs, or TARPs) and the extraordinarily rapid growth of demand for commodities from the BRICS countries. These TARPs and BRICS have spurred sudden and rapid shifts in commodity prices and capital flows, and they have spurred bursts of speculative investments into new "greenfield" mineral and hydrocarbon deposits. The broader consequences of these surges and plunges have yet to be fully explored.

Transformations

These new flows and technologies have articulated with national and subnational political economies of development in novel and transformative ways. The chapters presented here are a testament to these transformations. While the local and subnational transformations come through most forcefully, national transformations are not far behind. In Chapter 3, for instance, Perreault elicits the ways in which the identities and arguments mobilized in national political debates in Bolivia have been shot through with the idiom of gas—or, as Humphreys Bebbington (2010) phrases it, Bolivian politics have become "hydrocarbonized." In Chapter 5, Moore and Velásquez hint at similar if perhaps slightly less profound transformations of national political debate in Ecuador, and there can be no doubt at all that national politics in Peru have become dominated by the mining question. Meanwhile, the potential scale of gas and mining rents at stake has meant that national development models have also changed in significant and new ways. More than ever across the greater Andean region, one sees the emergence of a development model in which the extractive sector is being viewed as the backbone of a growth strategy that will generate the surplus to finance the social investment and cash transfer programs that are viewed as pivotal to government legitimacy. This model shows significant convergence across regimes of apparently very different hues: from twenty-first-century socialist Ecuador, to Morales' Bolivia, and even to the more clearly neoliberal regimes of Colombia and Peru (Bebbington and Humphreys Bebbington 2011).

Struggle is also at the center of these new articulations between extraction and political economy. There is much to be said here, and we address characteristics of these struggles further on, but at this point one particular aspect of these struggles merits comment. While the most significant struggles over access to resources in Latin America's twentieth century involved peasantries seeking to break up the concentration of property and wealth in the countryside, in this current round of struggles over extraction the converse applies: in many instances these are struggles triggered by a progressive reconcentration of rural property and wealth. Moreover, while struggles over land in the mid-twentieth century addressed critical issues of resource access and social justice, they did not call into question a model of national economic development. Indeed, one of the reasons why land reform occurred in many instances was precisely because the *latifundia* economy was no longer central to, or even functional to, the main pillars of national economic strategy. In contrast, many contemporary struggles over extraction challenge the core of the national models of accumulation and social investment outlined above. In this regard, the political resonance and analytical significance of these struggles are substantially different from those of yesteryear.

The Subsoil and "New" Political Ecologies

In the opening chapter we argued that the subsoil should be a central concern for political ecology. We gave various reasons to support this claim: modern economic systems depend entirely on the products of the subsoil for their functioning and, in that sense, the subsoil is a constituent of the political economy; as they pass through the surface and across a range of boundaries, subsoil materials transform social life and environmental relationships; and the subsoil has a particular resonance in the constitution of social and political identities. We went on to argue that several themes would be foundational in the conduct of such political ecologies of the subsoil: the explicit combination of ecological and political analysis; the articulation of global value chains and territorial processes; the interactions among the state, social struggle, and processes of enclosure; and human responses to the transformations triggered by extraction. Finally we suggested that a political ecology of the subsoil would imply certain forms of practice.

Taken together, the chapter authors have covered much of this ground.

Rather than retrace all of this, we draw attention to the ways that they have elaborated several elements of these themes: the analytical significance of boundaries and frontiers; the nature and complexity of struggle and identities; the relationships between the state and the subsoil; and matters of practice.

Frontiers and Boundaries

The significance of boundaries and frontiers has been a recurring theme across the chapters, as has the analytical purchase that can come from focusing on processes that both create and move across these dividing lines. Indeed, in Chapter 9, Postigo, Montoya, and Young argue explicitly that boundaries between particular layers of the geosphere-biosphere should constitute the core of a subsoil political ecology. They invoke a field that would focus on the socio-natural implications of flows across the frontier separating Earth's surface and subsurface. In this approach, "water resources and an assortment of edaphic, hydrological, and geological processes can be used to inform the further study of power relations, land security, environmental concerns, and basic human rights." Specifically they suggest that political ecology could focus on the "critical zone," defined as "a cross section of the uppermost part of the Earth's surface, including the groundwater, soil, vegetation, and the boundary (lowermost) layer of the atmosphere." Within this critical zone, the soil appears as a particularly important boundary, separating not only distinct biogeophysical processes, but also completely different tenure systems of the surface and the subsurface as well as domains of social action, for only very few social actors have the potential to delve deep into the subsurface.

Fluxes across this boundary bring together and at the same time disturb different physical and social processes. As the metabolism of contemporary capitalism drives processes that pull the subsurface into the domain of human interaction and then push the waste materials of this metabolic process back underground, into watercourses, or into the atmosphere, new socio-natural complexes are produced that can only be adequately grasped through a combination of biophysical and social analysis. Indeed, while the National Research Council (2001) has identified this critical zone as a priority focus of attention, discussion of such fluxes has involved extremely little social science. Yet, as made clear in this collection, social processes—allocation of property, forms of governance, struggle and conflict, and decisions about trade-offs such as "water for gold"—have an acute effect on social and physical processes alike. Focusing on such issues could be a remarkably fruitful domain for a political ecology of the subsoil, exploring political economic, land use, and environmental and climate change (among others) through the forces that determine the nature of fluxes across this boundary.

While "boundaries" such as these invoke a notion of dividing lines, "frontiers" invoke a notion of "edges"—of points reached but not yet surpassed. Such a notion of "frontier" is mobilized in several of the chapters to talk about the expansion of the extractive economy. Many of these frontiers are defined by the outer edges of extraction as it moves into new regions or as it spreads its reach within areas that already have long mining and hydrocarbon histories. For instance, in Chapter 4, Bury and Norris emphasize "the power of resource extraction frontiers to transform both societies and environments," and understand these frontiers "as edges of change that are harbingers of both material and cultural transformation" and "as places where new scalar relationships are forged in response to shifting global forces and where struggles over meaning and materiality occur." Such frontiers are simultaneously material and cultural, and in the authors' enunciation of impending change they also mark fault lines of friction, conflict, and transformation. Of course, not all such frontiers are extractive, and much attention is paid in Chapter 4 to the frontiers of a quite different vision for Andean development, a vision combining private conservation areas and low-end trekking tourism within the same sort of low-intensity, capitalist use of rural resources that is viewed by Moore and Velásquez (Chapter 5) as characterizing the aspirations of farmers in Azuay. Bury and Norris's particular interest (Chapter 4) is in the friction that occurs as these two frontiers have converged on the same spaces in the Huayhuash mountain range of Peru. While they conclude that the mining frontier will ultimately prevail, the analysis is helpful for revealing how this overlapping of frontiers is also an overlap between different ways of making sense of the world, imagining futures, and combining the material and the social in pursuit of life and livelihood. Such an insight is part of a broader tradition in studies that have emphasized "encounters at the interface" of development and rural society (Long 1989), as well as processes of hybridization at these interfaces (Escobar 2001).

Other frontiers, however, lie in the future. These are the uncertain frontiers that will mark out, in space and time, how far this ongoing extractive super cycle finally reaches. While all of the authors focus on the edges of the recent expansion of extractive operations—discoveries of natural gas and the construction of pipelines across Bolivia's lowlands, gold and silver in the Ecuadorian páramos, copper in the remote Cordillera Condor, polymetallic deposits among the glaciers of the Cordillera Huayhuash in Peru, and hydrocarbons throughout the Amazon basin—they say much less regarding how long this expansion will last, how far and how deep it may reach, and what new frictions, conflicts, and transformations its future frontiers might generate. Might, for instance, this recent "boom" in extractive activities ultimately collapse in a "bust" of prices and production? Five centuries of extraction in the region indicate that this is quite likely. Furthermore, what will be the effects of ongoing global economic and political instability on the foreign capital flows that seek out new extractive opportunities across the region? What will be the geopolitical effects of accelerating investment and demand from BRICS countries? How far down beneath the surface will extractive activities reach and with what consequences? As noted in Chapter 2, the deepening subterranean reach of capital and technology has uncovered vast new submarine petroleum salt dome deposits off the coast of Brazil and "tight" natural gas deposits throughout the Devonian shales of the Southern Cone countries. As the impacts of "super deep" submarine drilling operations and hydraulic fracturing have already galvanized deep discord in many countries, particularly in the United States, how will they affect social mobilization in Latin America? What might be the implications of these discoveries for regional political and economic relationships within Latin America and between Latin America and the rest of the world? Finally, as we conclude in Chapter 2, what will be the consequences as new "bioextractive" and geotechnical technologies are more widely deployed across the region? While they allow for ever deeper and more profound extraction of mineral and hydrocarbon resources, they have also begun to spur new configurations of socionatural relations.

Still other frontiers stalk the chapters of this book: legal frontiers between tenure rules governing the surface and those governing the subsurface; land use frontiers between agriculture and extraction; imagined frontiers between different views of nation in Bolivia; and "live" frontiers between Peru and Ecuador. Over and again, it becomes clear that these frontiers are tense and conflictive, and that the processes of translation and articulation that must occur across these frontiers are complex and difficult. In a managerial and policy sense, it is palpably evident that governments, companies, civil society organizations, and researchers have given far too little thought as to how to facilitate this translation and articulation. The institutional mechanisms for this are simply not in place, and we recognize that the sorts of boundary organizations (Jasanoff 1987; Cash et al. 2003) that we consider to be so vital emerge more by accident than they do by design (Bebbington and Bury 2009; see also Chapter 9 by Postigo, Montoya, and Young). Hence, we see across the region chaotic and disarticulated initiatives to establish dialogues (*mesas de dialogo*), consultations, and conflict management mechanisms — all exercises in the management of frontiers and boundaries. Only in a few cases (e.g., El Salvador) has the anticipation of these conflictive articulations been addressed proactively and strategically. Elsewhere this articulation has been managed in ways that tack back and forth between the reactive and the authoritarian.

What the existence of these multiple, tense frontiers indicates is the co-existence across the region of very many differing views of how things should be. Analytically, this demands study of these different understandings and of the ways in which they affect each other, become politically mobilized, and ultimately affect the ways in which resources, people, and landscapes are governed.

Subterranean Struggles and Hidden Identities

The notion of "subterranean" struggle was meant to draw attention not only to the fact that these are struggles mediated by the subsoil, but also that they themselves are hidden and difficult to penetrate. Indeed, the chapters reveal the authors trying to understand the layered memories, buried motivations, and underlying political projects that drive these struggles. Many of these struggles are also buried in the often subconscious dimensions of everyday affairs (Chapter 6 by Warnaars). Indeed, even the collective action underlying more organized struggle is a sporadic affair, and most people who partici-pate in mobilizations live most of their lives in everyday activities having to engage in the same calculations that Warnaars recounts, as well as the self-doubt that Moore and Velásquez (Chapter 5) hint at in part of their narra-tive. In other instances, organized struggles *are* sustained over time, but here, too, they pass through phases of latency or quiescence that create space for the steady work needed to build capacities, instruments, and icons—whether these are the water quality studies of residents of Victoria del Portete, Tarqui, and Tenguel, the digitized maps of the Nación Camba, or the pipeline surveys of the Chiquitanos. Importantly, these struggles can also involve long peri-ods of negotiation, and then of waiting, to see whether what is negotiated is finally delivered. Indeed, as the case of the Achuar in Río Corrientes suggests, negotiation can be a component part of struggle and may well be the pathway through which the fruits of struggle are finally delivered. These processes can be painfully slow, lasting years and decades. More than anything else, then, successful struggle seems to be a sublime combination of chance openings, pressure, and dogged endurance—enduring the wait to see if negotiations reach agreements, enduring the wait until those agreements are finally deliv-ered, and enduring the uneasy everyday life that occupies most waking hours in the process. Struggle, as portrayed in these chapters, is not romantic—it is, instead, bloody hard work.

As the authors explore dimensions of struggle that have often been hidden from view in political ecological analysis, they have revealed other reasons to avoid being starry-eyed about struggle. Moore and Velásquez insist that those who struggle against extraction should not be viewed as "part of a romantic subaltern class." In Azuay and El Oro, many who resist mining, and who have in some cases been tried and/or sent to prison, are capitalist farmers who sell their milk to urban dairies or their organic bananas to European markets. These are protestors whose interests evidently do *not* hinge on being "anti-market." Instead, as Moore and Velásquez suggest, these movements' "defense of life, water, and farming represents understandings of development that are both market-oriented and ethically minded." In a similar vein, in El Pangui (Chapter 6) some protestors are or once were miners, and others are market-oriented colonist farmers. Meanwhile, the cases discussed in Chapter 10 by Bebbington et al. reveal movements that are anything but anti-state: instead they are demanding a stronger, more rule-driven, Weberian, and democratically accessible state. Other movements discussed in the chapters are yet further removed from "romantic" visions of the subaltern. These include the Nación Camba movement discussed by Perreault, protests articulated by small-scale entrepreneurs in search of contracts from extractive enterprises, as well as the darker, vigilante sorts of movement that Moore and Velásquez discuss in Tenguel.

So any conceptualization of struggle should avoid the normative trap of presuming that it is heroic, pretty, or progressive (cf. McCarthy and Watts 1997). Indeed, taken together, the authors suggest that the larger story about extraction and struggle is that the expanding extractive frontier catalyzes a range of movements with diverse constituencies and motivations. Some of these seek alternatives of greater or lesser degrees of radicalism, some seek access to the rents produced by extraction, and others seek to take advantage of issues raised by extraction and make them functional to the political projects that they are already pursuing.

That said, these struggles are not only to be understood in terms of strategic, goal-oriented actions. They are also about complex and buried identities. Perreault and Warnaars are the most explicit about this, but in some sense each of the authors is struggling to theorize exactly what it is that people are identifying with in these struggles. Are these direct identifications with the material of the subsoil? Do ideas of the subsoil become constitutive of identity? This seems to be part of the argument of Chapter 3 by Perreault, and it is certainly the case that the notion of *Pachamama* (Mother Earth) is invoked often in identity politics and debates over extraction in Bolivia. In Chapter 6 by Warnaars, however, mobilized identities seem primarily related to ethnicity and territory, while others are labor based, as in the case of the one-time informal miners turned environmentalists. In these cases, identities appear to be catalyzed or reworked by extraction but less obviously constituted through the subsoil. In other instances, the identities mobilized during struggles seem more clearly related to historical experiences and memories of exclusion, domination, contamination, and pillage that are brought to bear on extraction, leading to particular interpretations of mining and hydrocarbon activity and particular types of struggle. These questions and uncertainties about identity are of crucial importance because claims regarding the legitimacy or illegitimacy of identities are at the forefront of struggles over extraction. Companies and governments recurrently question the "honesty" of popular environmentalism, suggesting that protestors use environmental arguments when what really motivates them are partisan ideologies and a desire to access rents. Meanwhile, local protestors will question the motivations of national governments and vice versa, and on a more legal terrain, questions of indigeneity are central to how far certain international conventions can be invoked. These observations do not mean that political ecological analysis should seek to determine "real" identities—a theoretically futile and absurd task. They do suggest, however, how important it is to probe very deeply when discussing the relationships between identities and the subsoil, and to make claims very cautiously.

Making sense of the diverse projects in these struggles through one combined framework is a challenge and may well be inappropriate; it might simply constitute an effort to crunch too much diversity into one way of viewing the world. That said, our sense is that certain general statements can be made. In particular, the struggles as documented in this collection reflect efforts to defend particular interests in the face of deeper contradictions in society. While the contradictions at play vary, as described in these chapters, they all share an important spatial dimension, in that distinct political economic projects lay claim to the same spaces and the resources within those spaces. The consequence of this is that in many of these spaces, these different projects cannot coexist, either because they need exactly the same resources or because the by-products of one project undermine the viability of the other, as when mining activity pollutes water sources used by organic farming downstream. These contradictions manifest themselves as the conflicts around which the struggles documented here are waged. Some of these struggles reflect efforts to work the contradiction in one direction or another (i.e., towards control of space and resources by local populations or by the extractive enterprise), while others reflect efforts to cultivate and take advantages of possibilities made available by these contradictions, as when political leaders position themselves so as to benefit from struggles over extraction.

The State and the Subsoil

The state has been central to the cases discussed in these chapters. Taken together, they make clear the extent to which the subsoil cannot be separated from the state and that struggles cannot be sensibly interpreted separately from the state. The subsoil is so intimately bundled with the state in part because the state is its de facto owner. While the subsoil may, de jure, be constitutionally defined as property of the nation, the state is the trustee of this property and so has a critical role in determining its allocation and use. The government of the moment then uses the apparatus of the state to pursue its own objectives and agendas and, as made clear in most chapters, realizing the economic value of the subsoil is essential for the political programs of many governments of the region. Governments have, therefore, sought to use the state apparatus—in the form of ministries, the executive office, the military, the police, and the judiciary—as a vehicle to ensure that this value can indeed be realized. This is made painfully clear in the chapters. The state is shown using the discretionary authorities of ministries to allocate rights in the subsoil or rights to transport its fruits, as well as ministries' powers to approve questionable environmental impact statements. In other instances, the authors show the state using violence to quell protest, the courts to weaken activists, or the office of the president to delegitimize social movements and those who question the extractive model. And finally—albeit of less analytical interest and significance in these chapters—special interests have made (often illegal) use of the state in pursuit of their private agendas.

The discursive power of the state is also apparent. The authors show different ways in which the offices of the state are used in an attempt to define the contours of public and political debate on extractive industry. The state is an important, if not the only, source of arguments regarding the necessity and inevitability of extraction, the need to prioritize growth over conservation, or the priority of technical and economistic languages in any analysis of the case for extraction. This power to define the terms of discussion has forced certain movements to engage in debates on the state's preferred terms. Moore and Velásquez (Chapter 5), for instance, show activists pulling in technical experts to counter the technical arguments of the mining sector, and in some regard, Bebbington and Scurrah (Chapter 7) suggest that only when local health concerns were documented in the technical language of the regional offices of the health ministry did they have any resonance.

So the authors give us multiple insights into the centrality of the state in a political ecology of the subsoil and the need to understand its role in the exercise of legal, physical, discursive, and bureaucratic power. That said, they also present insights into the complexity of the state. While there is little doubt of the *general* orientation of the state — one that favors extraction, appropriation of rent, reinvestment of rent for sociopolitical purposes, and a weakening of rights to protest — the authors also reveal other faces of the state. Perhaps the clearest instance of this is the Ombudsman's office in Peru that played such a critical role in defending Achuar rights to health and a safe environment in Río Corrientes (Chapter 7 by Bebbington and Scurrah). Other examples noted in the book, however, include certain moments within Ecuador's Ministry of Energy and Mines and Constituent Assembly, as well as some of its provincial governments (see Chapter 5 by Moore and Velásquez, and Chapter 6 by Warnaars). That these parts of the state pull in other directions reflects the extent to which they are occupied by professional and/or political interests that do not align with those of government.

The state emerges, therefore, as both a directly interested party (it controls rights in the subsoil) and also as a clear terrain of struggle. While dominant powers in this struggle control larger parts of the government and the state, this control is always incomplete. This incompleteness may exist because the very rules of the state are obstacles to such control (for instance, the rules that determine the independence of the Peruvian Ombudsman's office from the Executive) or because human behavior within the state cannot be subject to total regulation, meaning that staff and professionals may act in ways that work against executive preference.

Practicing Geographies of Extraction

Going back just a decade to the year 2000, published works on the geography and anthropology of Latin American mining and hydrocarbons were limited indeed, especially in English. By 2006, the ranks of June Nash, Ricardo Godoy, Suzanna Sawyer and Laura Rival (all anthropologists) had been joined by the likes of Jeff Bury, Bret Gustafson, Tom Perreault, and Gavin Bridge. Yet the research was still limited. The chapters in this book reflect the step-change that has occurred since then, as well as the now impressive levels of research activity on the subsoil. In this sense, the very *practice* of research on extractive industry is itself a largely new phenomenon — and interestingly one that has emerged subsequent to Walker's (2006, 2007) challenges to the practice of political ecology. There is little doubt that this research will continue to boom, as younger and older political ecologists are drawn to these old and new extractive frontiers. Simple indicators of this continuing boom are the growing number of presentations on mining, hydrocarbons, and large-scale infrastructure at recent conferences of the Association of American Geographers (AAG), the Latin American Studies Association (LASA), and the American Anthropological Association (AAA), as well as the many doctorates that are currently underway.

Indicative of the still relative newness of the topic, we also see a range of ways of conducting such research. This diversity is also reflected in this book. Some of the chapters reflect work conducted in close contact with indigenous and local organizations (e.g., Hindery, Warnaars, Moore and Velásquez), some are based on work conducted jointly with nongovernmental research centers (Bebbington and Scurrah, Hindery, and Bebbington et al.), and some are based on research conducted more or less independently of such alliances (Perreault, Bury and Norris, and Postigo, Montoya, and Young). Some of this work has been done by individual scholars, and other parts have been completed by teams.

Likewise, different methods are reflected in the chapters, though all are qualitative in orientation. These methods range from reconstruction on the basis of clinical and careful analysis of legal and other documents (Hindery) and of discourses (Perreault), through to extended ethnographic research (Moore and Velásquez, Warnaars, Bury and Norris, and Bebbington et al.) and comparative qualitative research (Bebbington and Scurrah, Postigo, Montoya, and Young, and Bebbington et al.). Other mixed methods have also been deployed to varying degrees across the chapters. This includes the integration of geospatial data and techniques that illustrate larger patterns of land use change (Bury and Norris, and Hindery), and insights from biologic and hydrologic methods (Postigo, Montoya, and Young).

Finally, the authors reveal different modes of interacting with political and policy debates around extraction, both within Latin America and in the broader context of international governance networks. Common to these modes of engagement, however, is that while conducting their research the authors have each established wide-reaching networks across state, market, and civil society organizations. These networks include community organizations, regional federations and defense fronts, NGOs, national organizations and political leaders, parts of government, international multilateral agencies, and news agencies. As the complexity of these networks implies, in conducting political ecologies of extraction the boundaries between research, politics, policy, and public debate are especially blurred and porous.

Yet beyond all these differences, there is also a common feeling running through these chapters that to engage with extraction produces modes of enquiry that genuinely challenge and contribute to the field of political ecology. The sense is that dealing with the subsoil necessitates mixed, investigative, and deeply embedded research methods. The chapters in this collection could not have been told by armchair political ecologists; indeed, the levels of engagement of these authors almost seem to require activist research to collect the data that is presented here. If this is so, then a political ecology of the subsoil helps speak back to the challenges of ecology, politics, and policy thrown down to the field by Walker's thought-provoking reviews of the field (Walker 2005, 2006, 2007).

Looking Ahead: Research Themes and Challenges

Notwithstanding uncertainties as to how this current "super cycle" of investment in extraction will work out, we close this book by identifying several possible directions for future research. This agenda will be driven by the mutually constitutive relationship between social mobilization and the behavior of extractive operations, as well as by broader geopolitical and economic transformations. As such, any future research directions should be attentive to shifting and often contingent cross-scalar relationships while being firmly embedded in local social and ecological systems.

One area for future research lies firmly in the empirical domain. In Chapter 1 we noted the long-standing tradition of qualitative fieldwork in political and cultural ecology that is reflected in the other chapters in this collection. Looking forward, however, the use of mixed qualitative and quantitative approaches will allow scholars to address broader audiences and policymakers, to evaluate broader arrays of biophysical and social data, and to "scale up" their findings to larger spatial domains. Scholars may also be attentive to the ways in which geospatial data analyses can provide critical insights into landscape-level questions, which are typically the scale at which contemporary, large-scale extractive activities operate. There is also scope to further develop field methods and observational techniques. In particular, new training and techniques directed towards evaluating the impacts of extractive industries on key ecological parameters such as hydrologic processes, biodiversity, and soil productivity would strengthen many analyses. Moreover, more comprehensive evaluations at the scale of the household and community may incorporate more detailed data related to health and human welfare, as well as learning and cognition (e.g., King 2010). More detailed human interaction and social network analyses may also provide better insights into the dynamics of social change and the ways in which social movements are linked to broader assemblages and social networks. Finally, as the first phase of the post-1990s boom in extraction draws to a close, the region will begin to see a round of mine closures that are, because of the sheer scale of operations, without precedent in Latin America. Studying these processes of closure, their implications for and the possibilities of ecological restoration, and the consequences for local and regional societies will be a vitally important research contribution.

One methodological component present in many of the chapters in this volume but deserving further attention is the longer-term processes of environmental and social change with which extractive activities articulate. As recent research illustrates (Bridge 2009; Moore 2010), environmental histories that seek to understand the long-term evolution of regional economies and landscapes and the ecological legacies of extractive industries could inform many policy and theoretical debates. Future research may also build upon the observational record of previous scholars in order to extend the depth of our insights into social and environmental change. While some key elements of the most current round of extractive industries are indeed relatively new phenomena, their ecological impacts are part of longer-term processes whose implications for human well-being and environmental services are not well understood.

Methodological innovations aimed at grappling with so-called "coupled" natural and human systems are also likely to deliver conceptual insights and open up new hypotheses and avenues of inquiry. Collaborative, transdisciplinary work on extractive industries is particularly important because of the complex ecological and social relationships at play. For example, addressing the effects of oil and natural gas operations on biodiversity in the Amazon Basin, the behavior of mercury in water columns and its impact on animals and human health, or the implications of gold mining for environmental services at the watershed level are tasks that fall far beyond the ability of individual researchers but are among the most salient questions for the shifting, contemporary political ecology of Latin America. In a similar vein, understanding the implications and causal powers of those new technologies that are likely to be deployed in the extractive sector will require researchers to broaden their skills or more likely expand their networks of collaboration so that they include these specializations.

Finally, the relations among extraction, water, and climate are ripe for analysis. Because extractive industries rely significantly on water resources for their operations, they are also linked to wider ecological, economic, and political relationships affecting water use and governance. In relatively dry areas, contestation over water rights and the impacts of mining and hydrocarbons on water quality are likely to be constant features of social struggles. Climate change is another broader area of inquiry linked to water resources, petroleum-intensive extractive techniques, and land cover change. Governance struggles over water are already emerging in the Central Peruvian Andes, particularly because climate change and the use of water by extractive industries are both affecting hydrologic resources (Baraer et al. 2012; Bury et al. 2011). However, the interactions among extractive industries, hydrologic processes, and climate change might also have unexpected effects. For instance, because climate change is increasing the recession rates of glaciers and ice around the planet, it is also uncovering new and highly lucrative deposits of minerals and hydrocarbons. This has spurred the rapid growth of extractive operations in many remote areas such as Greenland, the Arctic, and high in the Andes. Furthermore, the interaction effects of climate change and extractive industries can intensify environmental problems, such as water quality, particularly in areas that have been heavily impacted by extractive industries over long periods of historical time (Fortner et al. 2011). Broader issues related to extractive industries, and climate governance, as Bridge (2010a) illustrates, also include the fact that extractive industries are both direct sources of new carbon emissions through their operations and, in the case of hydrocarbons operations, indirect sources through their extraction of petroleum and natural gas.

These are just some of the themes we see on the horizon. While new avenues of inquiry are already being advanced by scholars such as Moore (2010), Himley (2010) and Huber (2011), increasing economic volatility and rapidly shifting capital flows, the emergence of new extractive techniques such as biomining, recent discoveries of vast petroleum and shale gas reserves, the presence of new state and economic actors in extractive networks, and the further extension of the extractives complex across Latin America are all areas that merit more detailed examination.

A Final Word: Water for Gold?

The evocative title to the chapter written by Jen Moore and Teresa Velásquez captures a concern shared by all our authors: namely that in the rush to promote extraction, Latin American governments may be trading too much. For Moore and Velásquez, and the protestors whose struggles they narrate, the great fear is that the search for gold by small and large-scale miners alike may compromise the long-term viability of water supplies, agricultural production, and human health. In a similar vein, Tom Perreault quotes Watts' (2001, 205) use of the Faust metaphor to suggest that Bolivia has entered into an ill-advised pact "in which a national project (modernity, development, citizenship)—is purchased at the expense of sovereignty, autonomy, independence, tradition, and so on. . . . [I]t is precisely against the terms of this Faustian pact that social movements across the political spectrum are reacting." While not all movements might be so motivated—indeed in Perreault's own chapter it is not at all clear that the struggle of the Nación Camba is in any way a fight against Bolivia's commitment to natural resource-driven economic growth— many of the authors describe movements of people who worry about the implications of the extractive economy for their livelihoods, territories, health, and environments. They also worry about the implications that a commitment to extractive industry will hold for their rights to associate or to participate in the elaboration and governance of development options. What is more, the authors show why such concerns seem absolutely justified. High concentrations of lead in the blood of the Achuar, hepatitis rates among the Kandozi, water pollution in Tenguel, forest loss in the Chiquitanía, and fish kills in Llamac all give substance to populations' environmental and health concerns. Meanwhile, violence and deaths in Piura and Cajamarca, lack of transparency and apparent company-government subterfuge in Santa Cruz, government failure to keep promises in Azuay and Tenguel, and seeming executive disinterest in conditions in Río Corrientes each suggests that populations' concerns about the implications of extractive industry expansion for their rights and for the quality of democracy are likewise well founded.

Whether the subterranean struggles documented here will be effective in countering companies' "subterranean techniques" (Sawyer 2003) and so help affected populations secure their concerns is less clear. Some authors suggest that struggle has helped ameliorate conditions. The clearest example of this would be the Acta de Dorissa in Río Corrientes. However, for the most part our authors seem doubtful. Moore and Velásquez point to the continuing duplicity of Ecuador's government, Bury and Norris note the huge asymmetries of power between the extractive project and the private-conservation-with-tourism project in Ancash, and Hindery shows sustained collusion among companies, government, and international financial institutions. Meanwhile Warnaars, Bebbington et al., and Moore and Velásquez draw attention to the ever-present struggles that go on *among* those who are also struggling *against* others. Of course, governments and even companies also have their internal divisions, but when already in a position of disadvantage within asymmetric power relations, these fractures within movements greatly weaken the capacity of struggle to foster change. The likelihood of significant change seems all the more remote, to the extent that these are struggles against economic activities that are so integral to broader economic models in the region.

Whether this is a bleak conclusion depends on whether one believes extraction constitutes a viable development model for the region, and on this point positions are deeply divided in the region, albeit far less so among our contributors. Normative positions aside, what is very clearly suggested in these chapters is that in much of Latin America, the mutually constitutive relationships among struggle, extraction, grievance, state formation, and territorialization will continue into the foreseeable future, transforming landscapes and livelihoods and marking the political economies within which social and environmental research is conducted. And so we close the book insisting that resource extraction constitutes a vital domain of research that will push the frontiers of political ecology while political ecologists make important contributions to understanding its causes, nature, and consequences.

Notes

1. We paraphrase the question here, but convey the sense.
2. See www.caretas.com.pe/Main.asp?T=3082&idE=994&idS=639 for original quotation in online edition.

Bibliography

Abbott, Mark B., and Alexander P. Wolfe. 2003. "Intensive Pre-Incan Metallurgy Recorded by Lake Sediments from the Bolivian Andes." *Science* 301 (5641): 1893–1895.

Abbott, Mark B., Brent B. Wolfe, Alexander P. Wolfe, Geoffrey O. Seltzer, Ramon Aravena, Brian G. Mark, Pratigya J. Polissar, Donald T. Rodbel, Harry D. Rowe, and Mathias Vuille. 2003. "Holocene Paleohydrology and Glacial History of the Central Andes Using Multiproxy Lake Sediment Studies." *Palaeogeography, Palaeoclimatology, Palaeoecology* 194 (1–3): 123–138.

Acción Ecológica and Friends of the Earth. 1999. "Ecuador no será un país minero." Documento para la reunión anual de Amigos de la Tierra (FOE) Campaña de Minería [Paper for the annual meeting of the Friends of the Earth Mining Campaign], 10–14 November 1999.

Adams, William M., and Jon Hutton. 2007. "People, Parks and Poverty: Political Ecology and Biodiversity Conservation." *Conservation and Society* 5 (2): 147.

Agrawal, Arun, and Clark C. Gibson. 1999. "Enchantment and Disenchantment: The Role of Community in Natural Resource Conservation." *World Development* 27 (4): 629–649.

AIDESEP. 2006. "¡No más petroleras en territorio achuar… gobernabilidad indígena en territorio indígena!" Comunicado de la Asociación Interétnica de Desarrollo de la Selva Peruana—AIDESEP. SERVINDI, 10 October 2006, http://www.servindi.org/actualidad/1177/1177.

Albro, Robert. 2006. "Actualidades Bolivia's 'Evo Phenomenon': From Identity to What?" *Journal of Latin American Anthropology* 11 (2): 408–428.

Ali, Saleem. 2003. *Mining, the Environment and Indigenous Development Conflicts.* Tucson: University of Arizona Press.

Álvarez, José Luis, Maribel Arroyo, Lida Carhuallanqui, James Copestake, Martín Jaurapoma, Tom Lavers, Miguel Obispo, Edwin Paúcar, Percy Reina, and Jorge Yamamoto. 2008. "Resources, Conflict, and Social Identity in Context." In *Wellbeing and Development in Peru: Local and Universal Views Confronted*, edited by J. Copestake. New York: Palgrave Macmillan.

Alvarez, Sonia, Evelina Dagnino, and Arturo Escobar, eds. 1998. *Cultures of Politics,*

Politics of Culture: Re-Visioning Latin American Social Movements. Boulder, CO: Westview.

Amundson, Ronald, Daniel D. Richter, Geoff S. Humphreys, Esteban G. Jobbágy, and Jérôme Gaillardet. 2007. "Coupling Between Biota and Earth Materials in the Critical Zone." *Elements* 3 (5): 327–332.

Anderson, Benedict. 1991. *Imagined Communities*. London: Verso.

Anderson, Elizabeth, Mariana Montoya, Aldo Soto, Hernán Flores, and Michael McCain. 2009. "Challenges and Opportunities for Management of a Migratory Fish (*Prochilodus nigricans*) in the Peruvian Amazon: The Case of Lake Rimachi." In *Challenges for Diadromous Fishes in a Dynamic Global Environment*, edited by A. Haro, K. L. Smith, R. A. Rulifson, C. M. Moffitt, R. J. Klauda, M. J. Dadswell, R. A. Cunjak, J. E. Cooper, K. L. Beal, and T. S. Avery. Bethesda, MD: American Fisheries Society.

Anderson, Scott. 2008. "Kinross to Buy Aurelian for C\$1.2 Billion." Reuters, 24 July 2008.

Anderson, Suzanne Prestrud, Roger C. Bales, and Christopher J. Duffy. 2008. "Critical Zone Observatories: Building a Network to Advance Interdisciplinary Study of Earth Surface Processes." *Mineralogical Magazine* 72 (1): 7–10.

Andolina, Robert. 2003. "The Sovereign and Its Shadow: Constituent Assembly and Indigenous Movement in Ecuador." *Journal of Latin American Studies* 35: 721–750.

ANH. 2011. *Oil and Gas Lots*. Bogota, Colombia: National Hydrocarbons Agency.

Arellano-Yanguas, Javier. 2012. "Mining and Conflict in Peru: Sowing the Minerals, Reaping a Hail of Stones." In *Social Conflict, Economic Development and the Extractive Industries: Evidence from South America*, edited by A. Bebbington. London: Routledge.

Arsel, Murat, and Bram Büscher. 2012. "Nature™ Inc.: Changes and Continuities in Neoliberal Conservation and Market-Based Environmental Policy." *Development and Change* 43 (1): 53–78.

Asher, Kiran, and Diana Ojeda. 2009. "Producing Nature and Making the State: *Ordenamiento Territorial* in the Pacific Lowlands of Colombia." *Geoforum* 40: 292–302.

Atkinson, Giles, and Kirk Hamilton. 2003. "Savings, Growth and the Resource Curse Hypothesis." *World Development* 31 (11): 1793–1807.

Auer, Klaus, and Tim Norris. 2001. "'ArrierosAlife': A Multi-Agent Approach Simulating the Evolution of a Social System: Modeling the Emergence of Social Networks with 'Ascape'." *Journal of Artificial Societies and Social Simulation* 4 (1).

Auty, Richard M. 2001. *Resource Abundance and Economic Development*. New York: Oxford University Press.

Báez, Sara, Pablo Ospina, and Galo Ramón. 2004. *Una breve historia del espacio ecuatoriano: Desarrollo local con énfasis en la gestión de los recursos naturales*. Quito: Consorcio Camaren.

Bagrow, Leo, and R. A. Skelton. 2009. *History of Cartography*. 2nd ed. New Brunswick, NJ: Transaction Publishers.

Baker, Paul A., Geoffrey O. Seltzer, Sherilyn C. Fritz, Robert B. Dunbar, Matthew J. Grove, Pedro M. Tapia, Scott L. Cross, Harold D. Rowe, and James P. Broda. 2001. "The History of South American Tropical Precipitation for the Past 25,000 Years." *Science* 291 (5504): 640–643.

Baker-Hughes. 2011. *Worldwide Rig Count*. Houston, TX: Baker-Hughes Incorporated.

Bakewell, Peter J. 1984a. *Miners of the Red Mountain: Indian Labor in Potosí, 1545–1650*. Albuquerque: University of New Mexico Press.

———. 1984b. "Mining in Colonial Spanish America." In *The Cambridge History of Latin America*, edited by L. Bethell. Cambridge: Cambridge University Press.

———. 1997. *Mines of Silver and Gold in the Americas*. Vol. 19. *An Expanding World*. London: Variorum.

Bakker, Karen, and Gavin Bridge. 2006. "Material Worlds? Resource Geographies and the Matter of Nature." *Progress in Human Geography* 30 (1): 5–27.

Ballard, Chris, and Glenn Banks. 2003. "Resource Wars: The Anthropology of Mining." *Annual Review of Anthropology* 32: 287–313.

Banco Mundial. 2005. *Riqueza y sostenibilidad: Dimensiones sociales y ambientales de la minería en el Perú*. Lima: World Bank—Unidad de Gestión del País—Perú, Desarrollo Ambiental y Social Sostenible, Región Latinoamérica y El Caribe.

Baraer, Michel, Bryan Mark, Jeffrey McKenzie, Thomas Condom, Jeffrey Bury, Kyung-In Huh, Cesar Portocarrero, Jesus Gómez, and Sarah Rathay. 2012. "Glacier Recession and Water Resources in Peru's Cordillera Blanca." *Journal of Glaciology* 58 (207): 134–150.

Barbieri, F. L., A. Cournil, and J. Gardon. 2009. "Mercury Exposure in a High Fish Eating Bolivian Amazonian Population with Intense Small-Scale Gold Mining Activities." *International Journal of Environmental Health* 19 (4): 267–277.

Barclays. 2009. *The Original E&P Spending Survey*. New York: Barclays Capital.

———. 2011. *Global 2012 E&P Spending Outlook*. New York: Barclays Capital.

Barnechea, Alfredo. 2012. "Alegato por el Gasoducto Surandino." *Caretas*, 26 January 2012.

Barragán R., Rossana. 2009. "De hegemonías y ejemonías: Una perspectiva histórica sobre los recursos del estado." In *Tensiones irresueltas*, edited by J. Crabtree, G. G. Molina, and L. Whitehead. La Paz: Plural.

Barrick. 2010. *Pascua-Lama 2010 Responsibility Report: Barrick Mining Company*.

Barry, Roger G. 2006. "The Status of Research on Glaciers and Global Glacier Recession: A Review." *Progress in Physical Geography* 30 (3): 285–306.

Barthlott, Wilhelm, Alexandra Hostert, Gerold Kier, Wolfgang Küper, Holger Kreft, Jens Mutke, M. Daud Rafiqpoor, and Jan Henning Sommer. 2007. "Geographic Patterns of Vascular Plant Diversity at Continental to Global Scales." *Erdkunde* 61 (4): 305–315.

Bassett, Tom J. 1988. "The Political Ecology of Peasant-Herder Conflicts in the Northern Ivory Coast." *Annals of the Association of American Geographers* 78 (3): 453–472.

Bassett, Tom, and Karl Zimmerer. 2003. "Cultural Ecology." In *Geography in America at the Dawn of the Twenty-First Century*, edited by G. L. Gaile and C. J. Willmott. New York: Oxford University Press.

Battistelli, Stefania, and Yvan Guichaoua. 2012. "Diamonds for Development? Querying Botswana's Success Story." In *The Developmental Challenges of Mining and Oil: Lessons from Africa and Latin America*, edited by Rosemary Thorp, Stefania Battistelli, Yvan Guichaoua, Jose Carlos Orihuela, and Maritza Paredes, 44–79. New York: Palgrave Macmillan.

Baviskar, Amita. 1995. *In the Belly of the River: Tribal Conflicts over Development in the Narmada Valley*. Delhi and New York: Oxford University Press.

BCR. 2009. *Reporte de inflación: Panorama actual y proyecciones macroeconómicas*. Lima: Banco Central de Reserva del Perú.

Bebbington, Anthony. 1999. "Capitals and Capabilities: A Framework for Analyzing Peasant Viability, Rural Livelihoods and Poverty." *World Development* 27 (12): 2021–2044.

———. 2007a. "Elementos para una ecología política de los movimientos sociales y el desarrollo territorial en zonas mineras." In *Minería, movimientos sociales y respuestas campesinas: Una ecología política de transformaciones territoriales*, edited by A. Bebbington. Lima, Peru: Instituto de Estudios Peruanos (IEP) and Centro Peruano de Estudios Sociales (CEPES).

———, ed. 2007b. *Minería, movimientos sociales y respuestas campesinas: Una ecología política de transformaciones territoriales*. Lima: Instituto de Estudios Peruanos (IEP) and Centro Peruano de Estudios Sociales (CEPES).

———. 2009. "The New Extraction: Rewriting the Political Ecology of the Andes?" *NACLA Report on the Americas* 42 (5): 12–20.

———, ed. 2012a. *Social Conflict, Economic Development and the Extractive Industries: Evidence from South America*. London: Routledge.

———. 2012b. "Underground Political Ecologies: The Second Annual Lecture of the Cultural and Political Ecology Specialty Group of the Association of American Geographers." *Geoforum* 43 (6): 1152–1162. http://dx.doi.org/10.1016/j.geo forum.2012.05.011.

Bebbington, Anthony, Ricardo Abramovay, and Manuel Chiriboga. 2008. "Social Movements and the Dynamics of Rural Territorial Development in Latin America." *World Development* 36 (12): 2874–2887.

Bebbington, Anthony J., and Simon P. Batterbury. 2001. "Transnational Livelihoods and Landscapes: Political Ecologies of Globalization." *Ecumene* 8 (4): 369–380.

Bebbington, Anthony J., and Jeffrey T. Bury. 2009. "Institutional Challenges for Mining and Sustainability in Peru." *Proceedings of the National Academy of Sciences (PNAS)* 106 (41): 17296–301.

Bebbington, Anthony, H. Carrasco, L. Peralvo, G. Ramón, V. H. Torres, and J. Trujillo. 1992. *Los actores de una decada ganada: Tribus, comunidades y campesinos en la modernidad*. Quito: Comunidec/Abya Yala.

Bebbington, Anthony, Michael Connarty, Wendy Coxshall, Hugh O'Shaughnessy, and Mark Williams. 2007a. *Minería y desarrollo en el Perú, con especial referencia al Proyecto Río Blanco, Piura*. Lima: Instituto de Estudios Peruanos (IEP), OXFAM Internacional, Centro de Investigación y Promoción del Campesinado (CIPCA), Peru Support Group.

———. 2007b. *Mining and Development in Peru, with Special Reference to the Río Blanco Project, Piura*. London: Peru Support Group.

Bebbington, Anthony, Leonith Hinojosa, Denise Humphreys Bebbington, Maria Luisa Burneo, and Ximena Warnaars. 2008. "Contention and Ambiguity: Mining and the Possibilities of Development." *Development and Change* 39 (6): 887–914.

Bebbington, Anthony, and Denise Humphreys Bebbington. 2011. "An Andean Avatar: Post-Neoliberal and Neoliberal Strategies for Securing the Unobtainable." *New Political Economy* 15 (4): 131–145.

Bebbington, Anthony, Denise Humphreys Bebbington, Jeffrey Bury, J. Lingan, J. P. Muñoz, and Martin Scurrah. 2007. "Movimientos sociales, lazos transnacionales, y desarrollo territorial rural en zonas de influencia minera: Cajamarca-Perú y Cotacachi-Ecuador." In *Minería, movimientos sociales y respuestas campesinas: Una ecología política de transformaciones territoriales*, edited by A. Bebbington, 163–230. Lima: Instituto de Estudios Peruanos.

Bebbington, Anthony, Denise Humphreys Bebbington, Jeffrey Bury, Jeannet Lingan, Juan Pablo Muñoz, and Martin Scurrah. 2008. "Mining and Social Movements: Struggles Over Livelihood and Rural Territorial Development in the Andes." *World Development* 36 (12): 2888–2905.

Beck, Ulrich. 2005. *Power in the Global Age: A New Global Political Economy*. Cambridge: Polity Press.

Becker, David G. 1983. *The New Bourgeoisie and the Limits of Dependency: Mining, Class, and Power in 'Revolutionary' Peru*. Princeton, NJ: Princeton University Press.

Beltrán, Harvey. 2003. "Protesters threaten Sanchez de Lozada's mining interests." *Business News Americas*, 14 October 2003, http://www.bnamericas.com/news /mining/Protesters_threaten_Sánchez_de_Lozada%27s_mining_interests.

Bennett, Jane. 2009. *Vibrant Matter: A Political Ecology of Things*. Durham, NC: Duke University Press.

Benson, Peter, and Stuart Kirsch. 2010. "Corporate Oxymorons." *Dialectical Anthropology* 34 (1): 45–48.

Berkes, Fikret. 2007. "Community-Based Conservation in a Globalized World." *Proceedings of the National Academy of Sciences (PNAS)* 104 (39): 15188–15193.

Bernstein, Marvin D. 1964. *The Mexican Mining Industry 1890–1950*. 1st ed. Syracuse, NY: State University of New York (SUNY).

Bethell, Leslie. 1995. *The Cambridge History of Latin America*. Vol. 6. Cambridge, MA: Cambridge University Press.

Bhakta, Pragna, and Brian Arthur. 2002. "Heap Bio-Oxidation and Gold Recovery at Newmont Mining: First-Year Results." *Journal of the Minerals, Metals and Materials Society* 54 (10): 31–34.

Binford, Michael W., Alan L. Kolata, Mark Brenner, John W. Janusek, Matthew T. Seddon, Mark Abbott, and Jason H. Curtis. 1997. "Climate Variation and the Rise and Fall of an Andean Civilization." *Quaternary Research* 47 (2): 235–248.

Blaikie, Piers M. 1985. *The Political Economy of Soil Erosion in Developing Countries*. New York: Longman.

———. 1999. "A Review of Political Ecology: Issues, Epistemology and Analytical Narratives." *Zeitschrift für Wirtschaftsgeographie* 43 (3/4): 131–147.

———. 2005. "Is Small Really Beautiful? Community-Based Natural Resource Management in Malawi and Botswana." *World Development* 34 (11): 1942–1957.

———. 2010. "Should Political Ecology Be Useful?" Paper read at Cultural and Political Ecology Specialty Group Lecture, Annual Meeting of the Association of American Geographers, 16 April 2010, Washington, DC.

Blaikie, Piers, and Harold Brookfield. 1987. *Land Degradation and Society*. London: Routledge.

Bodenlos, Alfred John, and George Edward Ericksen. 1955. *Lead-Zinc Deposits of Cordillera Blanca and Northern Cordillera Huayhuash, Peru*. Washington, DC: U.S. Government Printing Office.

Bolpress. 2007. "El Complejo Metalúrgico Vinto vuelve a manos del Estado." 9 February 2007.

Brading, D. A., and Harry E. Cross. 1972. "Colonial Silver Mining: Mexico and Peru." *The Hispanic American Historical Review* 52 (4): 545–579.

Brantley, Susan L., Martin B. Goldhaber, and K. Vala Ragnarsdottir. 2007. "Crossing Disciplines and Scales to Understand the Critical Zone." *Elements* 3 (5): 307–314.

Breuilly, John. 2008. "Introduction." In *Nations and Nationalism*, edited by E. Gellner. Ithaca, NY: Cornell University Press.

Bridge, Gavin. 2000. "The Social Regulation of Resource Access and Environmental Impact: Production, Nature and Contradiction in the US Copper Industry." *Geoforum* 31 (2): 237–256.

———. 2001. "Resource Triumphalism: Postindustrial Narratives of Primary Commodity Production." *Environment and Planning A* 33 (12): 2149–2174.

———. 2004a. "Contested Terrain: Mining and the Environment." *Annual Review of Environment and Resources* 29 (1): 205.

———. 2004b. "Gas, and How to Get It." *Geoforum* 35: 395–397.

———. 2004c. "Mapping the Bonanza: Geographies of Mining Investment in an Era of Neoliberal Reform." *The Professional Geographer* 56 (3): 406–421.

———. 2008. "Global Production Networks and the Extractive Sector: Governing Resource-Based Development." *Journal of Economic Geography* 8 (3): 389–419.

———. 2009. "The Hole World: Spaces and Scales of Extraction." *New Geographies* 2, 43–48.

———. 2010a. "Geographies of Peak Oil: The Other Carbon Problem." *Geoforum* 41 (4): 523–530.

———. 2010b. "Resource Geographies I: Making Carbon Economies, Old and New." *Progress in Human Geography* 35 (6): 820–834.

Bridge, Gavin, and Phil McManus. 2000. "Sticks and Stones: Environmental Narratives and Discursive Regulation in the Forestry and Mining Sectors." *Antipode* 32 (1): 10–47.

Bridge, Gavin, and Tom Perreault. 2009. "Environmental Governance." In *Companion to Environmental Geography*, edited by N. Castree, D. Demeritt, D. Liverman, and B. Rhoads. Oxford: Blackwell Publishing.

Brierley, C. L. 2008. "How Will Biomining Be Applied in Future?" *Transactions of Nonferrous Metals Society of China* 18 (6): 1302–1310.

Brockington, Dan, and Rosaleen Duffy. 2010. "Capitalism and Conservation: The Production and Reproduction of Biodiversity Conservation." *Antipode* 42 (3): 469–484.

Brogden, Mette J., and James B. Greenberg. 2003. "The Fight for the West: A Political Ecology of Land Use Conflicts in Arizona." *Human Organisation* 62 (3): 289–298.

Brondizio, Eduardo S., Elinor Ostrom, and Oran R. Young. 2009. "Connectivity and the Governance of Multilevel Social-Ecological Systems: The Role of Social Capital." *Annual Review of Environment and Resources* 34: 253–278.

Brooks, T. M., R. A. Mittermeier, G. A. B. da Fonseca, J. Gerlach, M. Hoffmann, J. F. Lamoreux, C. G. Mittermeier, J. D. Pilgrim, and A. S. L. Rodrigues. 2006. "Global Biodiversity Conservation Priorities." *Science* 313 (5783): 58–61.

Browman, David L. 1990. "High Altitude Camelid Pastoralism of the Andes." In *The*

World of Pastoralism: Herding Systems in Comparative Perspective, edited by J. G. Galaty and D. L. Johnson. New York: The Guilford Press.

Brown, Kendall. 1994. "The Spanish Imperial Mercury Trade and the American Mining Expansion under the Bourbon Monarchy." In *The Political Economy of Spanish America in the Age of Revolution, 1750–1850*, edited by Kenneth J. Adrienne and Lyman L. Johnson. Albuquerque: University of New Mexico Press.

Bryant, Raymond L. 1992. "Political Ecology: An Emerging Research Agenda in Third-World Studies." *Political Geography* 11 (1): 12–36.

Bryant, Raymond L., and Sinéad Bailey. 1997. *Third World Political Ecology*. London: Routledge.

Buffen, Aaron M., Lonnie G. Thompson, Ellen Mosley-Thompson, and Kyung In Huh. 2009. "Recently Exposed Vegetation Reveals Holocene Changes in the Extent of the Quelccaya Ice Cap, Peru." *Quaternary Research* 72 (2): 157–163.

Bulte, Erwin H., Richard Damania, and Robert T. Deacon. 2005. "Resource Intensity, Institutions, and Development." *World Development* 33 (7): 1029–1044.

Burger, Richard L., and Ramiro Matos Mendieta. 2002. "Atalla: A Center on the Periphery of the Chavín Horizon." *Latin American Antiquity* 13 (2): 153–177.

Burkholder, Mark A., and Lyman L. Johnson. 2008. *Colonial Latin America*. New York: Oxford University Press.

Burneo, María Luisa, and Anahí Chaparro. 2010. "Poder, comunidades campesinas e industria minera: El gobierno comunal y el acceso a los recursos en el caso de Michiquillay." *Antropológica* 28 (Suplemento 1): 85–110.

Bury, Jeffrey. 2004. "Livelihoods in Transition: Transnational Gold Mining Operations and Local Change in Cajamarca, Peru." *The Geographical Journal* 170 (1): 78–91.

———. 2005. "Mining Mountains: Neoliberalism, Land Tenure, Livelihoods and the New Peruvian Mining Industry in Cajamarca." *Environment and Planning A* 37 (2): 221–239.

———. 2007. "Mining Migrants: Transnational Mining and Migration Patterns in the Peruvian Andes." *Professional Geographer* 59 (3): 378–389.

———. 2008a. "New Geographies of Tourism in Peru: Nature-Based Tourism and Conservation in the Cordillera Huayhuash." *Tourism Geographies* 10 (3): 312–333.

———. 2008b. "Transnational Corporations and Livelihood Transformations in the Peruvian Andes: An Actor-Oriented Political Ecology." *Human Organization* 67 (3): 307–321.

Bury, Jeffrey T., Bryan G. Mark, Jeffrey M. McKenzie, Adam French, Michel Baraer, Kyung In Huh, Marco Alfonso Zapata Luyo, and Ricardo Jesús Gómez López. 2011. "Glacier Recession and Human Vulnerability in the Yanamarey Watershed of the Cordillera Blanca, Peru." *Climatic Change* 105 (1–2): 179–206.

Business News Americas. 2003. "Comsur Transfers Equipment to Don Mario." February 14, 2003, http://www.bnamericas.com/news/oilandgas/Comsur_trans fers_equipment_to_Don_Mario.

Business Wire. "Manhattan Minerals Corp.: Comments on Inrena Preliminary Review of EIA." 20 May 2003, http://www.businesswire.com/news/home/2003052000 5724/en/Manhattan-Minerals-Corp.-Comments-Inrena-Preliminary-Review.

Caballero Martín, Víctor. 2009. *El rayo que no cesa: Conflicto y conflictividad social*. Lima, Peru: Asociación Servicios Educativos Rurales (SER).

————. 2011. "Conflictos sociales y socioambientales en el sector rural y su relación con el desarrollo rural: SEPIA XIII." In *Perú: El problema agrario en debate*, edited by P. Ames and V. Caballero. Lima: SEPIA.

Caballero Martín, Víctor, and Teresa Cabrera Espinoza. 2008. "Conflictos sociales en el Perú, 2006–2008." *Perú Hoy*, 100–130.

CEC (California Energy Commission). 2008. *LNG Marine Terminals*. Sacramento: California Energy Commission.

Calle, Isabel, and Manuel Pulgar-Vidal. 2006. *Manual de legislación ambiental*. Lima: Sociedad Peruana de Derecho Ambiental.

Campbell, Bonnie. 2003. "Factoring in Governance Is Not Enough. Mining Codes in Africa, Policy Reform and Corporate Responsibility." *Minerals and Energy* 18 (3): 2–13.

————. 2006. "Good Governance, Security and Mining in Africa." *Minerals and Energy* 21 (1): 31–44.

————. 2008. "Reform Processes in Africa: Issues and Trends." Paper read at Second International Study Group Meeting, Economic Commission for Africa, 19–21 May, 2008, at Addis Ababa, Ethiopia.

Campese, Jessica, Grazia Borrini-Feyerabend, Michelle de Cordova, Armelle Guigner, Gonzalo Oviedo, Marcus Colchester, Maurizio Farhan Ferrari, and Barbara Lassen. 2007. "Editorial: 'Just' Conservation? What Can Human Rights Do for Conservation . . . and Vice Versa?!" *Policy Matters*, http://cmsdata.iucn.org/down loads/pm15.pdf.

Cardoso, Fernando Henrique, and Enzo Faletto. 1979. *Dependency and Development in Latin America*. Berkeley: University of California Press.

Carr, Edward R., and Brent McCusker. 2009. "The Co-production of Land Use and Livelihoods Change: Implications for Development Interventions." *Geoforum* 40 (4): 568–579.

Carvajal, Miguel, and José Rivadeneira. 1997 (May). "Perspectiva socioeconómica de la pequeña minería y la minería artesanal: Estudio de caso de Nambija y Ponce Enríquez." Quito: PRODEMINCA, Ministry of Energy and Mines.

Cash, David W., William C. Clark, Frank Alcock, Nancy M. Dickson, Noelle Eckley, David H. Guston, Jill Jäger, and Ronald B. Mitchell. 2003. "Knowledge Systems for Sustainable Development." *Proceedings of the National Academy of Sciences* 100 (14): 8086–8091.

Castree, Noel. 2007. "Capitalism, the Left and the New World (Dis)Order." *Progress in Human Geography* 31 (4): 563–570.

————. 2008a. "Neoliberalising Nature: Processes, Effects, and Evaluations." *Environment and Planning A* 40 (1): 153–173.

————. 2008b. "Neoliberalising Nature: The Logics of Deregulation and Reregulation." *Environment and Planning A* 40 (1): 131–152.

CAT (Caterpillar Inc.). 2010. *785D Mining Truck*. Peoria, IL: Caterpillar Inc.

CEADES (Colectivo de Estudios Aplicados al Desarrollo Social). 2006. *Propuesta base de los pueblos indígenas y originarios de Bolivia*. Santa Cruz: Colectivo de Estudios Aplicados al Desarrollo Social.

CEJIS (Centro de Estudios Jurídicos e Investigación Social). 2008. *Consulta y participación de pueblos indígenas originarios y comunidades campesinas en actividades hidrocarburíferas*. Santa Cruz: Centro de Estudios Jurídicos e Investigación Social.

CEPES (Centro Peruano de Estudios Sociales). 2007. "Caso Carhuancho: Fallo del Tribunal Latinoamericano del Agua en favor de comunidades." *La Revista Agraria* 90, diciembre (December) 2007: 13.

Cerrate de Ferreyra, E. 1979. *Vegetación del valle de Chiquian.* Lima: Universidad Nacional Mayor de San Marcos.

Chapin, Mac. 2004. "A Challenge to Conservationists." *World Watch* 17 (6): 17–32.

Chirif, Alberto. 2006. *La lucha del pueblo achuar del Corrientes.* SERVINDI, 6 October 2006, http://www.servindi.org/actualidad/opinion/1167/1167.

———. 2010a. "Los achuares del Corrientes: El Estado ante su propio paradigma." *Antropológica* 28 (1): 289–309.

———. 2010b. "Perú: El perro glotón y su misterioso capital. La propiedad comunal en la mira." SERVINDI, http://www.servindi.org/actualidad/22625.

CIA. 2010. *World Factbook 2010.* Washington, DC: Potomac Books.

Cisneros-Lavaller, Alberto. 2007. "Resource Nationalism Now and Then in Latin America: Demystifying Its Comparison." *Geopolitics of Energy* 29 (12): 1–12.

Cleary, David. 1990. *Anatomy of an Amazonian Gold Rush.* Iowa City: University of Iowa.

Cockburn, Alexander, and James Ridgeway. 1979. *Political Ecology.* New York: Times Books.

Cole, Jeffrey A. 1985. *The Potosí Mita, 1573–1700: Compulsory Indian Labor in the Andes.* Palo Alto, CA: Stanford University Press.

Collier, Paul, and Anke Hoeffler. 2004. "Greed and Grievance in Civil War." *Oxford Economic Papers* 56 (4): 563–595.

———. 2005. "Resource Rents, Governance, and Conflict." *Journal of Conflict Resolution* 49 (4): 625–633.

Columbus, Christopher. 1892. *The Letter of Columbus on the Discovery of America: A Facsimile of the Pictorial Edition, with a New and Literal Translation.* Translated by W. Eames. New York: Lenox Library.

Compliance Advisor/Ombudsman. 2003. *Assessment Report: Complaint Regarding COMSUR/Don Mario Mine Bolivia.* Office of the Compliance Advisor/Ombudsman of the International Finance Corporation and the Multilateral Investment Guarantee Agency.

———. 2004. *Cover Letter for Capacity Report.* Office of the Compliance Advisor/Ombudsman of the International Finance Corporation and the Multilateral Investment Guarantee Agency July 1, 2004.

Conaghan, Catherine M., James M. Malloy, and Luis A. Abugattas. 1990. "Business and the 'Boys': The Politics of Neoliberalism in the Central Andes." *Latin American Research Review* 25 (2): 3–30.

Coney, Peter J. 1964. *Geology and Geography of the Cordillera Huayhuash, Peru.* Albuquerque: University of New Mexico.

Conservation International. 2002. "Historic U.S.-Peru Debt-for-Nature Swap Gets Boost from Major Conservation Groups." http://www.conservation.org/global/gcf/news/Pages/2002_peru_debt_for_nature.aspx.

Consorcio Prime Engenharia, Museo Noel Kempff Mercado, and Asociación Potlatch. 2000. *Estudio de evaluación de impacto ambiental (EEIA) y evaluación ambiental estratégica del corredor Santa Cruz-Puerto Suárez.*

Contreras, Carlos, and Ali Diaz. 2007. *Los intentos de reflotamiento de la mina de azogue de Huancavelica en el siglo XIX*, documentos de trabajo. Lima: Pontificia Universidad Católica del Perú.

Cook, Noble David, and W. George Lovell, eds. 1992. *Secret Judgments of God: Old World Disease in Colonial Spanish America (Civilization of the American Indian)*. Norman: University of Oklahoma Press.

Cooke, Colin A., Mark B. Abbott, Alexander P. Wolfe, and John L. Kittleson. 2007. "A Millennium of Metallurgy Recorded by Lake Sediments from Morococha, Peruvian Andes." *Environmental Science & Technology* 41 (10): 3469-3474.

Cooke, Colin A., Prentiss H. Balcomb, Harald Biesterc, and Alexander P. Wolfe. 2009. "Over Three Millennia of Mercury Pollution in the Peruvian Andes." *Proceedings of the National Academy of Sciences of the United States of America (PNAS)* 106 (22): 8830-8834.

Cooke, Colin A., Prentiss H. Balcomb, Charles Kerfoot, Mark B. Abbott, and Alexander P. Wolfe. 2010. "Pre-Colombian Mercury Pollution Associated with the Smelting of Argentiferous Ores in the Bolivian Andes." *Ambio* 40 (1): 18-25.

Cooke, Colin A., Alexander P. Wolfe, and William O. Hobbs. 2009. "Lake-Sediment Geochemistry Reveals 1400 Years of Evolving Extractive Metallurgy at Cerro de Pasco, Peruvian Andes." *Geology* 37 (11): 1019-1022.

CooperAcción. 2010. *Observatorio de conflictos mineros en el Perú*. Grufides, Fedepaz, CooperAcción 2010, 13 December 2010, http://www.muqui.org/observatorio /Observatorio_OCTUBRE2010/Observatorio_OCTUBRE2010.htm.

Coordinadora de Pueblos Étnicos de Santa Cruz. 2003. "Non-compliance with World Bank's Operational Guidelines in the Don Mario Mining Project in Bolivia." Letter to Compliance Advisor/Ombudsman, World Bank.

Coordinadora Nacional de Radio. 2009. *ONU solicita explicaciones al Gobierno por contaminación en la selva*. SERVINDI, 20 March 2008, http://www.servindi.org /actualidad/3643/3643.

Coronil, Fernando. 1997. *The Magical State: Nature, Money, and Modernity in Venezuela*. Chicago: University of Chicago Press.

Crosby, Alfred W. 1972. *The Columbian Exchange: Biological and Cultural Consequences of 1492*. Westport, CT: Greenwood Publishing Company.

Curreli, L., G. Loi, R. Peretti, G. Rossi, P. Trois, and A. Zucca. 1997. "Gold Recovery Enhancement from Complex Sulphide Ores Through Combined Bioleaching and Cyanidation." *Minerals Engineering* 10 (6): 567-576.

Dames and Moore. 1996. *Environmental Impact Study for the Bolivia-Brazil Gas Pipeline Project (Bolivian Portion). Final Report Prepared for: YPEB, Enron Corp., Petrobras & BTB*. Cochabamba, Bolivia: Dames and Moore.

Davis, Graham A., and John E. Tilton. 2005. "The Resource Curse." *Natural Resources Forum* 29: 233-242.

Davis, Graham A., and Arturo L. Vásquez Cordano. 2011. "International Trade in Mining Products." *Journal of Economic Surveys* 27 (1): 74-97.

deB. Richter, Jr., Daniel, and Megan L. Mobley. 2009. "Monitoring Earth's Critical Zone." *Science* 326 (5956): 1067-1068.

de Cieza de León, Pedro. 1864. *The Travels of Pedro de Cieza de Leon, A.D. 1532-50. Contained in the First Part of his Chronicle of Peru*. Translated by Sir Clements R. Markham, with Introduction. London: Printed for the Hakluyt Society. Original text from 1553.

———. 1883. *The Second Part of the Chronicle of Peru*. Translated by Sir Clements R. Markham, with Introduction. London: Printed for the Hakluyt Society.

de Echave, José. 2007. "La minería en el Perú: Entre la transformación de los conflictos y el desafío programático." Paper read at Seminar on Territory, Conflicts and Development, 22 October 2007, Manchester, UK.

Defensoría del Pueblo. 2007. *Los conflictos socioambientales por actividades extractivas en el Perú (Informe extraordinario)*. Lima: Defensoría del Pueblo.

de la Jara Basombrío, Ernesto, and Alberto Pizango Chota. 2010. "Letter: Pedido de Información." SERVINDI, 15 octubre (October) 2010. www.servindi.org/pdf/Carta%20MINEM0001%5b1%5d.pdf.

de las Casas, Bartolomé. 1971. *History of the Indies*. Vol. 2. Translated by A. Collard. New York: HarperCollins Publishers. Original text from 1540.

———. 1992. *A Short Account of the Destruction of the Indies*. Translated by Nigel Griffin with Introduction by Anthony Pagden. London: Penguin Classics. Original text from 1542.

de la Vega, Garcilaso, Francisco L. Urquizo, and Carlos Araníbar. 1967. *Comentarios reales de los Incas*. Lima: Fondo de Cultura Económica. Original text from 1617.

del Castillo, Laureano. 2009. Interview with Timothy Norris, November 2009. Lima: CEPES.

del Castillo, L., F. Eguren, P. Castillo, and CEPES. 2008. "Los decretos legislativos vinculados a la actividad agraria." *Informativo Legal Agrario Segunda Epoca* (December): 17–21.

Democracy Center, The. 2009. "The Trial of Gonzalo Sanchez de Lozada." 19 May 2009 (retrieved 8 April 2012), http://www.democracyctr.org/blog/2009/05/trial-of-gonzalo-sanchez-de-lozada.html.

Denevan, William M. 1992a. "The Pristine Myth: The Landscape of the Americas in 1492." *Annals of the Association of American Geographers* 82 (3): 369–385.

———. 1992b. *The Native Population of the Americas in 1492*. Madison: University of Wisconsin Press.

Deng, Tianlong, and Mengxia Liao. 2002. "Gold Recovery Enhancement from a Refractory Flotation Concentrate by Sequential Bioleaching and Thiourea Leach." *Hydrometallurgy* 63 (3): 249–255.

Descola, Philippe. 1985. "Del habitat disperso a los asentamientos nucleados: Un proceso de cambio socio-económico." In *Amazonía ecuatoriana: La otra cara del progreso*. Quito: Abya Yala.

Desforges, Luke. 2000. "State Tourism Institutions and Neo-liberal Development: A Case Study of Peru." *Tourism Geographies* 2 (2): 177–192.

de Soto, Hernando. 2000. *The Mystery of Capital: Why Capitalism Triumphs in the West and Fails Everywhere Else*. New York: Random House.

Deustua, José. 2000. *The Bewitchment of Silver: The Social Economy of Mining in Nineteenth-Century Peru*. Monographs in International Studies, Latin America Series No. 31. Athens: Ohio University Press.

Dietz, Thomas, Elinor Ostrom, and Paul C. Stern. 2003. "The Struggle to Govern the Commons." *Science* 302 (5652): 1907–1912.

Dillehay, Tom D. 2008. "Profiles in Pleistocene History." In *The Handbook of South American Archaeology*, edited by H. Silverman and W. H. Isbell. New York: Springer.

————. 2009. "Probing Deeper into First American Studies." *Proceedings of the National Academy of Sciences (PNAS)* 106 (4): 971–978.

Dinerstein, Eric, David M. Olson, Douglas J. Graham, Avis L. Webster, Steven A. Primm, Marnie P. Bookbinder, and George Ledec. 1995. *A Conservation Assessment of the Terrestrial Ecoregions of Latin America and the Caribbean.* Washington, DC: World Bank.

Dirección de Ecología y Protección del Ambiente. 2006. *Evaluación de resultados del monitoreo del río Corrientes y toma de muestras biológicas, en la intervención realizada del 29 de junio al 15 de julio del 2005.* Lima: Dirección General de Salud Ambiental.

Dore, Elizabeth. 1988. *The Peruvian Mining Industry: Growth, Stagnation, and Crisis.* Series in Political Economy and Economic Development in Latin America. Boulder, CO: Westview Press.

Dorea, J. G., A. C. Barbosa, I. Ferrari, and J. R. De Souza. 2003. "Mercury in Hair and in Fish Consumed by Riparian Women of the Rio Negro, Amazon, Brazil." *International Journal of Environmental Health Research* 13 (3): 239–248.

Dorr, John Van Nostrand, and Francis Lawrence Bosqui. 1950. *Cyanidation and Concentration of Gold and Silver Ores.* New York: McGraw-Hill.

Dourojeanni, Marc, Alberto Barandiarán, and Diego Dourojeanni. 2009. *Amazonía peruana en 2021. Explotación de recursos naturales e infraestructuras: ¿Qué está pasando? ¿Qué es lo que significan para el futuro?* Lima: ProNaturaleza.

Downey, Liam, and Susan Strife. 2010. "Inequality, Democracy, and the Environment." *Organization & Environment* 23 (2): 155–188.

EarthRights International (ERI), Racimos de Ungurahui, and Amazon Watch. 2007. *A Legacy of Harm: Occidental Petroleum in Indigenous Territory in the Peruvian Amazon.* Edited by Emily S. Goldman, Lily La Torre López, and María Lya Ramos. Lima: ERI.

EarthRights International (ERI), Racimos de Ungurahui, Amazon Watch, and WWF Perú. 2007. *Un legado de daño: Occidental Petroleum en territorio indígena de la Amazonía peruana,* edited by Emily S. Goldman, Lily La Torre López, and María Lya Ramos. Lima: ERI.

Eaton, Kent. 2004. *Politics Beyond the Capital: The Design of Subnational Institutions in South America.* Palo Alto, CA: Stanford University Press.

————. 2007. "Backlash in Bolivia: Regional Autonomy as a Reaction Against Indigenous Mobilization." *Politics & Society* 35 (1): 71–102.

Ecuador Times. 2010. "Enfrentamiento entre policías y mineros deja 4 heridos." 15 September 2010, http://www.ecuadortimes.net/es/2010/09/15/enfrentamiento -entre-policias-y-mineros-deja-4-heridos-en-zamora/.

Eerkens, Jelmer W., Kevin J. Vaughn, and Moises Lineras Grados. 2009. "Pre-Inca mining in the Southern Nasca Region, Peru." *Antiquity* 83 (321): 738–750.

Eerkens, Jelmer W., Kevin J. Vaughn, Moises Lineras Grados, and Matthew J. Edwards. 2008. "La Ballena: A Mining Base Camp in the Southern Nasca Region, Peru." *Antiquity* 82 (315), http://www.antiquity.ac.uk/projgall/eerkens315/.

Eguren, Fernando. 2006. "Reforma agraria y desarrollo rural en el Perú." In *Reforma agraria y desarrollo rural en la región andina,* edited by F. Eguren. Lima: Centro Peruano de Estudios Sociales.

El Comercio. 2007. "Las ofertas del Ministro Acosta no convencen." 9 June 2007.

Elliott, John H. 2007. *Empires of the Atlantic World: Britain and Spain in America 1492–1830*. New Haven, CT: Yale University Press.

Ellis, Robert Evan. 2009. *China in Latin America: The Whats and Wherefores*. Boulder, CO: Lynne Rienner Publishers.

El Mercurio. 2007. "Vías del Austro están nuevamente bloqueadas." 26 June 2007.

———. 2008a. "Habra 'reglas justas' para explotar minas." 20 April 2008.

———. 2008b. "Ministro marca un antes y un después." 10 January 2008.

El Mundo. 2006. "El izquierdista Correa dobla en votos a su rival conservador en Ecuador." 27 November 2006. http://www.elmundo.es/elmundo/2006/11/26/internacional/1164579186.html.

El Nacional de Machala. 2008. "Rechazo a decisión de asambleístas." 30 April 2008.

Emel, Jody. 2002. "An Inquiry into the Green Disciplining of Capital." *Environment and Planning A* 34 (5): 827–844.

Emel, Jody, Gavin Bridge, and Rob Krueger. 1994. "The Earth as Input." In *Geographies of Global Change: Remapping the World in the Twentieth Century*, edited by R. Johnston, P. Taylor, and M. Watts. Oxford: Blackwell Publishing.

Emel, Jody, and Matthew T. Huber. 2008. "A Risky Business: Mining, Rent and the Neoliberalization of 'Risk'." *Geoforum* 39 (3): 1393–1407.

Engerman, Stanley L., and Kenneth L. Sokoloff. 2005. *Colonialism, Inequality, and Long-Run Paths of Development*. Cambridge, MA: National Bureau of Economic Research (NBER).

Erickson, Clark L. 1999. "Neo-environmental Determinism and Agrarian 'Collapse' in Andean Prehistory." *Antiquity* 73 (281): 634–642.

Ernst & Young. 2010. *Global E&P Benchmark Study*. Ernst & Young, http://www.ey.com/US/en/Industries/Oil-Gas/US-oil-and-gas-E-P-benchmark-study.

Escobar, Arturo. 2001. "Culture Sits in Places: Reflections on Globalism and Subaltern Strategies of Localization." *Political Geography* 20: 139–174.

Estete, Miguel. 1535. *La relación del viaje que hizo el Señor Capitán Hernando Pizarro por mandado del señor gobernador, su hermano, desde el pueblo de Caxamalca a Parcama y de allí a Jauja, Verdadera relación de la conquista del Perú*.

Estete, Miguel, and Tristán Ravines. 1986. *La prisión del inca en Cajamarca. Noticia y memoria de Cajamarca 1532–1950*. Lima: National Cultural Institute.

Evans, Peter B., Dietrich Rueschemeyer, and Theda Skocpol, eds. 1985. *Bringing the State Back In*. Cambridge: Cambridge University Press.

Ewing, Andrew, and Susan Goldmark. 1994. "Privatization by Capitalization: The Case of Bolivia—A Popular Participation Recipe for Cash-Starved SOEs." In *World Bank FPD Note* No. 31. November 1994: World Bank.

Farriss, Brandie. 2007. "Finding Common Ground: Conservation, Development and Indigenous Livelihoods in the Huascarán Biosphere Reserve, Peru." PhD diss., University of North Carolina at Chapel Hill.

FECONACO. 2005. "Pronunciamiento de la Federación Nativa del Río Corrientes—FECONACO, Perú: Indígenas del Río Corrientes rechazan operaciones petroleras." SERVINDI, 24 November 2005, http://www.servindi.org/actualidad/164/164.

———. 2006. "¡Victoria de los pueblos indígenas achuar, quichua y urarina del Río Corrientes!" SERVINDI, 24 October 2006, http://www.servindi.org/actualidad/1221/1221.

———. 2009. "Informe del Proyecto de Monitoreo Integral e Independiente de FECONACO." Iquitos: FECONACO, October 2009.

Fernández Terán, Roberto. 2009. *Gas, petróleo e imperialismo en Bolivia.* La Paz: Plural/CESU.

Financial Times. 2009. "Oil Nationalism." Editorial. 29 May 2009, www.ft.com.

Finer, Matt, Clinton N. Jenkins, Stuart L. Pimm, Brian Keane, and Carl Ross. 2008. "Oil and Gas Projects in the Western Amazon: Threats to Wilderness, Biodiversity, and Indigenous Peoples." *PLoS ONE* 3, no. 8, www.plosone.org.

Finer, Matt, and Martí Orta-Martínez. 2010. "A Second Hydrocarbon Boom Threatens the Peruvian Amazon: Trends, Projections, and Policy Implications." *Environmental Research Letters* 5 (January-March).

Fisher, John R. 1977. *Silver Mines and Silver Miners in Colonial Peru, 1776–1824, Monograph Series.* Liverpool: Centre for Latin-American Studies, University of Liverpool.

Fjeldså, J., and N. Krabbe. 1990. *Birds of the High Andes.* Denmark: University of Copenhagen.

FONCODES (Fondo de Cooperación para el Desarrollo Social). 2006. *Mapa de la pobreza 2006.* See http://www.foncodes.gob.pe/portal/index.php/institucional/institucional-documentos/institucional-documentos-mapapobreza.

Forbes. 2003. "The Global 2000." 2 July 2003, http://www.forbes.com/2003/07/02/internationaland.html.

Forsyth, Tim. 2003. *Critical Political Ecology: The Politics of Environmental Science.* New York: Routledge.

Fortner, Sarah K., Bryan G. Mark, Jeffrey M. McKenzie, Jeffrey Bury, Annette Trierweiler, Michel Baraer, Patrick J. Burns, and LeeAnn Munk. 2011. "Elevated Stream Trace and Minor Element Concentrations in the Foreland of Receding Tropical Glaciers." *Applied Geochemistry* 26: 1792–1801.

Foweraker, Joe. 1995. *Theorizing Social Movements.* London: Pluto Press.

Fry, Matthew. 2008. "Concrete Block Farmers in Mexico." *Geographical Review* 98 (1): 123–132.

Fukuyama, Francis 1992. *The End of History and the Last Man.* New York: Avon Books.

Fuller, David. 2004. "The Production of Copper in 6th Century Chile's Chuquicamata Mine." *Journal of the Minerals, Metals and Materials Society* 56 (11): 62–66.

Gaddis, John Lewis. 2006. *The Cold War: A New History.* New York: Penguin Group USA.

Galeano, Eduardo. 1970. *Las venas abiertas de América Latina.* México: Siglo Veintiuno Editores.

———. 1973. *Open Veins of Latin America: Five Centuries of the Pillage of a Continent.* New York: Monthly Review Press.

———. 2003. "El país que quiere existir." *La Opinión* (reprint), 21 October 2003.

Gandarillas, Marco, Marwan Tahbub, and Gustavo Rodríguez Cáceres. 2008. *Nacionalización de los hidrocarburos en Bolivia: La lucha de un pueblo por sus recursos naturales.* Barcelona, Spain: Icaria Editorial.

García, Pedro. 2007. *Informe de Trabajo: Proyecto territorialidad indígena. Río Morona, pueblo shapra; Río Pastaza, pueblo kandozi.* Lima: CIPTA-AIDESEP.

Garner, Richard L. 1988. "Long-Term Silver Mining Trends in Spanish America:

A Comparative Analysis of Peru and Mexico." *The American Historical Review* 93 (4): 898–935.

————. 2006. *Where Did All the Silver Go? Bullion Outflows 1570–1650: A Review of the Numbers and the Absence of Numbers.* Unpublished manuscript.

GasOcidente. 2010. "Quantities of Gas Scheduled and Delivered to Reception and Delivery Points." http://www.gasocidentemt.com.br/pagina.asp?cod=31#Quanti dadePrograma da.

Geddicks, Al. 1993. *The New Resource Wars.* Boston: South End Press.

Geertz, Clifford. 1963. *Agricultural Involution: The Process of Ecological Change in Indonesia.* Berkeley: University of California Press.

Gellner, Ernest. 1983. *Nations and Nationalism.* Ithaca, NY: Cornell University Press.

GFD (Global Financial Data). 2011. *Global Financial Data and Statistics.* San Juan Capistrano, CA: Global Financial Data.

Gijseghem, Hendrik Van, Kevin J. Vaughn, Verity H. Whalen, Moises Linares Grados, and Jorge Olano Canales. 2011. "Prehispanic Mining in South America: New Data from the Upper Ica Valley, Peru." *Antiquity* 85 (328).

Gil, Vladimir. 2009. *Aterrizaje minero.* Lima: Instituto de Estudios Peruanos.

Gobierno Provincial del Azuay y la Universidad del Azuay. 2007. *Atlas de la Provincia del Azuay* printed in *El Mercurio*, November 2007. Cuenca, Ecuador.

Godoy, Ricardo. 1990. *Mining and Agriculture in Highland Bolivia: Ecology, History, and Commerce Among the Jukumanis.* Tucson: University of Arizona Press.

Goldman, Michael. 2005. *Imperial Nature: The World Bank and Struggles for Social Justice in the Age of Globalization.* New Haven, CT, & London: Yale University Press.

GOP (Government of Peru). 1987. *Ley N° 24656: Ley General de Comunidades Campesinas.* Lima, Peru: El Peruano.

————. 1995. *Ley N° 26505: Ley de la inversión privada en el desarrollo de las actividades económicas en las tierras del territorio nacional y de las comunidades campesinas y nativas.* Lima, Peru: El Peruano.

————. 2001. *Decreto Supremo No 038–2001–AG: Reglamento de la Ley de Areas Naturales Protegidas.* Lima, Peru: El Peruano.

————. 2002. *Memoria De Gestión Parlimentaria—Legislatura 2001* (agosto 2001–julio 2002). Lima, Peru: Comisión de Ambiente, Ecología, y Amazonía.

Gorriti, G. 2004. "Yanacocha: El campo y la mina." *Ideele* 166: 12–25.

GRADE. 2002. "Dos vetas por explorar para la minería peruana." *Boletin* No 6 (6).

Graffam, Gray, Mario Rivera, and Alvaro Carevič. 1996. "Ancient Metallurgy in the Atacama: Evidence for Copper Smelting During Chile's Early Ceramic Period." *Latin American Antiquity* 7 (2): 101–113.

Gramsci, Antonio. 1971. *Selections from the Prison Notebooks.* Translated by Q. Hoare and G. N. Smith. New York: International Publishers.

Green, Duncan. 2003. *Silent Revolution: The Rise and Crisis of Market Economics in Latin America.* 2nd ed. New York: Monthly Review Press.

Grenyer, Richard, C. David L. Orme, Sarah F. Jackson, Gavin H. Thomas, Richard G. Davies, T. Jonathan Davies, Kate E. Jones, Valerie A. Olson, Robert S. Ridgely, Pamela C. Rasmussen, Tzung-Su Ding, Peter M. Bennett, Tim M. Blackburn, Kevin J. Gaston, John L. Gittleman, and Ian P. F. Owens. 2006. "Global Distribution and Conservation of Rare and Threatened Vertebrates." *Nature* 444 (7115): 93–96.

Guaman Poma de Ayala, Felipe. 1980. *El primer nueva crónica y buen gobierno*. Translated by J. L. Urioste, edited by J. V. Murra and R. Adorno. 3rd ed. Mexico: Siglo XXI Editores. Original text from 1613.

Guardian. 2009. "Lithium Reserves Could Help Transform Bolivia's Economy." *Guardian*, 2 February 2009, www.guardian.co.uk/world/2009/feb/02/bolivia-lith ium-evo-morales.

Guimaraes, J. R., O. Betancourt, M. R. Miranda, R. Barriga, E. Cueva, and S. Betancourt. 2011. "Long-Range Effect of Cyanide on Mercury Methylation in a Gold Mining Area in Southern Ecuador." *Science of the Total Environment* 409 (23): 5026–5033.

Guriev, S., A. Kolotilin, and K. Sonin. 2008. High Oil Prices and the Return of 'Resource Nationalism': VOX-Research-Based Policy Analysis and Commentary from Leading Economists, www.voxeu.org/index.php?q=node/1050.

Gustafson, Bret. 2006. "Spectacles of Autonomy and Crisis: Or, What Bulls and Beauty Queens Have to Do with Regionalism in Eastern Bolivia." *Journal of Latin American Anthropology* 11 (2): 351–379.

———. 2008. "By Means Legal and Otherwise: The Bolivian Right Regroups." *NACLA Report on the Americas* 41 (1): 20–25.

———. 2011. "Flashpoints of Sovereignty: Natural Gas and Territorial Conflict in Bolivia." In *Domination: An Anthropology of Oil*, edited by A. Behrends, S. P. Rayna, and G. Schlee. London: Berghahn Books.

Haarstad, Håvard. 2009. "FDI Policy and Political Spaces for Labour: The Disarticulation of the Bolivian Petroleros." *Geoforum* 40: 239–248.

Haas, Jonathan, Winifred Creamer, and Alvaro Ruiz. 2004. "Dating the Late Archaic Occupation of the Norte Chico Region in Peru." *Nature* 432 (7020): 1020–1023.

Habashi, F. 1987. "One Hundred Years of Cyanidation." *Canadian Mining And Metallurgical Bulletin* 80 (905): 108–114.

Habermas, Jürgen. 1994. *The Theory of Communicative Action: Reason and the Rationalization of Society*. Vol. 1. Boston. Boston: Beacon Press.

Hammer, Joshua. 1996. "Nigeria Crude: A Hanged Man and an Oil-Fouled Landscape." *Harpers* 293: 58–70.

Hardin, Garrett. 1968. "The Tragedy of the Commons." *Science* 162 (3859): 1243–1248.

Harding, Colin. 1975. "Land Reform and Social Conflict in Peru." In *The Peruvian Experiment: Continuity and Change Under Military Rule*, edited by A. F. Lowenthal. Princeton, NJ: Princeton University Press.

Hardt, Michael, and Antonio Negri. 2000. *Empire*. Cambridge, MA: Harvard University Press.

Harvey, David. 1985. *The Urbanization of Capital*. Baltimore: Johns Hopkins University Press.

———. 2003. *The New Imperialism*. New York: Oxford University Press.

———. 2005. *A Brief History of Neoliberalism*. New York: Oxford University Press.

———. 2006. *The Limits to Capital*. New York: Verso. First published 1982 by University of Chicago Press.

Hayes, Tanya Marie. 2007. "Does Tenure Matter?: A Comparative Analysis of Agricultural Expansion in the Mosquitia Forest Corridor." *Human Ecology* 35 (6): 733–747.

Hearn, Adrian H., and José Luis León. 2011. *China Engages Latin America: Tracing the Trajectory*, edited by A. H. Hearn and J. L. León. Boulder, CO: Lynne Rienner Publishers.

Hecht, Susanna, and Alexander Cockburn. 1990. *The Fate of the Forest: Developers, Destroyers and Defenders of the Amazon*. New York: Harper Perennial.

Heckscher, Eli F., and Bertil G. Ohlin. 1991. *Heckscher-Ohlin Trade Theory*. Cambridge, MA: MIT Press.

Hemming, John. 1970. *The Conquest of the Incas*. London: Macmillan.

Hentschel, Thomas, Felix Hruschka, and Michael Priester. 2002. "Global Report on Artisanal and Small-Scale Mining." Working Paper 70, Mining, Minerals and Sustainable Development (MMSD) Project. London: International Institute for Environment and Development (IIED).

Hepworth, Nick, Julio C. Postigo, Bruno Güemes Delgado, and Petra Kjell. 2010. *Drop by Drop: Understanding the Impacts of the UK's Water Footprint Through a Case Study of Peruvian Asparagus*. London: Progressio/CEPES/Water Witness International.

Heynen, Nik, James McCarthy, Scott Prudham, and Paul Robbins. 2007. *Neoliberal Environments: False Promises and Unnatural Consequences*. London: Routledge.

Heynen, Nik, and Paul Robbins. 2007. "The Neoliberalization of Nature: Governance, Privatization, Enclosure and Valuation." *Capitalism Nature Socialism* 16 (1): 5-8.

Hidrandina. 1988. *Inventario de glaciares de Perú*. Huaraz: Hidrandina S.A.

Hilson, Gavin, and Sadia Mohammed Banchirigah. 2009. "Are Alternative Livelihood Projects Alleviating Poverty in Mining Communities? Experiences from Ghana." *Journal of Development Studies* 45 (2): 172-172.

Hilson, Gavin, Christopher J. Hilson, and Sandra Pardie. 2007. "Improving Awareness of Mercury Pollution in Small-Scale Gold Mining Communities: Challenges and Ways Forward in Rural Ghana." *Environmental Research* 103 (2): 275-287.

Hilson, Gavin, and Natalia Yakovleva. 2007. "Strained Relations: A Critical Analysis of the Mining Conflict in Prestea, Ghana." *Political Geography* 26 (1): 98-119.

Himley, Matthew. 2008. "Geographies of Environmental Governance: The Nexus of Nature and Neoliberalism." *Geography Compass* 2 (2): 433-451.

———. 2009. "Nature Conservation, Rural Livelihoods, and Territorial Control in Andean Ecuador." *Geoforum* 40 (5): 832-842.

———. 2010. "Global Mining and the Uneasy Neoliberalization of Sustainable Development." *Sustainability* 2 (2010): 3270-3290.

Hindery, Derrick. 2003. "Multinational Oil Corporations in a Neoliberal Era: Enron, Shell, and the Political Ecology of Conflict Over the Cuiabá Pipeline in Bolivia's Chiquitanía." PhD diss., University of California, Los Angeles.

———. 2004. Social and Environmental Impacts of World Bank/IMF-Funded Economic Restructuring in Bolivia: An Analysis of Enron and Shell's Hydrocarbons Projects. *Singapore Journal of Tropical Geography* 25 (3): 281-303.

———. 2013. *From Enron to Evo: Pipeline Politics, Global Environmentalism and Indigenous Rights in Bolivia*. Tucson: University of Arizona Press.

Hirsch, Robert L. 2008. "Mitigation of Maximum World Oil Production: Shortage Scenarios." *Energy Policy* 36 (2): 881-889.

Hirsch, Seev. 1974. "Capital or Technology? Confronting the Neo-factor Proportions and Neo-technology Accounts of International Trade." *Review of World Economics* 110 (4): 535–563.

Hobsbawm, Eric. 1990. *Nations and Nationalism Since 1780: Programme, Myth, Reality.* Cambridge: Cambridge University Press.

———. 1995. *The Age of Extremes: A History of the World, 1914–1991.* New York: Vintage Books.

Hodell, David A., Jason H. Curtis, and Mark Brenner. 1995. "Possible Role of Climate in the Collapse of Classic Maya Civilization." *Nature* 375 (6530): 391–394.

Horowitz, Leah S. 2008. "Destroying God's Creation or Using What He Provided?: Cultural Models of a Mining Project in New Caledonia." *Human Organization* 67 (3): 292–306.

———. 2010. "'Twenty Years Is Yesterday': Science, Multinational Mining, and the Political Ecology of Trust in New Caledonia." *Geoforum* 41 (4): 617–626.

Huaranga, Guillermo Arbaiza. 2008. *Narraciones costumbristas del pueblo de Llamac.* Huancayo, Peru: Gráfica Belén.

Huber, Matthew T. 2008. "From Lifeblood to Addiction: Oil, Space, and the Wage-Relation in Petro-Capitalist USA." *Human Geography* 1: 42–45.

———. 2009. "Energizing Historical Materialism: Fossil Fuels, Space and the Capitalist Mode of Production." *Geoforum* 40 (1): 105–115.

———. 2011. "Enforcing Scarcity: Oil, Violence, and the Making of the Market." *Annals of the Association of American Geographers* 101 (4): 816–826.

Huber, Matthew T., and Jody Emel. 2008. "Fixed Minerals, Scalar Politics: The Weight of Scale in Conflicts Over the 1872 'Mining Law' in the United States." *Environment and Planning A* 41 (2): 371–388.

Human Rights Watch. 2012. "Bolivia Country Summary," http://www.hrw.org/sites /default/files/related_material/bolivia_2012.pdf.

Humboldt, Alexander von, and Aimé Bonpland. 2008. *Personal Narrative of Travels to the Equinoctial Regions of America, During the Years 1799–1804.* Adelaide, Australia: The University of Adelaide Library.

Humphreys, Macartan, Jeffrey D. Sachs, and Joseph E. Stiglitz. 2007. *Escaping the Resource Curse.* New York: Columbia University Press.

Humphreys Bebbington, Denise. 2010. "The Political Ecology of Natural Gas Extraction in Southern Bolivia." PhD diss., University of Manchester.

———. 2012a. "Extraction, Inequality and Indigenous Peoples: Insights from Bolivia." *Environmental Science & Policy.* DOI: http://dx.doi.org/10.1016/j.envsci .2012.07.027.

———. 2012b. "State-Indigenous Tensions Over Hydrocarbon Development in the Bolivian Chaco." In *Social Conflict, Economic Development and the Extractive Industries: Evidence from South America*, edited by A. Bebbington. London: Routledge.

Humphreys Bebbington, Denise, and Anthony Bebbington. 2010. "Anatomy of a Regional Conflict: Tarija and Resource Grievances in Morales' Bolivia." *Latin American Perspectives* 37 (4): 140–160.

Hylton, Forrest, and Sinclair Thomson. 2005. "The Chequered Rainbow. *New Left Review* 35 (Sept.–Oct.): 41–64.

IAMGOLD. 2007. "IAMGOLD reaches agreement on environmental protection in Ecuador." Press release. 15 November 2007.

————. 2008. "IAMGOLD releases Quimsacocha Pre-feasability Study." Press release. 29 July 2008.

ICMM. 2006. *Resource Endowment Initiative: Synthesis of Four Country Case Studies.* London: International Council on Mining and Metals.

————. 2007. *The Challenge of Mineral Wealth: Using Resource Endowments to Foster Sustainable Development.* Peru Country Case Study. London: International Council on Mining and Metals.

IDB (Inter-American Development Bank). 2010. *India: Latin America's Next Big Thing?* Washington, DC: Inter-American Development Bank.

IFC (International Finance Corporation). 2006. *A Guide to Biodiversity for the Private Sector: Why Biodiversity Matters and How It Creates Business Value.* Washington, DC: International Finance Corporation, World Bank.

IFP Energies. 2011. *Panorama 2011: Exploration-Production: Activities and Markets.* Lyon, France: IFP Energy News.

Igoe, Jim, Katja Neves, and Dan Brockington. 2010. "A Spectacular Eco-Tour around the Historic Bloc: Theorising the Convergence of Biodiversity Conservation and Capitalist Expansion." *Antipode* 42 (3): 486–512.

IMF (International Monetary Fund). 2001. *Peru: Selected Issues, IMF Staff Country Reports.* Washington, DC: International Monetary Fund.

————. 2010. *World Economic Outlook.* Washington, DC: International Monetary Fund.

INEI (Instituto Nacional de Estadística e Informática). 2005. *Compendio estadístico 2005.* Lima: Instituto Nacional de Estadística e Informática.

INGEMMET (Instituto Geológico Minero Metalúrgico). 2010. *Mining Concessions for Peru.* Lima: Instituto Geológico Minero Metalúrgico.

————. 2011. *Mining Concessions and Hydrocarbon Lots: GIS dataset.* Lima: Instituto Geológico Minero Metalúrgico.

INRENA (Instituto Nacional de Recursos Naturales). 2006. *Reserva Paisajistica Nor Yauyos Cochas: Plan Maestro 2006–2011.* Lima: Instituto Nacional de Recursos Naturales.

Jasanoff, Sheila S. 1987. "Contested Boundaries in Policy-Relevant Science." *Social Studies of Science* 17 (2): 195–230.

Jerez, Carlos A. 2009. "Metal Extraction and Biomining." *Encyclopedia of Microbiology* 1: 407–420.

Jiang, Julie, and Jonathan Sinton. 2011. *Overseas Investments by Chinese National Oil Companies.* Paris: International Energy Agency.

Jordan, Tim. 2005. "Social Movements and Social Change." In *Centre for Research on Socio-Cultural Change.* CRESC Faculty of Social Sciences, the Open University.

Joseph, Miranda. 2002. *Against the Romance of Community.* Minneapolis: University of Minnesota Press.

Kamphuis, Charis. 2010. "The Convergence of Public and Corporate Power in Peru: Yanacocha Mine, Campesino Dispossession, Privatized Coercion." Research Paper No. 11/2010, Comparative Research in Law & Political Economy Research Paper Series. Toronto: Osgoode Hall Law School, York University.

Kaplan, Robert D. 2009. "The Revenge of Geography." *Foreign Policy* (May/June), www.foreignpolicy.com/story/cms.php?story_id=4862&print=1.

Karoon Gas Australia Ltd. 2010. *Onshore Marañón Basin.* Karoon Gas Australia Ltd.,

February 2010, http://www.karoongas.com.au/Projects/OnshoreMaranonBasin /tabid/91/Default.aspx.

Kaup, Brent Z. 2008. "Negotiating Through Nature: Resistant Materiality and the Materiality of Resistance in Bolivia's Natural Gas Sector." *Geoforum* 39: 1734–1742.

———. 2010. "A Neoliberal Nationalization: The Constraints on Natural Gas-Led Development in Bolivia." *Latin American Perspectives* 37 (3): 123–138.

King, Brian. 2010. "Political Ecologies of Health." *Progress in Human Geography* 34 (1): 38–55.

Kirsch, Stuart. 2006. *Reverse Anthropology: Indigenous Analysis of Social and Environmental Relations in New Guinea.* Palo Alto, CA: Stanford University Press.

———. 2010. "Sustainable Mining." *Dialectical Anthropology* 34 (1): 87–93.

Klarén, Peter Flindell. 2000. *Peru: Society and Nationhood in the Andes.* New York: Oxford University Press.

Klein, Herbert S. 1992. *Bolivia: The Evolution of a Multi-Ethnic Society.* 2nd ed. New York: Oxford University Press.

Kohl, Benjamin. 2002. "Stabilizing Neoliberalism in Bolivia: Popular Participation and Privatization." *Political Geography* 21: 449–472.

Kohl, Benjamin, and Linda C. Farthing. 2006. *Impasse in Bolivia: Neoliberal Hegemony and Popular Resistance.* London: Zed Press.

———. 2012. "Material Constraints to Popular Imaginaries: The Extractive Economy and Resource Nationalism in Bolivia." *Political Geography* 31 (4): 225–235.

Kolff, Adam. 2000. "The Political Ecology of Mining and Marginalization in the Peruvian Andes: A Case Study of the Cordillera Huayhuash." MA Thesis, University of Colorado Boulder.

Kolff, Adam, and Jim Bartle. 1998. *Cordillera Huayhuash: Perú.* Lima: Nuevas Imagenes.

Körner, Christian, Masahiko Ohsawa, Eva Spehn, Erling Berge, Harald Bugmann, Brian Groombridge, Lawrence Hamilton, Thomas Hofer, Jack Ives, Narpat Jodha, Bruno Messerli, Jane Paratt, Martin Price, Mel Reasoner, Alan Rodgers, Jillian Thonell, Masatoshi Yoshino, Jill Baron, Roger Barry, Jules Blais, Ray Bradley, Robert Hofstede, Valerie Kapos, Peter Leavitt, Russell Monson, Laszlo Nagy, David Schindler, Rolf Vinebrooke, and Teiji Watanabe. 2005. "Mountain Systems." In *Ecosystems and Human Well-Being: Current State and Trends.* Vol. 1, edited by R. Hassan, R. Scholes, and N. Ash. Washington, DC: Island Press.

Kosek, Jake. 2006. *Understories: The Political Life of Forests in Northern New Mexico.* Durham, NC: Duke University Press.

Kosich, Dorothy. 2008. "Vinto Tin Smelter Seizure Negotiations Extended Until February." *Mineweb,* 7 January 2008, www.mineweb.com/mineweb/view/mineweb/en /page60?oid=43778&sn=Detail.

Krueger, Rob. 2002. "Relocating Regulation in Montana's Gold Mining Industry." *Environment and Planning A* 34 (5): 867–882.

Kuecker, Glen David. 2007. "Fighting for the Forests: Grassroots Resistance to Mining in Northern Ecuador." *Latin American Perspectives* 34 (2): 94–107.

Kuentz, Adèle, Marie-Pierre Ledru, and Jean-Claude Thouret. 2011. "Environmental Changes in the Highlands of the Western Andean Cordillera, Southern Peru, During the Holocene." *The Holocene,* published online 22 July 2011, DOI: 10.1177/0959683611409772.

Larson, Brooke. 2004. *Trials of Nation Making: Liberalism, Race and Ethnicity in the Andes, 1810–1910.* Cambridge: Cambridge University Press.

La Torre, Lily, and Dora A. Napolitano. 2007. "The Achuar and 'Production Waters'." *EcoHealth* 4: 110–114.

La Torre López, Lily, and Beatriz Huertas. 1999. *All We Want Is to Live in Peace: Lessons Learned from Oil Operations in Indigenous Territories of the Peruvian Amazon.* Lima: IUCN/Racimos de Ungurahui.

La Verdad. 2009. "Se formó un nuevo directorio de PEPISCO." *La Verdad*, Seminario Regional, 17 September 2009, http://laverdadiquitos.blogspot.com/2009/09/la-verdad-edicion-n-347_17.html.

La Voz del Pueblo. 2008. "Constatando la inmisericorde contaminación que produce la actividad minera, ministro de minas y oetróleos visita la zona de Ponce Enríquez y Tenguel." *La Voz del Pueblo*, May 2008.

Le Billon, Phillippe. 2001. "The Political Ecology of War: Natural Resources and Armed Conflicts." *Political Geography* 20 (5): 561–584.

———. 2004. "The Geopolitical Economy of 'Resource Wars'." *Geopolitics* 9 (1): 1–28.

———. 2008. "Diamond Wars?: Conflict Diamonds and Geographies of Resource Wars." *Annals of the Association of American Geographers* 98 (2): 345–372.

Leach, Melissa, Robin Mearns, and Ian Scoones. 1997. "Environmental Entitlements: A Framework for Understanding the Institutional Dynamics of Environmental Change." Discussion papers. Sussex: Institute of Development Studies (IDS), University of Sussex.

———. 1999. "Environmental Entitlements: Dynamics and Institutions in Community-Based Natural Resource Management." *World Development* 27 (2): 225–247.

Lederman, Daniel, Marcelo Olarreaga, and Guillermo Perry, eds. 2009. *China's and India's Challenge to Latin America Opportunity or Threat?* Washington, DC: World Bank.

Lemke, Thomas. 2011. *Biopolitics: An Advanced Introduction.* Translated by E. F. Trump. Preface by M. J. Casper and L. J. Moore. New York: New York University Press.

Lemos, M. C., and A. Agrawal. 2006. "Environmental Governance." *Annual Review of Environment and Resources* 31: 297–325.

Leys, Peter. 2010. "What Is the Role of the Ombudsman's Institution in Conflicts, within the Margins of the Expanding Political Economy of Copper?: The Case of Peru's Southern Andes." Master's thesis, Social Sciences and International Development Studies, Roskilde University, Denmark.

Liebenthal, Andres, Roland Michelitsch, and Ethel Tarazona. 2005. *Extractive Industries and Sustainable Development: An Evaluation of World Bank Group Experience.* Washington, DC: World Bank.

Little, Paul. 2001. *Amazonia: Territorial Struggles on Perennial Frontiers.* Baltimore: Johns Hopkins University Press.

Liverman, Diana. 2004. "Who Governs, at What Scale and at What Price? Geography, Environmental Governance, and the Commodification of Nature." *Annals of the Association of American Geographers* 94 (4): 734–738.

Liverman, Diana M., and Silvina Vilas. 2006. "Neoliberalism and the Environment in Latin America." *Annual Review of Environment and Resources* 31: 327–363.

Lockhart, James, and Stuart B. Schwartz. 1983. *Early Latin America: A History of Colonial Spanish America and Brazil*. Cambridge: Cambridge University Press.

Long, Norman, ed. 1989. *Encounters at the Interface: A Perspective in Social Discontinuities in Rural Development*. Wageningse Sociologische Studies 27. Wageningen, The Netherlands: Wageningen Agricultural University.

Long, Norman, and Bryan Roberts. 1984. *Miners, Peasants, and Entrepreneurs: Regional Development in the Central Highlands of Peru*. Cambridge: Cambridge University Press.

Los Tiempos. 2009. "Suprema pide autorización para abrir proceso por caso Enron." 27 April 2009.

Lowenthal, Abraham F. 1975. "Peru's Ambiguous Revolution." In *The Peruvian Experiment: Continuity and Change Under Military Rule*, edited by A. F. Lowenthal. Princeton, NJ: Princeton University Press.

———, ed. 1975. *The Peruvian Experiment: Continuity and Change Under Military Rule*. Princeton, NJ: Princeton University Press.

Lu, Graciela María Mercedes. 2009. "The Río Corrientes Case: Indigenous People's Mobilization in Response to Oil Development in the Peruvian Amazon." Master's thesis, International Studies Department, University of Oregon, Eugene.

Lucero, José Antonio. 2008. *Struggles of Voice: The Politics of Indigenous Representation in the Andes*. Pittsburgh, PA: University of Pittsburgh Press.

Luong, Pauline J., and Erika Weinthal. 2006. "Rethinking the Resource Curse: Ownership Structure, Institutional Capacity, and Domestic Constraints." *Annual Review of Political Science* 9: 241–263.

Machado, Iran F., and Silvia F. De M. Figueiroa. 2001. "500 years of Mining in Brazil: A Brief Review." *Resources Policy* 27 (1): 9–24.

Magrin, G., C. Gay García, D. Cruz Choque, J. C. Giménez, A. R. Moreno, G. J. Nagy, C. Nobre, and A. Villamizar. 2007. "Latin America." In *Climate Change 2007: Impacts, Adaptation and Vulnerability*. Contribution of Working Group II to the Fourth Assessment Report of the Intergovernmental Panel on Climate Change, edited by M. L. Parry, O. F. Canziani, J. P. Palutifok, P. J. van der Linden, and C. E. Hanson. Cambridge: Cambridge University Press.

Mann, Charles C. 2006. *1491: New Revelations of the Americas Before Columbus*. New York: Vintage Books.

Mansfield, Becky. 2004. "Neoliberalism in the Oceans: 'Rationalization,' Property Rights, and the Commons Question." *Geoforum* (35): 313–326.

———. 2007. "Privatization: Property and the Remaking of Nature-Society Relations: Introduction to the Special Issue." *Antipode* 39 (3): 393–405.

———. 2012. "Environmental Health as Biosecurity: 'Seafood Choices,' Risk, and the Pregnant Woman as Threshold." Special Issue on the Geography of Health, September 2012, *Annals of the Association of American Geographers* 102 (5): 969–976.

Manson, Steven M. 2008. "Does Scale Exist? An Epistemological Scale Continuum for Complex Human-Environment Systems." *Geoforum* 39 (2): 776–788.

Markham, Sir Clements R. 1872. *Reports on the Discovery of Peru: I. Report of Francisco de Xeres, Secretary to Francisco Pizarro. II. Report of Miguel de Astete on the Expedition to Pachacamac. III. Letter of Hernando Pizarro to the Royal Audience of Santo Domingo. IV. Report of Pedro Sancho on the Partition of the Ransom of Atahuallpa*. Berkeley, CA: Printed for the Hakluyt Society.

———. 1893. *The Journal of Christopher Columbus (During his First Voyage, 1492–93) and Documents Relating the Voyages of John Cabot and Gaspar Corte Real.* Vol. 86. London: Printed for the Hakluyt Society.

———. 1910. *The Incas of Peru.* New York: Dutton.

Marston, Sallie A., John Paul Jones III, and Keith Woodward. 2005. "Human Geography Without Scale." *Transactions of the Institute of British Geographers* 30 (4): 416–432.

Martínez-Alier, Joan. 2002. *The Environmentalism of the Poor: A Study of Ecological Conflicts and Valuation.* Cheltenham, UK: Edward Elgar Publishing.

Martínez Cano, Melinda. 2003. "Proyecto minero Pallca: Etnografía de una experiencia." *Revista de Antropología* (1): 239–252.

Marx, Karl. 1867. *Capital: The Process of Production of Capital.* 4th German ed. Moscow: Progress Publishers.

Marx, Karl, and Friedrich Engels. 1867. *Capital: A Critique of Political Economy.* 1967 (reprinted 1992) ed. New York: International Publishers.

Mayer, Enrique. 2002. *The Articulated Peasant: Household Economies in the Andes.* Boulder, CO: Westview Press.

McCarthy, James. 2002. "First World Political Ecology: Lessons from the Wise Use Movement." *Environment and Planning A* 34 (7): 1281–1302.

———. 2004. Privatizing Conditions of Production: Trade Agreements as Neoliberal Environmental Governance. *Geoforum* 35 (3): 327–341.

———. 2005. "Scale, Sovereignty, and Strategy in Environmental Governance." *Antipode* 37 (4): 731–753.

———. 2007. "States of Nature: Theorizing the State in Environmental Governance." *Review of International Political Economy* 14 (1): 176–194.

McCarthy, James, and Scott Prudham. 2004. "Neoliberal Nature and the Nature of Neoliberalism." *Geoforum* 35 (3): 275–283.

McCarthy, James, and Michael Watts. 1997. "Nature as Artifice, Nature as Artifact: Development, Environment and Modernity in the Late Twentieth Century." In *Geographies of Economies*, edited by R. Lee and J. Wills. London: Edward Arnold.

McClain, Michael E., and Robert J. Naiman. 2008. "Andean Influences on the Biogeochemistry and Ecology of the Amazon River." *BioScience* 58 (4): 325–339.

MCD (Mine Cost Data). 2012. *Yanacocha Annual Production.* Wilmington, DE: MCD.

McSweeney, Kendra. 2004. "The Dugout Canoe Trade in Central America's Mosquitia: Approaching Rural Livelihoods Through Systems of Exchange." *Annals of the Association of American Geographers* 94 (3): 638–661.

Mehlum, Halvor, Karl Moene, and Ragnar Torvik. 2006. "Institutions and the Resource Curse." *Economic Journal* 116 (508): 1–20.

MEG (Metals Economics Group). 2010. *Copper Reserves Replacement Strategies.* http://www.metalseconomics.com/.

———. 2011. *World Exploration Trends.* http://www.metalseconomics.com/.

MEM (Ministerio de Energía y Minas). 1998. *Evaluación ambiental territorial de las Cuencas de los ríos Tigre-Pastaza.* Lima: Ministerio de Energía y Minas.

———. 2000. *Ten Decades of Mineral Production.* Lima: Ministerio de Energía y Minas.

———. 2007. *Resumen del Informe Proyecto Quimsacocha IAMGOLD Ecuador S.A.* 14 November 2007. Lima: Ministerio de Energía y Minas.

———. 2008. *Convenio de Cooperación para el desarrollo y la convivencia pacífica suscrito entre la comunidad campesina de Llamac y la Compañía Minera Santa Luisa S.A.* Lima: Ministerio de Energía y Minas. http://intranet2.minem.gob.pe/web/archivos/dgss/publicaciones/actas/ANCASH/27052008.pdf.

———. 2010. *Reporte de variables macroeconómicas y mineras.* Lima: Ministerio de Energía y Minas.

———. 2011. Executive Report on Economic Variables and Mines. Lima: Ministerio de Energía y Minas.

MINAG (Ministerio de Agricultura). 1998. *Directorio de comunidades campesinas del Perú 1998.* Lima: Proyecto Especial de Titulación de Tierras.

MINCETUR (Ministerio de Comercio Exterior y Turismo). 2005. *Perú: Plan estratégico nacional de turismo 2005–2015.* Lima: Ministerio de Comercio Exterior y Turismo.

———. 2010. *Movimiento de pasajeros por todas las Oficinas de Control Migratorio del Perú.* Lima: Ministerio de Comercio Exterior y Turismo.

———. 2012. *Movimiento de pasajeros por todas las Oficinas de Control Migratorio del Perú.* Lima: Ministerio de Comercio Exterior y Turismo.

Ministerio de Desarrollo Sostenible y Planificación. 2002. Declaratoria de Impacto Ambiental (Licencia Actualizada). Empresa Minera Paititi. MDSP-VMARNDF-DGICSA-UPCA-DIA No. 1091: Área Viceministerial de Medio Ambiente, Recursos Naturales y Desarrollo Forestal (Bolivia).

———. 2003. Aprobación del Tramite de Registro y Licencia para Actividades con Sustancias Peligrosas (LASP). 24 October 2003: Viceministerio de Recursos Naturales y Medio Ambiente (Bolivia).

Ministerio de Gobierno. 2002. Certificado de Inscripción, Empresa Minera Paititi. S.A.—EMIPA11/26/2002: Viceministerio de Defensa Social, Dirección General de Sustancias Controladas (Bolivia).

Ministerio de Salud (Ministry of Health). 2006. *Visita de reconocimiento para la evaluación de la calidad sanitaria de los recursos hídricos y muestreo biológico en las comunidades de la Cuenca del río Corrientes.* Lima, Informe No. 995-2006/DEPA-APRHI/DIGESA.

Miranda Pacheco, Carlos. 2009. "La importancia del gas en la economía boliviana." In *Tensiones irresueltas: Bolivia, pasado y presente*, edited by J. Crabtree, G. G. Molina, and L. Whitehead. La Paz: Plural.

Mitchell, Timothy. 2002. *Rule of Experts: Egypt, Techno-Politics, Modernity.* Berkeley: University of California Press.

Mittermeier, Russell A., Patricio Robles Gil, Michael Hoffman, John Pilgrim, Thomas Brooks, Cristina Goettsch Mittermeier, John Lamoreux, and Gustavo A. B. da Fonseca. 2004. *Hotspots Revisited: Earth's Biologically Richest and Most Endangered Ecoregions.* Mexico City, MX: CEMEX.

Mlachila, Monfort, and Misa Takebe. 2011. *FDI from BRICs to LICs: Emerging Growth Driver?*, IMF Working Paper WP/11/178. Washington, DC: International Monetary Fund.

MOFCOM (Ministry of Foreign Commerce). 2011. *Statistical Bulletin of China's Outward Foreign Direct Investment.* Beijing: Ministry of Foreign Commerce.

Molina, Wilder. 2008. *Estado, identidades territoriales y autonomías en la región amazónica de Bolivia.* La Paz: Programa de Investigación Estratégica en Bolivia.

Montero Gil, R. 2011. "Mining—the Andean Perspective." Paper read at Workshop on Socio-ecological Inequalities in Mountain Environments: The Andes and Alps in Comparative Perspective, 18 July 2011, at Obergürgl, Austria.

Montoya, Mariana. 2010. *How Access, Values, and History Shapes the Sustainability of a Social-Ecological System: The Case of the Kandozi Indigenous Group of Peru.* PhD diss., the University of Texas at Austin.

Moog Rodrigues, Maria Guadalupe. 2004. *Global Environmentalism and Local Politics: Transnational Advocacy Networks in Brazil, Ecuador, and India.* Albany: State University of New York Press.

Moore, Donald. 1996. "Marxism, Culture, and Political Ecology." In *Liberation Ecologies: Environment, Development, Social Movements,* edited by R. Peet and M. Watts. London & New York: Routledge.

Moore, Jason W. 2010. "'This Lofty Mountain of Silver Could Conquer the Whole World': Potosí and the Political Ecology of Underdevelopment, 1545–1800." *Journal of Philosophical Economics* 4 (1): 58–103.

Moore, Jennifer. 2007. "Ecuador's Mining Prospects and the Conflict with Affected Communities." Agencia Latinoamericana de Información (ALAI), http://alainet .org/active/18420&lang=es.

Morales, Evo. 2009. "Morales denuncia estrategias para evitar exploración de hidrocarburos en Bolivia." Agencia Boliviana de Información, 10 July 2009.

Morse, Stephen, and Michael Stocking, eds. 1995. *People and Environment.* London: University College London Press.

MRNR (Ministerio de Recursos Naturales no Renovables [National Ministry of Nonrenewable Resources]). 2011. *National Petroleum Contracts.* Quito: Ministerio de Recursos Naturales no Renovables.

Naito, Koh, Felix Remy, and John P. Williams. 2001. *Review of Legal and Fiscal Frameworks for Exploration and Mining.* London: Mining Journal Books Ltd.

Nash, June. 1979. *The Mines Eat Us and We Eat the Mines: Dependency and Exploitation in Bolivian Tin Mines.* New York: Columbia University Press.

National Geospatial-Intelligence Agency. 2010. *World Port Index.* Springfield, VA: National Geospatial-Intelligence Agency.

National Research Council. 2001. *Basic Research Opportunities in Earth Science.* Washington, DC: National Academy Press.

Neumann, Roderick P. 1996. "Dukes, Earls, and Ersatz Edens: Aristocratic Nature Preservationists in Colonial Africa." *Environment and Planning D: Society and Space* 14 (1): 79–98.

———. 1998. *Imposing Wilderness: Struggles Over Livelihood and Nature Preservation in Africa.* Berkeley: University of California Press.

———. 2004. "Nature-State-Territory: Towards a Critical Theorization of Conservation Enclosures." In *Liberation Ecologies: Environment, Development, Social Movements,* edited by R. Peet and M. Watts. London and New York: Routledge.

———. 2005. *Making Political Ecology.* New York: Hodder Arnold.

———. 2009. "Political Ecology: Theorizing Scale." *Progress in Human Geography* 33 (3): 398–406.

Nietschmann, Bernard. 1973. *Between Land and Water: The Subsistence Ecology of the Miskito Indians, Eastern Nicaragua.* New York: Seminar Press.

North, Douglass. 1991. "Institutions." *Journal of Economic Perspectives* 5 (1): 97–112.

North, Liisa, Timothy David Clark, and Viviana Patroni. 2006. *Community Rights and Corporate Responsibility: Canadian Mining and Oil Companies in Latin America.* Toronto: Between the Lines.

Nriagu, Jerome O. 1993. "Legacy of Mercury Pollution." *Nature* 363 (6430): 589–589.

Nuthall, Keith, and Jonathan Dyson. 2012. "Resource Nationalism: Comibol Boss Claims Bolivian Zinc-Tin Mine Will Triple Output After Nationalisation." *Metal Bulletin Weekly,* 20 July 2012.

O'Connor, James. 1998. *Natural Causes: Essays in Ecological Marxism.* New York: The Guilford Press.

OICH (Organización Indígena Chiquitana) and CEADES (Centro de Estudios Aplicados a los Derechos Economicos, Sociales y Culturales). 2005. *Informe indígena sobre la mina Don Mario de COMSUR S.A.: Monitoreo indígena independiente por las comunidades indígenas de la PC Turubo CCICHT—OICH—CPESC.* Santa Cruz, Bolivia: OICH and CEADES.

———. 2007. *Editorial: Los impactos socio-ambientales por la construcción de la Carretera Bioceanica Santa Cruz–Puerto Suarez.* Santa Cruz, Bolivia: OICH and CEADES.

Olson, G. J., J. A. Brierley, and C. L. Brierley. 2003. "Bioleaching Review Part B: Progress in Bioleaching: Applications of Microbial Processes by the Minerals Industries." *Applied Microbiology and Biotechnology* 63 (3): 249–257.

ONERN (Oficina Nacional de Evaluación de Recursos Naturales). 1984. *Inventario y evaluación de recursos naturales de la microregión Pastaza-Tigre.* Lima: Oficina Nacional de Evaluación de Recursos Naturales.

One World. 2012. "One World International Human Rights Guide." See http:// uk.oneworld.net/guides/humanrights, or http://www.oneworldgroup.org/.

Oré, María Teresa. 2005. *Agua: Bien común y usos privados. Riego, estado y conflictos en la Achirana del Inca.* 1st ed. Lima: Universidad Católica del Perú.

Oré, María Teresa, Laureano del Castillo, Saskia van Orsel, and Jeroen Vos. 2009. *El agua, ante nuevos desafíos: Actores e iniciativas en Ecuador, Perú y Bolivia.* 1st ed. Lima: Oxfam Internacional and Instituto de Estudios Peruanos.

Orgáz García, Mirko. 2002. *La guerra del gas: Nación versus transnacionales en Bolivia.* La Paz: OFAVIN.

Orlove, Benjamin S. 1982. "Native Andean Pastoralists: Traditional Adaptations and Recent Changes." In *Contemporary Nomadic and Pastoral Peoples: Africa and Latin America,* edited by P. C. Salzman. Williamsburg, VA: College of William and Mary.

Orlove, Benjamin S., and Glynn Custred. 1980. "The Alternative Model of Agrarian Society in the Andes: Households, Networks, and Corporate Groups." In *Land and Power in Latin America: Agrarian Economies and Social Processes in the Andes,* edited by B. S. Orlove and G. Custred. New York: Holmes & Meier.

Orta Martínez, Martí, Dora A. Napolitano, Gregor J. MacLennan, Cristina O'Callaghan, Sylvia Ciborowski, and Xavier Fabregas. 2007. "Impacts of Petroleum Activities for the Achuar People of the Peruvian Amazon: Summary of Existing Evidence and Research Gaps." *Environmental Research Letters* 2 (4): 045046, doi:10.1088/1748-9326/2/4/045006.

Orvana Minerals Corporation. 2002. *Orvana Announces Commencement of Development at Don Mario Gold Project and Executive Appointments.* 4 March 2002.
——. 2003. Annual Information Form, Fiscal Year Ended 30 September 2003. 16 February 2004.
——. 2009. Annual Information Form, Fiscal Year Ended 30 September 2009. 21 December 2009.
——. 2010. *NI 43-101 Technical Report on the Don Mario Upper Mineralized Zone Project, Eastern Bolivia.* Bolivia: Orvana Minerals Corporation.
Ospina Peralta, Pablo. 2009. "Corporativismo, estado y revolución ciudadana: El Ecuador de Rafael Correa." In *Estado, movimientos sociales y gobiernos progresistas,* edited by Instituto de Estudios Ecuatorianos. Quito: Instituto de Estudios Ecuatorianos.
Ostrom, Elinor. 1990. *Governing the Commons: The Evolution of Institutions and Collective Action.* New York: Cambridge University Press.
——. 1996. "Crossing the Great Divide: Coproduction, Synergy, and Development." *World Development* 24 (6): 1073–1087.
——. 2007. "A Diagnostic Approach for Going Beyond Panaceas." *Proceedings of the National Academy of Sciences (PNAS)* 104 (39): 15181–15187.
Ostrom, Elinor, and Harini Nagendra. 2006. "Insights on Linking Forests, Trees, and People from the Air, on the Ground, and in the Laboratory." *Proceedings of the National Academy of Sciences (PNAS)* 103 (51): 19224–19231.
Otto, James M. 1997. "A National Mineral Policy as a Regulatory Tool." *Resources Policy* 23 (1-2): 1–7.
Parker III, Theodore A., Alwyn H. Gentry, Robin B. Foster, Louise H. Emmons, and J. V. Remsen, Jr. 1993. *The Lowland Dry Forests of Santa Cruz, Bolivia: A Global Conservation Priority.* Washington, DC: Conservation International.
Pastor, Robert A. 1992. *Whirlpool: U.S. Foreign Policy Toward Latin America and the Caribbean.* Princeton, NJ: Princeton University Press.
Peet, Richard, and Michael Watts, eds. 1996. *Liberation Ecologies: Environment, Development, Social Movements.* 1st ed. London and New York: Routledge.
——. 2004. *Liberation Ecologies: Environment, Development, Social Movements.* 2nd ed. London and New York: Routledge.
Pegram, Thomas. 2008. "Accountability in Hostile Times: The Case of the Peruvian Human Rights Ombudsman 1996—2001." *Journal of Latin American Studies* 40: 51–82.
Peluso, Nancy Lee, and Michael Watts, eds. 2001. *Violent Environments.* Ithaca, NY: Cornell University Press.
Pennington, R. Toby, Matt Lavin, Tiina Särkinen, Gwilym P. Lewis, Bente B. Klitgaard, and Colin E. Hughes. 2010. "Contrasting Plant Diversification Histories within the Andean Biodiversity Hotspot." *Proceedings of the National Academy of Sciences (PNAS)* 107 (31): 13783–13787.
Pérez, Carlos, and Hernán Loyola. 2007. *Informe de la comisión designada por el Señor Presidente de la República para el análisis y revisión de las concesiones mineras en el Azuay: Proyecto minero Kimsacocha de las áreas Río Falso, Cerro Casco y Cristal concesionado a la Compañía IAMGOLD S.A. Ecuador.* 30 August 2007.
Perreault, Thomas. 2002. *Movilización política e identidad en el Alto Napo.* Quito: Abya Yala.

———. 2006. "From the Guerra del Agua to the Guerra del Gas: Resource Governance, Neoliberalism and Popular Protest in Bolivia." *Antipode* 38 (1): 150-172.

Perreault, Thomas, and Barbara Green. 2013. "Reworking the Spaces of Indigeneity: The Bolivian Ayllu and Lowland Autonomy Movements Compared." *Environment and Planning D: Society and Space* 31 (1): 43-60.

Perreault, Thomas, and Patricia Martin. 2005. "Geographies of Neoliberalism in Latin America." *Environment and Planning A* 37 (2): 191-201.

Perreault, Thomas, and Gabriela Valdivia. 2010. "Hydrocarbons, Popular Protest and National Imaginaries: Ecuador and Bolivia in Comparative Context." *Geoforum* 41 (5): 689-699.

PeruPetro. 2010. "Lotes de contratos de operaciones petroleras y cuencas sedimentarias." PeruPetro, 23 Nov 2010, http://www.perupetro.com.pe/wps/wcm/connect /perupetro/site/InformacionRelevante/MapaLotes/Mapa%20de%20Lotes.

———. 2011. *Petroleum Operations Contract Lots and Sedimentary Basins.* Lima: Peru-Petro S.A.

Petropress. 2000. "Los grandes negocios de Enron en Bolivia." 1 July 2000, http:// www.rebanadasderealidad.com.ar/enron-1.htm.

Pinedo, D. 2000. "Manejo comunal de pastos, equidad y sostenibilidad en una comunidad de la Cordillera Huayhuash." In *Perú: El problema agrario en debate, SEPIA VII,* edited by I. Hurtado, V. Agreda, C. Trivelli, A. Díez, A. Brack, and M. Glave. Lima: Soluciones Practicas.

Pizarro, Pedro. 1921. *Relation of the Discovery and Conquest of the Kingdoms of Peru.* New York: Cortes Society.

Platts Insight. 2012. "Asia Gains Traction: Platts Top 250 Global Energy Company Rankings Reviewed." November 2012: 50-63.

Polanyi, Karl. 1944. *The Great Transformation: The Political and Economic Origins of Our Time.* Boston: Beacon Press.

Postero, Nancy Grey. 2007. *Now We Are Citizens: Indigenous Politics in Postmulticultural Bolivia.* Palo Alto, CA: Stanford University Press.

Postigo, Julio C. 2010. "El capitalismo neoliberal del segundo gobierno de Alan García." In *Peru hoy: Desarrollo, democracia y otras fantasías,* edited by Desco. Lima: Desco.

Postigo, Julio C., and Mariana Montoya. 2009. "Conflictos en la Amazonía: Un análisis desde la ecología política." *Debate Agrario* 44: 129-158.

Postigo, Julio C., Kenneth R. Young, and Kelley A. Crews. 2008. "Change and Continuity in a Pastoralist Community in the High Peruvian Andes." *Human Ecology* 36 (4): 535-551.

Prescott, William H. 1843. *The History of the Conquest of Mexico.* New York: Harper & Brothers.

Prudham, Scott. 2004. "Poisoning the Well: Neoliberalism and the Contamination of Municipal Water in Walkerton, Ontario." *Geoforum* 35 (3): 343-359.

Puhakka, Maarit, Risto Kalliola, Marjut Rajasilta, and Jukka Salo. 1992. "River Types, Site Evolution and Successional Vegetation Patterns in Peruvian Amazonia." *Journal of Biogeography* 19 (6): 651-665.

Purser, W. F. C. 1971. *Metal-Mining in Peru, Past and Present.* New York: Praeger Publishers.

Quarles, Mark. 2009. *Evaluación del éxito de los esfuerzos de remediación ambiental en los sitios impactados por la actividad petrolera en la región de Corrientes en el norte de Perú.* Santa Fe, NM: E-Tech International.

Queropalca. 2007. *Plan Maestro Area Conservación Privada Jirishanca.* Lauricocha, Huánuco, Perú.

Rabe, Stephen G. 1988. *Eisenhower and Latin America: The Foreign Policy of Anticommunism.* Chapel Hill: University of North Carolina Press.

Rabinow, Paul, and Nikolas Rose. 2006. "Biopower Today." *BioSocieties* 1 (2): 195-217.

Radcliffe, Sarah A., and Sallie Westwood. 1996. *Remaking the Nation: Place, Identity and Politics in Latin America.* New York: Routledge.

Raffles, Hugh. 2002. *In Amazonia: A Natural History.* Princeton, NJ: Princeton University Press.

Raimondi, Antonio. 2006. *El departamento de Ancachs y sus riquezas minerales, 1873.* Serie Clásicos sanmarquinos, v. 2. Lima: Fondo Editorial Universidad Nacional Mayor de San Marcos, Asociación Educacional Antonio Raimondi, Antamina, COFIDE.

Räsänen, Matti, Ron Neller, Jukka Salo, and Hogne Jungner. 1992. "Recent and Ancient Fluvian Deposition Systems in the Amazonian Foreland Basin, Peru." *Geological Magazine* 129 (3): 293-306.

Rasmussen, Craig, Peter A. Troch, Jon Chorover, Paul Brooks, Jon Pelletier, and Travis E. Huxman. 2009. "An Open System Framework for Integrating Critical Zone Structure and Function." *Biogeochemistry* 102 (1-3): 1-15.

Rawlings, Douglas E., and Barrie D. Johnson. 2007. *Biomining.* New York: Springer Verlag.

Redclift, Michael R. 2006. *Frontiers: Histories of Civil Society and Nature.* Cambridge, MA: MIT Press.

Redford, Kent H. 1991. "The Ecologically Noble Savage." *Cultural Survival Quarterly* 15 (1): 46-48.

Renjifo, Luis Miguel, Grace P. Servat, Jacqueline M. Goerck, Bette A. Loiselle, and John G. Blake. 1997. "Patterns of Species Composition and Endemism in the Northern Neotropics: A Case for Conservation of Montane Avifaunas." *Ornithological Monographs* 48: 577-594.

Ribot, Jesse C., and Nancy Lee Peluso. 2003. "A Theory of Access." *Rural Sociology* 68 (2): 153-181.

Ricardo, David. 1891. *Principles of Political Economy and Taxation.* London: G. Bell and Sons.

Rival, Laura M. 2002. *Trekking Through History: The Huaorani of Amazonian Ecuador.* New York: Columbia University Press.

Robbins, Paul. 2000. "The Rotten Institution: Corruption in Natural Resource Management." *Political Geography* 19 (4): 423-443.

———. 2004. *Political Ecology: A Critical Introduction.* Malden, MA: Blackwell Publishing.

———. 2007. *Lawn People: How Grasses, Weeds, and Chemicals Make Us Who We Are.* Philadelphia, PA: Temple University Press.

———. 2012. *Political Ecology: A Critical Introduction.* 2nd ed. Malden, MA: Blackwell Publishing.

Robinson, James A., Ragnar Torvik, and Thierry Verdier. 2006. "Political Foundations of the Resource Curse." *Journal of Development Economics* 79 (2): 447-468.

Robles Mendoza, Roman. 2006. "Explotación de recursos en la Cordillera Huayhuash: la minería y el turismo." *Investigaciones sociales: Revista del Instituto de Investigaciones Histórico Sociales* (16): 93–126.

Roca, José Luís. 1979. *Fisonomía del regionalismo boliviano.* La Paz: Plural.

Rocheleau, Dianne, and David Edmunds. 1997. "Women, Men and Trees: Gender, Power and Property in Forest and Agrarian Landscapes." *World Development* 25 (8): 1351–1371.

Roddaz, Martin, Patrice Baby, Stephane Brusset, Wilber Hermoza, and Jose Maria Darrozes. 2005. "Forebulge Dynamics and Environmental Control in Western Amazonia: The Case Study of the Arch of Iquitos (Peru)." *Tectonophysics* 399: 87–108.

Rodríguez Cáceres, Gustavo. 2007. "Luces y sombras de la nacionalización de hidrocarburos en Bolivia." In CEDIB, *Monopolios petroleros en América Latina y Bolivia: Repsol y otras transnacionales europeas.* Proceedings of International Symposia in El Alto, La Paz, Cochabamba, and Santa Cruz. Bolivia: Centro de Documentación e Información Bolivia, 22–28 August 2007.

Roett, Riordan, and Guadalupe Paz, eds. 2008. *China's Expansion into the Western Hemisphere: Implications for Latin America and the United States.* Washington, DC: Brookings Institution Press.

Rohwerder, T., T. Gehrke, K. Kinzler, and W. Sand. 2003. "Bioleaching Review Part A: Progress in Bioleaching: Fundamentals and Mechanisms of Bacterial Metal Sulfide Oxidation." *Applied Microbiology and Biotechnology* 63 (3): 239–248.

Romero, Simón. 2009. "In Bolivia, Untapped Bounty Meets Nationalism." *New York Times,* 3 February 2009, A1.

Rose, Nikolas S. 1999. *Powers of Freedom: Reframing Political Thought.* Cambridge: Cambridge University Press.

Ross, Catherine. 2009. "Case Study: Natural Gas Project in Peru." In *Globalizing Social Justice: The Role of Non-Government Organizations in Bringing about Social Change,* edited by J. Atkinson and M. Scurrah. Oxford: Palgrave MacMillan.

Ross, Michael L. 1999. "Review: The Political Economy of the Resource Curse." *World Politics* 51 (2): 297–322.

———. 2004. "How Do Natural Resources Influence Civil War? Evidence from Thirteen Cases." *International Organization* 58 (01): 35–67.

———. 2008. "Mineral Wealth, Conflict, and Equitable Development." In *Institutional Pathways to Equity: Addressing Inequality Traps,* edited by A. J. Bebbington, A. Dani, A. de Haan, and M. Walton. Washington, DC: World Bank.

Rosser, Andrew. 2006. *The Political Economy of the Resource Curse: A Literature Survey.* IDS Working Paper 268. Brighton, UK: Institute of Development Studies (IDS).

Rowe, John Howland. 1957. "The Incas Under Spanish Colonial Institutions." *The Hispanic American Historical Review* 37 (2): 155–199.

Rubenstein, Steven. 2004. "Steps to a Political Ecology of Amazonia." *SALSA Tipití* 2 (2): 131–176.

Rubin, Jeffrey. 1998. "Ambiguity and Contradiction in a Radical Popular Movement." In *Cultures of Politics, Politics of Culture: Revisioning Latin American Social Movements,* edited by S. Alvarez, E. Dagnino, and A. Escobar. Boulder, CO: Westview.

Rudel, Thomas K., Diane Bates, and Rafael Machinguiashi. 2002. "Ecologically

Noble Amerindians? Cattle Ranching and Cash Cropping Among Shuar and Colonists in Ecuador." *Latin American Research Review* 37 (1): 144–159.

Russett, Bruce M. 1995. *Grasping the Democratic Peace: Principles for a Post-Cold War World*. Princeton, NJ: Princeton University Press.

Sachs, Jeffrey D., and Andrew M. Warner. 1995. "Natural Resource Abundance and Economic Growth." NBER Working Paper No. 5398. Cambridge, MA: NBER.

Sack, Robert David. 1986. *Human Territoriality: Its Theory and History*. Cambridge: Cambridge University Press.

Sala de Prensa José Peralta. 2008. "Mandato Minero obtuvo un amplio respaldo en la Asamblea." 18 Abril (April) 2008, http://constituyente.asambleanacional.gov.ec /index.php?option=com_content&task=view&id=7041.

Salidjanova, Nargiza. 2011. *Going Out: An Overview of China's Outward Foreign Direct Investment*. Washington, DC: U.S.-China Economic & Security Review Commission.

Samame, Mario Boggio. 1984. *Peru: A Mining Country*. Lima: Instituto Geológico, Minero y Metalúrgico.

Sánchez-Albornoz, Nicolás. 1984. "The Population of Colonial Spanish America." In *The Cambridge History of Latin America*, edited by L. Bethell. Cambridge: Cambridge University Press.

Sandbu, Martin E. 2006. "Natural Wealth Accounts: A Proposal for Alleviating the Natural Resource Curse." *World Development* 34 (7): 1153–1170.

Sandweiss, Daniel H., Ruth Shady Solís, Michael E. Moseley, David K. Keefer, and Charles R. Ortloff. 2009. "Environmental Change and Economic Development in Coastal Peru between 5,800 and 3,600 Years Ago." *Proceedings of the National Academy of Sciences (PNAS)* 106 (5): 1359–1363.

Santiago, Myrna I. 2006. *Ecology of Oil: Environment, Labor and the Mexican Revolution, 1900–1938*. Cambridge: Cambridge University Press.

Santiso, Javier. 2007. *The Visible Hand of China in Latin America*. Paris: Development Centre of the Organisation for Economic Co-Operation and Development (OECD).

Santos, G. M., M. I. Bird, F. Parenti, L. K. Fifield, N. Guidon, and P. A. Hausladen. 2003. "A Revised Chronology of the Lowest Occupation Layer of Pedra Furada Rock Shelter, Piauí, Brazil: The Pleistocene Peopling of the Americas." *Quaternary Science Reviews* 22 (21–22): 2303–2310.

Sauer, Carl O. 1969. *Seeds, Spades, Hearths, and Herds*. Cambridge, MA: MIT Press.

Sawyer, Suzana. 2003. "Subterranean Techniques: Corporate Environmentalism, Oil Operations, and Social Injustice in the Ecuadorian Rain Forest." In *In Search of the Rain Forest*, edited by C. Slater. Durham, NC: Duke University Press.

———. 2004. *Crude Chronicles: Indigenous Politics, Multinational Oil, and Neoliberalism in Ecuador*. Durham, NC: Duke University Press.

Sawyer, Suzana, and Edmund Terence Gomez. 2008. *Transnational Governmentality and Resource Extraction: Indigenous Peoples, Multinational Corporations, Multinational Institutions and the State*. Geneva, Switzerland: UNRISD.

Schroeder, Kathleen. 2007. "Economic Globalization and Bolivia's Regional Divide." *Journal of Latin American Geography* 6 (2): 99–120.

Schroeder, Richard A. 2010. "Tanzanite as Conflict Gem: Certifying a Secure Commodity Chain in Tanzania." *Geoforum* 41 (1): 56–65.

Schultze, Carol A., Charles Stanish, David A. Scott, Thilo Rehren, Scott Kuehner, and James K. Feathers. 2009. "Direct Evidence of 1,900 Years of Indigenous Silver Production in the Lake Titicaca Basin of Southern Peru." *Proceedings of the National Academy of Sciences (PNAS)* 106 (41): 17280–17283.

Scott, James C. 1985. *Weapons of the Weak: Everyday Forms of Peasant Resistance.* New Haven, CT: Yale University Press.

———. 1998. *Seeing Like a State: How Certain Schemes to Improve the Human Condition Have Failed.* New Haven, CT: Yale University Press.

Scurrah, Martin, Claudia Bielich, and Anthony Bebbington. 2010. "El caso Río Corrientes: Un hito en la emergencia del movimiento indígena amazónico." Working paper. Lima.

Sen, Amartya Kumar. 1981. *Poverty and Famines: An Essay on Entitlement and Deprivation.* Oxford: Clarendon Press.

SERNANP (Servicio Nacional de Áreas Naturales Protegidas). 2011. "Sistema Nacional de Areas Naturales Protegidas." GIS dataset. Lima, Peru: Servicio Nacional de Areas Naturales Protegidas.

SERVINDI. 2010a. "Perú: Denuncian el paso de la hepatitis B a cáncer hepático en población candoshi." 20 septiembre (September) 2010, http://www.servindi.org /actualidad/31576.

———. 2010b. "Perú: El exterminio de los kandozi y los shapra por la hepatitis B y la indiferencia pública. 12 abril (April) 2010, http://www.servindi.org/actuali dad/24237?utm_source=feedburner&utm_medium=email&utm_campaign=Feed %3A+Servindi+%28Servicio+de+Informaci%C3%B3n+Indigena%29.

Siddiqui, Mohd Haris, Ashish Kumar, Kavindra Kumar Kesari, and Jamal M. Arif. 2009. "Biomining: A Useful Approach Toward Metal Extraction." *American-Eurasian Journal of Agronomy* 2 (2): 84–88.

Sikkink, Kathryn. 1997. "Development Ideas in Latin America: Paradigm Shift and the Economic Commission for Latin America." In *International Development and the Social Sciences. Essays in the History and Politics of Knowledge,* edited by Frederick Cooper and Randall Packard, 228–256. Berkeley: University of California Press.

Silver, Douglas B. 2008. "Super Cycle: Past, Present and Future." *Mining Engineering* 60 (6): 72–77.

Smith, Adam. 1776. *The Wealth of Nations.* Glasgow ed. Indianapolis, IN: Liberty Fund.

Smith, Anthony. 1991. *National Identity.* London: Penguin Books.

Smith, Neil. 2008. *Uneven Development: Nature, Capital, and the Production of Space.* Athens: University of Georgia Press. Originally published 1984, London: Blackwell.

Smith, Peter H. 1996. *Talons of the Eagle: Dynamics of U.S.-Latin American Relations.* Oxford: Oxford University Press.

Smith, Richard Chase. 2008. "Las reformas liberales y la propiedad comunitaria." *Perú Económico* October: 17–19.

———. 2009. "Bagua: La verdadera amenaza." *Poder 360°,* July 2009, www.poder360 .com/article_detail.php?id_article=2208.

Sokoloff, Kenneth L., and Stanley L. Engerman. 2000. "History Lessons: Institutions, Factor Endowments, and Paths of Development in the New World." *The Journal of Economic Perspectives* 14 (3): 217–232.

Solano, Pedro. 2005a. *La esperanza es verde: Áreas naturales protegidas en el Perú*. Lima: SPDA.

———. 2005b. *Manual de instrumentos legales para la conservación privada en Perú.* Lima: Sociedad Peruano de Derecho Ambiental.

Solis, Ruth Shady, Jonathan Haas, and Winifred Creamer. 2001. "Dating Caral, a Preceramic Site in the Supe Valley on the Central Coast of Peru." *Science* 292 (5517): 723–726.

Soltani, Atossa, and T. Osborne. 1997. *Arteries for Global Trade, Consequences for Amazonia*. Malibu, CA: Amazon Watch.

Soto, Aldo, Mariana Montoya, and Hernán Flores. 2010. "Conservation in Amazonian Indigenous Territories: Finding a Common Agenda in the Wetlands of the Abanico del Pastaza." In *Indigenous Peoples and Conservation: From Rights to Resource Management*, edited by K. Walker, A. B. Rylands, A. Woofter and C. Hughes. Arlington, VA: Conservation International.

Spronk, Susan. 2007. "Bolivia: A Movement Toward or Beyond 'Statism'?" *Monthly Review* (March 29).

Stanish, Charles, Edmundo de la Vega, Michael Moseley, Patrick Ryan Williams, Cecilia Chávez J., Benjamin Vining, and Karl LaFavre. 2010. "Tiwanaku Trade Patterns in Southern Peru." *Journal of Anthropological Archaeology* 29 (4): 524–532.

Stanislaw, Joseph A. 2009. "Power Play: Resource Nationalism, the Global Scramble for Energy, and the Need for Mutual Interdependence." White Paper. Washington, DC: Deloitte Center for Energy Solutions.

Stein, Stanley J., and Barbara H. Stein. 2000. *Silver, Trade, and War: Spain and America in the Making of Early Modern Europe*. Baltimore: Johns Hopkins University Press.

Stevens, Paul, and Evelyn Dietsche. 2008. "Resource Curse: An Analysis of Causes, Experiences and Possible Ways Forward." *Energy Policy* 36 (1): 56–65.

Stevens, Stan. 1997. *Conservation Through Cultural Survival*. Covelo, CA: Island Press.

Striffler, Steve. 2002. *In the Shadows of State and Capital: United Fruit Company, Popular Struggle, and Agrarian Restructuring in Ecuador, 1900–1995*. Durham, NC: Duke University Press.

Sundberg, Juanita. 1998. "NGO Landscapes in the Maya Biosphere Reserve, Guatemala." *The Geographical Review* 88 (3): 388–390.

Superintendencia Forestal. 2002. *Plan de desmontes para fines no agropecuarios*. Unidad Operativa de Bosque San José, RU-SJC-PDM-p-023/2002.

———. 2005. *Plan de desmontes para fines no agropecuarios*. Unidad Operativa de Bosque San José, RU-SJC-PDM-p-055/2005.

Surralles, Alexandre. 2007. "Candoshi." In *Guía etnográfica de la Alta Amazonía*. Vol. 6, *Achuar/Candoshi*. Edited by F. Santos and F. Barclay. Lima: Smithsonian Tropical Research Institute, Instituto Francés de Estudios Andinos.

Swyngedouw, Eric, and Nikolas C. Heynen. 2003. "Urban Political Ecology, Justice and the Politics of Scale." *Antipode* 35 (5): 898–918.

Taylor, Anne-Christine. 1985. "La riqueza de Dios: Los achuar y las misiones." In *Amazonía ecuatoriana: La otra cara del progreso*. Quito: Abya Yala.

Telmer, Kevin H., and Marcelo M. Veiga. 2009. "World Emissions of Mercury from Artisanal and Small Scale Gold Mining." In *Mercury Fate and Transport in the Global Atmosphere*, edited by N. Pirrone and R. Mason. New York: Springer Science.

TePaske, John Jay. 1998. "New World Gold Production in Hemispheric and Global

Perspective, 1492–1810." In *Monetary History in Global Perspective, 1500–1801*, edited by C. E. Nuñez. Seville: University of Seville.

TePaske, John Jay, Herbert S. Klein, and Kendall W. Brown. 1982. *The Royal Treasuries of the Spanish Empire in America*. Vol. 1. *Peru*. Durham, NC: Duke University Press.

Thompson, Lonnie G., Ellen Mosley-Thompson, Henry Brecher, Mary Davis, Blanca Leon, Don Les, Ping-Nan Lin, Tracy Mashiotta, and Keith Mountain. 2006. "Abrupt Tropical Climate Change: Past and Present." *Proceedings of the National Academy of Sciences* (*PNAS*) 103 (28): 10536–10543.

Thorp, Rosemary. 1998. *Progress, Poverty, and Exclusion: An Economic History of Latin America in the 20th Century*. Baltimore: Johns Hopkins University Press.

Thorp, Rosemary, and Geoffrey Bertram. 1978. *Peru, 1890–1977: Growth and Policy in an Open Economy*. London: MacMillan Press Ltd.; New York: Columbia University Press.

TMI (The Mountain Institute). 2001. *Plan de ordenamiento turístico de la Cordillera Huayhuash*. Lima: The Mountain Institute.

Torero, M. 2001. *The Social Impact of Privatization and the Regulation of Utilities in Peru*. Lima: GRADE.

TRC (Truth and Reconciliation Commission for Peru). 2003. *Truth and Reconciliation Final Report*. Lima: TRC.

Tschakert, Petra. 2009. "Digging Deep for Justice: A Radical Re-imagination of the Artisanal Gold Mining Sector in Ghana." *Antipode* 41 (4): 706–740.

Tschakert, Petra, and Kamini Singha. 2007. "Contaminated Identities: Mercury and Marginalization in Ghana's Artisanal Mining Sector." *Geoforum* 38 (6): 1304–1321.

Tsing, Anna Lowenhaupt. 2000. "Inside the Economy of Appearances." *Public Culture* 12 (1): 115–144.

———. 2005. *Friction: An Ethnography of Global Connection*. Princeton, NJ: Princeton University Press.

Tubb, Rita. 2011. 2011 "Worldwide Pipeline Construction Report." *Pipeline & Gas Journal* 238 (1): 1–5.

Turner, Billie L., and Paul Robbins. 2008. "Land-Change Science and Political Ecology: Similarities, Differences, and Implications for Sustainability Science." *Annual Review of Environment and Resources* 33: 295–316.

Turner, Frederick Jackson. 1920. *The Frontier in American History*. New York: Holt.

Turner, Terence. 1995. "An Indigenous People's Struggle for Socially Equitable and Ecologically Sustainable Production: the Kayapo Revolt against Extractivism." *Journal of Latin American Anthropology* 1 (1): 98–121.

UNCTADSTAT. 2011. UNCTAD Statistics Database: United Nations Trade and Development Program.

UNICEF (United Nations Children's Fund). 2005. *Kandozi y shapra frente a la hepatitis B: El retorno de lo visible*. Lima: Fondo de las Naciones Unidas para la Infancia (UNICEF).

UNECLAC (United Nations Economic Commission on Latin America and the Caribbean). 2001. *Mining in Latin America in the Late 1990s*. Santiago, Chile: UNECLAC.

———. 1984. *The Politics of Adjustment and Renegotiation of External Debt in Latin America*. Santiago, Chile: UNECLAC.

———. 2010. *International Maritime Transport in Latin America and the Caribbean in 2009 and the First Half of 2010.* Natural Resources and Infrastructure Division, UNECLAC.

———. 2011a. *Foreign Direct Investment in Latin America.* Santiago, Chile: UNECLAC.

———. 2011b. *India and Latin America and the Caribbean: Opportunities and Challenges in Trade and Investment Relations.* Santiago, Chile: Division of International Trade and Integration, UNECLAC.

UNEP (United Nations Environment Programme). 2011. *Environment for Development Perspectives: Mercury Use in ASGM.* Nairobi, Kenya: UNEP.

Urton, Gary. 2008. "The Inca Khipu: Knotted-Cord Record Keeping in the Andes." *The Handbook of South American Archaeology* 19 (3): 831–843.

Urton, Gary, and Carrie J. Brezine. 2005. "Khipu Accounting in Ancient Peru." *Science* 309 (5737): 1065–1067.

U.S. Congress. 2005. *China's Influence in the Western Hemisphere: Hearing Before the Subcommittee on the Western Hemisphere of the Committee on International Relations, House of Representatives,* 109th Congress, First session, 6 April 2005. Washington, DC: U.S. GPO.

U.S. Government. 2000. *World Port Index.* Bethesda, MD: National Imagery and Mapping Agency, U.S. Government.

USAID (U.S. Agency for International Development). 2009. "Tropical Forest Conservation Act (TFCA) Program Descriptions," http://transition.usaid.gov/our_work/environment/forestry/tfca_descs.html.

USEIA (U.S. Energy Information Administration). 2011a. *Petroleum and Other Liquids.* Washington, DC: U.S. Energy Information Administration.

———. 2011b. *World Shale Gas Resources: An Initial Assessment of 14 Regions Outside the United States.* Washington, DC: U.S. Energy Information Administration.

———. 2012. *World Energy Outlook.* Washington, DC: U.S. Energy Information Administration.

USGS (U.S. Geological Survey). 2006. *Mineral Operations of Latin America and Canada.* Reston, VA: U.S. Geological Survey.

———. 2009. *Mineral Operations of Latin America and Canada.* Reston, VA: U.S. Geological Survey.

———. 2010. *Mineral Operations of Latin America and Canada.* Reston, VA: U.S. Geological Survey.

———. 2011. *Mineral Operations of Latin America and Canada.* Reston, VA: U.S. Geological Survey.

———. 2012. *Mineral Commodity Summaries.* Reston, VA: U.S. Geological Survey.

Valdivia, Gabriela. 2008. "Governing Relations Between People and Things: Citizenship, Territory, and the Political Economy of Petroleum in Ecuador." *Political Geography* 27: 456–477.

Valdivia, Sonia M., and Cassia M. L. Ugaya. 2011. "Life Cycle Inventories of Gold Artisanal and Small-Scale Mining Activities in Peru." *Journal of Industrial Ecology* 15 (6): 922–936.

Valenzuela, Lissette, An Chib, Simon Bearda, Alvaro Orella, Nicolas Guiliania, Jeff Shabanowitz, Donald F. Hunt, and Carlos A. Jerez. 2006. "Genomics, Metagenomics and Proteomics in Biomining Microorganisms." *Biotechnology Advances* 24 (2): 197–211.

Valera, Jose L. 2007. "Special Report: Changing Oil and Gas Fiscal and Regulatory Regimes in Latin America." *Oil and Gas Journal* 105 (45): 20–22+24.

Van Buren, Mary, and B. H. Mills. 2005. "Huayrachinas and Tocochimbos: Traditional Smelting Technology of the Southern Andes." *Latin American Antiquity* 16 (1): 3–25.

VanCott, Donna Lee. 2005. *From Movements to Parties in Latin America: The Evolution of Ethnic Politics.* Cambridge: Cambridge University Press.

Van Gijseghem, Hendrik, Kevin J. Vaughn, Verity H. Whalen, Moises Linares Grados, and Jorge Olano Canales. 2011. "Prehispanic Mining in South America: New Data from the Upper Ica Valley, Peru." *Antiquity* 85 (328).

Vaughn, Kevin J., Moises Linares Grados, Jelmer W. Eerkens, and Matthew J. Edwards. 2007. "Hematite Mining in the Ancient Americas: Mina Primavera, a 2,000 Year Old Peruvian Mine." *Journal of the Minerals, Metals and Materials Society* 59 (12): 16–20.

Veiga, Marcello, Peter A. Maxson, and Lars D. Hylander. 2006. "Origin and Consumption of Mercury in Small-Scale Gold Mining." *Journal of Cleaner Production* 14 (3–4): 436–447.

Viale, Claudia, and Carlos Monge. 2010. "¿Se puede despetrolizar la Amazonía?" Mimeo. Lima: Revenue Watch International.

Wagener, Thorsten, Murugesu Sivapalan, Peter A. Troch, Brian L. McGlynn, Ciaran J. Harman, Hoshin V. Gupta, Praveen Kumar, P. Suresh C. Rao, Nandita B. Basu, and Jennifer S. Wilson. 2010. "The Future of Hydrology: An Evolving Science for a Changing World." *Water Resources Research* 46. doi: 10.1029/2009WR008906.

Walker, Peter A. 2005. "Political Ecology: Where Is the Ecology?" *Progress in Human Geography* 29 (1): 73–82.

———. 2006. "Political Ecology: Where Is the Policy?" *Progress in Human Geography* 30 (3): 382–395.

———. 2007. "Political Ecology: Where Is the Politics?" *Progress in Human Geography* 31 (3): 363–369.

Wallerstein, Immanuel. 1974. *The Modern World-System.* Bingley, UK: Emerald Group Publishing.

Walton, Timothy R. 1994. *The Spanish Treasure Fleets.* Sarasota, FL: Pineapple Press.

Warhurst, Alyson, and Gavin Bridge. 1997. "Economic Liberalisation, Innovation, and Technology Transfer: Opportunities for Cleaner Production in the Minerals Industry." *Natural Resources Forum* 21 (1): 1–12.

Waszkis, Helmut. 1993. *Mining in the Americas: Stories and History.* Cambridge: Woodhead.

Waterton, Richard, John Maynard Smith, and Jon Fjeldså. 1998. *An Oxford University Expedition to the High Altitude Polylepis Forests of the Cordillera Huayhuash, Central Peru.* Unpublished manuscript.

Watling, H. R. 2006. "The Bioleaching of Sulphide Minerals with Emphasis on Copper Sulphides: A Review." *Hydrometallurgy* 84 (1–2): 81–108.

Watts, Michael J. 1983. *Silent Violence: Food, Famine and Peasantry in Northern Nigeria.* Berkeley: University of California Press.

———. 1994. "Development II: The Privatization of Everything?" *Progress in Human Geography* 18 (3): 371–371.

———. 1999. "Collective Wish Images: Geographical Imaginaries and the Crisis of National Development." In *Human Geography Today*, edited by D. Massey, J. Allen, and P. Sarre. Cambridge: Polity Press.

———. 2001. "Petro-Violence: Community, Extraction, and Political Ecology of a Mythic Commodity." In *Violent Environments*, edited by N. L. Peluso and M. Watts. Ithaca, NY: Cornell University Press.

———. 2004a. "Antinomies of Community: Some Thoughts on Geography, Resources and Empire." *Transactions of the Institute of British Geographers* 29: 195–216.

———. 2004b. "Resource Curse? Governmentality, Oil and Power in the Niger Delta, Nigeria." *Geopolitics* 9 (1): 50–80.

———. 2004c. "Violent Environments: Petroleum Conflict and the Political Ecology of Rule in the Niger Delta, Nigeria." In *Liberation Ecologies: Environment, Development, Social Movements*, edited by R. Peet and M. Watts. London and New York: Routledge.

———. 2005. "Righteous Oil? Human Rights, the Oil Complex, and Corporate Social Responsibility." *Annual Review of Environment and Resources* 30: 373–407.

———. 2009. *Crude Politics: Life and Death on the Nigerian Oil Fields*. Berkeley: University of California Press.

———. 2010. "Now and Then." *Antipode* 41 (1): 10–26.

Watts, Michael, and Ed Kashi. 2008. *Curse of the Black Gold: Fifty Years of Oil in the Niger Delta*. New York: Powerhouse.

Webb, R., and G. F. Baca. 1993. *Anuario estadístico Perú en números 1993*. Lima: Instituto Cuánto.

Webber, Jeffery R. 2006. "Evo Morales' Historic May Day: Bolivia's Nationalization of Gas!" *Counterpunch*, 3 May 2006, http://www.counterpunch.org/2006/05/03/bolivia-s-nationalization-of-gas/.

———. 2008. "Rebellion to Reform in Bolivia. Part I: Domestic Class Structure, Latin American Trends, and Capitalist Imperialism." *Historical Materialism* 16 (2): 23–58.

Weberbauer, A. 1945. *El mundo vegetal de los Andes peruanos*. Lima: Ministerio de Agricultura.

Weber-Fahr, Monika. 2002. "Treasure or Trouble? Mining in Developing Countries." Mining and Development Series. Washington, DC: World Bank and International Finance Corporation.

WGC (World Gold Council). 2011. *World Gold Reserves*. London: World Gold Council.

Williamson, John H. 1993. "Democracy and the 'Washington Consensus'." *World Development* 21 (8): 1329–1336.

Wilson, Fiona. 2004. "Towards a Political Economy of Roads: Experiences from Peru." *Development and Change* 35 (3): 525–546.

WMCDE (World Mine Cost Data Exchange). 2011. *Yanacocha Mineral Production*. Wilmington, DE: World Mine Cost Data Exchange.

Wolf, Eric. 1972. "Ownership and Political Ecology." *Anthropology Quarterly* 45: 201–205.

———. 1982. *Europe and the People Without History*. Berkeley: University of California Press.

World Bank. 1994a. *Capitalization Program Adjustment Credit, Project ID 6BOLPA064.* Washington, DC: World Bank.

———. 1994b. *Bolivia: Capitalization Program Adjustment Credit Initiating Memorandum.* Washington, DC: World Bank.

———. 1994c. *Capitalization TA Project, Project ID BOPA06178.* Washington, DC: World Bank.

———. 2000. *Bolivia-Hydrocarbon Sector Social and Environmental Management Capacity Building Project—Learning and Innovation Loan (LIL): Project ID BOPE65902.* Washington, DC: World Bank.

———. 2009. *World Development Report 2009: Reshaping Economic Geography.* Washington, DC: World Bank.

———. 2010. *World Development Report 2010: Development and Climate Change.* Washington, DC: World Bank.

———. 2012. *World Development Report 2012: Gender Equality and Development.* Washington, DC: World Bank.

Wu, Kang. 1994. "Emerging Energy Security Issues." In *Energy Investment Advisory Series Report No. 2.* Honolulu, HI: Program on Resources—Energy and Minerals, East-West Center.

Wu, Kang, and Shiva Pezeshki. 1995. "Recent Hydrocarbon Developments in Latin America: Key Issues in the Downstream Oil Sector." In *Energy Investment Advisory Series Report No. 4.* Honolulu, HI: Program on Resources—Energy and Minerals, East-West Center.

Xerez, F. 1917. *Reports on the Discovery of Peru.* Translated and edited by C. R. Markham. London: Hakluyt Society. Originally published 1872, as *Verdadera relación de la conquista del Perú y provincia del Cuzco llamada la Nueva-Castilla. Colección de libros y documentos referentes a la historia del Perú, Ser. I.*

Yashar, Deborah. 2005. *Contesting Citizenship in Latin America: The Rise of Indigenous Movements and the Postliberal Challenge.* Cambridge: Cambridge University Press.

Young, Kenneth R., Carmen Ulloa Ulloa, James L. Luteyn, and Sandra Knapp. 2002. "Plant Evolution and Endemism in Andean South America: An Introduction." *The Botanical Review* 68 (1): 4–21.

Zavaleta Mercado, René. 2008. *Lo nacional-popular en Bolivia.* La Paz: Plural.

Zegada, María Teresa. 2007. *En nombre de las autonomías: Crisis estatal y procesos discursivos en Bolivia.* La Paz: Programa de Investigación Estratégica en Bolivia (PIEB).

Zimmerer, Karl S. 2004. "Cultural Ecology: Placing Households in Human-Environment Studies: The Cases of Tropical Forest Transitions and Agrobiodiversity Change." *Progress in Human Geography* 28 (6): 795–806.

———. 2006. "Cultural Ecology: At the Interface with Political Ecology: The New Geographies of Environmental Conservation and Globalization." *Progress in Human Geography* 30 (1): 63–78.

———. 2007. "Cultural Ecology (and Political Ecology) in the 'Environmental Borderlands': Exploring the Expanded Connectivities within Geography." *Progress in Human Geography* 31: 227–244.

Zimmerer, Karl S., and Thomas J. Bassett. 2003. *Political Ecology: An Integrative Approach to Geography and Environment-Development Studies.* New York: The Guilford Press.

Contributors

About the Editors

Anthony Bebbington is Milton P. and Alice C. Higgins Professor of Environment and Society and Director of the Graduate School of Geography, Clark University. He is also a Research Associate of the Centro Peruano de Estudios Sociales, Peru, and a Professorial Research Fellow at the University of Manchester. He is a member of the U.S. National Academy of Sciences and has held fellowships from the Center for Advanced Studies in the Behavioral Sciences, Stanford, the Free University and Ibero-American Institute of Berlin, the UK Economic and Social Research Council, the United Nations Food and Agricultural Organization, the Fulbright Commission, and the Inter-American Foundation. His work addresses the political ecology of rural change, with a particular focus on extractive industries and socioenvironmental conflicts, social movements, indigenous organizations, and livelihoods. He has worked throughout South and Central America, though primarily in Peru, Ecuador, and Bolivia, and more recently in El Salvador.

Jeffrey T. Bury is an Associate Professor of Environmental Studies at the University of California–Santa Cruz. He is a geographer with broad training in development studies, political science, and environment–society traditions in geography. His research interests include the impacts of transnational mining in Peru, climate change and glacier recession in the Central Andes, and new models of conservation in Latin America. He began studying the impacts of transnational gold mining operations in the Peruvian highlands in 1997 and has since completed more than a decade of fieldwork in Latin America. His research has been funded by the National Science

Foundation, Economic and Social Research Council, Social Science Research Council, Academy for Educational Development, and the Fulbright Foundation. His recent publications appear in *The Annals of the Association of American Geographers*, *The Proceedings of the National Academy of Sciences*, *Climatic Change*, *Environment and Planning D*, *The Geographic Journal* and *The Professional Geographer*.

About the Contributors

Emily Gallagher is a doctoral candidate in the Graduate School of Geography at Clark University, and has an MS in Horticulture from Cornell University. Her research interests include development geography, rural land use planning, and resource governance in mixed agroforest landscapes. Her current work studying extension services and cocoa-forest mosaics in Ghana is funded by the Institute of International Education (IIE) and the Andrew W. Mellon Foundation, as well as the National Science Foundation.

Derrick Hindery is Assistant Professor in the Departments of International Studies and Geography at the University of Oregon. His research examines the impacts of global economic restructuring on indigenous peoples and the environment in Latin America and the United States. His work has appeared in *Land Use Policy* and *The Singapore Journal of Tropical Geography*, and he has recently authored a book on indigenous mobilization, hydrocarbons conflicts, and the environment in Bolivia, as part of the First Peoples publishing initiative (2013, University of Arizona Press).

Leonith Hinojosa (PhD, University of Manchester) is Research Fellow at The Open University and Associate Fellow at the University of Manchester, UK. Her research addresses the spatial dimensions of growth and development, social policies, extractive industries, and sustainable impact assessment of international trade. She has consulted for UNRISD, IFAD, and other development organizations and has worked with Peruvian nongovernmental organizations.

Denise Humpreys Bebbington is Research Assistant Professor of International Development and Director of the Women and Gender Studies program at Clark University. Previously she was Latin America Coordinator for Global Greengrants Fund, and Inter-American Foundation Representative to Peru. Her research addresses the expansion of extractive industry and infrastructure development in South America, the responses of social-environmental movement organizations, and the political ecology of natural resource extraction. Her publications have appeared in *World Development, Development and Change*, and *Latin American Perspectives*, among others.

María-Luisa Burneo is a researcher at the Instituto de Estudios Peruanos and a PhD student in Social Anthropology and Ethnology at the École des Hautes Etudes en Sciences Sociales in Paris, from which she also holds an MA in Anthropology. She has worked for various rural development NGOs in Peru, with a particular emphasis on work with peasant communities in the coastal and highland regions. Her research interests focus on dynamics of change in rural societies, in particular as they relate to territory and land tenure. She has previous work experience coordinating projects across Peru that aim to strengthen decentralization processes.

Mariana Montoya has a PhD in Geography from the University of Texas at Austin. Her doctoral research was focused on the sustainability of socio-ecological systems in the Peruvian Amazon. She is currently the Science Director of the Wildlife Conservation Program, a position that entails the management of landscape conservation programs in Peru in the light of potential impacts from infrastructure projects and extractive industries. Previously she worked extensively on biodiversity conservation, development, and resource management in Peru, serving as program manager for NGOs and for the government.

Jennifer Moore is the Latin America Program Coordinator for Mining-Watch Canada. Previously she worked as a journalist. She has reported extensively on extractive industries, social movements, and social and environmental justice issues.

Timothy Norris is a doctoral student in the Department of Environmental Studies at the University of California–Santa Cruz. His has lived and worked in Peru for more than a decade, in the central Peruvian Andes. His research has been funded by the National Science Foundation and National Geographic. His research interests include extractive industries, community conservation, and participatory GIS.

Tom Perreault is Associate Professor in the Department of Geography at Syracuse University. His work focuses on resource governance, extractive industries, and social mobilization in the Andes. He has written on water conflicts and natural gas in Bolivia, as well as on indigenous movements in Ecuador, and he has been a Fulbright Fellow in Bolivia. His works have appeared in leading geography journals, including *Environment and Planning D*, *Environment and Planning A*, *Antipode*, and *Annals of the Association of American Geographers*. His most recent project examines the relationship between mining, water, and rural livelihoods on the Bolivian altiplano.

Julio C. Postigo is a Postdoctoral Fellow at the National Socio-Environmental Synthesis Center (SESYNC) at the University of Maryland, College Park. He received a PhD in the Department of Geography and the Environment at the University of Texas at Austin and is also Research Associate at the Centro Peruano de Estudios Sociales (CEPES). His current research addresses the effects of global environmental change on pastoral social-ecological systems in the Global South. His publications include, amongst others, an edited book on climate change, social movements, and public policy in Latin America, *Change and Continuity in a Pastoralist Community in the High Peruvian Andes*, *El capitalismo neoliberal del segundo gobierno de Alan García*, and *Capitalismo, cambio climático, y las trampas de las soluciones locales*.

Martin Scurrah is Senior Researcher in the Peruvian Center for Social Studies (CEPES) in Lima. He has recently published a book on social movements and poverty in Peru with Anthony Bebbington and Claudia Bielich. His current research interests include the possible relationship between social conflict and institutional innovation in the extractive industries, and the design of strategies for the transition to a post-extractivist society.

Teresa Velásquez is Assistant Professor of Anthropology at California State University, San Bernardino, and has a PhD from the University of Texas at Austin. Her research examines the political and cultural transformations experienced by rural farmers as a result of their mobilizations against a gold mining project in the southern Ecuadorian Andes. She is the recipient of awards from the National Science Foundation and the Inter-American Foundation.

Ximena Warnaars is an anthropologist/activist and a PhD student in the School of Environment and Development at the University of Manchester. Her work focuses on territory, social movements, indigenous people, and environmental justice related to mining and oil conflicts in the Peruvian and Ecuadorian Amazon. She is currently based in Lima, Peru, and works as Amazon Program Coordinator for Earth Rights International.

Kenneth R. Young is a professor in the Department of Geography and the Environment of the University of Texas at Austin. He does research on the biogeography of tropical organisms and ecosystems, focusing on landscape change in relation to vegetation dynamics, human land use, and climate variability. He coedited (with Thomas Veblen and Antony Orme) the 2007 volume entitled *The Physical Geography of South America*, published by Oxford University Press, and is the author of more than 80 research articles.

Index

Page numbers followed by "f" indicate figures; those followed by "t" indicate tables. See pages vii–xi for abbreviations list.

Lightning Source UK Ltd.
Milton Keynes UK
UKHW012002021021
391359UK00009B/426